Collecting Qualitative Data

This book provides a practical and accessible guide to collecting qualitative data that moves beyond the traditional focus on face-to-face interviews. It emphasises a range of textual, media and virtual methods that provide interesting twists on, and are less resource-intense than, established methods, thereby offering the researcher alternative techniques for collecting data. Divided into three parts, textual, media and virtual, the book provides step-wise guidance on methods that are underutilised within qualitative research and offers new and interesting angles on widely used techniques. Contributors share their experiences of implementing each particular technique and highlight both its potentials and pitfalls. What unites all the methods featured in this book is that they are ideally suited to student projects and resource-limited research. The book will be of interest to readers both new to qualitative research and established researchers seeking to broaden their methodological repertoire.

Virginia Braun is Professor in the School of Psychology at The University of Auckland, New Zealand. A feminist and critical psychologist, her research explores gender, bodies, sex/sexuality and health, and she has published extensively in these areas. She is co-author of the award-winning textbook *Successful Qualitative Research: A Practical Guide for Beginners*, as well as numerous other methodological works. Notably, with Victoria Clarke, she developed an approach to thematic analysis which has become one of the most widely used qualitative methods in the social and health sciences.

Victoria Clarke is Associate Professor in Qualitative and Critical Psychology at the University of the West of England, Bristol, UK. She has published three prize-winning books, including most recently *Successful Qualitative Research: A Practical Guide for Beginners*. She has conducted Economic and Social Research Council- and British Academy-funded research on family and relationships and has published on topics including appearance psychology, human sexuality, LGBTQ psychology and qualitative methods. With Virginia Braun, she developed an approach to thematic analysis which has become one of the most widely used qualitative methods in the social and health sciences.

Debra Gray is Reader in Social Psychology at the University of Winchester, UK. She is a critical social psychologist whose work explores the intersecting areas of social, political and environmental psychology. She has published widely on many topics relating to participation in political, community and health settings and collective socio-spatial identities and intergroup relations. She has an ongoing interest in the intersection of research and practice, and works with many third-sector and public-sector organisations. She has expertise in a wide range of qualitative methods, and she is excited by creative (and multi-modal) ways to collect, analyse and use qualitative data.

Collecting Qualitative Data

A Practical Guide to Textual, Media and Virtual Techniques

VIRGINIA BRAUN

The University of Auckland

VICTORIA CLARKE

University of the West of England, Bristol

DEBRA GRAY

The University of Winchester

CAMBRIDGE
UNIVERSITY PRESS

CAMBRIDGE
UNIVERSITY PRESS

University Printing House, Cambridge CB2 8BS, United Kingdom

One Liberty Plaza, 20th Floor, New York, NY 10006, USA

477 Williamstown Road, Port Melbourne, VIC 3207, Australia

4843/24, 2nd Floor, Ansari Road, Daryaganj, Delhi – 110002, India

79 Anson Road, #06–04/06, Singapore 079906

Cambridge University Press is part of the University of Cambridge.

It furthers the University's mission by disseminating knowledge in the pursuit of education, learning, and research at the highest international levels of excellence.

www.cambridge.org
Information on this title: www.cambridge.org/9781107054974
DOI: 10.1017/9781107295094

First published 2017

Printed in the United Kingdom by Clays, St Ives plc

A catalogue record for this publication is available from the British Library.

Library of Congress Cataloging-in-Publication Data
Names: Braun, Virginia (Professor in Psychology), author. | Clarke, Victoria (Associate Professor in Qualitative and Critical Psychology), author. | Gray, Debra (Reader in Social Psychology), author.
Title: Collecting qualitative data : a practical guide to textual, media and virtual techniques / Virginia Braun, The University of Auckland, Victoria Clarke, University of the West of England, Debra Gray, the University of Winchester.
Description: Cambridge, UK ; New York, NY : Cambridge University Press, 2017.
Identifiers: LCCN 2016033205| ISBN 9781107054974 (hardback) | ISBN 9781107662452 (paperback)
Subjects: LCSH: Qualitative research – Methodology. | Social sciences – Research – Methodology.
Classification: LCC H62 .B71496 2016 | DDC 001.4/2–dc23
LC record available at https://lccn.loc.gov/2016033205

ISBN 978-1-107-05497-4 Hardback
ISBN 978-1-107-66245-2 Paperback

Contents

Figures, Tables and Boxes

Chapter 2

Chapter 3

Chapter 4

Chapter 5

Chapter 6

Chapter 7

Chapter 8

Chapter 9

Chapter 13

Acknowledgements

This book, *Collecting Qualitative Data* (*CQD*), developed out of a seminar – Qualitative Research in an Age of Austerity – which took place at the University of the West of England in October 2012. We are very grateful to the Qualitative Methods in Psychology Section of the British Psychological Society for the seminar competition award that enabled the event to take place, and to our seminar co-organisers, Nikki Hayfield and Naomi Moller. And we were delighted that Cambridge University Press *got* our vision for the book and came on board.

The five-year interval between that seminar and the publication of this book means it will come as no surprise that we have to thank our contributors for bearing with us when health problems and work overload got in the way of us being the efficient and 'on it like a scotch bonnet' (thanks Nikki!) editors we ideally aspire to be. With this in mind, we particularly thank Tim Kurz, who joined us for the early stages of the adventure sailed by the good ship *CQD*. Sadly, work also got in the way of his involvement, and he jumped overboard and swam back to safe harbour. His early involvement is much appreciated!

We were thrilled that two titans of the world of qualitative research – Professor Brendan Gough and Professor Ruthellen Josselson – agreed to provide wise words that set us off on (BG), and welcomed us back from (RJ), the *CQD* adventure. Thanks to our students, especially our supervisees (past and current), for being enthusiastic co-adventurers in messing around with qualitative methods. And it goes without saying (but we're saying it) that we extend a very warm 'huzzah!' to all the people who have mentored, inspired and collaborated with us over the years.

Debra wants to say a special thank you to her chapter co-authors – Helen and Bronwen – for their help in navigating the wilds of vignette research; to her PhD supervisor – Kevin Durrheim – for introducing her to qualitative methods in the first place, and for encouraging her to ask critical questions and find critical answers. And Ginny and Victoria want to say a special thank you to

Celia Kitzinger and Sue Wilkinson, their PhD supervisors at Loughborough University, for fanning the flames of their love of qualitative research, encouraging them, and giving them the confidence, to become adventurers, to 'experiment' (in the broadest sense), with qualitative methods. Their chapters in this book are heavily indebted to Sue and Celia's groundbreaking work.

Contributors

Martha Augoustinos is Professor of Psychology at the University of Adelaide, Australia. Martha has published widely in the field of social psychology and discourse, in particular on the nature of racial discourse in Australia. This has included an analysis of how Indigenous Australians are constructed in everyday conversation and political rhetoric. She is co-author of *Social Cognition* with Iain Walker and Ngaire Donaghue and co-editor with Kate Reynolds of *Understanding Prejudice, Racism and Social Conflict*.

Laura Favaro is a doctoral student at City University London, UK. Her thesis examines constructions of gender, sex, sexuality and intimate relationships in UK- and Spain-based commercial women's online magazines, integrating analyses of the editorial content, user forum discussions and interviews with producers. Laura convenes the Gender & Sexualities Research Forum at City.

Fiona Fox is a researcher with the Ethnography team at the National Institute for Health Research Collaborations for Leadership in Applied Health Research and Care West (NIHR CLAHRC West), UK. Prior to that, she studied and worked at the three universities in Bristol and Bath, gaining a BSc from the University of Bristol; a PhD from the Centre for Appearance Research at the University of the West of England; and a great deal of postdoc experience from the Department for Health, at the University of Bath. Fiona has used qualitative approaches for a variety of applied health research topics, as well as supervising, reviewing and teaching qualitative research methods.

Lucy Gibson is Lecturer in Applied Health and Social Care at Edge Hill University, UK. Her doctoral research explored popular music and the life course and investigated themes of cultural commitment, lifestyles and identities amongst fans of northern and rare soul, rock, and electronic dance music (EDM). Lucy has published and presented academic work on popular music and ageing, the extension of youth cultural practices in adulthood, using email interviews to investigate music and memory, and the ageing body. Her research interests broadly focus on ageing, youth culture, community engagement, well-being and online research methods.

David Giles is Reader in Media Psychology at the University of Winchester, UK. He has published several books on the influence of media and celebrity and numerous papers on the social dynamics of online communication, with particular reference to mental health. He is one of the founders of the multidisciplinary MOOD (Microanalysis of Online Data) network, which organises an annual international workshop on the development of methods for performing close qualitative analyses of a broad range of online materials incorporating text, visual content, hyperlinks and other uniquely digital phenomena.

Rosalind Gill is Professor of Social and Cultural Analysis at City University London, UK. She is interested in gender, media, and intimate life, as well as in new technologies and cultural and creative labour. She is author or co-editor of several books including *Gender and the Media, Secrecy and Silence in the Research Process* with Roisin Ryan Flood and *New Femininities* with Christina Scharff.

Brendan Gough is Professor of Social Psychology in the School of Social, Psychological and Communication Sciences at Leeds Beckett University, UK. Brendan has published numerous papers on gender identities and relations, mostly on health and well-being (weight, alcohol consumption, smoking, diet and aspects of men's health). He is co-founder and co-editor of the journal *Qualitative Research in Psychology*, and he edits the Critical Psychology section of the journal *Social & Personality Psychology Compass*. He has also co-authored *Critical Social Psychology* and co-edited *Men, Masculinities and Health* and *Reflexivity*.

Paul Hanna is a Chartered Psychologist and Lecturer in Sustainable Tourism at the University of Surrey, UK. His main research interests are identity, well-being, sustainability, pro-environmental behaviours and research methodologies. His work has been published in a range of journals, including *GeoJournal, Journal of Consumer Culture, Theory & Psychology, Qualitative Research, Qualitative Research in Psychology* and *Environmental Economics*. He is currently working on a range of research projects exploring spatial, affective, social and individual elements of sustainable behaviour in relation to leisure and tourism.

Scott Hanson-Easey is Research Fellow in the School of Population Health at the University of Adelaide, Australia. He has a formal background in social psychology, and his research, employing discourse analysis and social representations theory, has addressed social issues such as intergroup relations, the language of racism and intercultural risk communication. Recently, his work has focused on the social construction of climate change risk and adaptation.

Laura Harvey is Lecturer in Sociology at the University of Surrey, UK. Her work takes an interdisciplinary approach, drawing on sociology, gender studies, social psychology and cultural studies. Her research interests include everyday intimacies and inequalities, research with young people, sexualities, the mediation of sexual knowledge, feminist methodologies and discourse analysis.

Nikki Hayfield is Senior Lecturer in Social Psychology in the Department of Health and Social Sciences at the University of the West of England, Bristol, UK. Her PhD was an exploration of bisexual women's visual identities and bisexual marginalisation. In her research, she uses qualitative methodologies to explore lesbian, gay, bisexual and heterosexual sexualities, relationships and (alternative) families.

Nicholas Hookway is currently Lecturer in Sociology within the School of Social Sciences at the University of Tasmania, Australia. Nick's principal research interest is morality and social change in conditions of late modernity. His other research interests are kindness, religion and spirituality, and online research technologies.

Ruthellen Josselson is Professor of Clinical Psychology at the Fielding Graduate University, US, and a psychotherapist in private practice. Her research focuses on women's identity and on human relationships. She received both the Henry A. Murray Award and the Theodore R. Sarbin Award from the American Psychological Association as well as a Fulbright Fellowship. She has been active in group relations work for many years, consults to organisations, and lectures and conducts workshops both nationally and internationally. She is the editor of the journal *Qualitative Psychology* and the author of numerous books including, most recently, *Interviewing for Qualitative Inquiry*.

Pamela J. Lannutti is Associate Professor of Communication and Director of the Graduate Programs in Professional and Business Communication at La Salle University, Philadelphia, US. Her research focuses on communication in personal relationships. Much of her recent work has focused on same-sex marriage, and she is the author of *Experiencing Same-Sex Marriage*.

Helen Malson is Associate Professor of Social Psychology in the Department of Health and Social Sciences at the University of the West of England, UK. Her research focuses on critical feminist analyses of 'eating disorders' and, more broadly, on issues of gendered embodiment. Her methodological expertise lies in critical discourse analytic approaches in analysing a variety of different data types. Her research has been funded by the Arts Research Council, the New South Wales Department of Health and the Westmead Millennium Trust. Her publications include *The Thin Woman* and, with Maree Burns, *Critical Feminist Approaches to Eating Dis/Orders*.

Paula Meth is Senior Lecturer in the Department of Urban Studies and Planning at Sheffield University, UK. Her work encompasses Social Geography, Urban Studies and Development Studies and is focused on gender, violence and housing in South Africa. Paula is the co-author of *Geographies of Developing Areas*, and she has published various papers on issues relating to qualitative methodology, particularly in relation to the ethics of working on violence as well as the use of diaries and mixed methods in research.

Naomi Moller is a Chartered Psychologist and Lecturer in Psychology at the Open University, UK. Trained as a counselling psychologist, she has a long-standing interest in research, teaching research methods and supervising research for almost a decade, and recently co-edited with Andreas Vossler *The Counselling and Psychotherapy Research Handbook*. Her research interests include perceptions and understandings of counsellors and counselling, relationship and family research, including infidelity. Naomi is co-director of the Families, Relationships and Communities research group at the Open University, and is on the editorial board of various journals including the British Association of Counselling and Psychotherapy's *Counselling and Psychotherapy Research*.

Shadreck Mwale is a medical sociologist and Lecturer in Sociology and Social Policy at the University of Brighton, UK. His research interests are in human involvement in clinical trials, regulation of medical innovations, inequalities and health, and research methodologies. He has recently completed his PhD and is working on a number of publications derived from his research on ethical and regulatory dimensions of healthy volunteer involvement in Phase 1 clinical trials.

Bronwen Royall graduated from the University of the West of England with a degree in psychology and is currently studying for an MSc in neuropsychology at the University of Bristol, UK. Her research interests are predominantly focused on issues in mental health following her work as an assistant psychologist.

The Story Completion Research Group includes Victoria Clarke, Nikki Hayfield, Naomi Moller and Irmgard Tischner and various postgraduate students including Iduna Shah-Beckley and Matthew Wood, both of whom have contributed to the writing of Chapter 3. Other students have given their permission for us to use their research as illustrative examples.

Gareth Terry is Senior Research Officer at the Centre for Person Centred Research at AUT University (Auckland, New Zealand). His research fits broadly in the areas of critical health and critical social psychologies, with particular interests in people's experiences of life with chronic health conditions, men's health, body image, reproductive decision-making, and masculine identities. He also has methodological interests in thematic analysis, critical discursive psychology and qualitative survey development, and has contributed to edited volumes in these areas.

Irmgard Tischner is Senior Lecturer at the Technical University of Munich, at the Chair of Sociology of Diversity. Focusing on poststructuralist, feminist and critical psychological approaches, her research interests include issues around embodiment and subjectivity, particularly in relation to (gendered) discourses of body size, health and physical activity in contemporary Western industrialised societies, as well as gendered issues of appearance and leadership in business and politics.

Foreword

Brendan Gough

Qualitative research is a rich, diverse field which is ever expanding and fragmenting. However, this diversity is all too often confined to specialist journals and conferences – the type of qualitative research featured in established journals is often quite formulaic, dry and dull (see Brinkmann, 2015). Students and early career researchers may be forgiven for thinking that qualitative research constitutes doing interviews and then attempting to generate some themes from the resulting transcripts. As the editors of this book and various other qualitative researchers have noted, however, interviews can be re-imagined in enriching and productive ways, whether facilitating the recruitment and engagement of otherwise hard-to-reach participants via communication technologies (messaging, Skype, etc.), or employing meaningful artefacts (e.g., photographs, treasured possessions) and activities (drawing, story completion) to help enliven and extend face-to-face interviews (e.g., Guillemin, 2004; Jowett, Peel and Shaw, 2011; Sheridan and Chamberlain, 2011).

Beyond interviews, there is a world of qualitative data to be sought, selected and/or collected, ranging from newspaper and magazine articles (and readers' responses to stories) to online sources, such as discussion forums, blogs and social media content. Moreover, the use of media and virtual data sources in qualitative research can be less time-consuming, less challenging and less ethically complex than more traditional face-to-face interviews and focus groups – and therefore appealing to novice qualitative researchers working on time-limited projects. A text like this is therefore to be welcomed, opening up a whole new repertoire of innovative methods which can engage current and future generations of qualitative researchers. As such, it builds on and extends recent calls to document, deploy and celebrate diversity in qualitative enquiry (e.g., Madill and Gough, 2008; Gough and Lyons, 2016).

Rather uniquely, this book foregrounds data collection. It is curious that most qualitative methods textbooks tend to emphasise different modes of analysis over data collection, and that, invariably, those methods of qualitative data collection that do feature are interviews and focus groups. In explicating different (and some novel) techniques of gathering, generating and finding qualitative data, current and potential qualitative researchers are provided with clear guidelines, illustrations and reflections which will help them make informed choices for their own research endeavours. All chapter contributors are experts in the methods they present, and offer valuable 'insider' insights into the particular practices, potential pitfalls and pleasures involved in their own brand of qualitative research.

Given that quantitative researchers are becoming more acquainted with qualitative research methods, it is refreshing to see a whole part of the book devoted to qualitative 'experimenting' with conventional quantitative tools, such as surveys and vignettes. Qualitative surveys, for example, present a series of open questions in order to encourage participants to provide more detailed accounts of the topic in question than would be gathered using traditional numerical scales and tick-box questionnaires. The qualitative survey can also empower the researcher/s by delivering high sample sizes and large datasets, which many mainstream journals expect from submitting authors. The other methods covered showcase creative modes of eliciting personal accounts from participants; the use of hypothetical scenarios (story completion; vignettes) may engage participants to explore personal experiences without feeling exposed, while bespoke diary methods allow participants to develop meaningful accounts and reflections over time.

It is also pleasing to see a part on media materials – resources too often left to the margins of qualitative research or to interdisciplinary fields such as media studies, where theoretical preferences can often override methodological rigour. Because we live in a world which is media-saturated, it would be strange if qualitative researchers did not attend to media content. A focus on print and broadcast media can tell us much about contemporary (and competing) norms, and it is great to see coverage of newspapers and magazines (representations) as well as radio material (social interaction) in Part II. The availability of media content online makes such data easily accessible for qualitative researchers, with the opportunities for feedback online for readers, viewers and listeners offering further data seams for qualitative researchers to mine. The production of accounts online, whether through blogs or discussion forums, allows access to often personal stories which might be difficult to generate using face-to-face interviews, and it is good to see chapters which draw on these online sources.

The online environment is the focus of the final part, with the emphasis on ways in which the researcher can interact with participants using available digital technologies. Various modes of communication are promoted: interviewing via email, messaging and Skype, as well as online focus groups. As such, the classic qualitative methods of individual and group interviews are reworked, enabling remote dialogue with participants while also presenting some challenges. Again, the advice and examples presented will be welcomed by qualitative researchers interested in using diverse digital means of encountering participants.

In sum, this book breaks new ground by bringing together a collection of authors and methods which illuminate new and exciting ways of doing qualitative research. I expect it will be very popular and will prove to be an invaluable resource for novice and experienced researchers alike. I for one will be using it for teaching and research purposes, and will be encouraging my colleagues to do likewise.

References

Brinkmann, S. (2015). Perils and pitfalls in qualitative psychology. *Integrative Psychological and Behavioral Science*, *49*, 162–173.

Gough, B. and Lyons, A. (2016). The future of qualitative research in psychology: Accentuating the positive. *Integrative Psychological and Behavioral Science, 50*, 234–243.

Guillemin, M. (2004). Understanding illness: Using drawings as a research method. *Qualitative Health Research*, *14*, 272–289.

Jowett, A., Peel, E. and Shaw, R. L. (2011). Online interviewing in psychology: Reflections on the process. *Qualitative Research in Psychology*, *8*, 354–369.

Madill, A. and Gough, B. (2008). Qualitative research and its place in psychological science. *Psychological Methods*, *13*, 254–271.

Sheridan, J. and Chamberlain, K. (2011). The power of things. *Qualitative Research in Psychology*, *8*, 315–332.

1 Collecting Textual, Media and Virtual Data in Qualitative Research

Virginia Braun, Victoria Clarke and Debra Gray

Why This Book?

Imagine you pay a visit to your university library to read and learn about qualitative research methods. After a few hours of sitting at a table surrounded by piles of books, you will likely draw the conclusion that data collection is fairly straightforward, that all you need to know about collecting qualitative data is how to do a (face-to-face) interview, and maybe how to run a focus group. In a discipline like psychology (our discipline), and in many other social and health science disciplines, methods texts often emphasise (qualitative) data analysis over data collection, with qualitative data collection often limited to face-to-face interviews, and increasingly focus groups. This limited approach creates two impressions: that data *collection* isn't that important, or certainly less important than data *analysis*, and that qualitative researchers use only a limited range of methods to collect data.

Neither of these is true. Data analysis is (arguably) only as good as the data that are collected. What's more, face-to-face interviews and focus groups are not über-methods, suitable for any and all purposes, and without limitations. They can be costly with regard to time and resources, they require certain interactional skills to get the best out of data collection and they aren't always the best way to address the range of research questions that interest qualitative researchers. Despite this, their frequent unquestioned dominance means that they – or face-to-face interviews in particular – occupy a position as the 'gold standard', 'go to' method for collecting qualitative data, often being used to address research questions that would arguably have been better tackled through the use of other data collection methods. This is not to say that face-to-face interviews and focus groups aren't important and useful methods for qualitative research – they very much are! But the range of possibilities for data collection, and thus forms of data, open to the qualitative researcher is much, much wider than just these two methods.

In this book, we aim to explore and expand qualitative research possibilities by providing an accessible and practical introduction to a wide array of data collection methods and sources. Importantly, the methods that we cover do not offer an inferior substitute for the 'gold standard' face-to-face interview and focus group, generating shorter and shallower data; instead, they offer an *alternative*, with different qualities and strengths, and are suited to different purposes. The book offers qualitative researchers an arsenal of (new) tools from which to explore innovative and exciting research questions. We advocate the importance of fit between your theoretical orientation, research question, participant group, analytic approach and the data collection method you use; this view is strongly supported in all the chapters in this book. What matters is selecting the right approach to data collection for your research question and participant group. A good fit will set you on the path towards excellent data.

The book is organised into three parts: Textual, Media and Virtual. *Textual* covers four methods that are typically more widely used in *quantitative* research – surveys, story completion, vignettes and diaries – but that hold great potential for *qualitative* research. Qualitative researchers have long been interested in the media as a source of data, but methodological discussion of this data source is scarce (outside of media studies). *Media* covers both 'traditional' broadcast and print media (radio, magazines and newspapers) and newer forms of social media (blogs, forums, online news, reader comments). *Virtual* covers techniques that harness the potential of the Internet (email, instant messaging (IM) and Skype interviews and online focus groups) to provide alternatives to traditional face-to-face interviews or focus groups. Many contributors in this and other parts of the book identify that the Internet has revolutionised qualitative research, opening up new avenues for recruiting participants and collecting data, as well as giving rise to new *forms* of data (see also Fielding, Lee and Blank, 2008; Mann and Stewart, 2000).

The methods discussed offer ways to collect data that are typically less resource-intensive than face-to-face interviews or focus groups. These methods and data sources enable researchers to conduct high-quality qualitative research, often without leaving the office. They also engage with, and provide possible solutions to, some thorny questions for qualitative researchers (especially in the contemporary academic climate):

(1) How can you access a geographically dispersed sample without it being prohibitively expensive?
(2) What methods can you use to best encourage participation from hidden and/or hard-to-reach populations?

(3) How best can you research sensitive issues, from the point of view of participant anonymity and inclination to participate, *and* from the point of view of researcher well-being?

(4) How can you viably conduct qualitative research with a large participant sample?

(5) How can you viably collect qualitative longitudinal data without an enormous budget?

(6) What are the benefits of non-researcher-generated data?

(7) How can the time and resources of a researcher best be balanced to maximise the chance of successful research completion?

These questions are particularly pertinent in an 'age of austerity' in the academy (e.g., Davies and O'Callaghan, 2014). Vast numbers of scholars within the health and social sciences use qualitative methods in their research. Many exist within economic and academic climates where research has become more pressured, in terms of time, financial resources and expectations of (quick) outcomes. This book invites those scholars to 'think outside the box' of their regular qualitative methods, offering in a single volume theoretical overviews and practical advice on ways to collect qualitative data differently. In presenting innovative ways data can be collected, new modes of scholarship and new research orientations are opened up to student researchers and established scholars alike.

The methods presented in this book will be particularly suitable for students doing research projects for two main reasons:

(1) They offer typically time-efficient methods, for research needing to be completed within a very clearly delimited time-frame.

(2) They require fairly minimal resources, a potentially important consideration for those conducting research on an extremely tight budget.

A note of caution: we don't cover everything in the wide, *wide* world of qualitative data collection in this book – that would require a whole book series, not just one volume! Nor do we cover many methods of data collection that can be regarded as 'innovative' (e.g., visual approaches; Margolis and Pauwels, 2011; Reavey, 2011; Rose, 2012). In the main, the methods we have selected represent new developments in qualitative data collection in the last decade or so, but retain a focus on the text. They provide interesting 'twists' on existing and established methods and offer alternative – often more practical – ways of addressing familiar research questions about participants' experiences or social processes, whilst at the same time opening up new avenues for qualitative inquiry.

We now provide a brief overview of the book – what it covers (we've already told you a bit about that!) and how it is structured – so that you can use it in a way that best suits your requirements. This is intertwined with a brief discussion of some of the key features of qualitative research as a 'map' for those new to this terrain.

What This Book Offers the Qualitative Researcher

Who Is This Book for?

This book is intended for readers across the social and health sciences – though of course read on, even if that isn't your area of interest! The editors and contributors come from different disciplines and fields of study, including psychology, sociology, public health, communication, psychotherapy, gender studies, social geography and more. As we aim to provide a practical and accessible *introduction* to a range of textual, media and virtual methods, the book is principally written for readers who are new to these methods, and we keep in mind that they may be new to qualitative research more broadly.

The book is also designed to accompany a course or lecture block on qualitative research and to provide a 'how to' guide for students undertaking research using one or more of the methods covered.

How to Read and Use This Book

You can start at the beginning and read this book from cover to cover! But you don't have to – each chapter has been designed to stand-alone. We do, however, recommend that you read the section below before progressing to the rest of the book, as it provides useful framing material, including a brief discussion of some of the key features and assumptions of qualitative research. All of the chapters have (broadly) the same structure – with slight variation when it doesn't fit well with the method or data source under discussion. They are generally organised as follows:

Overview: This section does what it says on the tin – it provides a brief overview of the chapter so you know what you will get out of it.

Introduction to the example study: At the start of each chapter you'll find a *box* that introduces an example study (or sometimes, studies) that provides a real-life illustration of the method/data source *in use*. The example studies aren't intended as perfect exemplars (if there ever were such things!) of how to use a particular method or data source. If you're new to research, know that the impression of a seamless research process that published journal articles and book chapters create is often far from reality. This book aims to provide a more authentic sense of the messy reality of the research process – and so the contributors share their false-starts, challenges and *complete failures*, as well as their successes! Each chapter as a whole *does* provide clear guidance on how (best) to implement the relevant method and equip you with strategies for dealing with challenges you might encounter.

Introduction to the method/data source: This section clearly defines what the method/data source is, its history and background, and some key characteristics.

What does the method/data source offer the qualitative researcher? This section provides a clear sense of when and why you would chose to use the relevant method, as well as highlighting the practical advantages it offers. Although it is important to have a clear rationale for your design choices that reflect the importance of conceptual 'fit' between your theoretical assumptions, research questions and methods (Willig, 2013), pragmatic considerations – such as 'Do I feel confident using this method?' or 'Will I be able to submit my dissertation by the deadline if I use this method?' – also play a role in research design. Recognising these factors, this section focuses on both theoretical and pragmatic considerations, with the latter particularly important in research that is time- or resource-limited.

What research questions suit the method/data source? The research process begins with a research question: this section provides a consideration of the types of research questions that can be addressed using the method or data source discussed. Whereas quantitative research tends to be guided by concrete and precise predictions and hypotheses, qualitative research questions tend to be fairly open. This is *not* the same as not having a research question! Even though qualitative research designs are characteristically organic, flexible and exploratory, developing an appropriate research question is a vital starting point (Braun and Clarke, 2013). This is not to say your research question can't evolve as the research progresses – in qualitative research, it often does; but qualitative research, like all research, has a clear sense of its purpose. One common focus for qualitative research is exploring the 'lived experience' of particular groups or individuals. However, research questions are not limited to people's thoughts, feelings and behaviours, or to how they experience and/or make sense of particular phenomena. Research questions can also focus on the interrogation of language and meaning, as well as examining the assumptions underpinning, and the implications and effects of, particular patterns and formations (Braun and Clarke, 2013). Thinking about research questions early on is important as some of the methods discussed particularly – or even only – suit specific kinds of research questions; others are more flexible with a wider range of applications.

Design, sampling and ethical issues: This section provides practical guidance on considerations involved in designing a piece of research using a particular method/data source, with a focus on sampling and ethical concerns. At first sight, qualitative research may seem like it doesn't need much in the way of 'designing'. After all, you're not administering lots of different measures, and you don't have to worry about things like standardising participant instructions and internal validity – or do you? Design and careful planning are just as important in qualitative research as they are in quantitative research, and some approaches do require extensive preparation (e.g., qualitative surveys, see Chapter 2). The key to effective qualitative design is conceptual 'fit' between the different elements of the project; 'a good qualitative research design is one in which the method of data analysis is appropriate to the research question, and where the method of data collection generates data that are appropriate to the method of analysis' (Willig, 2001: 21). Along with the section on suitable research questions, this section will help you to design a coherent project – one that exhibits good fit!

Steps to using the method/data source: Again, this section does what it says on the tin! It outlines the key steps involved in implementing a particular method/data source. This provides a useful checklist for when you come to use the method.

What can go wrong with the method/data source? It is exceedingly rare for a research project to run smoothly with no challenges or obstacles to overcome, or even what at the time can feel like complete disasters to manage. This section gives you a heads up on some of the common pitfalls associated with a particular method/data source and advice on potential ways to avoid or manage them. The key message across the book is *don't panic*! Things go wrong from time to time, but careful planning and design can help smooth your path and ensure that you are well equipped to deal with any challenges you may encounter. We are very grateful to the contributors for being willing to share their trials and tribulations; as we noted above, this is the kind of detail typically left out of seamless research reports (for other discussions, see Boynton, 2016; Hallowell, Lawton and Gregory, 2005), but doing so can create a false impression that published researchers are perfect at research and never get anything wrong (far from it!).

What methods of analysis suit the method/data source? The aim in this section is to provide you with an *overview* of analytic approaches appropriate for the data source/method, rather than in-depth guidance – plenty of other texts offer that. There is a broad range of analytic approaches available to the qualitative researcher: some are used widely, and across the social and health sciences (e.g., grounded theory, thematic analysis); others are associated with particular disciplines (e.g., interpretative phenomenological analysis has origins in psychology) but are increasingly taken up more broadly; others still are more 'idiosyncratic', associated primarily with a particular researcher or group of researchers. To add more complexity, some approaches come in lots of *different varieties*, both across and within disciplines. Discourse analysis, for instance, can refer to very *different*, and sometimes actually contradictory, approaches. This section of each chapter identifies a range of analytic approaches appropriate to the method/data source, focused mainly on approaches widely used across the social and health sciences: qualitative content analysis (Hsieh and Shannon, 2005), thematic analysis (Boyatzis, 1998; Braun and Clarke, 2006, 2012, 2013), interpretative phenomenological analysis (Smith, Flowers and Larkin, 2009), grounded theory (Birks and Mills, 2011), discourse analysis (Wetherell, Taylor and Yates, 2001a, 2001b), narrative analysis (Riessman, 2007) and conversation analysis (Ten Have, 2007). Some authors may also describe *particular* analytic traditions/approaches that have developed with regard to the method in slightly more depth.

Conclusion: Each chapter ends with a brief conclusion summing up the benefits of the particular method, and incorporates a boxed personal reflection of using the method.

A Guide to the Pedagogical Features in This Book

A key aim of this book is to provide a *practical* and *accessible* guide to collecting qualitative data. Various pedagogical features, designed to highlight key information and assist you in implementing the methods in your own research, are included:

(1) Each chapter finishes with a *have a go . . .* feature. This offers suggestions for *hands-on* activities for *trying out*, and developing a deeper and practical understanding of, the particular method or data source. This *have a go . . .* feature will also be useful for lecturers in planning seminar and workshop activities.

(2) Each chapter provides *further resources* to take you deeper into the method. Some of these are useful *online* resources; some are suggestions for *further reading*, including any published versions of the example studies discussed in the chapter. These provide what the authors see as key and accessible starting points for going deeper.

(3) In each chapter you'll also find a variety of *boxes*, *tables* and *figures* to highlight key information.

Qualitative research writing can appear rather jargon-loaded to the unin-
itiated, and even at times to the experienced qualitative researcher, so it's likely
you'll come across a term or terms you've never heard of before. We therefore
include a detailed *glossary* to provide pithy, confusion-busting definitions of
some of the key terms and concepts used in the book.

Overview of Chapters

Chapters are presented within three thematic parts, each focused on a particular
broad type of method/data source. There's naturally some overlap between
the three: many of the *textual* methods are also used online; likewise, media
data are increasingly accessed online – *textual, media* and *virtual*. . . . This means
the distinction between textual, media and virtual methods is not absolute, but the
methods/data sources described in each part share some core characteristics.

In Chapter 2, Gareth Terry and Virginia Braun kick off Part I focused on
textual data with an introduction to *qualitative survey methods*. Surveys have
traditionally been used by quantitative researchers to examine attitudes and
opinions; Terry and Braun argue that surveys can be used by qualitative
researchers to ask similar types of questions, as well as address distinctively
qualitative research questions about the lived experiences and practices of
particular groups. Unique among qualitative methods, surveys provide a
'wide angle' lens on the topic of interest, which is particularly useful in
research focused on documenting and exploring social norms, such as Terry
and Braun's research on body hair management and removal.

In Chapter 3, Victoria Clarke, Nikki Hayfield, Naomi Moller, Irmgard
Tischner and other members of the Story Completion Research Group discuss
their 'experiments' with *story completion* as a qualitative method. Story completion was first developed as a 'projective' technique, designed to uncover the
'hidden depths' of psychoanalytic psychotherapy clients, and later developed
as a quantitative research tool, with complex coding systems used to translate
stories into numerical data for statistical analysis. Clarke et al. argue that story
completion provides a compelling and creative way of exploring topics of
interest to qualitative researchers. Drawing on their research relating to gender,
sexuality, appearance and embodiment, they show how asking participants to
write stories, rather than asking them directly about their views and opinions,
opens up exciting new possibilities for qualitative research.

Another method that involves hypothetical scenarios and stories is the
vignette method. In Chapter 4, Debra Gray, Bronwen Royall and Helen
Malson provide an introduction to *vignettes as a qualitative, stand-alone*

method. Vignettes have long been used in quantitative survey research to measure participants' attitudes and beliefs about a particular topic. In qualitative research, vignettes have typically been used in combination with other methods, as a secondary elicitation tool. However, Gray et al. demonstrate that vignettes in and of themselves provide a productive way of exploring participants' sense-making around particular phenomena.

The final chapter in this part also discusses a method that requires participants to write or type their responses to a particular question or task but shifts from hypothetical scenarios and stories back to gathering first-person accounts of personal experience (like qualitative surveys do). In Chapter 5, Paula Meth explores the *solicited diary method*, where the researcher asks the participant to engage in diary writing for a specific purpose. She shows that diaries provide an invaluable way of gaining access to participants' hidden worlds and the unfolding of personal experience over time. Solicited diaries can therefore provide a relatively accessible tool for conducting longitudinal research, something not usually possible in time- and resource-limited research.

Part II focuses on *media* as a data source, exploring both traditional broadcast and print media and newer forms of social and online media. Laura Favaro, Rosalind Gill and Laura Harvey open this part with a broad focus on *media data* in Chapter 6, discussing newspapers, magazines and the increasingly pervasive 'reader comments' feature on online news sites. They outline the many advantages of media data for qualitative researchers, not least their ubiquity and (often free) accessibility, and the importance of engaging with such sources *as* data in an increasingly 'mediated' world. Their chapter not only offers specific guidance for visiting these media types, but also provides a good foundation for the other chapters in this part.

In Chapter 7, Scott Hanson-Easey and Martha Augoustinos discuss another kind of traditional media data – *talkback* or *talk radio*, where a listening audience is invited to 'call-in' to discuss a variety of 'everyday' concerns, opinions and views. Drawing on their own discourse analytic research, on constructions and representations of Sudanese refugees in Australia, they highlight how talkback radio can provide unique insight into how people 'make sense of' their social worlds. Moreover, they argue that talkback radio offers particular advantages for researchers who are interested in *language* and *talk-in-interaction.*

Nicholas Hookway shifts the focus onto newer forms of online social media data – in particular *blogs* – in Chapter 8. Drawing on his own experiences of using blogs in his research on everyday morality, he highlights the ways in which blogs provide qualitative researchers with uniquely multi-modal and multi-media data that are textual, audio, visual and interactive. He argues that blogs provide qualitative researchers with unique access to first-person textual accounts of everyday life, and therefore offer much potential for researchers interested in how people understand and experience the world, and the creative ways in which people express these understandings and experiences.

David Giles continues the discussion of online interactive media, with his overview of using *online discussion forums* as data in Chapter 9. He highlights the potential of these data for providing access to 'naturalistic' accounts of people's views and experiences (a common theme across the media chapters), and for providing key insights into social interaction and social identities, as well as the functioning of online communities. Drawing on his own discursive research in pro-ana and Asperger's online communities, he highlights the enormous potential of social media data for qualitative researchers, as well as key challenges around ethics and the status of online data.

Part III focuses on *virtual* interactive data collection, particularly the ways in which more traditional forms of qualitative data collection (e.g., interviews, focus groups) have evolved or been transformed by the move to virtual environments. In Chapter 10, Lucy Gibson provides an introduction to *email interviews*. Drawing on her own research with music fans, she demonstrates that email interviews offer an efficient, cost-effective and convenient means of gathering rich and detailed *written* data. They also offer specific benefits to the research participant, in that they are convenient and can be more acceptable to people who are unable, or do not want, to attend a face-to-face interview. Thus, email interviews can be very useful for reaching a geographically dispersed group, or for hard-to-find and/or hard-to-reach populations.

In Chapter 11, Pamela Lannutti takes us into the world of *Instant Messaging (IM) interviewing*, where people are asked to take part in a real-time, interactive, text-based chat (interview). She argues that, as IM interviews take place while the researcher and participant are simultaneously online, they confer many of the benefits of more traditional interview formats, whilst also offering many of the advantages of virtual methods: overcoming distance, convenience for the researchers and participants, increased possibility for data confidentiality and anonymity, and ease of data capture. Drawing on her research into same-sex marriage in the US, she highlights the potential of this method, but also some of its pitfalls – particularly in terms of some of the security concerns around collecting data in virtual spaces.

Chapter 12 explores one of the latest developments in interviewing – the use of video-calling technologies (in this instance Skype) to conduct virtual-but-visual interviews. Paul Hanna was the first researcher to write about the use of

Skype in interview research, and he is joined by his colleague Shadreck Mwale to discuss their experiences of using Skype to conduct interviews in two research projects – one on sustainable tourism and one on volunteer involvement in Phase I clinical trials. They argue that Skype interviews confound the distinction between face-to-face *spoken* interviews and virtual *written* interviews, by providing virtual and face-to-face interaction and data collection.

The final chapter, by Fiona Fox, moves us away from interviewing – providing an introduction to the world of *online focus group* (OFG) research. Drawing on her experience of a research project on young people with chronic skin conditions, she discusses both real-time (synchronous) and non-real-time (asynchronous) OFGs, and the practicalities of designing, recruiting, moderating and analysing both of these types of OFG. As with many of our chapters on virtual data collection, she argues that OFGs can be a feasible and attractive alternative to their offline counterpart and may even be more inclusive for, and attractive to, some participant groups.

The content chapters are 'bookended' by a Foreword (by Brendan Gough) and an Afterword (by Ruthellen Josselson) that provide an orientation to how this book sits in the greater field of qualitative research, as well as future directions in this domain.

Further Resources: Readings

For readers new to qualitative research, the following texts provide accessible introductions – even for readers outside of psychology:

Braun, V. and Clarke, V. (2013). *Successful qualitative research: A practical guide for beginners*. London: Sage Publications.
Howitt, D. (2012). *Introduction to qualitative methods in psychology* (2nd edn). Harlow, UK: Prentice Hall.
Vossler, A. and Moller, N. (eds.) (2014). *The counselling and psychotherapy research handbook*. London: Sage Publications.
Willig, C. (2013). *Introducing qualitative research in psychology* (3rd edn). Berkshire, UK: Open University Press.

References

Birks, M. and Mills, J. (2011). *Grounded theory: A practical guide*. London: Sage Publications.
Boyatzis, R. E. (1998). *Transforming qualitative information: Thematic analysis and code development*. Thousand Oaks, CA: Sage Publications.

Boynton, P. (2016). *The research companion: A practical guide for those in The social sciences and health and development* (2nd edn). London: Routledge.

Braun, V. and Clarke, V. (2006). Using thematic analysis in psychology. *Qualitative Research in Psychology, 3*(2), 77–101.

(2012). Thematic analysis. In H. Cooper, P. M. Camic, D. L. Long, A. T. Panter, D. Rindskopf and K. J. Sher (eds.), *APA handbook of research methods in psychology, Vol. 2: Research designs: Quantitative, qualitative, neuropsychological, and biological* (pp. 57–71). Washington, DC: American Psychological Association.

(2013). *Successful qualitative research: A practical guide for beginners.* London: Sage Publications.

Davies, H. and O'Callaghan, C. (2014). All in this together? Feminisms, academia, austerity. *Journal of Gender Studies, 23*(3), 227–232.

Fielding, N., Lee, R. M. and Blank, G. (eds.) (2008). *The SAGE handbook of online research methods.* Los Angeles: Sage Publications.

Hallowell, N., Lawton, J. and Gregory, S. (eds.) (2005). *Reflections on research: The realities of doing research in the social sciences.* Maidenhead, UK: Open University Press.

Hsieh, H. F. and Shannon, S. E. (2005). Three approaches to qualitative content analysis. *Qualitative Health Research, 15*(9), 1277–1288.

Howitt, D. (2012). *Introduction to qualitative methods in psychology* (2nd edn). Harlow, UK: Prentice Hall.

Mann, C. and Stewart, F. (2000). *Internet communication and qualitative research: A handbook for researching online.* London: Sage Publications.

Margolis, E. and Pauwels, L. (eds.) (2011). *The SAGE handbook of visual research methods.* London: Sage Publications.

Reavey, P. (ed.) (2011). *Visual methods in psychology: Using and interpreting images in qualitative research.* London: Routledge.

Riessman, C. K. (2007). *Narrative methods for the human sciences.* Thousand Oaks, CA: Sage Publications.

Rose, G. (2012). *Visual methodologies: An introduction to researching with visual materials.* Los Angeles: Sage Publications.

Smith, J. A., Flowers, P. and Larkin, M. (2009). *Interpretative phenomenological analysis: Theory, method and research.* London: Sage Publications.

Ten Have, P. (2007). *Doing conversation analysis: A practical guide* (2nd edn). London: Sage Publications.

Wetherell, M., Taylor, S. and Yates, S. J. (eds.) (2001a). *Discourse as data: A guide for analysis.* London: Sage Publications.

(2001b). *Discourse theory and practice: A reader.* London: Sage Publications.

Willig, C. (2001). *Introducing qualitative research in psychology: Adventures in theory and method.* Buckingham, UK: Open University Press.

(2013). *Introducing qualitative research in psychology* (3rd edn). Berkshire, UK: Open University Press.

Part I

Textual Data Collection

2 Short but Often Sweet

The Surprising Potential of Qualitative Survey
Methods

Gareth Terry and Virginia Braun

Overview

In qualitative surveys, participants respond in writing to a series of open-ended questions. This format can give participants the freedom to respond however they want to, determining the length, timing and location of their contributions. Although open-ended questions are often included in quantitative or 'mixed method' surveys (often with a quantitative analytic orientation, see Groves, 2009), *purely* qualitative surveys remain under-used and under-theorised. This chapter reflects our own experiences of using qualitative surveys (including what we learnt from our mistakes!) to produce rich, varied and textured data. Both *purely* qualitative surveys and mixed surveys that take the qualitative components seriously offer handy 'resource-lite' tools for qualitative researchers. Data are easy to collect, and the ability to gather responses from a great number of participants offers the researcher a wide-angle lens on topics of interest (Toerien and Wilkinson, 2004), which can be unusual in qualitative studies. The method is suitable for exploring people's experiences and their practices, their perceptions and their understandings about the research topic, and for researching sensitive topics.

In this chapter, we highlight the potential of qualitative surveys (and qualitative-dominated mixed surveys) and offer practical guidance for *collecting* data using such a method, including around 'traps for young players'. To illustrate points throughout, we draw on the qualitative elements of an online mixed survey we designed and used to examine body hair removal views and practices in New Zealand (see Box 2.1).

Introduction to Qualitative Surveys

In the qualitative survey, data are collected through a series of predetermined and fixed, open-ended questions, to which participants respond in writing. As such, it

---

Box 2.1 Introducing the 'body hair and its removal and alteration' (BHRA) survey

Hair removal for women has been normative in most 'Western' countries for some time, but body hair practices appear to have changed rapidly, with (younger) women removing hair in more places, and many (younger) men also removing their hair (Boroughs, 2012; Boroughs, Cafri and Thompson, 2005; Fahs, 2011, 2012, 2013; Toerien and Wilkinson, 2004; Toerien, Wilkinson and Choi, 2005). We were interested in understanding how younger people (18–35) in Aotearoa/New Zealand felt about body hair and its removal, and what they were actually doing with their own body hair, and developed a survey to address these questions (in 2012). Building on Virginia's previous qualitative survey research (Braun, Tricklebank and Clarke, 2013), and tools used by others in the field, our survey contained a mix of qualitative (open) and quantitative (fixed) response options. We use it as the example in this chapter for a few reasons – the research questions and survey itself were qualitatively oriented; the survey was qualitatively dominated (excluding the demographic section); the qualitative data generated were rich and diverse, and analysed in a fully qualitative way; and it was delivered online.

After piloting, the survey contained 92 questions, distributed across four sections: (1) Demographic Information (18 questions, *all quantitative*); (2) Body Hair and Men (19 questions, *mostly qualitative*); (3) Body Hair and Women (19 questions, *mostly qualitative*); and (4) Your Own Body Hair and Practices (36 questions, *mostly qualitative*). Over a short period of time, we gathered 1,000 responses, and of these 584 were complete surveys that fit the criteria for inclusion. Participants were identified as female (50.6%), male (48.9%) and 'other' (0.5%), gender-wise, and varied across a range of other demographics. The 584 participants generated so much qualitative (and quantitative) data that we're still exploring multiple aspects of body hair meaning and practice – watch this space! The first analysis – mostly of the *quantitative* data, since it proved quite surprising – has been published (Terry and Braun, 2013a; see also Terry and Braun, 2016).

---

is one of a cluster of methods that generate *textual* data from participants (see Braun and Clarke, 2013; see also Chapters 3, 4 and 5). *Quantitative* surveys (and questionnaires, their more 'robust' siblings; see Box 2.2) have a long history of use by social researchers (Groves, 2009). A quantitative focus is so common in survey research that it is often assumed or stated in texts devoted to survey development (e.g., Dal, 2011; Groves, 2009). That said, it is not uncommon for primarily quantitative surveys to contain some qualitative questions and for mixed surveys to combine qualitative and quantitative questions. However, the qualitative data generated from such questions are often treated in a very limited fashion, including reduction to quantified variables for statistical analysis. This does not need to be the case and, as our example will show,

---

Box 2.2 The qualitative *survey* or the qualitative *questionnaire* – are they the same?

We talk about the *survey*, but others often use the term *questionnaire* – are they the same? Not really. Although the terms 'survey' and 'questionnaire' both refer to a tool used to collect data, only survey refers to the *process* of sampling a population for information, opinions, experiences or practices. More importantly, however, questionnaires contain scales that generally require a process of question validation, reliability testing and other requirements (Groves, 2009), in fitting with positivist–empiricist research expectations. Surveys do not require this, and can be more open and explorative. Given general theoretical incompatibility between concerns around 'reliability' and qualitative research frameworks, we don't think it makes sense to talk about qualitative questionnaires.

---

qualitative data generated in mixed surveys can be analysed in a thoroughly qualitative way.

Although qualitative questions in largely quantitative surveys are common, the *purely qualitative* survey remains limited in uptake, and somewhat invisible. It doesn't always feature in qualitative textbooks or lists of qualitative methods (Toerien and Wilkinson, 2004), in the same way some version of 'interviews, observation and document analysis' do (Hewson and Laurent, 2008: 67). This *is* changing, and rightly so, as it offers an exciting tool for qualitative researchers (see Braun and Clarke, 2013). When we talk about a *qualitative* survey, we can refer to a data collection tool that collects *only* qualitative data, but qualitative survey data can be collected through a tool that also collects quantitative data (see Box 2.3, which outlines a range of 'qualitative purity' in survey tools). More important is whether the survey tool (and research project) is qualitative in its *orientation* – meaning the qualitative data are treated and analysed *as* qualitative data. A *qualitative* orientation has been described as a 'Big Q' approach to qualitative data (Kidder and Fine, 1987) in contrast to a 'small q' orientation, where research concerns (e.g., reliability, avoiding bias, generalisability) stem from a 'scientific' positivist–empiricist quantitative orientation.

What Do Qualitative Surveys Offer the Qualitative Researcher?

Qualitative surveys generate rich, detailed and varied data, and are suitable for exploring a wide range of topics. They work for analyses that aim to understand and explore participants' frameworks of meanings (an 'experiential' framework), and for analyses that seek to unpack and interrogate meaning (a 'critical'

Box 2.3 A typology of more- to less-qualitative surveys

(1) *The 'fully' qualitative survey* only includes qualitative questions, and is still relatively uncommon – even if we exclude the (typically quantitative) demographic information researchers collect as an ethical requirement (American Psychological Association, 2010). These surveys are often much shorter than mixed ones, with sometimes as few as three or four questions, such as Barrett's (2007) research on representations of BDSM in cinema (see also Frith and Gleeson, 2004, 2008). They can, however, be longer, such as Opperman, Braun, Clarke and Rogers' (2014) research on experiences around orgasm, which asked participants to respond to 16 questions.

(2) *The mixed (qualitative dominated) survey* is much more common; the primary focus is on the collection (and analysis) of *qualitative* data. Quantitative questions tend to be restricted to simple yes/no responses (and to the collection of demographic information) and function to support what is a predominantly qualitatively based analysis; there is no question that this is qualitative research. The openness of questions in this approach to surveys (and in the fully qualitative one) has some resonance with interview guides; indeed, Coyle and Rafalin (2001) used their interview schedule to develop a survey to explore Jewish gay men's negotiations around cultural, religious and sexual identities.

(3) *The fully mixed survey* reflects an interest in research questions answered by both qualitative and quantitative data; qualitative and quantitative questions are often fairly evenly balanced in number. Data of different types are sometimes analysed independently and sometimes in some combination – if so, a qualitative framework may dominate, or the quantitative data might predominate, with qualitative data supporting, illustrating or expanding the quantitative evidence. As noted in Box 2.1, we ended up treating our BHRA survey in this way, when the quantitative data proved really interesting, although we had intended it more as a 'type 2' survey.

(4) *The mixed (quantitative dominated) survey* is the most well-known version of surveys that collect qualitative data. Qualitative components only comprise a small proportion of questions. In some instances, qualitative questions might be added into an existing quantitative survey to add 'depth' of response or to elicit responses the researchers may not have anticipated, if a participant group – and/or topic – is under-researched. Fish and Wilkinson's (2003) survey about breast examinations among lesbian women works in this fashion.

---

framework; see Braun and Clarke, 2013). Moreover, they are less reliant on researcher 'craft skills' for data collection (Kvale and Brinkmann, 2009; Seale, 1999) than methods such as semi-structured interviews, making them suitable for use by qualitative data collectors of varied experience and skill.

Qualitative surveys mix openness with standardisation. They contain a fixed set of questions, asked of participants in the same order. However,

open responding means the critique of surveys as 'precluding the unexpected' (Willig and Stainton Rogers, 2008) no longer applies – responses
are not particularly delimited. Participants are required to put things in their
own words and are asked to respond from within their own sense-making
frameworks, albeit textually. As a (typically) self-administered tool
(Braun and Clarke, 2013), participants can often control the pace, time
and location of their involvement. Moreover, they respond typically in
a context of anonymity (Best and Krueger, 2008) – though this can vary by
modality. Survey data are primarily collected in one of three modalities:
paper hard copy, email or online. Each modality comes with pros and cons
(see Table 2.1).

For hard copy versions, participants may collect or return their survey,
presenting a 'face' of participation – although return can be anonymous if
posted. Emailed surveys typically provide a connection between an email
account and the completed survey emailed back, although this is fairly low-
level non-anonymity. Online delivery offers the most anonymity for participants, but tends not to be considered *fully anonymous* by ethics committees or
review boards, due to the retention of participants' unique IP addresses. Despite
IP-address tracing concerns, online delivery is *effectively* anonymised, and
certainly 'felt anonymity' is high. This potentially facilitates less inhibited
responses from participants than face-to-face methods (Jowett, Peel and
Shaw, 2011). It makes online surveys very useful for sensitive topics, such as
Opperman et al.'s (2014) experiences of orgasm survey, as well as for certain
marginalised populations, for whom identification may be a particular concern
(e.g., Barrett, 2007).

An additional benefit of *online* qualitative surveys is that they provide
a different way of recruiting and sampling, potentially extending participant
samples beyond the 'usual suspects' of much social science research: educated,
white, middle-class, straight people (Braun and Clarke, 2013). Inclusion of
participants from groups that have been identified as 'hard-to-reach', 'difficult-
to-engage' or marginalised *may* be facilitated by a method that doesn't necessarily require self-identification, or allows for recruitment beyond a geographi-
cally-based network (Evans, Elford and Wiggins, 2008; Levine et al., 2011;
Stewart and Williams, 2005). However, some of these groups may expect
researcher visibility, engagement and accountability, so don't just assume all
marginalised group members want anonymity and distance to participate in
research (Liamputtong, 2007; Smith, 2012). Online methods in general are
increasingly being used to collect data from 'hard-to-reach' populations
(Riggle, Rostosky and Reedy, 2005; Seymour, 2001; Stewart and Williams,
2005), from communities that exist only *as* online communities (e.g., work

Table 2.1 The pros and cons of hard copy, email and online survey formats

Type	Pros	Cons
Hard copy Delivered on paper Participants write responses by hand	Data can be collected in a structured way (e.g., student participants can complete surveys during a teaching session), which can increase sample size Easiest for participants to do 'drawing' tasks If postal distribution is used, can send reminders to increase participation	*Potentially* limited anonymity Data entry required Costs associated with postal distribution (e.g., to post 60 surveys in the UK, and include SAEs for returning the survey, would cost around £75 (2016 prices); further costs associated with sending reminders) Excludes participants with poor literacy skills
Email Sent via email (usually as an attached MS Word file) Participants usually type their responses Participants *can* print and complete the survey by hand	Handwriting or electronic completion options Good for geographically dispersed participants Potential for follow-up data collection (depending on research design and ethics) Can send reminders to increase participation	Potentially limited anonymity Participants need computer access and skills Risks excluding marginalised groups (those not online or with poor literacy skills) Data collation required If electronic completion, difficult for anything other than textual responses
Online Delivered through online survey software (e.g., Qualtrics; SurveyMonkey) Participants complete and submit survey entirely online	Quick and easy distribution Highest level of anonymity Good for geographically dispersed participants Great for using with (colour) images and audio and video clips Potentially very quick data collection No need for data entry or collation Potential to start data coding in the software program	Participants need computer access and skills Risks excluding marginalised groups Follow-up data collection and sending reminders less possible Difficult for anything other than textual responses Data output formats may be restrictive, especially if working with large samples

Source: Developed from Braun and Clarke (2013).

with asexual communities has been almost exclusively virtual; Przybylo, 2013), as well as from diversely spread populations.

There is potential to collect data from a large sample – with our body hair survey (the BHRA; see Terry and Braun, 2013a and Box 2.1), we collected nearly 600 completed surveys. Toerien and Wilkinson's (2004) UK body hair research collected close to 700. The size and breadth of the sample can provide some counterbalance for any loss of 'depth' in data, as compared with face-to-face methods (Toerien and Wilkinson, 2004) – although it is *not* the case that 'bigger is inherently better' for qualitative research samples. However, for some research questions, such as wanting to understand social norms or dominant practices, a larger sample provides a broad base, and *hopefully* a highly diverse sample, allowing you to explore the data and consider possible variation within responses. For instance, we *could* examine whether the patterns in men's body hair removal accounts were similar for men of various ages, of different ethnicities, straight and queer men, and even men of various political orientations. It's not only large samples that facilitate this comparative potential; in (some) qualitative survey research, the systematised mode of data collection makes comparison easier than with more flexibly applied data collection methods (e.g., semi-structured interviews).

Qualitative surveys are 'resource-lite', in that they can provide a quick and inexpensive mode for data collection – this can be useful for students with time-limited projects, and for academics in pressured university environments, where time and funding for research are increasingly squeezed. There are various other *practical* advantages associated with using qualitative surveys. Data can be collected simultaneously from many participants, meaning compressed time-frames for data collection are common. In our study, almost all data were collected over one weekend following a story about the survey in a national newspaper. Adding to the speed of data collection, in both emailed and online versions, data 'transcription' is unnecessary (and typing up hard copy surveys is also considerably quicker than audio-data transcription). These factors give the researcher more time for analysis, which can be advantageous, particularly in time-restricted projects (e.g., student projects). And, the standardised nature of responding makes it fairly straightforward for researchers to compile and collate data relevant to particular research questions or aspects of the project, such as all the responses related to men's back hair removal. This can assist in identifying both patterns and variation in responses. But a word of warning: be wary of assuming that material relevant to a particular topic or question will *only* appear in response to certain questions. Good qualitative research still requires a thorough assessment of the *whole* dataset, in relation to the analytic object of interest.

Finally, as a field, qualitative research is increasingly using and exploring visual elements in data collection (e.g., Banks, 2007; Rose, 2012). Qualitative surveys allow for the inclusion of visual or even audiovisual elements into research. With hard copy delivery, imagery can be included either as a point of reference or as a *task* for participants to respond to. In Braun et al.'s (2013) hard copy survey exploring views and perspectives on pubic hair, participants were asked to draw their idea for what constitutes 'little', 'typical' and 'lots' of pubic hair on three images of a generic male and of a generic female torso. They were then asked to indicate on another male and female torso the amount of pubic hair they perceived to be 'most attractive'. As this judgement is highly subjective and highly *visual*, graphic representation provided a far better insight than a numerical scale or a written description would have. In online or electronic (emailed) surveys, embedded or hyperlinked images, or even digital video or audio material, could be included as prompts or response materials. This creates an exciting multi-textuality in the method, which might particularly appeal to researchers interested in the ways individuals are both products and producers of culture (Wetherell and Edley, 1999). A word of warning, however: testing and ensuring consistency of experience across different web browsers and compatibility of software (e.g., Flash, JavaScript or Shockwave) with various platforms (e.g., PC/Mac vs. tablets) are essential. Software glitches may result in some participants quitting or only partially answering the survey (Best and Krueger, 2008). Existing software packages with built-in cross-platform functionality can alleviate some of this concern, but good IT support or knowledge in the research team will be important if you're doing things beyond a text-based survey. And, piloting and thorough testing across platforms are vital.

What Research Questions Suit Qualitative Surveys?

Qualitative surveys can be used to collect data to answer both *broad* and *specific* research questions, and in relation to a wide range of topics and *types* of research questions. Large surveys can generate data that allow you to answer more than one type of research question – the broad scope of our BHRA survey (Box 2.1) allowed us to address multiple research questions, such as what do people *do* in relation to body hair (Terry and Braun, 2013); how do women *feel* about body hair and body hair practices (Terry, Braun, Jayamaha and Madden, 2017); and what meanings are constructed around male body hair (Terry and Braun, 2016). For smaller projects, however, we recommend focusing on one research question, for cohesiveness and manageability. In Opperman et al.'s (2014) experiences of orgasm survey, for instance, the research question focused on young people's experiences of orgasm and the sense they made of those experiences. Although research questions can and do evolve and get refined during the process of qualitative research, the structured nature of data collection with qualitative *surveys* means that research questions do need to be fairly defined *before* the survey is finalised.

Qualitative researchers explore meaning and experience in many different ways, but research questions do tend to cluster into different 'types' (see Braun and Clarke, 2013; Willig, 2008). Qualitative surveys are a suitable or even desirable way of generating data to answer many of these. Qualitative surveys are an excellent tool to use if you're interested in understanding (or interrogating) people's *experiences* or their *practices*, such as Turner and Coyle's (2000) research on the experiences of being the offspring of a sperm donor, or Frith and Gleeson's (2004, 2008) work on men and clothing. With our BHRA survey, we were able to describe in rich detail the hair removal practices, and the variations in those practices, among our large sample, and could feel confident that we'd captured this well. Qualitative survey data from large samples can also provide useful 'baseline' knowledge about practices or experiences in an under-researched area, without delimiting the scope of response, as a quantitative survey would.

Qualitative surveys are also an excellent tool for gathering information on peoples' *views* and *perspectives* – many questions in our BHRA survey, for instance, produced data that allowed us to explore how people view hair on different bodies and body parts. This type of research question seems to align nicely with contemporary social media-influenced culture, where users often engage and express their opinions on issues online (Kamel Boulos and Wheeler, 2007) through the fairly ubiquitous (social) media comment box. This feature of Web 2.0-infused life makes qualitative surveys (particularly online) a potentially good fit; people's familiarity with this format through regular online 'social interaction' may assist in generating rich and varied data. It can, however, also detract from personal accounts, if more negative facets of social media life, such as 'trolling' (see Box 2.4), reflect a participant's preferred form of engagement. In our experience, however, there has been little of the negative, and more evidence of deep, thoughtful expressions of views and perspectives.

These types of research questions fit well with realist, critical realist and experiential frameworks around qualitative research; they tend to use data to map the recounted experiences or perspectives onto what *really* happens in the real world in a fairly straightforward way. Researchers aligned more with social constructionist or critical frameworks (Burr, 2003; Fox, Prilleltensky and

---

> **Box 2.4** Trolling and zingers
>
> 'Trolling' refers to comments 'designed' to provoke a negative reaction through 'objectionable' responses marked by misogyny, racism and heterosexism. They are prevalent on social media, and especially experienced by women (e.g., Chambers, 2013; Filipovic, 2007).
>
> 'Zingers' refers to short 'bite-sized' comments that are 'designed' to get a response on social media in the form of 'favouriting' or 'likes', and tend towards the superficial rather than the personal (Marwick and Boyd, 2011).

Austin, 2009; Gergen and Gergen, 2003) treat a straightforward relationship between language and reality as problematic and tend to ask questions related to *representation* or *meaning construction*. Researchers investigating such social meanings often focus on the conceptual frameworks people make use of to discuss their understandings of a particular social practice. Meanings explored through data are not treated as reflective of an underlying reality, but instead as helping to create the 'truth' of the object of research. Although it might seem counter-intuitive, we have found that qualitative surveys provide an excellent tool for this sort of research, especially if we understand individual responses as always embedded within social meanings (Gergen, 1997). For instance, in the BHRA study, we treated common descriptions of male back hair as 'gorilla-like' as reflecting *and reproducing* a social reality in which male back hair is interpreted as animalistic, brutish and disgusting (Terry and Braun, 2016).

Qualitative surveys, then, work well with *most* of the sorts of research questions qualitative researchers ask, and fit well with a range of different epistemological and ontological frameworks.

Design, Sampling and Ethical Issues

Qualitative survey design needs to occur at two key levels: (1) content and structure; and (2) formatting. Ideal design at the content and structure level intersects with survey mode (hard copy, emailed, online). For instance, online survey software can significantly shape how a survey looks and operates, which may require some rethinking of question structure and formatting. It's important to consider these design issues together, as you work through the process. Thinking about content and structure includes considering not just *what* you ask, but *how* questions are asked, and what answers they might produce, as well as how *many* questions and what order these will go in.

Guidelines for designing both quantitative surveys (e.g., Groves, 2009) and semi-structured interview guides (e.g., Braun and Clarke, 2013; Galletta, 2013; Smith, 1995) provide helpful tips, but note that pre- and post-testing for reliability and validity are not typically a concern in qualitative surveys (Toerien and Wilkinson, 2004).

Surveys need a title, instructions, content questions (generally open-ended) and demographic questions (usually a mix of tick or click box, with some open-ended). In addition, there are the participant information materials to develop and the consent process to consider.

The survey *title* needs to be clear, and signal to participants *what* they can expect to be asked about (e.g., 'Hair removal practices and perspectives in Aotearoa/New Zealand'). For hard copy and email surveys, designated space needs to be added on each page of the survey, to write/type in a participant code; online versions can assign one automatically. The title (and participant code) is followed by *completion instructions*, which need similarly to be clear, detailed, but not overly long, and enable participants to know what is expected of them (see Braun and Clarke, 2013, for examples). It may be necessary to provide additional question-specific instructions in some places throughout the survey (see 'what can go wrong with qualitative surveys' section). Ambiguity and confusing jargon create problems, so avoid, or offer *definitions* if you want all participants to understand a term in a certain way. But don't go overboard: you do not want to delimit or 'prime' participant responses too much. In our BHRA survey, we defined four key terms for participants (see Box 2.5) – these terms were integral to the survey, but don't necessarily have a universally shared meaning. In online surveys, where participants cannot easily refer back to a list of definitions, key ones should be restated at the top of every page, or at least as often as practicable (Best and Krueger, 2008).

Box 2.5 Definitions provided in the BHRA survey

When you're completing the rest of this survey, please keep the following definitions in mind.

Body hair alteration: any change to hair as it grows naturally on the body, including removal, trimming, bleaching

Body hair removal: removal of hair from the visible surface of the body (e.g., shaving, waxing, laser hair removal)

Body hair trimming/reduction: reducing in length the hair while still retaining visible hair

Currently: refers to practices typical of the last month or so

Typically, what comes next is the survey content – the *questions* you want responses to. Qualitative survey questions are *open-ended*: the participant can answer however they want, with as many or as few words as they choose. A vital factor in qualitative survey design is ensuring that questions are clear, as there's no opportunity to clarify or check for (mis)understanding once the survey has been distributed. As with interviews (Kvale and Brinkmann, 2009), short, clear, open questions that only ask *one thing* of the participants, but also invite explanation and elaboration, tend to work best. Such questions often begin with words such as 'how' or 'why', or include an invitation to 'please explain' – for instance, 'Why do you think women remove body hair?' Precise wording is important. In this instance, '*you think*' sets it up as about personal perspectives. Omitting these words would produce quite a different expectation, and requires the participant to 'know' the answer, potentially resulting in an unhelpful 'I don't know' response. So think carefully about *what* you are asking participants to respond to and *how* you are asking them to respond.

It's also useful to make deliberate choices about the *register* you're asking people to respond through – such as cognitive (thinking) or emotional (feeling). Again, it's potentially quite different to ask, 'What do you *think* when you see a woman with underarm hair?' and 'What do you *feel* when you see a woman with underarm hair?' The former invites cognitive explanations; the latter foregrounds emotional responses. In order to avoid signalling a register of response, we phrased our question: 'What sort of reaction (if any) would you have if you saw a woman with hairy underarms?' Our avoidance of presumption of *any* reaction was also important: we were looking for *their* sense-making about this issue; additionally, we didn't want to implicitly reinforce the idea that women with underarm hair are a 'freakfest'.

Generally, we recommend a minimum of 3–4 (see Frith and Gleeson, 2004, 2008, for examples) and a maximum of 25–30 (see Turner and Coyle, 2000, for an example) main questions for a qualitative survey, depending on focus and the depth of response expected. This maximum allows for a breadth of topic questions, and accounts for any inability to probe participants' answers, but it does not overburden them. Qualitative questions typically require more mental (and sometimes emotional) expenditure from the participant than quantitative questions, but regardless of type, overly long surveys risk: (1) roll-off – when a participant does not finish all the questions in a survey; and (2) haphazard answering of questions or not reading instructions, resulting in less thought-through and/or short responses (Best and Krueger, 2008). We think our own 'mega-survey' of 92 questions was very long and put a number of people off completion, but we took a calculated risk. We were as invested in 'proof of concept' as much as collecting data, – we were interested in assessing the limits of qualitative surveys. Although we were successful, this was probably because we knew what we were getting into, and the 'luck' of having a number of people invested enough in the topic to complete. Getting two to three friendly reviewers (including supervisors) to time themselves doing the survey during the piloting phase, and give honest feedback, can be vital for assessing if you're asking the right questions, too many, not enough or not generating the responses you want.

A survey *can* be too short if it doesn't deliver the amount of data you need to say anything meaningful, but it is important to recognise that *more* questions do not necessarily give you more (or better) data. A small number of *good* questions that elicit the depth, volume and type of data you need to answer your research question should always be considered superior to a long, overly detailed survey that gets limited responses. Your own research situation (time-frame, experience, etc.) needs to be balanced in this equation as well: we'd advise generally avoiding a complicated 25-question survey for a small project (e.g., undergraduate) that is your first experience of qualitative research; a longer survey would be fine for larger projects (e.g., for a Masters dissertation). Generally, closed (yes/no answer) questions should be used sparingly, and would almost always be followed up with an open-ended question to generate rich participant-led qualitative data that give more insight into the response. For example, in the BHRA survey, participants were typically asked to explain their response to closed questions (see Box 2.6).

The *flow* of questions throughout the qualitative survey is another important consideration – it needs to be logical and clear. This is less of an issue with surveys at the shorter end of the spectrum (i.e., 3–4 questions), but the implications of ordering still need to be considered. Typically, two good rules of thumb are: (1) move from the more general to the more specific; and (2) move from less- to more-personal questions (Kvale and Brinkmann, 2009). For longer surveys, separating questions into thematic sections can be useful, both to help participants keep 'on track' and understand the logic of question flow and for

---

Box 2.6 BHRA Question 32

32. Is it socially acceptable for men to leave their body hair in its natural state?
   □ Yes □ No □ It depends

Please explain

---

giving researchers distinct areas of focus when they come to analysis. Our BHRA survey content questions were split across three sections: (1) body hair and men; (2) body hair and women; and (3) your own body hair and practices. Following your planned questions, it is good practice to include a final 'Is there anything else you would like to add?' type open question. This allows the participant to express ideas or information relevant to the topic and that they deem important or interesting but that the rest of the survey doesn't explicitly ask about.

Demographic questions provide a description of the characteristics of your participants, and including this is often considered an ethical expectation (see American Psychological Association, 2010). Typical demographic questions include age, sex/gender, sexuality, race/ethnicity, occupation or education levels, but how much and what specifically you ask depends on what you want to do with the data, and what 'story' you want to be able to tell of your participants. Demographic questions are often quantitative, but can be open; there are two schools of thought about their placement in the overall survey. Traditionally, they appear at the end of the survey (e.g., Bradburn, Sudman and Wansink, 2004), because asking about personal details is considered threatening at the start of a survey, and people are thought to be more likely to answer these questions once they have finished answering ones about the topic. A different approach suggests that demographic questions can actually ease participants in to the survey and treats the assumption of 'threat' as problematic – especially if the survey is on a sensitive topic. If people have volunteered to answer in-depth sensitive and probing questions on a sensitive topic, questions about age and sex/gender and so on are potentially the least intrusive they will face. We found this second approach worked better for the BHRA in terms of consistency and quality of answers overall, but this insight was gained through piloting. We'd suggest that the traditional (end) mode of placement may be reflective of the dominance of quantitative questions in surveys, and that for qualitative surveys the reverse (beginning) placement can be better.

End your survey with a clear 'thank you' message signalling the end of the survey, and relevant contact details; if hardcopy or email, include clear 'return' instructions. If the survey has touched on potentially distressing topics, it is also important to provide details of relevant support services; the *participant information sheet* (PIS) might also contain these details, for example, university counselling services (for student samples), counselling hotlines (e.g., Lifeline or Youthline in New Zealand, the National Health Service 111 line or a third sector organisation such as Relate in the UK). You could also consider more specific services, such as LGBTQ counselling services or sexual violence hotlines. In the UK, where GP visits are free for the user, suggesting visiting your local practice may also be an option. Inclusion of support services may be an *ethical* requirement, depending on local ethics and the survey topic.

Ethics and Sampling

The standard ethical considerations for (qualitative) research (e.g., Braun and Clarke, 2013; Brinkmann and Kvale, 2008; Patton, 2002; Rice, 2009) apply to qualitative surveys, with some 'tweaks'. The researcher still needs to prepare a PIS to tell potential participants about the study. The PIS includes information about the researcher or research team and scope of the project, who is eligible to participate, confidentiality and anonymity, including issues associated with encryption (for using online surveys), the possibility or not of retrospective data withdrawal, and details about data storage and use. It also includes official information about ethical approval, university logos, etc. For hardcopy or email delivery, the PIS is sometimes provided to potential participants *before* they receive the survey. For online surveys, the PIS is usually the first information the potential participant sees, after – or as part of – a welcome page.

The process of consent with qualitative surveys varies by format and is some-what different from face-to-face methods, which usually require signed consent forms (American Psychological Association, 2010). As the specific requirements for ethical approval vary, comply with your local requirements. For hard copy and email delivery in Aotearoa/New Zealand, consent to participate is usually indi-cated by returning the completed survey. However, this is not always the case in the UK, where further participant consent can be required. For online surveys, consent is (also) indicated by submission of the completed survey, but an addi-tional step of 'click consent' is typically recommended after the PIS, before the participant is taken to the survey itself. This usually involves one or more click-boxes that indicate consent to, or agreement with, certain criteria around partici-pation (e.g., age; see Figure 2.1). Online surveys need to be set up to prevent access *without* the required boxes being clicked.

A sample size of up to 100 participants can work for smaller student projects (see, for instance, Opperman et al., 2014) and/or for researchers new to qualita-tive work, especially if a survey isn't very long and will generate a good breadth of responses. Larger sample sizes with longer surveys (e.g., our survey with over 500 participants) will likely produce rich complex datasets that allow for multiple different analyses, but if the topic is 'thin', such sizes may not be justified. In considering sample size, consider the likely breadth *and* depth, as well as the scope of, and resources for, the project. With a larger sample, collecting detailed demographics means you can potentially explore whether your data differ across certain broad demographic differences, such as whether those with

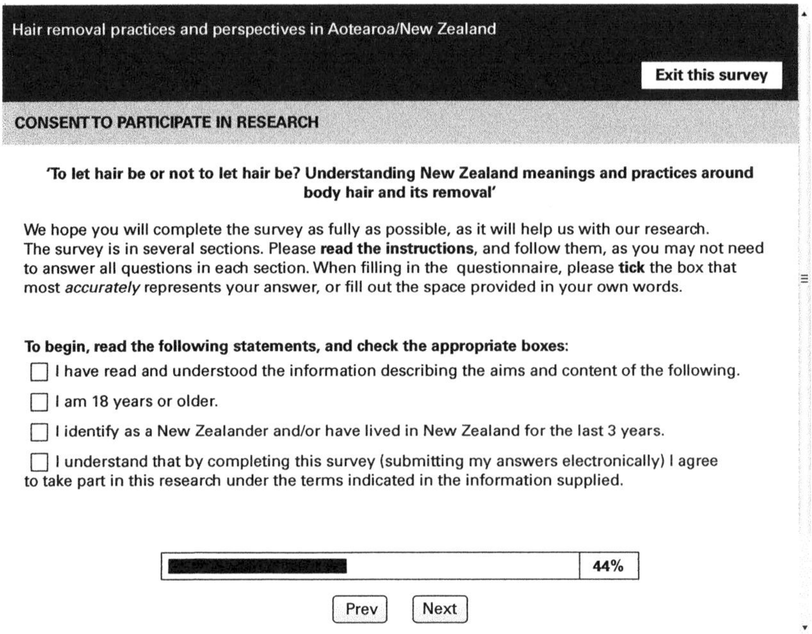
Hair removal practices and perspectives in Aotearoa/New Zealand

Exit this survey

CONSENT TO PARTICIPATE IN RESEARCH

'To let hair be or not to let hair be? Understanding New Zealand meanings and practices around body hair and its removal'

We hope you will complete the survey as fully as possible, as it will help us with our research. The survey is in several sections. Please **read the instructions**, and follow them, as you may not need to answer all questions in each section. When filling in the questionnaire, please **tick** the box that most *accurately* represents your answer, or fill out the space provided in your own words.

To begin, read the following statements, and check the appropriate boxes:

☐ I have read and understood the information describing the aims and content of the following.

☐ I am 18 years or older.

☐ I identify as a New Zealander and/or have lived in New Zealand for the last 3 years.

☐ I understand that by completing this survey (submitting my answers electronically) I agree to take part in this research under the terms indicated in the information supplied.

44%

Prev Next

Figure 2.1 Consent in the BHRA survey

conservative or liberal political views differ in how they represent body hair. But remember, qualitative researchers are not seeking a representative map of the general population in order to claim generalisability; rather, they aim to obtain rich, complex and textured explanations, and variability is valued (Patton, 2002; Willig and Stainton Rogers, 2008).

Specific Design Considerations

One important factor to consider – *particularly* for hard copy surveys – is the amount of space provided in response boxes. Experimental research has demonstrated that people provide longer and generally 'deeper' answers, when response box sizes are larger (Smyth, Dillman, Christian and McBride, 2009). Inappropriately designed boxes can result in respondents making (incorrect) assumptions about the types of answers expected from them (Christian, Dillman and Smyth, 2007). There are no hard and fast rules here, but it's important to consider what 'message' your response box might be sending, and how it might affect data quality. A pet hate of ours with online surveys is 'too small' boxes, where you cannot see the entirety of your answer; this makes reviewing and potentially editing one's response

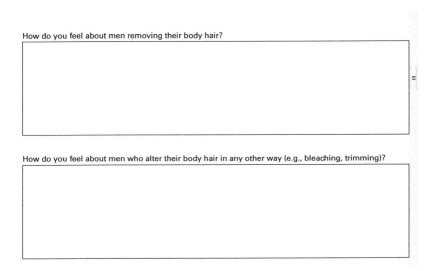

How do you feel about men removing their body hair?

How do you feel about men who alter their body hair in any other way (e.g., bleaching, trimming)?

Figure 2.2   An example of textboxes from the BHRA study

difficult (Figure 2.2 provides an example of text boxes from our BHRA survey – note that they allow multiple lines of text). In survey software we have used (e.g., Qualtrics, or SurveyMonkey), modification of box sizes is a straightforward process; this should be part of the process of learning how any software platform works.

As the software used in online surveys can shape the layout considerably, some basic HTML skills – or IT support within your institution – may allow you to modify the basic structures and templates offered by web-based tools, and create the 'right' look and layout (but this is not essential for doing online survey research).

Steps to Using Qualitative Surveys

Because surveys are a structured and fixed tool for data collection, preparation to get everything right before data collection is essential. A sequential process can ensure nothing is missed, and we've identified seven steps in the process:

(1) *Determine your research question.* We have already discussed different types of research questions. If you start with only a broad topic of interest (e.g., hair removal), *refining* your questions is important to focus your project, help define your target sample and clarify the scope of the qualitative survey.

(2) *Start to draft questions that will help answer research questions; these will form the basis for your survey.* Sometimes, you will develop these from scratch, but existing research – including your own work – can also inform question development. Knowing what has been asked, and *how* it has been asked, can help identify interesting gaps or problematic assumptions in existing research. We followed this strategy for the BHRA survey: looking across all existing qualitative and quantitative body hair surveys, we developed our own survey using a combination of newly developed, refined and existing questions.

(3) *Once you've drafted your questions, organise them into a draft survey, avoiding repetition and overlap.* For longer surveys, group questions into sections. There are often various ways questions could be grouped together, both overall and in terms of different sections. As noted earlier, we chose to cluster our BHRA survey questions around hair into sections divided by gender and other-/self-orientation (first we asked about men, then women, then the person's own practices; see Box 2.1). Grouping questions together by focus can help identify overlap, and where individual questions may need culling, or editing to make sure they 'fit' well within the context of surrounding questions, are *clear* in what they ask and don't cover issues already asked about. This applies even if they aren't grouped into specific sections.

(4) *The next step – piloting your survey – is absolutely* crucial, *as the fixed design means all kinks, quirks and confusions need to be ironed out before you give the survey to participants.* As participants don't get a chance to question you or clarify meaning, a poorly designed and non-piloted survey can ruin the whole project. Piloting typically involves testing the survey on a small sample of people similar to your participants (we generally aim for about 10%, but fewer might work for a smaller or 'hard-to-recruit' sample). The collected data can reveal whether or not the questions 'work' to provide the data you need to answer your research question; they can also identify questions that are unclear. The pilot stage for our BHRA survey involved 45 people (about 10% of our initially expected final sample of 400–500) as well as five people who timed themselves and gave feedback on the survey completion experience. We also asked six other researchers in the field to review the survey and provide feedback. This form of review isn't typical for all survey piloting, but given the scale, breadth and depth of the project, we wanted a thorough piloting process.

(5) *You then review your survey and revise if any changes are needed.* This applies both to individual questions, and to overall structure and design. Questions may be moved, removed, reworded for clarity, or new ones

added; new *sections* may be developed; whole sections may be removed or may be moved around. As we've noted, following piloting the BHRA survey, we decided to shift our demographic section to the start, against standard survey design advice, and we had a much higher percentage of completed demographics and completed qualitative questions than in the pilot.

(6) *Once revisions are made, you need to finalise and* proof *the final version.* It's very easy for slippages to occur between different versions of a survey – particularly if more than one person is making revisions. You need to make sure the final version is the correct one *and* that typographical or other errors haven't been introduced in the revision stage.

(7) *The final steps are to advertise for/recruit participants (see Box 2.7) and collect data.* For hardcopy and email survey formats, this is a sequential process, where participants make contact, and are provided with the survey to compete, and return it. For online surveys, the process occurs simultaneously, as recruitment typically takes the participant directly to the survey; you are likely not involved.

What Can Go Wrong with Qualitative Surveys?

Overall, qualitative surveys provide a fairly easy and straightforward tool for qualitative researchers, but things can go wrong, and there are pitfalls to be avoided. Two of the most likely problems are haphazard completion and roll-off (non-completion). For instance, although we collected almost 600 completed BHRA surveys, around 1,000 people started the survey. Most of those who didn't complete answered the demographic questions, but no others. The online format means we have no idea why this happened, but this high roll-off rate isn't dissimilar to what can happen with quantitative survey recruiting (Best and Krueger, 2008; Groves, 2009). We assume some of our roll-off related to the length of the survey – as noted already, length needs to be balanced against scope. However, the majority seemed to occur at the point participants were expected to *write answers*, rather than just click a box. The fact that qualitative surveys take time, effort and skills for participants needs to be recognised. Very clear guidelines in the PIS, which outline the expectations in terms of time-commitment and type of contribution, are important. For email format and hard copy format, where the participant gives you their details, reminder emails can facilitate completion and return (Braun and Clarke, 2013). Online survey tools also offer automated email reminders, but whether

---

Box 2.7 Recruit, recruit, recruit!

For the BHRA project, we recruited diversely. We placed advertisements in cafes, on university bulletin boards and in gyms, and created a Facebook page for the study; we 'hired' a number of recruiters with wide and diverse personal networks to publicise the research via social media and other methods. But media contacts and press releases proved the most successful strategy for recruitment, as we have found in other research we have conducted in New Zealand (see Braun and Clarke, 2013, for a description of Terry's vasectomy research recruitment). This strategy might not be viable in all geographic locations.

If roll-off is expected, and it may be, it needs to be built into recruitment; over-recruiting may be necessary, using strategies that fit with your epistemological stance. In the worst case scenario, you will get more data than expected!

A strategy to improve *completion* of recruited participants is providing some enticement *for completion*. With the BHRA survey, we offered the chance to be included in a draw for NZ$200 (£100) of shopping vouchers – a fairly substantial 'prize' – but details of how to enter the draw were only provided on submission of the *completed* survey:

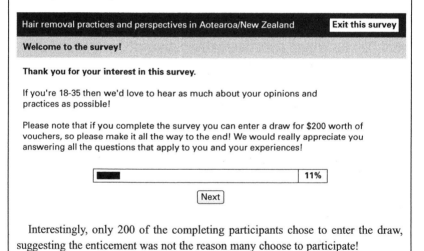

Interestingly, only 200 of the completing participants chose to enter the draw, suggesting the enticement was not the reason many choose to participate!

---

this facility is available to you depends on the structure of survey distribution, and how you have managed ethical concerns related to participant anonymity.

Another small risk, exacerbated by anonymity, is that people may not take the task seriously. With qualitative surveys, we rely on people's self-selection as indicating some investment in being a participant in the project, especially when they are delivered online with no researcher contact. People may feel more able to express themselves and their opinions more readily when they are not in a group or facing an interviewer (Stewart and Williams, 2005). The flipside of the very real benefit of anonymity, and greater freedom of expression, is the potential for 'trolling' or 'zingers' (see Box 2.4). In the BHRA survey, a small proportion of participants appeared invested in appearing 'humorous' rather than engaged – for example, when asked, 'Why do you think men remove their pubic hair?' one participant answered 'to make the tiger stand tall on the plain', when asked 'What sort of reaction (if any) would you have to a woman with hairy legs?' responses included, 'GET OUT THE WAXING STRIPS!', 'probably vomit on her' and 'Is she Chewbacca's sister or something?'. Fortunately this isn't typical of responses. Social desirability norms, and the ideals of research as a prosocial endeavour, may play a beneficial role in keeping participants 'on task' most of the time (Joinson, 1999). Such responses can provide humour during analysis, and although they're not necessarily great data, they do offer some insight into socially available meanings, *and* into rhetorical strategies deployed by people within online cultures. What all of these issues draw attention to is 'loss of control' by the researcher over the environment the survey is completed in, once a person gets or starts a survey (Kaczmirek, 2008). Including prompts or instructions such as 'please provide as much detail as you can', 'please take your time answering' or 'please give an answer that best reflects your own perspective' can also be a useful way of pre-empting too short or too flippant answers. Partly this may be about facilitating a sense of connection to a researcher, rather than a computer screen (Smyth et al., 2009). Using questions that orient the participant to you as researcher (e.g., 'tell *me* about . . .') can be a good strategy for producing in-depth answers.

What Methods of Analysis Suit Qualitative Survey Data?

Quite a bit of time can be spent on the analysis of qualitative survey data as they can be collected quickly, do not require much typing up and collation and/or data extraction in a usable form is easy. This is important, because although surveys often produce fairly 'straightforward' data, the datasets can also be large, and potentially overwhelming, especially for new researchers. Deep engagement can also be a challenge if the data appear 'thin', and the structuring of responses in a question/answer format can make it hard for researchers to look beyond 'answer to questions' to see patterns *across* the dataset (Braun and Clarke, 2013). Allowing time for familiarisation with the dataset is *vital*. As the researcher has not been involved in data collection in a way that embeds them in the ideas being generated, they start analysis completely removed from the data.

Thematic analysis (Braun and Clarke, 2006, 2012; Braun, Clarke and Terry, 2015) is a highly flexible method for 'systematically identifying, organising, and offering insight into patterns of meaning (themes)' in qualitative data (Braun and Clarke, 2012: 57). This provides a very straightforward and useful approach for the analysis of survey data, especially when working with large datasets. The structured nature of questions/answers in qualitative surveys can make initial coding – particularly if only studying the surface level of meaning – relatively straightforward. Thematic analysis can also enable a deeper engagement with some of the less obvious themes that cut across participants' responses. Further, thematic analysis gives the reader a tool to present an analysis of survey data that varies from the more descriptive (e.g., Fish, 2006; Fish and Wilkinson, 2003) through to the more theoretical/conceptual (for examples, see Braun et al. 2013; Clarke, 2016; Clarke and Smith, 2015; Clarke and Spence, 2012; Jowett and Peel, 2009; Opperman et al., 2014; Peel, 2010; Toerien and Wilkinson, 2004).

Other approaches that we (e.g., Terry and Braun, 2013b, 2015) have found amenable to survey data are poststructuralist forms of discourse analysis (Gavey, 1989; Willig, 2008) and less 'fine-grained' versions of discursive psychology, such as that advocated by Margaret Wetherell and Nigel Edley among others (Edley, 2001; Wetherell and Edley, 1999). These approaches orient the researcher to a view of language as productive, as helping create the realities it describes, and as accomplishing particular actions. They offer useful approaches for identifying the ideologies and cultural resources people use to make sense of a particular issue or problem in qualitative survey data, or the rhetorical strategies they employ, often with a closer focus on language and language use than that offered by even constructionist thematic analysis. This can be useful in unpacking the 'ready-made' explanations people can deploy in answering qualitative surveys. However, the brevity and lack of nuance that can be a feature of some qualitative survey data do limit the potential depth of such analysis.

Qualitative surveys aren't ideal for use with qualitative approaches that prioritise particular methodological requirements around data collection and the development of analysis (such as with interpretative phenomenological analysis (e.g., Smith, Flowers and Larkin, 2009) or grounded theory (e.g., Bryant and Charmaz, 2007)), although survey data are still sometimes analysed with these approaches. Similarly, if your analytic focus is closely on the way language is treated, as with narrative analysis (Riessman, 2007), discursive psychology (Potter and Wiggins, 2007) or conversation analysis (Wilkinson and Kitzinger, 2007), surveys generally do not provide appropriate data.

Conclusion

The qualitative survey provides an excellent tool for exploring many different sorts of research questions that qualitative researchers are interested in and opens scope to often fairly easily collect data from a large sample. Although considerable work goes in to the design of the survey, overall surveys are easy to use and fairly resource-lite. They have the potential to generate rich as well as broad data, and the pitfalls and risks are easily managed (see Box 2.8).

Box 2.8 Personal reflections on using qualitative surveys (from Gareth Terry)

Virginia had started developing a survey study based on her previous research in the area of hair removal practices and I was keen to be involved in the development and management of the project. I had done some work on survey development and (online) data collection in the past, but this was largely quantitative, so I was enthusiastic about exploring qualitative surveys, given that they fit more closely to my inclination towards qualitative research!

I found SurveyMonkey extremely straightforward to use for qualitative research – mostly as we had a 'full access' version, thanks to an institutional licence. Taking some time to learn some basic HTML meant I was able to tweak the look of the survey quite a bit, making the process more creative than simply cutting and pasting our Word version into the online survey. That's not to say developing the initial 'paper' version of the survey wasn't creative – and we brainstormed the development of the questions, speculating what kinds of data they might generate, and how to get the best possible responses, over good coffees in local cafes.

One of the first things that struck me, even in the piloting phase, was the investment participants seemed to have in the topic. Although textual formats can be seen as limited in terms of expression, newer forms of social media have provided a language and framework to enhance the communicative process. In various ways (e.g., CAPSLOCK, emoticons ☺, exclamation mark 'abuse'!!!!!!!!), participants indicated to us what was important (and unimportant) to them about hair removal. Some ideas were expressed time and again, evidencing culturally shared understandings, but often in ways that demonstrated creativity and variation within those understandings. The data produced were extremely rich, were easily coded, and *very* easy to read through for the most part.

The non-completions *were* quite frustrating, but once the newspaper articles hit the press, the sheer number of respondents more than compensated. I initially found the responses that seemed more about netiquette (McLaughlin and Vitak, 2012) than any attempt to provide a thoughtful response quite frustrating. Short 'zinger'-type answers were unfortunately the responses that seemed to 'stick' in my head. I worried whether most of our data would end up being like this (they weren't, so maybe it pays not to look at the data until they're all collected!). I found myself likening these sorts of answers to the comments section of newspaper articles, as my emotional responses were similarly 'extreme' – from laughing out loud to anger at outright misogyny! There were times I wanted to exclude these sorts of responses, but came to recognise that they had worth as data, that there was something interesting going on, irrespective of how superficial (and irritating) they seemed.

It was perhaps this mixture of data (rich and interesting, lending themselves to analysis vs. more superficial, 'twittery', humorous or trolling responses) that made the project so enjoyable. It began to feel like we were tapping into people's cultural sense-making resources at a number of levels, and in ways that I hadn't experienced in one space before. Not only were the data capturing the shape of hair removal practices in Aotearoa/New Zealand in quite unexpected ways (e.g., a distinct trend against *total* pubic hair removal among our participants, in contrast to popular claims and some empirical evidence; Herbenick, Schick, Reece, Sanders and Fortenberry, 2010), they were also providing a *new* form of qualitative data, informed by online cultures, but shaped by offline practices, and giving us insights that perhaps only an anonymous forum like a survey could provide.

Have a Go . . .

(1) Find an online quantitative survey on a topic that could be explored using a qualitative survey. Look at the types of questions they ask, and think about how you might: a) come up with a research question on the topic that fits a qualitative orientation; and b) rewrite the questions as qualitative survey questions/write new ones that cover the same areas. What information would you gain, and lose, through changing the survey to a qualitative one?

(2) Brainstorm a qualitative research question related to 'doing exercise' that suits qualitative survey research. Identify the key areas you'd want to ask people about, to answer your research question. Using the guidelines in this chapter, draft questions for each of these sections. Once you've put together a rough draft of your survey, pilot the tool on some classmates. Does it generate data that can answer your question(s)? Revise the survey as necessary.

(3) Box 2.9 contains data (not corrected in any way) from the BHRA survey. They are responses to the question: 'How do you feel about body hair on men?' Read the data once, noting any general thoughts that arise as you read them, then work through them a second time, more systematically, *coding* them as if you were doing a thematic analysis.

Box 2.9 BHRA data for coding exercise

P14: No strong feeling I think I am equally ok with men removing, keeping or trimming body hair. I can understand all three options and do a variety of all of the above

P17: Fine. Except sasquatch men

P22: I find it rather more than sexually arousing.

P23: On other men I find body hair that is tame and not excessive to be appealing. On myself however I strongly dislike it, and find it very depressing to have to 'see it'.

P31: Less is better but enough to be manly. don't like back hair

P33: I don't have a problem with it – if someone is comfortable with the way they look and how much body hair they have, that's their call.

P34: Should be maintained in certain areas by either trimming or shaving, back hair removed.

P37: Don't like body hair

P41: It is just hair, perfectly natural part of being a man if you happen to have it.

P42: I have no particular problem with body hair on men

P45: Awful. Should be banned

P46: It's normal, excessive amounts a bit off-putting.

P48: Don't mind hair but should be well groomed

P52: Well, i dislike the amount i have, but men are hairy. and yes nobody likes talking about it . . . especially back hair (when nobody even sees it that often under normal circumstances)

P55: Acceptable as long as it's not overly long or bushy, minimal in particular places. Has to be maintained properly.

P56: Fine. I used to feel a little self-conscious when hair began growing on my back, but was always resigned to having a hairy chest as my father and older brother do. Now I'm not too worried about it.

P59: Its okay, but not tooo much, back hair is a no no!

P60: normal, but excessive is pretty gross

P62: Chest hair is socially acceptable. I believe back hair or excessive hair is definitely on the way out and is not a good look.

P63: Personally, I dont like it, it causes smell and is ugly

P65: I think it looks masculine and sexy

P69: SOME is ok, as long its not thick/dark and monkey-like haha

Further Resources: Online

Some examples of qualitative surveys can be found online at: http://studysites.uk
.sagepub.com/braunandclarke/study/research.htm
There are a number of examples of qualitative survey data that can be analysed as practice
at: http://studysites.uk.sagepub.com/braunandclarke/study/qualitative.htm
For learning the basics of HTML in order to modify an existing template from a web
tool such as SurveyMonkey, we have found w3 schools extremely helpful:
www.w3schools.com/

Further Resources: Readings

For a broad 'how to' for qualitative research, and the first text to introduce qualitative surveys
as a stand-alone data generation method: Braun, V. and Clarke, V. (2013). *Successful
qualitative research: A practical guide for beginners*. London: Sage Publications.
For an example of a short survey which generated rich data: Frith, H. and Gleeson, K.
(2004). Clothing and embodiment: Men managing body image and appearance.
Psychology of Men & Masculinity, *5*(1), 40–48.
For an example of survey research on a sensitive topic: Opperman, E., Braun, V., Clarke, V.
and Rogers, C. (2014). 'It feels so good it almost hurts': Young adults' experiences of
orgasm and sexual pleasure. *Journal of Sex Research*, *51*(5), 503–515.
For an example of online survey research that uses critical/discursive approaches to
analysis: Clarke, V. and Smith, M. (2015). 'Not hiding, not shouting, just me': Gay
men negotiate their visual identities. *Journal of Homosexuality*, *62*(1), 4–32.

References

American Psychological Association. (2010). *Publication manual of the American
Psychological Association* (6th edn). Washington, DC: American Psychological
Association.
Banks, M. (2007). *Using visual data in qualitative research*. London: Sage Publications.
Barrett, J. (2007). You've made mistress very, very angry: Displeasure and pleasure in
media representations of BDSM. *Particip@tions*, *4*(1), online: http://www.partici
pations.org/Volume%204/Issue%201/4_01_barrett.htm.
Best, S. and Krueger, B. (2008). Internet survey design. In N. G. Fielding, R. M. Lee and
G. Blank (eds.), *The SAGE handbook of online research methods* (pp. 217–235).
London: Sage Publications.
Boroughs, M. S. (2012). *Body depilation among women and men: The association of body
hair reduction or removal with body satisfaction, appearance comparison, body
image disturbance, and body dysmorphic disorder symptomatology.* (Unpublished
PhD thesis). Tampa, FL: The University of South Florida. Retrieved from: http://sc
holarcommons.usf.edu/etd/3985
Boroughs, M., Cafri, G. and Thompson, J. (2005). Male body depilation: Prevalence and
associated features of body hair removal. *Sex Roles*, *52*(9–10), 637–644.

Bradburn, N. M., Sudman, S. and Wansink, B. (2004). *Asking questions: The definitive guide to questionnaire design – for market research, political polls, and social and health questionnaires*. San Francisco, CA: Jossey-Bass.

Braun, V. and Clarke, V. (2006). Using thematic analysis in psychology. *Qualitative Research in Psychology*, *3*(2), 77–101.

(2012). Thematic analysis. In H. Cooper, P. M. Camic, D. L. Long, A. T. Panter, D. Rindskopf and K. J. Sher (eds.), *APA handbook of research methods in psychology, Vol. 2: Research designs: Quantitative, qualitative, neuropsychological, and biological* (pp. 57–71). Washington, DC: American Psychological Association.

(2013). *Successful qualitative research: A practical guide for beginners*. London: Sage Publications.

Braun, V., Clarke, V. and Terry, G. (2015). Thematic analysis. In P. Rohleder and A. Lyons (eds.), *Qualitative research in clinical and health psychology* (pp. 95–113). Basingstoke, UK: Palgrave Macmillan.

Braun, V., Tricklebank, G. and Clarke, V. (2013). 'It shouldn't stick out from your bikini at the beach': Meaning, gender, and the hairy/hairless body. *Psychology of Women Quarterly*, *37*(4), 478–493.

Bryant, A. and Charmaz, K. (2007). *The SAGE handbook of grounded theory*. Thousand Oaks, CA: Sage Publications.

Brinkmann, S. and Kvale, S. (2008). Ethics in qualitative psychological research. In C. Willig and W. Stainton Rogers (eds.), *The SAGE handbook of qualitative research in psychology* (pp. 263–279). London: Sage Publications.

Burr, V. (2003). *Social constructionism* (2nd edn). London: Routledge.

Chambers, D. (2013). *Social media and personal relationships: Online intimacies and networked friendship*. London: Palgrave Macmillan.

Christian, L. M., Dillman, D. A. and Smyth, J. D. (2007). Helping respondents get it right the first time: The influence of words, symbols, and graphics in web surveys. *Public Opinion Quarterly*, *71*(1), 113–125.

Clarke, V. (2016). Wearing a gay slogan t-shirt in the higher education classroom: A cautionary tale. *Feminism & Psychology*, *26*(1), 3–10.

Clarke, V. and Smith, M. (2015). 'Not hiding, not shouting, just me': Gay men negotiate their visual identities. *Journal of Homosexuality*, *62*(1), 4–32.

Clarke, V. and Spence, K. (2012). 'I am who I am'? Navigating norms and the importance of authenticity in lesbian and bisexual women's accounts of their appearance practices. *Psychology of Sexuality*, *4*(1), 25–33.

Coyle, A. and Rafalin, D. (2001). Jewish gay men's accounts of negotiating cultural, religious, and sexual identity: A qualitative study. *Journal of Psychology & Human Sexuality*, *12*(4), 21–48.

Dal, M. (2011). Online data collection and data analysis using emergent technologies. In S. N. Hesse-Biber (ed.), *The handbook of emergent technologies in social research* (pp. 275–299). Oxford: Oxford University Press.

Edley, N. (2001). Analysing masculinity: Interpretative repertoires, ideological dilemmas and subject positions. In M. Wetherell, S. Taylor and S. Yates (eds.), *Discourse as data: A guide for analysis* (pp. 189–229). London: Sage Publications.

Evans, A., Elford, J. and Wiggins, D. (2008). Using the Internet for qualitative research. In C. Willig and W. Stainton Rogers (eds.), *The SAGE handbook of qualitative research in psychology* (pp. 315–333). London: Sage Publications.

Fahs, B. (2011). Dreaded 'otherness': Heteronormative patrolling of women's body hair rebellions. *Gender & Society, 25*(4), 451–472.

(2012). Breaking body hair boundaries: Classroom exercises for challenging social constructions of the body and sexuality. *Feminism & Psychology, 22*(4), 482–506.

(2013). Shaving it all off: Examining social norms of body hair among college men in women's studies courses. *Women's Studies 42*(5), 559–577.

Filipovic, J. (2007). Blogging while female: How Internet misogyny parallels 'real-world' harassment. *Yale Journal of Law and Feminism, 19*(1), 295–303.

Fish, J. (2006). Exploring lesbians' health behaviours and risk perceptions. *Diversity in Health & Social Care, 3*(3), 163–169.

Fish, J. and Wilkinson, S. (2003). Understanding lesbians' healthcare behaviour: The case of breast self-examination. *Social Science & Medicine, 56*(2), 235–245.

Fox, D., Prilleltensky, I. and Austin, S. (eds.). (2009). *Critical psychology: An introduction* (2nd edn). Thousand Oaks, CA: Sage Publications.

Frith, H. and Gleeson, K. (2004). Clothing and embodiment: Men managing body image and appearance. *Psychology of Men & Masculinity, 5*(1), 40–48.

(2008). Dressing the body: The role of clothing in sustaining body pride and managing body distress. *Qualitative Research in Psychology, 5*(1), 249–264.

Galletta, A. (2013). *Mastering the semi-structured interview and beyond: From research design to analysis and publication.* New York: New York University Press.

Gavey, N. (1989). Feminist poststructuralism and discourse analysis: Contributions to feminist psychology. *Psychology of Women Quarterly, 13*(4), 459–475.

Gergen, K. (1997). *Realities and relationships: Soundings in social construction.* Cambridge, MA: Harvard University Press.

Gergen, M. and Gergen, K. (eds.). (2003). *Social construction: A reader.* London: Sage Publications.

Groves, R. M. (2009). *Survey methodology.* Hoboken, NJ: Wiley.

Herbenick, D., Schick, V., Reece, M., Sanders, S. and Fortenberry, J. D. (2010). Pubic hair removal among women in the United States: Prevalence, methods, and characteristics. *The Journal of Sexual Medicine, 7*(10), 3322–3330.

Hewson, C. and Laurent, D. (2008). Research design and tools for internet research. In N. G. Fielding, R. M. Lee and G. Blank (eds.), *The SAGE handbook of online research methods* (pp. 58–78). Thousand Oaks, CA: Sage Publications.

Joinson, A. (1999). Social desirability, anonymity, and Internet-based questionnaires. *Behavior Research Methods, Instruments, & Computers, 31*(3), 433–438.

Jowett, A. and Peel, E. (2009). Chronic illness in non-heterosexual contexts: An online survey of experiences. *Feminism & Psychology, 19*(4), 454–474.

Jowett, A., Peel, E. and Shaw, R. (2011). Online interviewing in psychology: Reflections on the process. *Qualitative Research in Psychology, 8*(4), 354–369.

Kaczmirek, L. (2008). Internet survey software tools. In N. G. Fielding, RM. Lee and G. Blank (eds.), *The SAGE handbook of online research methods* (pp. 236–257). London: Sage Publications.

Kamel Boulos, M. and Wheeler, S. (2007). The emerging Web 2.0 social software: An enabling suite of sociable technologies in health and health care education. *Health Information & Libraries Journal, 24*(1), 2–23.

Kvale, S. and Brinkmann, S. (2009). *Interviews: Learning the craft of qualitative research interviewing*: Thousand Oaks, CA: Sage Publications.

Levine, D., Madsen, A., Wright, E., Barar, R. E., Santelli, J. and Bull, S. (2011). Formative research on MySpace: Online methods to engage hard-to-reach populations. *Journal of Health Communication, 16*(4), 448–454.

Liamputtong, P. (2007). *Researching the vulnerable: A guide to sensitive research methods.* London: Sage Publications.

Marwick, A. and Boyd, D. (2011). I tweet honestly, I tweet passionately: Twitter users, context collapse, and the imagined audience. *New Media & Society, 13*(1), 114–133.

McLaughlin, C. and Vitak, J. (2012). Norm evolution and violation on Facebook. *New Media & Society, 14*(2), 299–315.

Opperman, E., Braun, V., Clarke, V. and Rogers, C. (2014). 'It feels so good it almost hurts': Young adults' experiences of orgasm and sexual pleasure. *The Journal of Sex Research, 51*(5), 503–515.

Patton, M. Q. (2002). *Qualitative research & evaluation methods* (3rd edn). Thousand Oaks, CA: Sage Publications.

Peel, E. (2010). Pregnancy loss in lesbian and bisexual women: An online survey of experiences. *Human Reproduction, 25*(3), 721–727.

Potter, J. and Wiggins, S. (2007). Discursive psychology. In C. Willig and W. Stainton Rogers (eds.), *The SAGE handbook of qualitative research in psychology* (pp. 73–90). London: Sage Publications.

Przybylo, E. (2013). Producing facts: Empirical asexuality and the scientific study of sex. *Feminism & Psychology, 23*(2), 224–242.

Rice, C. (2009). Imagining the other? Ethical challenges of researching and writing women's embodied lives. *Feminism & Psychology, 19*(2), 245–266.

Riggle, E. D. B., Rostosky, S. S. and Reedy, C. S. (2005). Online surveys for BGLT research. *Journal of Homosexuality, 49*(2), 1–21.

Riessman, C. K. (2007). *Narrative methods for the human sciences.* Thousand Oaks, CA: Sage Publications.

Rose, G. (2012). *Visual methodologies: An introduction to researching with visual materials.* Los Angeles: Sage Publications.

Seale, C. (1999). Quality in qualitative research. *Qualitative inquiry, 5*(4), 465–478.

Seymour, W. S. (2001). In the flesh or online? Exploring qualitative research methodologies. *Qualitative Research, 1*(2), 147–168.

Smith, J. (1995). Semi-structured interviewing and qualitative analysis. In J. Smith, R. Harré and L. van Langenhove (eds.), *Rethinking methods in psychology* (pp. 9–26). London: Sage Publications.

Smith, J. A., Flowers, P., and Larkin, M. (2009). *Interpretative phenomenological analysis: Theory, method and research.* London: Sage Publications.

Smith, L. (2012). *Decolonizing methodologies: Research and indigenous peoples* (2nd edn). London: Zed Books.

Smyth, J. D., Dillman, D. A., Christian, L. M. and McBride, M. (2009). Open-ended questions in web surveys: Can increasing the size of answer boxes and providing extra verbal instructions improve response quality? *Public Opinion Quarterly, 73*(2), 325–337.

Stewart, K. and Williams, M. (2005). Researching online populations: The use of online focus groups for social research. *Qualitative Research, 5*(4), 395–416.

Terry, G. and Braun, V. (2013a). To let hair be, or to not let hair be? Gender and body hair removal practices in Aotearoa/New Zealand. *Body Image, 10*(4), 599–606.

(2013b). 'We have friends, for example, and he will not get a vasectomy': Imagining the self in relation to others when talking about sterilization. *Health Psychology*, *32*(1), 100–109.

(2016). 'I think gorilla-like back effusions of hair are rather a turn-off': Excessive hair and male body hair (removal) discourse. *Body Image*, *17*, 14–24.

Terry, G., Braun, V., Jayamaha, S. and Madden, H. (2017). Negotiating the hairless ideal in Aotearoa/New Zealand: Choice, awareness, complicity, and resistance in women's accounts of body hair removal. *Feminism & Psychology*. In press.

Toerien, M. and Wilkinson, S. (2004). Exploring the depilation norm: A qualitative questionnaire study of women's body hair removal. *Qualitative Research in Psychology*, *1*(1), 69–92.

Toerien, M., Wilkinson, S. and Choi, P. (2005). Body hair removal: The 'mundane' production of normative femininity. *Sex Roles*, *52*(5–6), 399–406.

Turner, A. J. and Coyle, A. (2000). What does it mean to be a donor offspring? The identity experiences of adults conceived by donor insemination and the implications for counselling and therapy. *Human Reproduction*, *15*(9), 2041–2051.

Wetherell, M. and Edley, N. (1999). Negotiating hegemonic masculinity: Imaginary positions and psycho-discursive practices. *Feminism & Psychology*, *9*(3), 335–356.

Wilkinson, S. and Kitzinger, C. (2007). Conversation analysis. In C. Willig and W. Stainton Rogers (eds.), *The SAGE handbook of qualitative research in psychology* (pp. 54–71). London: Sage Publications.

Willig, C. (2008). *Introducing qualitative research in psychology: Adventures in theory and method* (2nd edn). Maidenhead, UK: Open University Press.

Willig, C. and Stainton Rogers, W. (2008). Introduction. In C. Willig and W. Stainton Rogers (eds.), *The SAGE handbook of qualitative research in psychology* (pp. 1–12). London: Sage Publications.

3   Once Upon a Time . . .

Qualitative Story Completion Methods

Victoria Clarke, Nikki Hayfield, Naomi Moller, Irmgard
Tischner and the Story Completion Research Group

Overview

This chapter introduces the story completion (SC) method of collecting qualitative data, a novel technique that offers intriguing potential to the qualitative
researcher. Since the method is new to qualitative research, it has fewer
published research studies than some of the other methods covered in this
book. For this reason, the chapter aims not only to provide a description of the
method and recommendations for how best to use it, but also to explore some of
the unresolved theoretical and practical questions about SC. These questions
have been identified by the chapter authors, who comprise the Story
Completion Research Group. We are a group of researchers who have come
together to share our experience of using and further developing the method
(see Box 3.1). Our view is that SC has the potential to 'reach the parts that other
methods cannot reach' (Pope and Mays, 1995). It therefore has advantages over
and above being enticingly resource-lite in terms of data collection, although
that in itself is a sizeable benefit.

Introduction to Story Completion

SC originally developed as a form of projective test, for use by psychiatrists and
clinical psychologists (and other therapeutic practitioners), to assess the personality and psychopathology of clients (see Rabin, 1981). Projective tests
involve asking people to respond to ambiguous stimuli – such as inkblots, as in
the famous Rorschach inkblot test (Rorschach, Lemkau and Kronenberg, 1998
[1921]). The assumption is that because the respondent cannot know unequivocally what the stimulus 'is', they have to draw on their own understandings
(personality, needs, life experiences) to make sense of it, and 'fill in the blanks'.
In doing so – as the theory of projective tests goes – the participant reveals
things about themselves that they may not be conscious of, or would feel

> **Box 3.1** Exploring perceptions and constructions of gender, sexuality and appearance
>
> We have been 'experimenting', in the broadest sense, with SC for the last decade or so, and in this chapter we share what we have learnt about, and our enthusiasm for, the method, drawing on a wide range of different SC studies from our, and our students', research. The example studies reflect our interests in gender, sexuality, appearance and counselling and include research on perceptions of transgender parenting, sexual refusal in heterosexual relationships, the disclosure of non-heterosexuality to parents, non-normative body hair practices, same-sex infidelity, fat-therapists, weight-management, sexuality and appearance… Again, reflecting our shared interests in gender, most of these studies use a comparative design to explore gender variation – with regard to both the responses *of* male and female (or other gendered) participants, and participant responses *to* male and female (or other gendered) characters.

uncomfortable revealing if asked directly about. Projective tests are rooted in psychoanalytic theory (Rabin, 2001), which assumes that large portions of the self are blocked off to consciousness, and thus unavailable to both clients and clinicians through conventional means such as self-report. The psycho-dynamically informed promise of projective tests taps into this 'blocked off' information, providing what Murray (1971[1943]: 1) compares to 'an x-ray picture of [the] inner self'.

The key projective method of interest for the current chapter is the Thematic Apperception Test (TAT), the most famous – but not the first (Morgan, 2002) – projective test based on SC (Murray, 1971 [1943]). The TAT involves showing a client a series of evocative but ambiguous images and asking them to 'make up a story' for each picture presented. Although there are scoring methods available, the typical approach to the TAT in therapeutic settings is for the administrator to use their clinical judgement to interpret what the stories reveal about their clients.

Projective tests are used predominantly in clinical settings to provide insight into individual clients, rather than as an empirical method for research data collection. In other settings, however, projectives have also been used as a research method – for example, in consumer and business research (e.g., Donoghue, 2000; Soley and Smith, 2008) and developmental psychology (e.g., Bretherton, Oppenheim, Emde and the MacArthur Narrative Working Group, 2003; Bretherton, Ridgewa and Cassidy, 1990; George and West, 2012). Projectives are typically used in *quantitative* designs, where complex coding systems have been developed that allow researchers to iron out the variability in individual responses to the projective stimuli, and turn the rich narrative detail into numbers and categories suitable for quantitative analysis (e.g., Exner, 2002, for the Rorschach inkblot test). It is difficult not to regret the loss of valuable, in-depth information that taking a quantitative approach necessitates.

As highlighted, projective tests make the assumption that hidden truths are revealed about the test-takers: 'indeed it is often because projective methods are supposed to be *better* at getting at what people "really" think, that they are recommended' (Kitzinger and Powell, 1995: 349). For some, this is what underpins SC as a method, as it is assumed that there is *a* truth that can be *discovered* through the research process. Therefore, those who use projective methods such as SC in this way rely on a (post)positivist epistemology, taking an essentialist stance on the person and on the data. Such an approach doesn't sit well with many qualitative researchers, and we elaborate on an alternative approach to using SC in the rest of the chapter. First suggested in a 1995 study by two feminist psychologists (Kitzinger and Powell, 1995), this approach situates SC within a *qualitative* framework (Braun and Clarke, 2013).

Kitzinger and Powell (1995) used SC to examine how 116 undergraduate students made sense of infidelity in the context of a heterosexual relationship. In SC research, the (ambiguous) stimulus the participant has to respond to is the opening lines to a story (the 'story stem'), which they are instructed to complete. Kitzinger and Powell used a comparative design to explore differences in responses when the unfaithful person was a man versus a woman. The 'unfaithful male partner' version of the story stem read: 'John and Claire have been going out for over a year. Then Claire realises that John is seeing someone else' (p. 352). In the 'unfaithful female partner' version, the names in the second sentence were swapped.

Equal numbers of participants responded to each version of the story stem. The researchers also made sure that roughly equal numbers of male and female participants completed each version, to allow them to explore differences in how the male and female participants made sense of the scenarios. In contrast to existing frameworks, the authors suggested that it was not necessary to read the stories as (only) revealing the psychological 'truth' of the respondents: 'researchers can instead interpret these stories as reflecting contemporary discourses upon which subjects draw in making sense of experience' (Kitzinger and Powell, 1995: 349–350). This approach to SC is a social constructionist one that rejects the idea that it is possible to access 'real' or 'true' feelings or thoughts, and assumes instead that realities are discursively constructed (Burr, 2003).

Kitzinger and Powell (1995) illustrated the differences between the two approaches by contrasting an essentialist reading of their data, as revealing gender differences in 'attitudes' to infidelity, with a social constructionist one, in which the data were read as replicating various discourses about the meanings of infidelity for men and women. In this context, male participants' propensity to write more about sexual than emotional infidelity did not reveal 'young men's preoccupation with sex' (p. 350) but rather said something about their greater likelihood of being exposed to pornographic narratives of heterosexual sex than romantic fiction. One of the aims in the current chapter is similarly to hand researchers the choice of which 'lens' to apply to their data, something that makes the SC method eminently adaptable to a range of research questions and approaches to qualitative research.

What Does Story Completion Offer the Qualitative Researcher?

In common with all of the techniques and approaches discussed in this book, SC methods have the advantage of being less demanding of time and resources than established face-to-face interactive methods, such as interviews and focus groups. Hard copy stories, for instance, can be handed out to a large group of people and the completed stories returned in 30 minutes or so; online stories can be distributed (and then downloaded) with a few mouse clicks.

The advantages of SC are not limited to being resource-lite, however. We now outline some of the unique features that SC has to offer.

(1) *SC gives access to a wide range of responses, including socially undesirable ones.* Much qualitative research is based on self-report data – often generated by interviews and focus groups – in which small numbers of participants are asked to provide their experiences or understandings of the topic of concern (Braun and Clarke, 2013). SC offers an alternative approach to exploring participants' perceptions or understandings by asking about the *hypothetical* behaviour of *others* (Will, Eadie and MacAskill, 1996; also see Chapter 4, on vignette research). When participants are prompted to write hypothetically, and in the third-person, they do not have to take ownership of, or justify, their stories in the way they would if they were being asked directly about the topic. Therefore, they are more likely to 'relax their guard' and engage with the research topic with less reserve. This gives SC the unusual advantage of breaking down the 'social desirability "barrier" of self-report research' (Moore, Gullone and Kostanski, 1997: 372). Traditionally, this has posed a problem for essentialist research, which has sought to tap into participants' 'real' views or perceptions: participants not responding truthfully create a validity concern for

such research. (It's important to note that not *all* SC researchers ask participants to write in the third-person; an example of a first-person SC is discussed below.)

(2) *SC ideally suits sensitive topics.* SC also offers a particularly accessible way for participants to take part in research, because it does not necessarily require personal experience of the topic (also see Chapter 4, on vignette research). The use of hypothetical scenario story telling also means participants are slightly 'removed' from the topic. This makes SC *especially* useful for exploring sensitive topics – if questioned directly about their *own* experiences, some participants feel uncomfortable, or even unwilling, to discuss such topics. Sensitive topics that have been explored utilising SC include orgasmic 'absence' (Frith, 2013) and sex offending (Gavin, 2005).

(3) *SC gives participants control and allows for creativity.* Many qualitative researchers value methods – like focus groups – that are more participant-led and 'hand back' some of the control of the research to the participants (Wilkinson, 1999). SC is arguably a method that affords participants more control *and* creativity than other methods. The ambiguity of some story stems, for instance (see 'design' section), means that participants have lots of scope to choose the direction and style of their story. They are the sole authority of what and how they write.

(4) *SC research is theoretically flexible.* As noted previously, qualitative SC can be used in both essentialist and constructionist qualitative research. In essentialist SC research, the data are assumed to represent participants' real perceptions of a phenomenon. US psychologists Livingston and Testa (2000), for example, used qualitative SC within an *experimental* design to explore women's perceptions of their vulnerability to male aggression in a heterosexual dating scenario. The participants completed the story stem under different experimental conditions (one group was given alcohol to drink before completing the story, another a placebo and the third was not given a drink). The participants were presented with a first story stem with a male character Mark. They were told that 'you think he's really good looking' (p. 741); Mark later phones sounding drunk and then 'shows up at your door' (p. 741). Thus, the researchers asked women to imagine *themselves* as the female character in their story and to write in the *first-person*; they treated the women's responses as representing their beliefs about this topic.

Third-person SC has also been interpreted through an essentialist lens. Psychologist Moore (1995), for instance, explored girls' beliefs about menarche by asking Year Six (11-year-old) Australian girls to each complete five different menstruation story stems.

The second way in which SC data have been interpreted is through the identification of discourses, tropes, discursive repertoires or constructions, consistent with a social constructionist epistemology (Burr, 2003), as used by Kitzinger and Powell (1995), described previously. Another example is feminist psychologist Frith's (2013) constructionist research on orgasmic 'absence', which treated SC data as capturing the cultural discourses available to participants. She used two versions of a story stem, featuring a heterosexual couple – Lisa and Tom. In one version, Tom realises Lisa has not had an orgasm; in the other version, it is Lisa who realises Tom has not had an orgasm. Frith identified three themes in the data these stems generated. The analysis explored how the stories drew on and reinforced various gendered discourses, including women's responsibility to be sexually attractive to maintain men's sexual interest and the notion that men's sexual desire is unbridled and easy to satisfy.

Contextualist research, which sits somewhere between essentialism and constructionism, and where multiple truths or situated realities are understood to exist within particular contexts (Braun and Clarke, 2013), is also possible using SC. However, to date there are no published studies exemplifying this approach.

(5) *SC offers robust and easy-to-implement comparative design options.* This feature of SC (which also applies to vignettes; see Chapter 4) can be useful to explore differences between groups of participants, or between versions of the same story, and how they are made sense of. As outlined already, Kitzinger and Powell's (1995) groundbreaking study used a comparative design, as has most subsequent qualitative SC research. For example, critical psychologists Braun and Clarke (2013) used two versions of a story to explore people's perceptions of trans-parenting. The story stem described a parent telling their children that they are uncomfortable living within their assigned gender and want to start the process of changing sex. Roughly half of the participants completed a male parent (Brian) version and half an otherwise identical female parent (Mary) version. Having two versions enabled the researchers to compare the responses according to both the gender of the parent character and the gender of the participant. This was important because mothers and fathers tend to be perceived very differently in the wider culture, and women tend to be more tolerant of gender diversity and nonconformity than men (Braun and Clarke, 2013).

(6) *SC offers scope for methodological innovation.* Qualitative researchers have only recently begun to fully explore the possibilities that SC offers. For example, critical psychologists Hayfield and Wood (2014) piloted an SC using *visual* methodologies (Frith, Riley, Archer and Gleeson, 2005) in

their research on perceptions of appearance and sexuality (see 'steps' section). The stem described a dating scenario; once they had completed their stories, participants were directed to the website Bitstrips to create a cartoon image of the main character. A preliminary analysis of the images indicated that participants recognised the existence of lesbian and gay appearance norms, which was not necessarily *as* apparent in their written responses. Hence, visual data may provide an anchor for, or 'bring to life', textual responses, and can also be analysed in their own right. This allows the potential for different understandings of, insights into, and interpretations of, the main findings (Frith et al., 2005).

(7) *SC is useful for researching social categories.* These advantages of SC as a method – including the ease of implementing comparative designs – mean that it fits well with research focused on understanding the operation of social categories such as gender, race/ethnicity or sexuality. It enables researchers to explore any divergences in how different social groups make sense of a scenario, *and* whether participants respond differently to variations in, for example, the story character's gender or sexuality. We document examples of our and others' gender and sexuality research throughout the chapter to illustrate this point.

What Research Questions Suit Story Completion?

The flexibility of SC is one of its key advantages and, accordingly, it can be used to research a broad range of topics. SC is particularly suited to research exploring people's perceptions, understandings and social constructions. However, questions that focus on people's *lived experiences* are not well-suited to SC research, because this method does not gather stories about participants' *own* experiences (see 'analysis' section). When developing your research question(s), as in any qualitative project, you will need to ensure it is both focused on a specific topic and also broad and open-ended (typically asking exploratory 'what' or 'how' questions). For example, Kitzinger and Powell (1995: 345) aimed to 'explore young men's and women's representations of "unfaithful" heterosexual relationships' and Frith (2013: 312) examined 'how people account for and explain orgasmic absence during heterosex'. These questions are specific enough to guide the research and design, but open enough so that there is plenty of scope for fully exploring participants' responses. It is also important to ensure that the type of question you create 'fits' with your epistemological approach; 'perception' questions tend to be used in essentialist research, whereas 'construction' and

Table 3.1 Examples of existing story completion research, questions and theory

Topic area	Research question/focus	Theoretical framework
Internet infidelity	What are the perceived impacts of cyber-cheating on offline relationships? (Whitty, 2005)	Essentialist (perceptions)
Sexual aggression	How do women perceive their vulnerability to sexual aggression in (heterosexual) dating contexts? (Livingston and Testa, 2000)	Essentialist (perceptions)
Infidelity	How do women and men represent unfaithful heterosexual relationships? (Kitzinger and Powell, 1995)	Essentialist and constructionist
Sex offending	What cultural narratives do people draw on in stories about child sex offenders? (Gavin, 2005)	Constructionist (discursive constructions)
Eating disorders	How are 'anorexic' and 'bulimic' young women discursively constructed in stories written by young people who do not self-identify as 'eating disordered'? (Wlash and Walson, 2010)	Constructionist (discursive constructions)

'representation' questions are most often used in constructionist and critical research. Table 3.1 provides examples of existing SC studies that demonstrate this.

Design, Sampling and Ethical Issues

The most important design consideration in SC research is the design of the story stem: the 'start' of a story that participants are asked to complete. A careful balance needs to be struck between providing the participant with a *meaningful* story stem and leaving enough ambiguity for tapping into their assumptions (or 'perceptions' or 'psychological projections', in essentialist research). Braun and Clarke (2013) discussed six considerations in story stem design:

(1) *Length of the story stem.* How much of the beginning of the story will you write? There are no hard and fast rules here; it depends on your topic and participant group. If the story concerns something likely to be familiar to your participants, less detail is necessary for the scenario to be meaningful

to them. For example, in Clarke's (2014) research on young people's constructions of non-normative body hair practices, it was safe to assume the participants had knowledge of the topic, so a very short stem was used: 'Jane has decided to stop removing her body hair... (this is the female version)'. For a less familiar or more complex topic, such as one focused on the character's psychology, your participants may need more detail to understand the scenario that is the focus of the stem. For instance, critical psychologist Tischner's (2014) research on constructions of weight-loss used a slightly longer stem: 'Thomas has decided that he needs to lose weight. Full of enthusiasm, and in order to prevent him from changing his mind, he is telling his friends in the pub about his plans.' Although weight-loss is a familiar topic to most people, the main focus of the research was on social perceptions and interactions around weight-loss *intentions*; this necessitated the story stem including the protagonist's interaction with other people – that is, him telling his friends about his plans.

(2) *Authentic and engaging scenarios and characters.* Unless the story, its protagonists and the context resonate with your participants, it is unlikely they will write a useful story. Your stem should engage your participants and be easy for them to relate to. Using names and scenarios that sound authentic and believable will help your participants imagine or 'see' the characters and the scenario, and thus to write a rich and complex story.

(3) *Amount of detail.* The most difficult design decisions revolve around the issue of detail in the story stem. Too much detail and direction will potentially limit the variation in and richness of the data; not enough could mean the participants will not know 'where to take' the story, resulting in data that do not address your research question. You need to design a story stem that stimulates a range of complex and rich stories. To achieve this, give the participants adequate direction by giving them a context or background to the story, and some detail about the characters, what the topic of the story should be about (and what you are actually asking participants to do, which is discussed later). At the same time, you also want to avoid overly constraining their responses, by describing the background and characters in too much detail. Participants need to know what their story should be about, but you don't want to give them the plot or ending. So if you want them to write about *motivations* for exercise, for instance, a very open story stem like 'Toby decides to become more physically active ... What happens next?' may take the stories in too many, and possibly undesired, directions and not focus on Toby's motivations. On the other hand, giving participants a particular motivation in the story stem (e.g., 'Toby wants to develop a six-pack to attract a boyfriend ...')

could result in a lack of diversity in your data, as participants follow your lead and don't describe the range of understood motivations to take up exercise (a further example is given in the section 'What Can Go Wrong with Story Completion').

(4) *Use of deliberate ambiguity.* SC is particularly useful for the exploration of underlying, taken-for-granted assumptions around a topic – for example, the heteronormative assumption that a couple consists of a man and a woman. This can often be achieved by leaving certain elements of your story ambiguous, such as some demographic characteristics of your protagonists (e.g., class, sex, race, sexuality, age). However, if your research question necessitates focusing participants' attention on a particular detail of the story, this shouldn't be left ambiguous. For example, Clarke, Braun and Wooles' (2015) study comparing constructions of same-sex and different-sex infidelity in the context of a heterosexual relationship had to specify the gender of the characters in the story stem.

(5) *First- or third-person.* The final design consideration concerns the standpoint you want your participants to take. Do you want them to step into the shoes of, and empathise with, one particular protagonist, or assume the position of an omniscient narrator? Although to date qualitative SC has involved mostly third-person story stems, first-person stems are possible (e.g., Livingston and Testa, 2000). These can be useful if it is important for the participants to write from the perspective of a specific character. From a classical projective standpoint, first-person SC is assumed to prompt more socially desirable responses (Rabin, 1981). Therefore, if you want to gain a *broader* range of stories, including socially undesirable responses, we recommend using a third-person stem.

(6) *Completion instructions.* Think carefully about the completion instructions provided to participants (see 'steps' section also). Is it necessary that they write about a particular aspect of the scenario? Do you want to know about how the story develops (in the future)? Or the 'back story' to the scenario? For instance, if it's particularly important that your participants provide a description of the characters, you need to include this in your completion instructions. For example, the stem on weight-loss intentions discussed earlier (Tischner, 2014) was followed by the instructions: 'Please complete and expand on this story by describing Thomas to us, and telling us how the story unfolds: what is Thomas saying to his friends about his reasons and motivations, and how do they react?'

So how many participants or stories should you aim for? In existing SC research, there is a large variation in sample sizes – from 20 (Walsh and

Malson, 2010) to 234 (Whitty, 2005) participants. Sample size depends on a number of factors, including: (a) the complexity of your design – more stories generally require more participants to be able to say something meaningful about each version, especially if you intend to make comparisons; (b) the richness of individual stories – richer stories mean fewer participants (note, however, that you may not be able to predict in advance how rich the stories will be); and (c) the purposes of your research. For a small student project, with a one-stem design, and no comparison between different participant groups, around 20–40 participants are likely to provide you with data that are rich and detailed enough for a meaningful analysis. The more comparisons you make, the bigger your overall sample will need to be. Braun and Clarke (2013) advise recruiting *at least* ten participants per story stem variation, but should you aim to publish your report, you may find that journal editors and reviewers require higher participant numbers than that.

Of course, as with any research, recruiting enough participants can be a challenge, which is why many studies are carried out with a student population. Students, however, are a very specific population, and often not very diverse in terms of demographics. At the same time, students *are* used to discussing and describing ideas in writing, tend to be fairly literate and thus will not struggle with the task of writing a story (Kitzinger and Powell, 1995); the same cannot be assumed for all other participant groups. Think carefully about the needs and expectations of your participants. For example, busy professionals may require very clear but short instructions (see 'what can go wrong with story completion' section).

As a general rule, SC research raises fewer ethical concerns than research that involves direct interaction with participants and asking them about their personal lives; this is particularly the case for online SC studies that make it even easier for participants to be anonymous and reduce risk for both participants and researchers. However, participant comfort with the topic is still an important ethical consideration, particularly for sensitive topics, and standard accepted ethical practice still needs to be adhered to (e.g., British Psychological Society, 2009). Follow the relevant ethical guidance of your institution and/or professional body.

Steps to Using Story Completion

(1) *Decide if you want to use a comparative design*. With a comparative design you can explore and compare the assumptions made, or perceptions held, about certain social groups or scenarios. If this is your aim, you need to

design versions of your story which reflect the specific differences you are concerned with, and allocate roughly equal numbers of participants to each of these. For example, Tischner (2014) used a comparative design to explore the gendered constructions of body weight concerns and weight-loss motivations. This necessitated two story stems, with a male and female protagonist respectively. Clarke et al.'s (2014) research on infidelity employed a more complex comparative design. Their aim was to explore how same- *and* different-sex emotional *and* sexual infidelity were conceptualised in the context of heterosexual marriage. This required four story stems. We do, however, caution against having too many versions of a story in one study, and the use of overly complex designs, because qualitative research is primarily about understanding (potentially complex and dynamic) meaning, rather than compartmentalisation. Two to six is the manageable maximum number of stem versions for small and medium-sized projects, in terms of both participant recruitment and analysis.

Another level of comparison involves different participant groups, and exploring the differences between the stories written by people who are, for instance, from different genders, sexualities, generations, or cultural or educational backgrounds. This requires the recruitment of sufficient numbers of participants from each demographic category concerned. For example, counselling psychologist Moller's (2014) research on perceptions of fat-therapists (which will be described more in Step Four) included responses from 18- to 21-year-old undergraduate psychology university students and 16- to 18-year-old sixth formers. This design made it possible to consider both the salience of counsellor body weight for the whole group of young people and also how small differences in age and educational experience impacted on the expression of fat stigma. Whereas the stories of both groups clearly reiterated anti-fat cultural narratives, the younger cohort were much more direct in their expression.

(2) *Determine how many stories each participant will be asked to complete.* When using a comparative design with multiple versions of the story stem, you have the option of asking participants to complete one, or more than one, story. In psychologist Gavin's (2005) research on the social construction of sex offenders, each participant was asked to complete *six* different versions of a story stem. She did so to explore how individual participants' narratives surrounding sex offenders varied when presented with different situations. Similarly, in a study on adolescent risk-taking, the researchers asked all of the participants to respond to four short SC scenarios so that data could be collected on a variety of different aspects of the topic (Moore et al., 1997).

Asking participants to complete more than one stem may reflect a more pragmatic concern to maximise the number of stories in the dataset. For example, Shah-Beckley's doctoral research on therapists' and non-therapists' constructions of heterosex (see Boxes 3.2 and 3.3 below) asked participants to complete two versions of a story stem. This halved the number of participants she needed to recruit. One concern when asking participants to respond to multiple story stems is that there may be order effects, with participants writing their longest story for the first story stem. However, in Shah-Beckley's research, the opposite was true, with participants writing longer stories in response to the second stem.

(3) *Write your instructions*. After you have designed your story stem(s), you need to write completion instructions for participants. In the participant information sheet, you should provide participants with some information about the nature of the task, and what they are expected to do, emphasising the necessity of writing *a story*. Here's an example from Clarke's (2014) research on body hair:

> You are invited to complete a story – this means that you read the opening sentences of a story and then write what happens next. There is no right or wrong way to complete the story, and you can be as creative as you like in completing the story! I am interested in the range of different stories that people tell. Don't spend too long thinking about what might happen next – just write about whatever first comes to mind. Because collecting detailed stories is important for my research, you are asked to WRITE A STORY THAT IS AT LEAST 10 LINES/200 WORDS LONG. Some details of the opening sentence of the story are deliberately vague; it's up to you to be creative and 'fill in the blanks'!

Then, ideally just before or after you present participants with the story stem, you need to provide specific instructions on how they should complete the story (unless you do not want to constrain their responses in any way). Completion instructions can vary from the broad and open to the more prescriptive and directive. For example, Clarke (2014) instructed participants to simply 'read and complete the following story'. Another common instruction is to ask participants to write 'what happens next'. Hayfield and Wood's (2014) research on sexuality and appearance provides an example of a more prescriptive approach. Because they wanted participants to focus on the events before, during and after the female character's date, they instructed participants to write their story in three sections. Their story varied by character sexuality (bisexual, lesbian and heterosexual); this is the lesbian version:

> Jess is a 21-year-old lesbian woman. She has recently met someone, and they have arranged to go on a date.
> • Please write about the run-up to the date and how she prepared for it . . .
> • Please write about the date and how it went . . .
> • Please write about what happened next . . . (Please feel free to write as much as you like about the characters and as far into the future as you like)

You may also want to provide participants with clear instructions on the length of the story you wish them to write, or a time expectation, to help ensure you get the quality of data you need. For example, we have instructed participants to spend a certain amount of time writing their story (e.g., 'please spend at least 10 minutes'), or to write stories of a particular length (as in Clarke's, 2014 example). Such instructions are particularly important for participant groups who are not necessarily highly motivated, such as individuals who take part in order to access particular benefits associated with participation.

It is especially important to *pilot* SC story stems, and participant information and instructions, to assess whether participants interpret the stem and instructions in the way you intended (see step five). In Clarke's (2014) study, for instance, the instructions 'you are asked to WRITE A STORY THAT IS AT LEAST 10 LINES/200 WORDS LONG' were added after piloting, because the pilot stories were often very brief or did not seriously engage with the task.

Potential Step: Write additional questions. Although one of the key features of SC is that it provides an indirect approach, some researchers have combined the use of a story stem with a small number of direct questions (in a way that combines some aspects of vignette research; see Chapter 4). For example, Moller's (2014) research on perceptions of fat therapists used the following story stem and completion instructions:

Please read and complete the following story: Kate has been finding it really difficult to cope with life so she has decided to go for counselling. As she walks into the counselling room for the first time, her first thought is: 'Oh, my counsellor is fat!' What happens next? (Please spend at least 10 minutes writing your story.)

After completing the story, participants were asked a direct question about the counsellor featured in the story stem: 'What weight did you think the counsellor was?' The answers to this question allowed Moller to understand how the participants defined 'fat' – a variable construct – and provided a conceptual anchor for interpreting their stories.

You should also consider whether it is important to ask participants demographic questions beyond the 'standard' questions about age, sex/gender, race/ethnicity, sexuality, disability and social class (see Braun and Clarke, 2013). Such questions can provide a useful 'baseline' for interpreting and contextualising your stories. For example, in her research on body hair, Clarke (2014) asked a series of questions about whether participants had currently or previously removed or trimmed body hair in particular areas and their reasons for doing so. Given that for women, but increasingly for men too, body hair removal is a dominant social norm (Terry and Braun, 2013; Braun et al., 2013), an overview of the participants' own body hair practices provides important information for contextualising the data.

(4) *Determine mode of data collection.* Another consideration is whether to conduct your study using 'paper and pen' completion, or electronically, either online using (free or subscription) survey software such as Qualtrics (www.qualtrics.com) or SurveyMonkey (www.surveymonkey.com), or by emailing the SC to participants as an attachment or in the body of an email. An advantage of hard copy completion is that you can hand the SC directly to participants (for example, if you are recruiting on university campuses or at specific events), and, provided you have ethical approval, offer participants a small 'reward' (such as chocolate) for returning their story. However, you then need to manually type up participants' stories ready for analysis.

The key advantage of *electronic* data collection is that responses require little preparation for analysis – emailed stories will need to be cut and pasted so they are collated in a single document; online responses can be downloaded into a document almost instantly. Furthermore, participants can complete the study at a time and place that suits them. However, online SC research that requires participants to have Internet access can limit who can take part; it is the *least* privileged members of society that tend to have limited or no Internet access (Hargittai, 2010), and some groups (such as older participants) *may* be uncomfortable with, or find difficult to use, certain types of technology (Kurniawan, 2008). The fact that participants can now complete online studies on smartphones and tablets (e.g., there is a Qualtrics 'app' that users can download for free) *may* also impact on data quality. Mobile devices often utilise 'soft' keyboards that do not necessarily facilitate accuracy of typing, or indeed typing full stop. Features such as auto-correct may mean that unless participants look closely at their responses as they are typing, inaccurate 'corrections' can be made. Therefore, detailed (and coherent) responses may be restricted by the need to constantly check the screen, as well as by the impracticality of smaller keyboards and screens common to such devices. However, some research has indicated that as long as participants do not need to enter numerical as well as alphabetic data (thereby requiring switching between soft-keyboards), completion on mobile devices will not necessarily take participants much longer, nor impact on errors (Sears and Zha, 2003), and this may also apply to tablets which are generally larger and more 'typing-friendly' than mobile phones. Finally, another important consideration is achieving a good fit between your mode of data collection and your participant group. You don't have to restrict yourself to one mode – it may be most appropriate to ask some participants to complete the study online and others on hard copy.

(5) *Pilot your SC.* Given the open-ended and exploratory nature of SC research, piloting your stem and instructions to ensure they elicit relevant and useful data is vital (Braun and Clarke, 2013). We have often made minor (but transformative) amendments to story stems or instructions following piloting. The resource-lite nature of SC means that piloting is not generally an onerous task. We recommend piloting your stem on the equivalent of 10–20% of the intended final sample; the precise number should be determined in relation to the diversity within your participant group: greater diversity = larger pilot sample. You can pilot in one of two ways: (1) by treating early data collection as a pilot and using their responses to judge if the stem and your instructions have been interpreted in the way(s) you intended; or (2) by asking participants to both complete the study *and* comment on the clarity of the instructions and the study design. If you make no (or minimal) changes to the stem following piloting, the pilot data can be incorporated into your sample. Once all these steps are completed, you are ready to keep calm and collect your data!

What Can Go Wrong with Story Completion?

The generation of poor-quality data is a concern across most qualitative data collection methods; SC can also 'go wrong' in this way, and it can result from a number of different factors. Participants can sometimes 'refuse' the task by not completing the story as requested – for example, by not writing their response *as a story*. This *may* result from a simple failure to understand the task. For instance, in Shah-Beckley and Clarke's (2016) research comparing psychology students' and therapists' perceptions of sexual refusal in heterosexual relationships, a number of the therapist-participants wrote about what Ben and Kate might be feeling, and what might happen to their relationship, but not in the format of a story (see example 1 in Box 3.2). Therapists are busy professionals, and it seems likely that they did not spend much time reading the detailed participant information, and thus did not understand what was being asked of them. This shows the importance of providing clear but not overly long instructions, and repeating and highlighting key instructions.

Participants may also generate short or shallow stories (see example 2 in Box 3.2). This is often the result of low participant motivation – as noted we have found that individuals participating for reasons other than wanting to contribute to the study (e.g., benefits associated with participation, such as students gaining course credit) often write very short stories unless given explicit (and repeated) instructions to produce stories of a certain length. But such instructions

---

Box 3.2 Examples of story completion data

The story stem: 'Ben and Kate have been together for a few years. For quite some time they have not been having sex because Ben does not want to. Kate has tried talking to Ben but he has been reluctant to talk. Tonight Kate is making sexual advances but Ben says he is tired and turns over … What happens next?' (In a second version of the story Kate refuses sex.) We have corrected all the spelling errors and typos in the data.

(1) *Story 'refusal'*: 'If that will happen from now on, she will challenge him to talk about it and if he refuses she will divorce him.'
(2) *Example of a short and thin story:* 'Kate is then upset as she feels unattractive. Ben doesn't want to discuss it further so becomes defensive and dismissive. They have an argument and Kate makes Ben sleep downstairs.'
(3) *An excerpt from a longer and richer story:* 'Kate then decides that enough is enough – what's wrong with him? Am I unattractive? Is there someone else? Is he worried about something he hasn't told me? Kate challenges Ben, 'I can't keep doing this – you need to tell me what's going on. Is there something you're worried about? Something you feel you can't tell me? Please try – I just want to understand.' Ben sighs and turns back over to face Kate. He places his hand on her face and looks at her – 'It's not you', he says, 'I just feel like I've lost the urge to have sex…'' (The story continues for another 216 words.)

Source: Shah-Beckley and Clarke (2016)

---

can iron out variability in story length – eliminating both very short and longer, richer and more complex, and thus highly desirable, stories. One way to manage this is to over-recruit, so you can eliminate stories under a certain length from the final dataset.

Short or shallow responses can also result from the design of the story stem. Story stems that constrain participant's creativity in how they continue and complete the story, or suggest a very likely single outcome, often produce rather thin and narrow data. For example, a student project using a story stem about a student feeling anxious about giving an assessed presentation produced shallow stories, which mostly ended with the student successfully giving the presentation (Braun and Clarke, 2013). The data did not provide the basis for a rich and complex analysis. The lessons we have learned are that: (1) it is important to write story stems that allow for a range of possible outcomes, hence maximising the potential for participant creativity; and (2) piloting of the stem is crucial (as discussed).

Another potential problem is that participants can sometimes write stories that contain elements of humour and fantasy. Braun and Clarke (2013) found this in their research on perceptions of a parent coming out to their children as transgendered, with one story containing the memorable line 'Brian rubs his nipple and then David Beckham appears'. You don't need to know much about the study to appreciate the participant's failure to take the task seriously! Such stories may *potentially* reflect participant discomfort with the topic. In that study, the prevalence of 'transphobia' in the wider society (Nadal, Skolnik and Wong, 2012) and in the content of some of these stories ('Brian's ... over the moon that the tax payer is picking up the bill for a completely unnecessary procedure') suggest this as a potential explanation. However, 'fantasy' stories are only a *potential* problem; for some research questions and approaches, they may actually provide useful data. For example, in Clarke's (2014) social constructionist research on non-normative body hair practices, fantasy stories about Jane stopping removing her body hair and running away to live as a yeti in the wild were highly pertinent, providing useful information on the socio-cultural connotations of hairy women.

Such humorous or fantasy stories highlight another challenge with the SC method – the data are potentially more difficult to interpret than self-report data. We've noticed that some student-researchers get confused about what SC data represent, treating the fictional characters as real people and equating the stories with self-report data. For example, creative responses to hypothetical scenarios about a parent coming out to their children as transgender were treated by some students (analysing the data for an assignment) as providing information about the *real-world* impact of a parent undergoing a gender transition on child development. It's important to remember that SC produces just that – *stories* – which *may* (depending on your epistemological standpoint) reveal something about what participants think and feel about a particular topic. Because of the nature of SC data – in our qualitative context, creative stories about hypothetical scenarios rather than direct self-reports of personal experience – standard analytic approaches may need to be adapted somewhat to capture the full potential of SC data.

What Methods of Analysis Suit Story Completion Data?

To date, two methods have been used to analyse SC data – thematic analysis (TA) (e.g., Clarke et al., 2014; Frith, 2013; Livingston and Testa, 2000) and discourse analysis (DA) (Walsh and Malson, 2010). Following Kitzinger and Powell (1995), TA (Braun and Clarke, 2006, 2012) is often slightly adapted from its usual use with self-report data. That is, rather than simply identifying patterns across the stories as a whole, researchers have identified patterns in specific elements of the story (these can be thought of as a variant of *horizontal* patterning, in the sense that the patterns intersect the stories). For example, SC research on perceptions of relational infidelity has identified themes in how the relationship (both that between the primary partners and that between the unfaithful partner and the 'other' man/woman) is presented, how infidelity is accounted for, and how the responses to, and consequences of, infidelity are depicted (Kitzinger and Powell, 1995; Whitty, 2005). This means that SC researchers have identified particular questions they want to ask of the data (in advance of the analysis, or after data familiarisation) and used the techniques of TA to identify patterns in relation to these questions.

As noted previously, Kitzinger and Powell (1995) demonstrated that both essentialist and constructionist readings of SC data are possible, and TA has been used to analyse SC data in both essentialist and constructionist ways. Pattern-based DA is also an ideal analytic approach for constructionist approaches to SC (Braun and Clarke, 2013). For example, critical psychologists Walsh and Malson (2010) used poststructuralist DA (e.g., Wetherell, Taylor and Yates, 2001) to interrogate some of the ways in which their participants made sense of anorexia and bulimia, and constituted the causes of, and recovery from, eating disorders. They explored how the participants constructed 'dieting' as normal and healthy, for instance, and the ways in which recovery from an eating disorder was framed in terms of a return to 'normal' dieting rather than (say) a return to unrestricted eating or a lack of concern with body weight.

In addition to identifying *horizontal* patterning in the data, SC researchers have also examined *vertical* patterning – patterns in how stories unfold. One approach very useful for this type of 'narrative' analysis is Braun and Clarke's (2013) story mapping technique that involves distinguishing patterns in the key elements of a story's progression. Braun and Clarke provide the example of a study exploring perceptions of a young woman 'coming out' to her parents as non-heterosexual. The story map for this study identified patterns in: (1) the parent's initial reactions to the coming out; (2) the development of the stories; and (3) the ending or resolution of the stories. After an initial expression of shock, the parents' responses to their daughter coming out were categorised as either (broadly) positive or negative; the negative reaction stories either ended positively, negatively or ambiguously, and the positive reaction stories always ended positively (see Figure 3.1). Depending on your research question and approach, this story mapping technique can be a useful complement to a standard pattern-based analysis (e.g., TA), which helps the analysis to retain a sense of the storied nature of the data. This technique also lightly captures (Western) cultural conventions around storytelling (beginning, middle, end) and the dominance of particular genres (e.g., 'happily ever after', 'triumph over adversity').

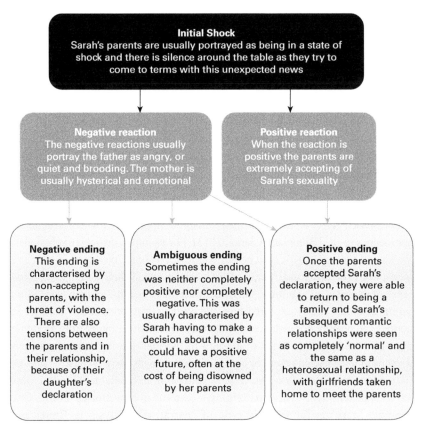

Initial Shock
Sarah's parents are usually portrayed as being in a state of shock and there is silence around the table as they try to come to terms with this unexpected news

Negative reaction
The negative reactions usually portray the father as angry, or quiet and brooding. The mother is usually hysterical and emotional

Positive reaction
When the reaction is positive the parents are extremely accepting of Sarah's sexuality

Negative ending
This ending is characterised by non-accepting parents, with the threat of violence. There are also tensions between the parents and in their relationship, because of their daughter's declaration

Ambiguous ending
Sometimes the ending was neither completely positive nor completely negative. This was usually characterised by Sarah having to make a decision about how she could have a positive future, often at the cost of being disowned by her parents

Positive ending
Once the parents accepted Sarah's declaration, they were able to return to being a family and Sarah's subsequent romantic relationships were seen as completely 'normal' and the same as a heterosexual relationship, with girlfriends taken home to meet the parents

Figure 3.1   An example of a story map
Source: Braun and Clarke (2013)

One analytic approach that has yet to be used to analyse SC data, but none-theless seems particularly apt, is narrative analysis (Riessman, 1993, 2007). Narrative techniques could be productively used to identify narrative types and genres, and the structures and styles of particular narrative types, thus extending and developing Braun and Clarke's (2013) story mapping technique.

Researchers who do qualitative research within a qualitative paradigm don't generally recommend the use of frequency counts in the analysis of self-report data, because of the organic and participant-responsive nature of self-report data collection (Braun and Clarke, 2013). However, frequency counts *are* often used in the analysis of SC data. For example, in their research on perceptions of infidelity, Kitzinger and Powell (1995) asked how many participants inter-preted Claire 'seeing someone else' as Claire being unfaithful – a full 10% rejected the implications of infidelity. When asking such concrete questions of the data (and when all participants have been set an identical task), reporting numbers or percentages, rather than using looser words such as 'most' or 'some', to capture patterning in the data is entirely appropriate.

Certain analytic approaches are not suited to the analysis of SC data, including approaches such as interpretative phenomenological analysis (Smith, Flowers and Larkin, 2009) and forms of narrative analysis focused on understanding participants' lived experiences (Riessman, 2007). Because participants are not asked for their views directly, and are often asked to write stories about things they may have little or no personal experience of, it's unclear whether SC data tell us anything meaningful about participants' lived experience. Without some big interpretative leaps, SC data would need to be combined with another data source to be suitable for use in research focused on lived experience. Grounded theory has similarly not been used to analyse SC data, and the focus on theory generation and the examination of the social processes and factors that shape particular phenomenon (Charmaz, 2006) suggest to us that it is unlikely to be an appropriate method for analysing SC data. Finally, approaches centred on the analysis of language practice – such as conversation analysis (e.g., Schegloff, 2007) and discursive psychology (e.g., Wiggins and Potter, 2010) – are not well-suited to SC data. These approaches typically focus on 'talk-in-interaction', the 'what' and 'how' of 'real' talk – both everyday 'real' talk and that produced in institutional contexts such as courtrooms or consulting rooms – which is rather different from written, storied data.

Box 3.3 Personal reflections on using story completion (Iduna Shah-Beckley)

I am completing a Professional Doctorate in Counselling Psychology. I have used SC for both a small project in my second year of study (focused on constructions of sexual refusal in heterosexual relationships; Shah-Beckley and Clarke, 2016) and now for my doctoral research, which explores how therapists and non-therapists make sense of heterosex. I have just finished collecting my data (200 stories) and begun the process of analysis informed by constructionist, poststructuralist, feminist and critical sexuality research. Before using SC, I only had experience of quantitative research, which often left me feeling very dissatisfied because the kind of data quantitative methods produced was simply not useful for addressing the kinds of research questions I was interested in. Broadly speaking, I am interested in how social norms around sexuality are produced and perpetuated, and the ways in which men's and women's sexuality are differentially shaped and constrained by social norms. SC is very useful for addressing these kinds of questions. For me, it's the best of both the quantitative and qualitative worlds, as it retains an 'experimental' element through the use of comparative designs, and it can generate a large amount of data, while also allowing for in-depth analysis.

For both of my studies, I have collected data online using the Qualtrics survey software, which has the huge practical advantage (compared to using face-to-face interviews or focus groups) of cutting out hours of transcribing time. The online environment grants participants maximum anonymity and allows people across the world to be reached. For me, the main challenge of using such a novel method as qualitative SC has been having to explain to other people why SC produces meaningful data. I have encountered questions and confusion from both quantitative and qualitative researchers, as well as lay people. So if you choose to use SC methods, you may encounter scepticism from other researchers. But this has really helped me to develop clear arguments about why I think SC really is a very exciting and useful method for qualitative (sexuality) research.

Conclusion

In sum, SC produces great data, and provides a major, and accessible, alternative to self-report methods of data collection. SC allows participants control and creativity, and the resulting data can be fun, rich and complex. SC also offers researchers new and exciting ways to generate data that provides compelling insights into the topic at hand.

Have a Go . . .

(1) Develop a research question suitable for use with SC and determine your participant group. Design a story stem that could be used to address this research question with this participant group. Think carefully about what details should be included (will your participants know anything about the topic?), and whether any aspects of the stem should be ambiguous.

(2) The following story is from Clarke's (2014) research on perceptions of non-normative body hair practices. Code the data in relation to the research question 'how do young people make sense of a woman stopping removing her body hair?' What are your main analytic observations about this story? Next, consider whether Braun and Clarke's (2013) story mapping technique could usefully be applied to this story? How would you code the opening, development and resolution of the story?

Jane has decided to stop removing her body hair... After years and years of shaving, waxing and bleaching. Jane has had enough of spending time removing her body hair. Jane has come to a point in her life where she is comfortable with her body and the way she looks. Jane does not feel the need to remove it as is now 65, happily married with old children. Jane does keep herself fit and healthy and wears make up and feels her husband loves her enough to not be worried about her body hair. Jane only removes her body hair on her legs and armpits in hot weather due to hygiene and how it looks in summer clothes. Jane also encourages older women to feel happy and comfortable in themselves and not worry and their body hair. Jane also like to encourage men to embrace their inner self and encourages them to embrace partners hair/non-haired bodies.

Further Resources: Online

The companion website for Braun and Clarke's (2013) book *Successful qualitative research: A practical guide for beginners* provides examples of SC research materials and a 'perceptions of a parent coming out as transgendered' SC datset to practice coding and analysis with: www.uk.sagepub.com/braunandclarke

Further Resources: Readings

The paper that introduced SC as a qualitative method: Kitzinger, C. and Powell, D. (1995). Engendering infidelity: Essentialist and social constructionist readings of a story completion task. *Feminism & Psychology, 5*(3), 345–372.

Braun and Clarke further developed the SC method for qualitative research (see Chapters 6 and 10): Braun, V. and Clarke, V. (2013). *Successful qualitative research: A practical guide for beginners*. London: Sage Publications.

Read about one of the examples discussed in more detail: Clarke, V., Braun, V. and Wooles, K. (2015). Thou shalt not covet another man? Exploring constructions of same-sex and different-sex infidelity using story completion. *Journal of Community & Applied Social Psychology, 25*(2), 153–166.

An example of a thematic analysis of SC data: Frith, H. (2013). Accounting for orgasmic absence: Exploring heterosex using the story completion method. *Psychology & Sexuality, 4*(3), 310–322.

An example of a discursive analysis of SC data: Walsh, E. and Malson, H. (2010). Discursive constructions of eating disorders: A story completion task. *Feminism & Psychology, 20*(4), 529–537.

References

Braun, V. and Clarke, V. (2006). Using thematic analysis in psychology. *Qualitative Research in Psychology, 3*(2), 77–101.

(2012). Thematic analysis. In H. Cooper, P. M. Camic, D. L. Long, A. T. Panter, D. Rindskopf and K. J. Sher (eds.), *APA handbook of research methods in psychology, Vol. 2: Research designs: Quantitative, qualitative, neuropsychological, and biological* (pp. 57–71). Washington, DC: American Psychological Association.

(2013). *Successful qualitative research: A practical guide for beginners.* London: Sage Publications.

Braun, V., Tricklebank, G. and Clarke, V. (2013). 'It shouldn't stick out from your bikini at the beach': Meaning, gender, and the hairy/hairless body. *Psychology of Women Quarterly, 37*(4), 478–493.

Bretherton, I., Ridgeway, D. and Cassidy, J. (1990). Assessing internal working models of the attachment relationship: An attachment story completion task for 3-year-olds. In M. T. Greenberg, D. Cicchetti and E. M. Cummings (eds.), *Attachment in the preschool years: Theory, research and intervention* (pp. 273–308). Chicago, IL: University of Chicago Press.

Bretherton, I., Oppenheim, D., Emde, R. N. and the MacArthur Narrative Working Group (2003). The MacArthur Story Stem Battery. In R. N. Emde, D. P. Wolfe and D. Oppenheim (eds.), *Revealing the inner worlds of young children: The MacArthur story stem battery and parent-child narratives* (pp. 381–396). New York: Oxford University Press.

British Psychological Society. (2009). *Code of ethics and conduct.* Leicester, UK: British Psychological Society.

Burr, V. (2003). *Social constructionism* (2nd edn). London: Psychology Press.

Charmaz, K. (2006). *Constructing grounded theory: A practical guide through qualitative analysis.* Thousand Oaks, CA: Sage Publications.

Clarke, V. (2014). Telling tales of the unexpected: Using story completion to explore constructions of non-normative body hair practices. Paper presented at Appearance Matters 6, 1–2 July, Bristol, UK.

Clarke, V., Braun, V. and Wooles, K. (2015). Thou shalt not covet another man? Exploring constructions of same-sex and different-sex infidelity using story completion. *Journal of Community & Applied Social Psychology, 25*(2), 153–166.

Donoghue, S. (2000). Projective techniques in consumer research. *Journal of Family Ecology and Consumer Sciences, 28*, 47–53.

Exner, J. E. (2002). *The Rorschach, a comprehensive system, Vol 1, basic foundations and principles of interpretation* (4th edn). Hoboken, NJ: Wiley.

Frith, H. (2013). Accounting for orgasmic absence: Exploring heterosex using the story completion method. *Psychology & Sexuality, 4*(3), 310–322.

Frith, H., Riley, S., Archer, L. and Gleeson, K. (2005). Editorial. *Qualitative Research in Psychology, 2*(3), 187–198.

Gavin, H. (2005). The social construction of the child sex offender explored by narrative. *The Qualitative Report, 10*(3), 395–415.

George, C. and West, M. L. (2012). *The adult attachment projective system, attachment theory and assessment in adults.* New York: The Guildford Press.

Hargittai, E. (2010). Digital na(t)ives? Variation in internet skills and uses among members of the 'net generation'. *Sociological Inquiry*, *80*(1), 92–113.

Hayfield, N. and Wood, M. (2014). Exploring sexuality and appearance using story completion and visual methods. Paper presented at Appearance Matters 6, 1–2 July, Bristol, UK.

Kitzinger, C. and Powell, D. (1995). Engendering infidelity: Essentialist and social constructionist readings of a story completion task. *Feminism & Psychology*, *5*(3), 345–372.

Kurniawan, S. (2008). Older people and mobile phones: A multi-method investigation. *International Journal of Human-Computer Studies*, *66*(12), 889–901.

Livingston, J. A. and Testa, M. (2000). Qualitative analysis of women's perceived vulnerability to sexual aggression in a hypothetical dating context. *Journal of Social and Personal Relationships*, *17*(6), 729–741.

Moller, N. (2014). Assumptions about fat counsellors: Findings from a story-completion task. Paper presented at Appearance Matters 6, 1–2 July, Bristol, UK.

Moore, S. M. (1995). Girls' understanding and social constructions of menarche. *Journal of Adolescence*, *18*(1), 87–104.

Moore, S. M., Gullone, E. and Kostanski, M. (1997). An examination of adolescent risk-taking using a story completion task. *Journal of Adolescence*, *20*(4), 369–379.

Morgan, W. G. (2002). Origin and history of the earliest Thematic Apperception Test pictures. *Journal of Personality Assessment*, *79*(3), 422–445.

Murray, H. A. (1971[1943]). *Thematic apperception test, manual*. Cambridge, MA: Harvard University Press.

Nadal, K. L., Skolnik, A. and Wong, Y. (2012). Interpersonal and systemic microaggressions toward transgender people: Implications for counseling. *Journal of LGBT Issues in Counseling*, *6*(1), 55–82.

Pope, C. and Mays, N. (1995). Reaching the parts other methods cannot reach: An introduction to qualitative methods in health and health services research. *British Medical Journal*, *311*(6996), 42–45.

Rabin, A. I. (ed.) (1981). *Assessment with projective techniques*. New York: Springer.
    (2001). Projective techniques at midcentury: A retrospective review of an introduction to projective techniques by Harold H. Anderson and Gladys L. Anderson. *Journal of Personality Assessment*, *76*(2), 353–367.

Riessman, C. K. (1993). *Narrative analysis*. Newbury Park, CA: Sage Publications.
    (2007). *Narrative methods for the human sciences*. Thousand Oaks, CA: Sage Publications.

Rorschach, H., Lemkau, P. and Kronenberg, B. (1998[1921]). *Psychodiagnostics: A diagnostic test based on perception* (10th rev. edn). Berne, Switzerland: Verlag Huber.

Schegloff, E. A. (2007). *Sequence organisation in interaction: A primer in conversation analysis*. New York: Cambridge University Press.

Sears, A. and Zha, Y. (2003). Data entry for mobile devices using soft keyboards: Understanding the effects of keyboard size and user tasks. *International Journal of Human-Computer Interaction*, *16*(2), 163–184.

Shah-Beckley, I. and Clarke, V. (2016). Exploring constructions of sexual refusal in heterosexual relationships: A qualitative story completion study. Manuscript under submission.

Smith, J. A., Flowers, P. and Larkin, M. (2009). *Interpretative phenomenological analysis: Theory, method and research*. London: Sage Publications.

Soley, L. and Smith, A. L. (2008). *Projective techniques for social science and business research*. Shirley, NY: The Southshore Press.

Terry, G. and Braun, V. (2013). To let hair be, or to not let hair be? Gender and body hair removal practices in Aotearoa/New Zealand. *Body Image, 10*(4), 599–606.

Tischner, I. (2014). Gendered constructions of weight-loss perceptions and motivations. Paper presented at Appearance Matters 6, 1–2 July, Bristol, UK.

Walsh, E. and Malson, H. (2010). Discursive constructions of eating disorders: A story completion task. *Feminism & Psychology, 20*(4), 529–537.

Wetherell, M., Taylor, S. and Yates, S. (2001). *Discourse theory and practice: A reader*. London: Sage Publications.

Whitty, M. T. (2005). The realness of cybercheating: Men's and women's representations of unfaithful internet relationships. *Social Science Computer Review, 23*(1), 57–67.

Wiggins, S. and Potter, J. (2010). Discursive psychology. In C. Willig and W. Stainton Rogers (eds.), *The SAGE handbook of qualitative research in psychology* (pp. 73–90). London: Sage Publications.

Wilkinson, S. (1999). Focus groups: A feminist method. *Psychology of Women Quarterly, 23*(2), 221–244.

Will, V., Eadie, D. and MacAskill, S. (1996). Projective and enabling techniques explored. *Marketing Intelligence & Planning, 14*(6), 38–43.

4   Hypothetically Speaking

Using Vignettes as a Stand-Alone Qualitative Method

Debra Gray, Bronwen Royall and Helen Malson

Overview

This chapter focuses on vignette research, where a hypothetical short story or narrative (*the vignette*) is presented to participants, who then respond in writing to a series of open-ended questions. In particular, we focus here on vignettes as a *stand-alone* method for qualitative research, rather than vignette use within other designs. Drawing on our experiences of using vignettes across a range of projects – and, particularly, a project on lay discourses of teenage 'anorexia' (see Box 4.1) – we argue that vignettes offer great potential for exploring participants' interpretations of a particular phenomenon, within a given context. They also offer a variety of *practical* benefits, not least of which is being able to collect data with relatively few resources. We explore both the theoretical and practical aspects of using vignettes and provide guidance and personal reflection on how to do research using this method.

Introduction to Vignettes

Vignettes have been widely used across the social and health sciences since at least the 1950s. They are predominantly used as a *quantitative* method, where the aim is usually to tap into participants' general attitudes or beliefs about a given situation or scenario (Finch, 1987). In *qualitative* research, they are typically used to complement other data collection methods, like interviews or focus groups – as a 'warm-up exercise' to get participants talking to each other, as an elicitation technique to focus conversation on a specific topic (e.g., Gray, Delaney and Durrheim, 2005; Gray and Manning, 2014; Fischer, Jenkins, Bloor, Neale and Berney, 2007) or as a way of exploring an issue in more detail and/or in different ways (e.g., Barter and Renold, 1999; Jenkins, 2006). In this chapter, we focus on what we see as a valuable, but relatively underused, type of vignette research – vignettes as a 'stand-alone' method, where data are

---

Box 4.1 Constructing the teenage 'anorexic'

This study was conducted by Bronwen Royall as her independent empirical project in the final year of her undergraduate degree course in psychology. The aim was to explore the ways in which teenage male and female 'anorexics' are discursively produced in 'lay' discourse, adding to the growing body of work that has looked at how 'anorexia' is constructed by the media, health professionals and those diagnosed with the condition themselves. Vignettes offered a specific set of advantages for this study, as it meant that: (1) participants did not need to have any direct experience of 'anorexia' themselves, capturing more 'lay' discourse; (2) we could research a potentially very sensitive issue in a relatively safe way; (3) participants' attention could be directed towards a specific group (in this case, teenagers); (4) we could capture how participants make sense of the presented scenarios in their own words; and (5) we could explore how gender featured in constructions of teenaged 'anorexics', which may have been more difficult using other data collection methods, where normative ideas of 'anorexia' as a problem of girls and women may have dominated.

For the study, two near-identical vignettes were developed. Each described one character, Harry or Hannah, who was diagnosed with 'anorexia nervosa' by their doctor (Box 4.2 shows the full vignette). Participants were allocated either the Harry or Hannah vignette, and asked to complete ten open-ended questions about the character. The questions were designed to be relatively broad, giving the participants considerable scope to present their own image of the character, and allowing them to provide relatively unconstrained and detailed responses. Data were collected online, using Qualtrics. In total, fifty-seven participants took part in the study, generating a substantial amount of in-depth data that highlighted the complex and often contradictory ways in which 'anorexic' teenagers are constructed and the ways in which gender featured in these constructions.

---

collected in textual form as a response to a series of open-ended questions about the vignette.

What counts as a vignette? A vignette can take many different forms. The most traditional – and perhaps most common – form of vignette is a written hypothetical or fictional story that is presented to participants with a set of questions about it. But vignettes can also be visual, including video-recorded (McKinstry, 2000; Morrison, 2015), and can be presented to participants on paper, on screen or online (Stolte, 1994; Taylor, 2006; Vitkovitch and Tyrell, 1995). Similarly, they can consist of 'real-life' stories, news stories (e.g., Gray, Delaney and Durrheim, 2005), geographic data (e.g., Gray and Manning, 2014) or could be materials taken from such things as public health campaigns, art or literature. Format-wise, vignettes can either follow a *staged* model, where the story is presented and developed across a number of stages, with each stage being followed by a series of questions (e.g., Jenkins, 2006; Fischer et al., 2007), or they can be presented as a single *complete* 'story', followed by one set of questions. Stories can be written using a first-person perspective (using 'I and me') or a third-person perspective (using 'him', 'her' or other (non) gendered pronouns such as 'ze'); participants can likewise be directed to answer as if they *were* the character, or from their own *personal* perspective. Participants can also be asked about how they, or a particular character in the story, *should ideally* act, or how they or the character *would realistically* act, focusing attention respectively on either more ideal dimensions of situations or on the more pragmatic (Finch, 1987).

The diversity of vignettes means that they can be used to address a wide range of different research topics and aims. In qualitative research this has included topics as varied as violence between children in residential care homes (Barter and Reynold, 2000; Barter, Renold, Berridge and Cawson, 2004), drug injectors' perceptions of HIV risk and safer behaviour (Hughes, 1998), social work ethics (Wilks, 2004) and perceptions of receiving and providing health-care (Brondani, MacEntee, Bryant and O'Neil, 2008). They can also be used across a variety of different theoretical approaches. For example, Jenkins, Bloor, Fischer, Berney and Neale (2010) propose a *phenomenological* approach for their research on user involvement in drug treatment decision-making and young people's injury-risking behaviours in leisure settings. This phenomenological approach explores the complex meanings and processes that are involved when participants are interpreting a situation, as well as their socially-acquired knowledge about a situation (in this case, drug treatment or leisure behaviours). O'Dell, Crafter, De Abreu and Cline (2012) propose a *dialogical* approach in their vignette work on young carers. This *dialogical* position argues that people's talk is 'multi-voiced', involving dialogue between different positions of identification. In vignette research, this may mean that participants will shift between discussing vignette characters as themselves, as someone else and/or in terms of what 'ought' to happen. They argue that it is valuable to identify these multiple voices and how they dialogue with one other, in order to understand how and why a particular voice is 'privileged' in a particular setting (O'Dell et al., 2012: 703).

In our own studies, we have approached vignettes from a *social construc-tionist* perspective (see also Wilks, 2004), and we have found vignettes to be a very valuable method for analysing how people construct (often multiple and contradictory) accounts of particular social categories and identities (such as the 'anorexic' teenage body). From our perspective, vignette methods are highly useful for generating data that help us understand discursive practices (cf. Potter and Wetherell, 1987) and rhetorical accounts (cf. Billig, 1991, 1996) – providing insight into (often multiple and contradictory) constructions of reality and the ways in which such constructions are socially and culturally situated. Vignette data allows us to attend to, for example, the multiple ways in which the teenage 'anorexic' is constructed in talk (e.g., as effeminate, as appearance-orientated, as destructive and as irrational), as well as the ways in which male and female teenage 'anorexics' are differently constructed (e.g., as normal/abnormal) in relation to (often Western) societal discourses about what it means to be gender appropriate.

What Do Vignettes Offer the Qualitative Researcher?

Vignettes offer researchers a uniquely flexible and highly creative way to explore participants' meanings and interpretations of a particular phenomenon, within a given context or situation. The researcher sets the context and focus of the research, by drawing up the parameters of the (hypothetical) story and by carefully choosing the material that will be used as the vignette. This can help researchers to manage complexity by 'isolating certain aspects of a given social issue or problem' (Barter and Renold, 2000: 312). Through open-ended questioning, participants are then asked to 'fill in the gaps' and to engage in processes of interpretation that can provide important insights into social phenomena and situations, such as teenage 'anorexia', violence between children (Barter and Renold, 2000) or drug injectors' HIV risk perceptions (Hughes, 1998). Participants 'discuss' the vignette scenario in their own words, thereby capturing elements of how participants themselves make sense of the story that they are presented with (Barter and Renolds, 1999; Hughes and Huby, 2004). In our example study (Box 4.1), this meant we could focus participants' attention on a specific aspect of 'anorexia' (its occurrence in male and female teenagers), while also capturing the terms participants themselves used to define 'anorexia', what they saw as central to being 'anorexic' and how they negotiated the various situations of the different actors in the vignettes.

Vignettes can be useful when participants might have little knowledge or understanding of the situation of interest (Hughes, 1998; Hughes and Huby, 2002). The fact that participants are (typically) asked to comment on a *hypothetical* scenario means that they don't need to have had any direct experience of the situation depicted in the vignette. This can be very useful if the topic of interest is not particularly well understood or well known in your participant group, or if you want to access your participants' spontaneously generated meanings and assumptions about some topic (Bendelow, 1993). A warning, however: it is unwise to make *assumptions* about the level of knowledge in your participant group. In our example study, for example, it turned out that over half of the participants (30/57) personally knew someone who had previously received a diagnosis for an eating disorder. So it's always a good idea to check this in the pilot phase of your research and when collecting your data (see 'steps' section).

Vignette methods can also be particularly good for exploring issues that could be potentially difficult for participants to discuss, as they allow participants to engage with them from a 'non-personal and therefore less threatening perspective' (Hughes, 1998: 383) and because they can help to 'desensitise' aspects of difficult topics (Hughes and Huby, 2002: 384). In studies where participants may be 'too close' to a delicate or sensitive topic – for example, where they may have personal experience of the topic being studied – they can be asked to comment on the story as if they were the character, as opposed to drawing *directly* on their own personal experiences. Vignettes also provide the opportunity for participants to have some control over the research process, by enabling *them* to determine at what stage, if at all, they introduce their own experiences to illuminate their responses (Barter and Renold, 2000; Barter et al., 2004; Thaler, 2012).

Another advantage is that vignettes can potentially help prevent 'socially desirable' responding (e.g., see Gould, 1996; Gourlay et al., 2014), as they introduce a sense of distance between the researcher and the participant. This is particularly the case if the study is done anonymously, as ours was. In our research, our *constructionist* position meant we were not concerned about social desirability in the more traditional sense – in terms of it obstructing participants faithfully reproducing their 'real' views – but we felt that vignettes might elicit opinions that could be somewhat socially 'unsafe' to express face-to-face, in some cases. And we did get 'socially undesirable' responses. For example, we got the following two responses about our Hannah and our Harry vignettes (note that these two responses are presented exactly as they were written by participants – we have not 'cleaned up' the spelling, grammar or typing errors):

I imagine Hannah to be a typical self-absorbed teenager. She probably feels egocentric, that all eyes are on her. Shes probably an avid watcher of music channels, celebrity get me out of here and the only ways is Essex. (HLR089)
I think people generally will see him as a silly boy who has taken his exercising to excess. They will think that he has done this out of vanity, and probably think he should just be able to change his habits and start eating normally immediately. They will think him wilful when he does not, and lose patience and have no sympathy for him. (BR574)

In the first of these extracts we see a quite derogatory portrayal of Hannah, as self-obsessed and concerned primarily with 'trivial' pop-media. In the second, we see similarly unsympathetic descriptions of Harry as silly, vain, willful and abnormal. Such unsympathetic descriptions are not generally socially sanctioned or socially desirable ways of talking about teenage 'anorexics'. Although we have no way of knowing if these same views would have been expressed using other data collection methods, such as in an interview or focus group, our experience of vignette methods across a range of studies is that they do access a much wider range of responses than would likely have been achieved if participants were asked to express their *own* views more openly or directly. This does not mean that vignettes *stop* participants from producing 'socially desirable' views! Rather, they (also) elicit views that might not be voiced easily in other contexts.

It is very easy when using vignettes to introduce an element of 'comparison' into the research design – between different features of the vignette and/or between different groups of participants. In our example study, the gender of the main *character* was easily changed. Alternatively, data could be collected and compared between men and women *participants*. In a more complex design, we could have varied both the gender of the character *and* the gender of the participants. Comparisons could similarly be done for age, ethnicity or any combination of these, or of other indices of identity, depending on relevance to the research question. Although comparison is not common in qualitative research, such designed comparisons can provide important insights into contrasting interpretations of otherwise uniform situations or contexts, or into contrasting interpretations of particular social groups (see also Chapter 3, on story completion). Indeed, our data showed a clear difference in how male and female 'anorexics' were described by our participants. Hannah was frequently portrayed as a normal or typical teenage girl, and attributed with stereotypically 'feminine' characteristics; Harry was more often imagined as an isolated and atypical teenage boy, described in terms that deviated significantly from a traditional masculine 'norm'. Vignettes thus helped us to understand how constructions of 'anorexia' are gendered, insights that would have been difficult to capture using data collection methods where comparative data are not as easily achieved. Thus, vignettes have the potential to generate data not easily accessed through other methods.

Vignettes also offer more *practical* advantages. Data can be collected from a relatively large sample of participants in a relatively short space of time, often with less expense than many other forms of qualitative data collection (Gould, 1996). In our example study, data were collected from fifty-seven participants in less than a month. Given that these data did not need to be transcribed, more time could be spent on analysis – and/or (in theory!) a more quickly completed study. Thus, vignettes can confer advantages of both time and cost for the researcher, when compared to the investment needed for traditional face-to-face interviews or focus groups.

If data are collected online, there can also be significant advantages in sampling and recruitment – typically allowing access to populations that are geographically dispersed. This was not important for our study, which was conducted with a mainly student sample. However, in other vignette studies, we have advertised online (e.g., by posting a link on a specialist forum) and recruited participants from all over the UK. Similarly, we have also used crowd-sourcing websites to collect vignette data – for example, Mechanical Turk in the US or CrowdFlower in the UK. These sites allow you to post studies that are completed by participants, who are then paid for their time. In our experience, this has worked well. The advantage of using crowd sourcing is that its participants tend to be demographically more diverse than standard Internet samples, and significantly more diverse than student samples in terms of age, gender and ethnicity (Buhrmester, Kwang, and Gosling, 2011). Data collection is also very fast (in our experience, less than a day!) and can involve participants from all over the world – this latter may be a pro or a con, depending on your research question and design. A key disadvantage is that you need to resource the participant payments, and this can be significant depending on your sample size.

What Research Questions Suit Vignettes?

The diversity and flexibility of the vignette method offers researchers the opportunity to address a wide variety of different types of research questions, beyond the traditional focus in (quantitative) vignette studies on attitudes, perceptions, beliefs or cultural norms (Finch, 1987; Hughes, 1998). Overall, a distinction can be made between research questions that aim to capture: (1) some aspect of practice, or what participants would *do* in a given situation, including what might influence particular actions; (2) participants' understandings or perceptions of a given situation or phenomenon, including their definitions or constructions of events, people, social groups and so forth; and (3) participants' ethical frameworks or moral codes.

The first type of research question is more common in quantitative vignette studies, but there are very good examples of qualitative research where vignettes have been used to address questions about what participants would do, or how participants might come to a decision about what to do, in a given situation. Examples include how health professionals make decisions on whether to withhold or withdraw life-prolonging treatments when faced with an advanced directive (Thompson, Barbour and Schwartz, 2003), how patient characteristics can influence the decisions that physicians make about diabetes management (Lutfey et al., 2008), and about the barriers to using HIV services in rural Tanzania (Gourlay et al., 2014). These demonstrate that qualitative vignettes can work well for such 'practice' oriented research questions.

The second type of research question is more common in qualitative vignette research and is typically concerned with how participants understand and make sense of the given (hypothetical) story or scenario, in order to understand something about participants' constructions, perceptions or assumptions about a particular phenomenon. Our study falls into this category: we were primarily concerned with how our participants would discuss the character of Hannah/Harry, so that we could explore how teenage 'anorexics' are constructed in lay discourse, and how gender features in these constructions. Research with this scope of interest can also sometimes explore meaning in relation to participants' own experiences – for example, young people's experiences of peer violence in children's homes (Barter and Renold, 2000).

Finally, vignettes can be useful in examining participants' ethical frameworks or moral codes (Finch, 1987; Wilks, 2004). In this kind of study, participants are presented with a moral, ethical or practical dilemma and then asked about how a particular *character* in the story *should* react to a particular situation and/or how *the participants themselves* should react to the situation. This can include research questions about, for example, how social workers make decisions about moral and ethical practice (Wilks, 2004) and the moral codes that inform children's thinking about post-divorce family life (Neale, Flowerdew, Smart and Wade, 2003).

There is much debate in the wider vignette literature about the gap between vignettes and social reality – for example, how the decision-making practices that are discussed in relation to a vignette may or may not mirror decision-making practices in real-life (Faia, 1979; Hughes and Huby, 2004; Parkinson and Manstead, 1993). As a general rule, this is not a concern for qualitative vignette research, where researchers are less focused on predicting people's responses to real-life situations and instead tend to prioritise exploring participants' meanings and interpretations. As this is a contentious issue, we caution against research which aims to elicit responses that mimic 'real-life' responses – it is not a strength of the vignette method, and they are considered to actually be of limited value in such projects (Hughes, 1998).

Design, Sampling and Ethical Issues

Somewhat surprisingly, there are few 'how to' guides for designing vignette studies, and this kind of research is not well represented in either qualitative or quantitative research methods texts. The central design concern is the construction of the vignette scenario and, crucially, providing participants with a scenario that seems meaningful, authentic and understandable (or at least not overly complicated), and is also sufficiently detailed and targeted to the specific issues that are of interest. The scenario needs to provide enough context and information for participants to have an understanding of the situation being depicted, but also needs to be vague in ways that compel participants to 'fill in' additional details (Hughes and Huby, 2001).

There are also a number of questions that researchers will need to answer about how to structure the vignette. Importantly, there are no right or wrong answers to these questions – rather, the vignette story needs to fit with the research question and work to elicit appropriate data. The chapters on story completion (Chapter 3) and qualitative surveys (Chapter 2) also provide helpful insights into some of these questions about structure. Key questions are:

(1) *Will you present the story to participants as a single story followed by questions, or incrementally, with questions following immediately after each section?* A single story has the advantage of being much simpler as all the information is presented at once (Hughes, 1998). However, this also means that you are more limited in the detail that you are able to provide. An incremental vignette can give the researcher more freedom (and control) around plot or character development, as different elements of the story can be introduced at different times. But, this also has the potential to confuse participants, who may not always follow your story arc (Finch, 1987). The choice of whether to provide a single or incremental story depends largely on your research question and the type of data you're hoping to collect. An incremental vignette is better if you're interested in participants' responses to more than one character, or to a particular plot development, such as the reactions of friends or family to a particular aspect of the story. These could be difficult to elicit using a single vignette story. On the other hand, you can choose to keep the story relatively uncomplicated, as you may want to introduce other sorts of variations in your vignette (using a comparative design; see next point). As we had two different versions of the vignette in our study, we decided additional story elements would over-complicate the study and so chose a single story design.

(2) *Do you want to make comparisons?* Do you want two (or more) versions of the vignette that vary in some way (e.g., different gender or age of characters)? Crucially, any variation needs a sound theoretical or empirical rationale. We decided to use gender as a comparison point between two vignettes (a girl and a boy version) for two reasons: (1) there is considerable evidence that 'anorexia' is not only much more frequently diagnosed in girls and women, but is also often seen as a 'feminine disorder' (Malson and Burns, 2009); and (2) boys experiences of 'anorexia' are often rendered invisible and potentially not real. Having two vignettes meant that we could explore these theoretical questions about how 'anorexia' is gendered in more depth. If using a comparative design, your vignette needs to be able to be varied without changing much other detail, so that you can be sure any conclusions about variation are clearly based on that factor. We were able to easily construct two versions of our vignette that differed *only* in terms of the main character's gender (see Box 4.2). This is often the most difficult part of a comparison, and if you cannot write two near-identical vignettes, then it is likely that a comparison is not appropriate.

(3) *How much detail do you want to provide about the characters or their situation?* Having some aspects of the vignette deliberately ambiguous can be very useful, particularly if you are looking to explore participants' assumptions (e.g., about gender, race, sexuality or age) (Hughes and Huby, 2001). Conversely, you may want to direct participants to focus on particular issues and include specific details about age, gender, ethnicity and so forth that locate their responses in some way – we did this in relation to gender and age.

(4) *Whose point of view do you want to emphasise?* Vignettes are typically written in either the first- or the third-person. First-person – asking participants to write from the point of view of the character – is useful if you want participants to empathise or sympathise with a particular character in the scenario. It can also help to encourage participants to see things from that character's point of view. Writing in the third-person – asking participants to write as if the character were someone else – can help to distance participants from the characters a little, and so can be useful if you want to probe more sensitive topics.

Once you have a vignette to present to participants, it is important to ensure that time and attention are devoted to constructing the *questions* you want to ask participants about the vignette (Box 4.2 gives an example). There is some overlap with the design of qualitative surveys here (see Chapter 2), although the questions that are asked in a vignette study must clearly relate to the story and

---

Box 4.2 Example of an 'anorexia' vignette: Hannah version

Hannah is fifteen years old and studying for her GCSEs. For the last few months Hannah has become preoccupied with her body weight and has recently lowered her daily food intake dramatically. Hannah regularly avoids meals, and some days she eats very little at all. Hannah has also begun a strict fitness regime, attending the gym once a day and regularly swimming at the local leisure centre. Hannah's recent eating habits and intense exercise programme have resulted in extreme weight loss, causing her family to insist on her seeing a doctor. After a consultation with the doctor, Hannah is diagnosed with the eating disorder anorexia nervosa.

Please answer the following questions, providing as much detail as possible:

(1) Please describe how you imagine Hannah – for example, her family and social background and the kind of personality, interests, habits and social life she might have.
(2) What do you imagine Hannah is likely to look like?
(3) Why do you think Hannah has become preoccupied with her body weight and changed her eating and exercise habits? What do you think might have caused this?
(4) How do you think Hannah is feeling?
(5) How do you think Hannah's family might feel about her weight loss and her new eating and exercise habits?
(6) How do you think Hannah's friends might react to her weight loss and her new eating and exercise habits?
(7) How will people generally view Hannah?
(8) Do you think Hannah needs help, and if so, what do you think might help Hannah?
(9) What do you imagine will happen to Hannah in the next two months?
(10) What do you imagine will have happened to Hannah a year from now?

The Harry version of the vignette was identical, with the name Harry substituted for Hannah and gendered pronouns changed.

---

so may be more directive than those typically found in a survey study. As with the design of the story, there are several questions that researchers are faced with at this point:

(1) *Do you want to ask participants about how a character should ideally act/feel and/or how they would realistically act or feel?* 'Should' questions direct participants to focus on the idealistic aspects of a situation; 'would' questions direct participants to focus on the pragmatic (Hughes, 1998). In most cases, researchers use a mixture of 'should' and 'would' questions to capture both idealistic and pragmatic aspects of a situation. In the

questions in Box 4.2, you can see that we tended to use 'might' questions rather than 'should' or 'would' questions. These kinds of questions effectively invite people to *imagine* others' feelings and thoughts and to articulate likely explanations for various aspects of a vignette scenario – in this they sit closer to 'should' type questions, but don't match them perfectly. For example, participants in our study provided some quite detailed accounts of why Hannah might have become preoccupied with body weight:

One of the reasons may be to do with the fact that she is studying for her GCSE's – it can be very stressful and she may be using her obsession with weight as a distraction. She may be nervous about the prospect of leaving school and feels a pressure to look a certain way for jobs, etc. She is also at the age where she is going to be starting to be keen on having a boyfriend – she probably believes that getting thin will help this. Also, if the majority of her friends are smaller than her then she is at an age where this is going to bother her – and therefore she may feel pressure to be the same as them (SP850).

Our use of a 'might' question here elicited a whole range of imagined explanations for Hannah's eating behaviour (e.g., about exams, stress, age, boys, peer pressure) and thus insight into the range of different ways that people construct the 'problem' of teenage anorexia (e.g., as being about appearance concerns). We found that 'might' questions offered a more open-ended way of inviting these kinds of responses than either 'should' or 'would' questions, which presuppose that there is a way that things 'should' or 'would' feel, happen, etc.

(2) *What story time-frame will you be asking about?* We used questions that framed time in different ways – for example, inviting people to think about what might happen to the character in two months, or in a year (see Box 4.2). This is useful if you are looking at how something is resolved (or not resolved) over time, and what this says about the issue you are interested in. This can also be useful if you choose to have a single story vignette, rather than an incremental one, as it can be a way of capturing additional detail about how participants see particular characters developing, albeit in a more constrained way.

(3) *Do you want to focus questions on the characters, or ask participants about how they themselves should or would act in the same situation?* We primarily used character-based questions that asked participants how they imagined the character would look, feel or act. This allowed us to investigate different aspects of our participants' perceptions and understandings of 'anorexic' teenagers, rather than capturing their own personal experiences of anorexia. Had we wanted to capture more of their experiences, we could have asked

more questions about how *they* would have thought, felt or acted in the same situation (Barter and Renold, 1999). This would be useful if, for example, we had recruited a sample of teenagers diagnosed with anorexia, and we wanted to know more about their own personal experiences and interpretations of their diagnosis, or, indeed, if we wanted to understand how eating issues might be present and play out in general student sample.

(4) *How many questions do you need?* There is no *ideal* number of questions for a vignette study. There is a trade-off to be made between the number of questions asked and the length and depth of the responses you are seeking *and* are likely to get (see also Chapter 2). In our experience, asking *ten* in-depth questions is quite a lot, particularly if they are presented in relation to a one-stage vignette scenario; responses to the latter questions can tail off in both depth and detail. Think about how much time a participant will be willing to spend completing the study, and only ask questions that you really want to gather data in relation to. Overly long – and overly complex – vignette studies can put participants off and therefore impact on data quality.

Whatever choices you make about your vignette questions, they need to be short, clear and precise. Participants should be able to understand immediately exactly *what* they are being asked. Ask single questions: multi-part questions that ask participants to do more than one thing can be confusing; at the very least, you're unlikely to get data that answer all aspects of the question. Make sure that you're thinking from your participants' perspective and orient questions to their language, knowledge and understandings.

In addition to the vignette-focused questions, it's a good idea to include an 'any other comments' question at the end. This can be a valuable way for participants to either feedback about the study or to address issues that you hadn't thought of.

There are no particular *sampling* issues related specifically to vignette methods – the different types of sampling used in qualitative research are suitable here (see Bryman, 2001; Patton, 2002). There are also few prescriptions in terms of sample size. In a vignette study, you trade some depth for breadth of responses, meaning in general you will need to collect data from more participants than is traditional in, for example, interview-based qualitative studies. The sample size you need will also largely be determined by your study design. If you have lots of different versions of your vignette, you will need more participants to gather enough data to make meaningful comparisons. Likewise, the more comparisons you want to make between participant groups (e.g., based on gender or age), then the more participants you will need to recruit. In general, a study with two vignettes (like ours) would need around sixty people (thirty in each version of the vignette) to provide sufficient data for analysis and comparison. However, with three versions of the vignette, you would probably need around ninety to make the comparison work. Similarly, if you had two versions of the vignette and wanted to compare two participant groups (e.g., men and women), then you may need 120. As you can see, this can lead to a large sample very quickly, and so you need to take this into account in designing your study – a key take home message from us is that more complex is not necessarily better!

The usual ethical processes for research (e.g., British Psychological Society, 2013) apply, including providing participants with a participant information sheet and requiring some process of consent. Care does need to be taken in how the study is described to potential participants. You don't want participants to be faced with a (potentially distressing) vignette scenario they were not expecting, and so a brief description of what topic(s) the vignette will cover is necessary. If your study is online, consent can be in the form of a tick box accompanied by a short declarative statement, for example, 'by ticking this box I indicate that I have read the information about this study and I agree to take part'. You can also manage participant access to the study, so that they cannot see the vignette or the questions until *after* they have given consent. This is a good idea as it ensures all participants *have* given their consent to take part (see also Chapter 2). If your study is offline, you can give your participants a hard copy of your information sheet and ask them to sign a hard copy consent form, before you give them the vignette and the accompanying questions.

Participants are generally entitled to withdraw their data during, and for some time after, taking part in research (British Psychological Society, 2013), although in practice this can be hard to manage, and in some instances exemptions tend to be used. If your study is online, withdrawal is usually managed by participants simply closing the browser window, at which point none of their data are stored. To enable withdrawal *after* taking part in an online vignette study, online survey software can generate a unique participant ID for each participant. Participants can then email this ID to the researcher and request that their data be deleted. If the data are collected offline, then the researcher can give each participant a unique ID that they can use to withdraw. If this is the case, then all electronic and hard copy data should be destroyed (e.g., deleted; shredded). As noted above, although it is considered good ethical practice, it is not mandatory that participants be allowed to withdraw their data after taking part (British Psychological Society, 2013). If you do wish to allow participants to withdraw (or your ethics body requires it), it is a good idea to set a time limit on this – for instance, one month after participation or by a particular date – after which participants cannot withdraw their data from the study anymore. This should be a date that will enable you to realistically complete your analysis and finalise your report, without the impact of data withdrawal.

Steps to Using Vignettes

The steps in vignette studies are similar to many other qualitative methods:

(1) *Understanding the background.* A thorough review of the literature in your research area is *particularly* important in vignette research, to help you design your vignette and write your open-ended questions. It will help you to make decisions about what kinds of things would seem plausible or authentic in this context, and what kinds of details are important to empha-sise – or *not*! Examples from other studies could help form the basis of a compelling and realistic vignette scenario, and you can often find good questions in previous studies in the same area.

(2) *Designing and writing the vignette scenario and questions.* This stage is all about making some of the decisions discussed above in the section on design. These decisions will be shaped by what you discover in Step 1 (e.g., there may be known differences between different ages or genders that you want to focus on) and by your research question.

(3) *Deciding on a mode of data collection.* The choice here is primarily between offline and online modes of data collection. Offline vignettes are typically presented in hard copy with participants responding in writing. Online modes of data collection typically involve either email or survey software (e.g., Qualtrics or SurveyMonkey, discussed more in Chapter 2). The choice to use online or offline depends on your population and what kind of access you have to them. An online mode is appropriate when you know your sample has access to the Internet, as ours did. However, an offline mode could be more appropriate if you are hoping to access your sample in a specific location or at specific time – for example, in a school lesson. *Online* delivery also facilitates more easy inclusion of audio-visual elements into the vignette. Therefore, if you know that your scenario will contain visual or audio data (or is *solely* visual or audio data, e.g., McKinstry, 2000), then this may be a better choice for your study.

(4) *Deciding on format.* In this stage, you decide how to format your vignette study. If you are presenting your study online, you need to consider how many questions to present to participants at a time. One per 'page' generally works

well, as it focuses participants on each question. It also means that participants won't have to scroll down too much, and potentially miss important questions. If you are conducting your study offline, then you need to think about how much *space* to allow participants for each question. Overall, half an A4 page per question is a good rule of thumb – although you want to provide one or two spare pages where participants can continue their thoughts and ideas if they want to (see also Chapter 2 for more discussion on this).

(5) *Piloting and revision.* Vignettes are a type of 'fixed' data collection (along with qualitative surveys (Chapter 2), story completion tasks (Chapter 3) and many qualitative diaries (Chapter 5)): they do not allow revision to take place once data collection has started. This makes it *really* important to pilot your vignette before data collection begins, usually on a small sample of 5–10 participants like those you plan to recruit – in our case students. In the piloting phase, the vignette should be presented *exactly* as it will be presented to participants. However, it can be useful to add some questions at the end asking for feedback on the vignette, the questions, and any other pertinent aspect. This will help you to see the vignette from the perspective of your participants answering the questions. If piloting indicates things are not clear, or you are not getting the type of data you anticipated or need, you need to go back and make revisions to the vignette, following the guidance above.

(6) *Collecting data.* Once you have piloted and revised your vignette, it's time to collect your data! It is useful to do a thorough and final proof check before making your vignette study 'live' to participants – especially if you've revised it following piloting. After this, you will probably be focused on participant recruitment and monitoring responses as they come in. It can be difficult to decide when to stop data collection. You may reach your target sample (e.g., sixty participants) and decide to stop on this basis. Or you may reach a point when you feel you have collected enough data to ensure an in-depth exploration of the research question (Spencer, Ritchie, Lewis and Dillon, 2003). Either way, it is likely that, by this point, you will have quantities of rich qualitative data ready for analysis.

What Can Go Wrong with Vignettes?

In general, there is little that can go very wrong with vignettes, but where problems do occur they are typically related to the scenario provided. If the scenario doesn't seem plausible or authentic to participants, then they may not take it seriously enough, or may get annoyed by it and provide sketchy or nonsensical answers (Hughes 1998). Likewise, the scenario may not be sufficiently meaningful or familiar to participants to elicit rich data. For example, asking participants to respond to stories about characters who are markedly older or younger than they are often doesn't work well (Hughes and Huby, 2001; Swartzman and McDermid, 1993). Our study might not have worked so well if we had asked our participants (who were mainly in their early twenties) to answer questions about a much older character, as they may have found it difficult to imagine their experiences. Matching the vignette with the participant group helps to avoid this problem.

Non- or shallow responses are another concern. It is sometimes the case that participants might not answer particular questions, or answer questions in a fairly shallow way, which leaves you with limited data. In our study, some questions did not always prompt the kinds of in-depth responses we wanted. For instance, in response to the question "How do you think Harry/Hannah is feeling" we got some one-line answers:

'Isolated. Alone'
'Really stressed and upset'
'Out of control, stressed, unsure'.

In our experience, length of answer differs across questions as well as across participants. Also, it became clear that having ten questions, all expecting detailed responses, was quite demanding of participants. Many responses became less detailed towards the end of the set of questions, suggesting that fewer questions could have elicited fuller responses. In retrospect, an incremental vignette might have worked better, as it may have engaged people for longer, or re-engaged them at different times. Such issues need to be considered in the design phase and serve to highlight the importance of piloting.

What Methods of Analysis Suit Vignette Data?

Analytic methods aimed at identifying meaning patterns across datasets, like thematic analysis (e.g., Braun and Clarke, 2006), work well with vignettes, offering a systematic way of coding and identifying patterns of meaning in the data. Thematic analysis can be particularly useful if your study has a comparative element and you are interested in different groups of people's interpretations of a given situation. You can compile and analyse your data in a variety of different ways, but also compare codes, categories or themes across groups in order to see if there are broad differences in patterns of meaning. It can be difficult for (particularly novice) researchers to look beyond the 'structure' that is provided by the format of the vignette questions and to code for patterns present *across* participant responses, or to engage meaningfully with the less obvious elements of the data, but it generally results in a richer analysis. To help with this, you could consider detaching the data from the questions in the initial stages of data analysis (e.g., during coding) and then reintegrating the questions at a later point, as needed.

Versions of discourse analysis can also work well with vignette data, offering insights into how particular social issues (e.g., 'immigration'), social groups (e.g., 'anorexics') or social problems (e.g., 'poverty') are discursively constructed (Burman and Parker, 1993; Potter and Wetherell, 1987; Wiggins and Potter, 2008). We have used discourse analysis (Potter and Wetherell, 1987) and rhetorical psychology (Billig, 1991, 1996) to analyse our data (see Box 4.3); we have found vignettes enable interesting insights into how people 'make sense of' particular social phenomena (e.g., the teenage 'anorexic'), as well as how such sense-making practices draw on broader social and cultural resources (e.g., medical discourses) to construct identities, experiences and so forth in various ways. We have also found vignettes to be useful for examining how such constructions may re-produce and/or challenge particular social power relations, for example, gender ideologies (Wilks, 2004). Vignettes can be particularly good at enabling researchers to analyse a relatively large number of (anonymously expressed) responses, and to thus capture a broad range of discursive constructions about the social issue, group or problem you are interested in.

Conclusion

Vignettes offer qualitative researchers a highly creative and flexible method, with great potential for exploring participants' meanings and interpretations, grounded within particular situations and contexts. They can be used to collect data from a fairly large sample of people, relatively quickly and with few required resources. Overall, the approach has few dangers or pitfalls for the novice researcher and can be an excellent way to start to collect and analyse qualitative data. Data collected are generally rich and elaborative and can be analysed in a variety of different ways.

Box 4.3 Personal reflections on using vignettes (from Bronwen Royall)

When researching 'lay' perceptions of the teenage 'anorexic', it felt important to adopt a method that would provide insight into the variety of different ways that participants talked about male and female teenage 'anorexics' – particularly how they expressed these constructions using their own language. I chose to use a stand-alone vignette as I felt that offering a scenario (in contrast to interviews or focus groups) would provide participants with a specific context that would provide direction and focus for the research – making it easier for participants to understand what I wanted them to focus on, and therefore helping me to answer my research question. Although I found the process of designing the vignette easy, it did require a significant amount of research and consideration. I read numerous personal accounts from teenagers who identified as 'anorexic' to ensure that the characters and scenarios depicted within the vignette were authentic and based around others' realities. I felt it was important to ensure that the scenario was sufficiently detailed to enable participants to become immersed within the story, while simultaneously leaving the situation open to interpretation, providing participants with the opportunity to generate their own image of the character based upon their own underlying social, cultural and historic beliefs.

Overall, I was pleased with the responses I got to my vignette. Lots of participants provided elaborate responses to the questions, creating a rich source of data and a solid foundation for a comprehensive analysis. However, some responses were far more limited, some being only partially completed, and many consisting of one-word answers. Initially, I found these responses frustrating and challenging to analyse. In hindsight, however, this unelaborated, straightforward data did provide a good starting point for analysing such a large dataset by providing brief, unequivocal 'labels' that often presented a 'boiled down' version of lengthier responses.

Having done this research, there is no doubt in my mind of the virtue of the stand-alone vignette as a data collection method. As with all research methods, it cannot be denied that there are certain limitations. However, in my opinion, vignettes provide an opportunity for generating rich qualitative data, while maintaining a degree of structure, which is especially useful for researchers new to qualitative methods.

Have a Go . . .

(1) Brainstorm a qualitative research question that you could answer using the vignette method. Remember that vignettes are well-suited to exploring people's perceptions, views and opinions of a social phenomenon.

(2) Write a vignette *story*. Remember to keep your story meaningful to participants (written in clear, appropriate language), as well as vivid, engaging

and authentic (make the characters feel like real people). Think carefully about what research question(s) you are looking to answer and/or assumptions you are attempting to uncover by getting participants to 'fill in the blanks' and provide their own interpretation of the hypothetical scenario.

(3) Write three to four questions that will follow your vignette. Remember that the questions should be open-ended and should be related directly to your vignette scenario.

(4) Produce a finalised version of the vignette and questions, and ask three or four people to complete it for you as a piloting exercise. Ask your participants for feedback on your story and questions, and consider how you could improve these.

(5) Revise the vignette and/or questions in response to this feedback, to come up with a 'ready to go' data collection tool.

Further Resources: Online

The companion website for Braun and Clarke's (2013) Successful Qualitative Research: A practical guide for beginners provides an introduction to the vignette method and examples of research materials for a vignette task on trans parenting: www.uk.sagepub.com/braunandclarke/study/additional.htm

Further Resources: Readings

For a good overview of the use of vignettes in social research, including some of the more general theoretical and practical issues with conducting vignette research, see Hughes, R. (1998). Considering the vignette technique and its application to a study of drug injecting and HIV risk and safer behaviour. *Sociology of Health & Illness*, *20*(3), 381–400; Hughes, R. and Huby, M. (2004). The construction and interpretation of vignettes in social research. *Social Work & Social Sciences Review*, *11*(1), 36–51.

For an example of vignette research with children and in conjunction with an interview method, see Barter, C. and Renold, E. (2000) 'I wanna tell you a story': Exploring the application of vignettes in qualitative research with children and young people. *International Journal of Social Research Methodology*, *3*(4), 307–323.

For an example of vignette research that used a news story format in conjunction with an interview method, see Gray, D., Delany, A. and Durrheim, K. (2005). Talking to 'real' South Africans: An investigation of the dilemmatic nature of nationalism. *South African Journal of Psychology*, *35*(1), 127–146.

For an example of using visual data in vignette research, see Morrison, T. L. (2015). Using visual vignettes: My learning to date. *The Qualitative Report*, *20*(4), 359–375.

References

Barter, C. and Renold, E. (1999). The use of vignettes in qualitative research. *Social Research Update, 25*. Retrieved from: http://sru.soc.surrey.ac.uk/SRU25.html

(2000). 'I wanna tell you a story': Exploring the application of vignettes in qualitative research with children and young people. *International Journal of Social Research Methodology, 3*(4), 307–323.

Barter, C., Renold, E., Berridge, D. and Cawson, P. (2004). *Peer violence in children's residential care*. Basingstoke, UK: Palgrave Macmillan.

British Psychological Society (2013). *Ethics guidelines for Internet-mediated research*. Leicester, UK: British Psychological Society.

Brondani, M. A., MacEntee, M. I., Bryant, S. R. and O'Neill, B. (2008). Using written vignettes in focus groups among older adults to discuss oral health as a sensitive topic. *Qualitative Health Research, 18*(8), 1145–1153.

Bendelow, G. (1993). Pain perceptions, emotions and gender. *Sociology of Health & Illness, 15*(3), 273–294.

Billig, M. (1991). *Ideology and opinions*. London: Sage Publications.

(1996). *Arguing and thinking: A rhetorical approach to social psychology* (2 edn). Cambridge: Cambridge University Press.

Braun, V. and Clarke, V. (2006). Using thematic analysis in psychology. *Qualitative Research in Psychology, 3*(2), 77–101.

(2013). *Successful qualitative research: A practical guide for beginners*. London: Sage Publications.

Bryman, A. (2001). *Social research methods*. Oxford: Oxford University Press.

Buhrmester, M., Kwang, T. and Gosling, S. D. (2011). Amazon's Mechanical Turk: A new source of inexpensive, yet high-quality, data? *Perspectives on Psychological Science, 6*(1), 3–5.

Burman, E. E. and Parker, I. E. (1993). *Discourse analytic research: Repertoires and readings of texts in action*. London: Routledge.

Faia, M. A. (1979). The vagaries of the vignette world: A comment on Alves and Rossi. *American Journal of Sociology, 85*(4), 951–954.

Finch, J. (1987). The vignette technique in survey research. *Sociology, 21*(2), 105–114.

Fischer, J., Jenkins, N., Bloor, M., Neale, J. and Berney, L. (2007). *Drug user involvement in treatment decisions*. York, UK: Joseph Rowntree Foundation.

Gould, D. (1996). Using vignettes to collect data for nursing research studies: How valid are the findings? *Journal of Clinical Nursing, 5*(4), 207–212.

Gourlay, A., Mshana, G., Birdthistle, I., Bulugu, G., Zaba, B. and Urassa, M. (2014). Using vignettes in qualitative research to explore barriers and facilitating factors to the uptake of prevention of mother-to-child transmission services in rural Tanzania: A critical analysis. *BMC Medical Research Methodology, 14*(1), 21–31.

Gray, D., Delany, A. and Durrheim, K. (2005). Talking to 'real' South Africans: An investigation of the dilemmatic nature of nationalism. *South African Journal of Psychology, 35*(1), 127–146.

Gray, D. and Manning, R. (2014). 'Oh my god, we're not doing nothing': Young people's experiences of spatial regulation. *British Journal of Social Psychology, 53*(4), 640–655.

Hughes, R. (1998). Considering the vignette techniques and its application to a study of drug injecting and HIV risk and safer behaviour. *Sociology of Health & Illness*, *20*(3), 381–400.

Hughes, R. and Huby, M. (2002). The application of vignettes in social and nursing research. *Journal of Advanced Nursing*, *37*(4), 382–386.

(2004). The construction and interpretation of vignettes in social research. *Social Work & Social Sciences Review*, *11*(1), 36–51.

Jenkins, N. (2006). *Misfortune or misadventure? A study of young people's leisure-related accidents* (Unpublished PhD thesis). Cardiff, UK: Cardiff University.

Jenkins, N., Bloor, M., Fischer, J., Berney, L. and Neale, J. (2010). Putting it in context: The use of vignettes in qualitative interviewing. *Qualitative Research*, *10*(2), 175–198.

Lutfey, K. E., Campbell, S. M., Renfrew, M. R., Marceau, L. D., Roland, M. and McKinlay, J. B. (2008). How are patient characteristics relevant for physicians' clinical decision making in diabetes? An analysis of qualitative results from a cross-national factorial experiment. *Social Science & Medicine*, *67*(9), 1391–1399.

Malson, H. and Burns, M. (eds.) (2009). *Critical feminist approaches to eating dis/orders*. London: Routledge.

McKinstry, B. (2000). Do patients wish to be involved in decision making in the consultation? A cross sectional survey with video vignettes. *British Medical Journal*, *321*(7265), 867–871.

Morrison, T. L. (2015). Using visual vignettes: My learning to date. *The Qualitative Report*, *20*(4), 359–375.

Neale, B., Flowerdew, J., Smart, C. and Wade, A. (2003). *Enduring families? Children's long term reflections on post-divorce family life*. Research Report for ESRC project no. R000239248.

O'Dell, L., Crafter, S., de Abreu, G. and Cline, T. (2012). The problem of interpretation in vignette methodology in research with young people. *Qualitative Research*, *12*(6), 702–714.

Parkinson B. and Manstead, A. S. R. (1993). Making sense of emotion in stories and social life. *Cognition and Emotion*, *7*, 295–323.

Patton, M. Q. (2002). *Qualitative evaluation and research methods*. Newbury Park, CA: Sage Publications

Potter, J. and Wetherell, M. (1987). *Discourse and social psychology: Beyond attitudes and behaviour*. London: Sage Publications.

Spencer, L., Ritchie, J., Lewis, J. and Dillon, L. (2003). *Quality in qualitative evaluation: A framework for assessing research evidence*. London: Government Chief Social Researcher's Office, Prime Minister's Strategy Unit.

Stolte, J. F. (1994). The context of satisficing in vignette research. *The Journal of Social Psychology*, *134*(6), 727–733.

Swartzman, L. C. and McDermid, A. J. (1993). The impact of contextual cues on the interpretation of and response to physical symptoms: A vignette approach. *Journal of Behavioral Medicine*, *16*(2), 183–198.

Taylor, B. J. (2006). Factorial surveys: Using vignettes to study professional judgement. *British Journal of Social Work*, *36*(7), 1187–1207.

Thaler, K. (2012). Norms about intimate partner violence among urban South Africans: A quantitative and qualitative vignette analysis. CSSR Working Paper (302).

Thompson, T., Barbour, R. and Schwartz, L. (2003). Adherence to advance directives in critical care decision-making: Vignette study. *British Medical Journal*, *327*(7422), 1011.

Vitkovitch, M. and Tyrrell, L. (1995). Sources of disagreement in object naming. *The Quarterly Journal of Experimental Psychology*, *48*(4), 822–848.

Wilks, T. (2004). The use of vignettes in qualitative research into social work values. *Qualitative Social Work*, *3*(1), 78–87.

Wiggins, S. and Potter, J. (2008) Discursive psychology. In C. Willig and W. Stainton Rogers (eds.), *The SAGE handbook of qualitative research in psychology* (pp. 72–89). London: Sage Publications.

5   'Coughing Everything Out'

The Solicited Diary Method

Paula Meth

Overview

With the solicited diary method, you ask participants to engage in diary writing, with some guidelines, and these diaries are then used as a source of qualitative data. Solicited diaries provide insight into the writer's feelings, views and experiences and have been fruitfully employed to address a wide range of research questions, including sensitive, private or difficult topics (Eidse and Turner, 2014; Elliott, 1997; Harvey, 2011; Meth and McClymont, 2009). In this chapter, I draw on my own experiences of using solicited diaries in two related projects on gender and violence in South Africa (see Box 5.1). Diaries yielded extensive data they facilitated access to the relatively hidden worlds of participants and provided longitudinal insights over varying periods of time. Diaries can also be cathartic and stimulate personal reflection, and thus contribute to transformative research aims. What follows is an overview of what solicited diaries offer the qualitative researcher, a discussion of practical issues relating to their design, a step-by-step guide for researchers wanting to use solicited diaries in their research and some reflections on their use.

Introduction to Solicited Qualitative Diaries

The *solicited diary* is a form of data collection that commonly uses written/ typed accounts of individuals' lives – although other forms, such as audio, video, photographic and drawing, have also been used (Gibson et al., 2013; Odendaal, Hausler, Tomlinson, Lewin and Mtshizana, 2012). Solicited diaries are written by a participant at the *request* of the researcher, with the participant fully aware from the outset that the diary, as a finished product, is not for private use. This is in contrast to unsolicited diaries, which are often historical in nature and usually written for private consumption (Alaszewski, 2006). It is a significant feature of solicited diaries, because it establishes that

---

Box 5.1 Domestic violence in violent contexts

I used solicited diaries in two related studies on gender and violence in South Africa. The first, a study with women living in Durban, focused on experiences of domestic violence in a context characterised by high rates of crime and violence (see Meth, 2003). My study aimed to determine: (1) the nature of the links between domestic violence and general violence; and (2) where and why women locate their fear. Focusing on women who were insecurely housed (i.e., sleeping on the streets, or at market stalls, or in informal housing, or living in substandard housing in a formal township), the study used a mix of interviews, solicited diaries and focus groups. I examined the geographies of women's fears and experiences and showed the pervasive nature of their fear, as well as the real threats they faced on a daily basis. As part of the study, we conducted evaluative interviews with some women to assess the relative advantages of the different qualitative methods used; participants valued diaries, in particular, as they felt they offered therapeutic benefits.

A second study was subsequently conducted with men, who as a generic category were not only the most commonly identified perpetrators of violence against women, but also victims themselves of high crime and violence rates. This study examined men's experiences of violence, and similarly had a methodological assessment built in to its focus. My key research questions were: (1) Are solicited diaries an effective method to use with men in determining their understandings of violence? (2) How do men make sense of living in contexts of extreme violence? Diaries again proved highly effective with these men, delivering not only insights into men's fraught emotions (see Meth, 2009), and first-hand experiences of violence as victims *and* perpetrators, but the persistence of their patriarchal views of society.

---

knowledge is purposefully produced through engagement with a researcher's agenda. The knowledge or data that are generated is, to some extent, negotiated between the researcher and the participant, in that the researcher has established, perhaps unilaterally or through consultation, the focus and boundaries of the research (i.e., the topic to be explored), and the participant engages with this topic through their writing. Solicited diaries, therefore, are not necessarily evidence of a participant's 'world view', or their most pressing concerns; rather, they should be understood as a solicited response to an issue.

To give an example of this, you may be approached by a researcher who asks you to record your daily travel practices: how you get to university, how long it takes you; how much it costs; what you think about it; and why you make the choices you do. You may be willing to complete this task, and you may enjoy writing about how sustainable you are as an avid cyclist, and how traffic jams are generally not a problem in your life. The researcher will learn about elements of your life through this exercise, but they will not necessarily learn about what ideologies or micro-issues drive your everyday existence. They may learn nothing about your childhood, or about your attitudes towards society. Diaries are not therefore unbounded insights into the full lives of participants; they are necessarily selective and partial. This partial insight is not a problem. The key is to recognise the limitations and possibilities of methods and to factor these in to your research strategies. Recognising these is vital in determining if a method is suitable for your particular research aim(s).

Diary accounts can range from semi-structured to entirely unstructured, depending on the aims of the study and the nature of the participants. Some studies may require participants to frequently address specific issues (e.g., daily food consumed), and thus some form of structuring and directing may be necessary. Particular participants can also find a more structured format easier to respond to – children, for example (see O'Donnell et al., 2013), or participants who find writing reflective accounts unfamiliar and/or daunting. This was the case in my study with men, where I used a set of instructions (see Box 5.2) to guide diary accounts; participants found this useful as the task was very unfamiliar to them. With different research aims and/or participants, largely unstructured diary entries may work perfectly.

The qualitative diary method has particular temporal qualities, which distinguishes it from most other qualitative methods – asynchronous email interviews (see Chapter 10) being a notable exception. Participants' thoughts and interpretations can be recorded in current or 'real' time – particularly if the participant is diligent about recording events relatively frequently. This can mean participants have to rely less on memory than they might in an interview, for instance, making recall easier (Kenyon, 2006). Additionally, the method can offer *longitudinal* insights, and this is one of its key advantages over most other qualitative methods. Diaries are written over a period of time (e.g., a number of weeks or even months) – contrast this with a one-off interview, which captures a singular account of a participant's views at a particular moment in time (e.g., 2–3pm on X day). Diaries therefore provide the participant with the time and space to build, amend, elaborate and rehearse their views over time, and to capture relevant changes (e.g., changing views on parenting, health or well-being). Diary writing is also intermittent, as entries are written at different times, which may allow for flexibility as well as variation in the writer's entries and interpretations of events. This discontinuity is a positive feature of diaries, reflecting the messiness of real-life perhaps more fully than some other methods.

A final feature to note about solicited diaries is that they are employed within both qualitative and quantitative studies. These different research traditions use somewhat distinct diary formats, and the literature on diaries is differentiated as a result. This chapter focuses on *qualitative* solicited diaries, but diaries are currently more commonly used in *quantitative* studies in disciplines such as health and transport studies. Quantitative diaries are more likely to record factual information, and participants are usually provided with tightly pre-scribed data entry sheets or online templates, and are asked to fill out schedules or diaries on a daily, or even hourly, basis (e.g., Roth et al., 2014; Kenyon, 2006). These more prescriptive forms of diary method contrast with the qualitative solicited diary, as used in my own studies, which provides the diarist with blank notebooks or online documents and the freedom to write as much or as little as they wish, and in any form of writing style. Knowing that this differentiated literature (and approach to using diaries) exists is important to help prioritise and filter useful sources.

What Do Solicited Qualitative Diaries Offer the Qualitative Researcher?

Diaries offer a lot! They can facilitate (partial) access to participants' inner thoughts and understandings and provide freedom of expression – bearing in mind the limitations imposed by writing, tiredness, the need for lighting, etc. (Meth, 2003). Because writing is necessarily a creative process, and because the participants' accounts can be built up over time, diaries provide their writers with the opportunity to generate knowledge at a time and in a manner suitable to them. This can work well for sensitive topics, where diarists might need to be 'emotionally ready' to share difficult experiences, or where the space of the diary might allow for revelations that are harder to express in person. This was apparent in both of my projects (detailed in Box 5.1). For example, in the first study, women diarists explained how diaries allowed them to detail private, often traumatic events for the very first time – 'I couldn't talk about this problem to my family; I kept it within me. I'm the only one that knows about it' (ZN, Diary 34); 'I never told anyone about this is the first time I'm talking about it' (F, Diary 11) (Meth, 2004: 162).

Diaries also allow participants the chance to 'gather their own thoughts', rather than responding on the spot – they can also stop and start entries, reflect, pause and erase. This offers a fairly high degree of control over their own engagement with the research. As another example from my women's study, Mrs F explained: 'I found it better to write the diary than talking during the group interview because I wrote at my own pace. There was no rush. I had time to memorize. ... It helps to have all the things you cannot talk about written down.' Thus, diaries compare favourably in many ways with other methods which often have strong time constraints attached to them (e.g., a one-hour interview slot, a two-hour focus group).

The solicited diary method can provide researchers with access to *spaces, experiences* and *times* that are often (otherwise) inaccessible. Most obviously, diary writing can be conducted within the home, or spaces of employment or leisure – spaces which may be the epicentre of key events and practices being researched. For example, Eidse and Turner's (2014) used solicited diaries in their work with street vendors in Hanoi – a banned economic practice – to document their daily interactions with the police and vendors' struggles to resist and mark out a space for themselves in the city. Morrison's (2012) analysis of love in the home drew on women's diary accounts to examine the meaning of home in relation to their heterosexual relationships. In these examples, the *location* is central to participants' subjective understandings of their lives, and the diary method facilitates a close engagement with these locations. Even ethnographic methods may exclude access to some of these spaces, as certain practices and performances, such as of love in the home, fall outside of the limits of ethical ethnography.

Diaries also offer unique *temporal* access, as researchers can access data produced outside typical data collection times, such as the middle of the night, or early on a weekend morning. In my own work, participants wrote their diaries whenever they chose, including at such times. In the context of South African informal living, the weekends and night-times are often times of insecurity, as alcohol consumption increases and a lack of street lighting and policing makes residents anxious. Capturing diary accounts at these more fraught times enhanced the 'in the moment' reality of the experiences. For researchers trying to understand processes that have particular temporal dimensions, such as loneliness, love, fear and ill health, such potential can be significant (Meth and McClymont, 2009; Morrison, 2012).

The solicited diary method can also potentially contribute to realising wider *transformative* aims through research. In Renzetti's (1997) principles of feminist methodologies, transformative aims included the capacity for research to provide participants – particularly those who are marginalised – with a voice, using research to build empowering relationships between the researcher and the researched. The qualitative diary method is powerfully suited to both of these. My two studies drew on a feminist geographer's perspective on the intersection and co-constitution of gender, place and society (McDowell, 1999). With a focus on their daily lived experience of violence, poverty and inequality, diaries provided participants with a voice, revealing private and often painful insights into their stressful lives. Participants may find writing down private, emotional or shameful concerns in a diary easier than voicing them directly to another individual. In addition, diary writing can be particularly *cathartic* for the diary writer, potentially being both enjoyable and psychologically beneficial (Bell, 1998; Meth, 2003; Meth and McClymont, 2009; Munyewende and Rispel, 2014), providing an opportunity to dispel particular burdens through the process of writing. An example of this can be seen in the following extract from an interview with Mrs F, who was part of my study with women in Durban:

In my heart I felt that in our suffering we were given an opportunity to talk about our feelings and how we would tell the world how 'stormy' are our lives. Writing the diary was a task I liked to do . . . . I also felt relieved. It was like a big luggage has been removed from my shoulders . . . Writing the diary made me feel good because I had an opportunity to revise and cough out everything that was haunting me all my life. I felt really good; in some instances I even laughed. There is somewhere in the diary where I write about employment issues. That thing was really eating me inside but I couldn't talk about it to anyone . . . but it, having written about them is like telling the world about these things and it makes me feel better. (Meth, 2003: 201)

Returning to Renzetti's (1997) feminist principles, this cathartic quality of diary writing can be an explicit function of a participant's power position within society – for those who are marginalised, the relief of sharing painful memories or realities can be immense (Meth, 2003).

Equally significantly, diaries, because of their highly reflective nature, can offer space for *personal transformation* of the participant (Harvey, 2011). Diaries can engender change in self-understanding, and the very process of writing, and also reflecting on, their entries can assist in encouraging participants to pursue particular practices, or can help participants to reinterpret existing practices in more meaningful ways. For example, in a diary study of sexual practices, Harvey (2011: 671) described the case of Joy, who through the process of diarising changed her own 'perception of sexual health risk, [displayed] an increased sense of self-esteem and identification with feminist discourses of female empowerment'. As with any method, the reverse is always possible, and solicited diaries can foster anxiety. This ethical issue and measures to manage it are discussed below.

What Research Questions Suit Solicited Qualitative Diaries?

The solicited diary method is remarkably flexible and has the capacity to address a wide range of research questions and aims. The qualitative studies I've referred to in this chapter already cover a wide spectrum of research questions, but share an interest in understanding feelings, experiences, insights and emotions. As detailed in Box 5.1, I used diaries to question the interrelationship between social phenomenon (e.g., domestic violence, violence and housing), as well as to ask questions about residents' experiences and interpretations – and about what happened, why, when and where.

However, diaries are more limited than methods like interviews for providing researchers with an opportunity to question, in a different way, a particular comment that a participant makes – a tactic used in interviewing to deepen, or extend, discussion, or to clarify an interviewee's statement. Thus, for research questions wishing to *unpick* 'why' a particular event occurred, or why a perception is held, diaries may prove less useful. However, diaries used alongside follow-up interviews can resolve some of these concerns (discussed further later).

Design, Sampling and Ethical Issues

The solicited diary method requires careful initial design, but is relatively straightforward thereafter. This is not to argue that it's an *easy* option, but rather to acknowledge that the researcher sets up a writing framework for the participants, who then make the bulk of the decisions, as they're the ones writing the diary. The framework is, however, very important and easy to get wrong: participants can misunderstand the purpose of diary writing or lose interest rapidly and not participate in the task.

In designing the framework, researchers must decide on the *purpose* and *format* of the diary. Whether you are using a handwritten or an electronic diary format, you must choose one of two approaches – one more open, one more guided. The more open approach involves providing one set of instructions at the start of the diary (e.g., inside the front cover of a handwritten diary) without any further guidance or structuring – the rest of the diary remains blank. Box 5.2 illustrates advice I provided for male diary users in this style – it was glued to the inside cover of blank notebooks. The more guided approach involves providing not only instructions at the beginning but also guidelines for each entry, or even proformas, where each entry is prescribed to some extent through the provision of headings, columns or other such devices (for examples of this approach, see Aleszewski, 2006; Kenyon, 2006). The first approach tends to work best with more narrative, qualitative diaries, which aim to encourage more unstructured, open and fluid accounts. The second approach is more likely to be useful for research that seeks to gain more consistent and regular input (although still qualitative in nature), such as information about travel behaviour. The advantage of a more open design is that researchers maximise the voice, agency and expression of the participants. This makes it suitable for research exploring individuals' experiences and interpretations of issues. However, the lack of structure/regular guidance *could* leave participants feeling confused and unsupported. This could be ameliorated by providing participants with researcher contact details in order to seek advice, or to build in visits or 'check-ups' with diary writers during their period of writing. Eidse and Turner (2014), for example, conducted 'check-in interviews' with diarists a few days after introducing the diary writing task to them, to ensure the participants were 'on track'.

Questions of *sampling* have varying significance for the qualitative diary method, and the best approach(es) will depend on your research aims, as well as on practical considerations of access, time and budget (see Chapter 3 in Braun and Clarke, 2013, for a discussion of qualitative sampling). In my own work, I aimed to gain deep insights into the lives of particular women and men living in particular places, in order to comment on gendered experiences of violence in these places. This approach to sampling might be termed 'sampling illustratively or evocatively' (Mason, 2002: 126) and required making decisions over who we felt would make 'the 'best illustration' of experiences of gender and violence. In order to try and vary these illustrations, we aimed to select participants who ranged in age, but because of their location – and South Africa's racial history – they were all ethnically similar. Furthermore, because of the need to use facilitators to access residents living informally, we had less control over our selection than we might otherwise.

The *number* of participants must be determined by the design and logic of your study and the key question is how many diaries you require to build an argument – something that will also depend on your analytic approach, and will be shaped by the project's time constraints and budgets, and the period of writing. My projects solicited thirty diaries with women and twenty diaries with men, each over a period of four weeks. In both, the amount of data produced by each participant over this time varied extensively: from around 4,000 to around 31,000 words, with the majority writing over 10,000 words. I recently experimented with diaries written over a two-week period; these yielded word lengths of between 5,500 and 13,000 words, indicating that period of time does largely match diary length.

Arguably, using larger samples of participants (e.g., more than 20) can aid in producing deeper understandings of your topic, as well as suggesting the 'generality' of diary contents. If particular – perhaps unexpected – issues are raised by multiple individual diary writers, this suggests something that may be relevant for a wider group. For example, I did not anticipate reference to the roles played by witch doctors and Christianity in shaping residents everyday lives, providing solutions to personal and criminal concerns, and offering a way of understanding the world, yet it was discussed in many of the diary contributions as significant. These repeated references, accessed through a larger sample, suggested to me that this was an important issue for understanding violence in this context. However, as with all qualitative research, be wary of unreflexive claims of generalisability!

Questions of sampling and selection do raise ethical concerns, not least because not all participants are equally able to consent and participate in diary writing. One obvious challenge with written diaries is that of illiteracy or lack of confidence over literacy skills. This can be managed in different ways: either by screening participants before inviting them to write diaries, although this risks excluding participants, or by allowing participants to use family or friends to do the writing for them. This latter solution can be effective, but does raise questions of privacy, and means the data are produced through a different process, and hence are something different to personally-produced narratives. Based on my own experiences, I suggest employing common-sense ethical guidance and sensitivity (Meth, 2003) to make a decision about how best to proceed. If you take this approach, you should discuss the implications for privacy at the outset, and adult participants can choose or reject it. If used, participants should be assured that if it becomes compromising for either them or their 'scribe', they are free to end participation. Alternatively, participants could use other forms of diary keeping, perhaps audio, photographic or video, which may circumvent literacy or other difficulties (e.g., see Worth, 2009). In addition, if this is relevant and an option, writers should be encouraged to write in the language they are most comfortable with (see Figure 5.1 for an example in Zulu, with accompanying English translation).

Researchers must also be mindful of the time constraints and effort of writing a diary (see Eidse and Turner, 2014, who voiced such concerns about their street vendor study), and factor this into decisions about the length of time participants are expected to spend on diary entries, and the total time-frame of diary collection. In my two projects, we asked diarists to spend four weeks on their diary writing; Eidse and Turner asked vendors in Vietnam to write them for one week. Alongside participant considerations, the choice of timing is based on researcher practicalities such as how long you are 'in the field' for, the length of the project, and other methods of data collection being employed, in combination with reflecting carefully on what kinds of information the researcher hopes to gain, and considering how much time might be needed to access the best data for their study. You should also consider whether any 'compensation' for time is appropriate. The issue of 'payment' is ethically

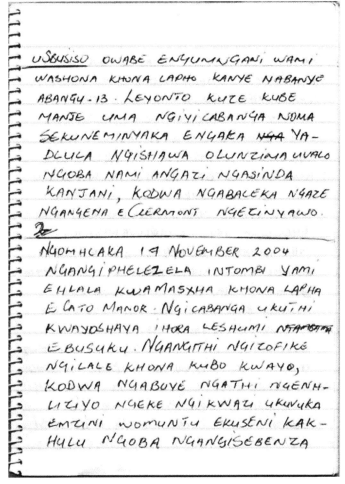

Figure 5.1   An example diary entry – written in Zulu by a male participant

Translation:

'Sibusiso was one of my friend died together with 13 people. That incident happened years ago but in my heart still not goes away or forgets. If I'm thinking about that incident my heart is beating fast because I don't know how I become safe as I was there with my friend but I ran until I get to Clermont by my feet

2

On the 17 of November 2004, I accompany my girlfriend to her home; she lives at Masxha in Cato Manor. It was around ten at night. I was planning to sleep over there but in my heart I feel so lazy to wake up early in the morning in someone house as I'm working' sensitive (Hammett and Sporton, 2012), and you should consider this issue carefully and justify any compensation within your ethics application. Payments, where made, should be locally appropriate! We compensated diarists around £10 per completed diary as this was felt appropriate compensation for their efforts. However, recognise that even payment of a small amount, particularly in contexts of poverty, can reinforce unequal power relations (Hammett and Sporton, 2012) and possibly act as a 'coercion' to continue participation if otherwise reluctant.

Diaries can pose significant challenges for privacy, and potentially even the safety, of participants. From a researcher perspective, all participants' entries must be kept anonymous, and you should avoid citing entries in ways which could accidentally reveal the writer's identity. For participants, diaries (especially if particularly private) may need to be kept hidden from other members of a household during the writing period, and researchers must consider the implications for participant safety if such diaries are found and read. Advising participants of these risks (i.e., thinking through the consequences of an 'unwanted' person reading the diary), as well as of strategies to manage and dilute such risks, is ethically necessary. In my own work, asking women, and then men, to write about violence, including in the home, meant that writing diary entries in the home-space was risky: other householders, including any perpetrators or victims of violence, might see or read what the diarist was writing. Some diarists discussed writing late at night, or hiding their diaries under other household items, to avoid such concerns. If this is an issue, researchers might suggest alternative venues for writing (such as a local library, or pre-arranged times at a community venue), consider modes of diary entries that may be more private (e.g., electronic, perhaps) or employ another method altogether (such as interviews).

Finally, writing diaries can cause participants a range of emotional responses, including anxiety, as difficult memories are written about and reflected on. This was expressed by Philani, one of the male participants, in our interview with him:

There are stories [that made] me sad, that story of [being] arrested and losing the job. The time I was writing I feel the anger of that . . . [and] sometime I was sad because other stories was reminding me [of] the thing I tried to forget in my life.

Prior to the study, researchers should encourage participants to only share what they are comfortable with and remind them that withdrawal from the project is possible if involvement proves problematic. However, as the researcher is not present when diary writing occurs, it can be harder to provide support and advice than some face-to-face methods. Ensuring the participant has some way of contacting the researcher, or building in occasional contact, can counter this issue.

Steps to Using Solicited Qualitative Diaries

Before embarking on using solicited diaries, be clear about your intended focus, as this will help you identify what material the diaries should concentrate on, and who you should seek to involve in your study. Once these are decided, the following steps walk you through the diary research process:

(1) *Identify the target participants for your project, bearing in mind potential challenges of access.* If permission or facilitation from 'gatekeepers' is required for access, work on building contacts and seeking this permission. In my own work, access was gained through community representatives who helped to find willing participants. We were not required to gain permission per se, but certainly access would have been impossible without our representatives' assistance.

(2) *Identify how many participants you need to approach.* Bear in mind that not all diarists will complete the task! Although there are no clear data on drop-out rates for research using qualitative solicited diaries, my advice would be to invite more participants than your ideal sample size – such as 10% more – and/or offer some compensation, if appropriate. In my studies, we achieved 100% participation, but this was undoubtedly shaped by monetary compensation (as noted, we offered £10 per diary).

(3) *Determine mode of collection and prepare all the materials needed.* Decide first which mode of collection you will use (e.g., a handwritten, typed or audio diary) as this will determine what materials need to be prepared – such as pens and blank booklets for handwritten diaries, a tablet or computer for typed diaries, though participants may be able to make use of their own technology (computers, phones, tablets, etc.). Avoid assumptions about access to technology and willingness to use it, as these risk excluding participants because of cost and/or possible shame of revealing this.

(4) *Identify the appropriate writing period.* This needs to satisfy the aims of your research *and* be acceptable to your participants. For some diary studies, a particular period of time may be vital (e.g., one week, month or year) to reveal cycles, patterns and/or processes over a certain period – for instance, if you were interested in use of monthly income, or emotions

over changing seasons. This clearly depends on topic – and for longer time-frames, you need also to decide how *regularly* you expect your participants to complete an entry.

(5) *Draft and re-draft any necessary 'instructions' for participants, explaining the task very clearly, perhaps even giving an example of what they might write* (see Box 5.2 for an example; Alaszewski, 2006, also provides good examples of various types of instruction). Make sure to avoid 'leading information', which prejudges the participant's feelings or experiences, such as 'describe why you dislike this area'. The advice you provide here is *critical*, as, following initial meetings with participants, the written instructions may be the only connection between the participant and the researcher during data collection – especially if 'check-ins' have not been pre-arranged. If the instructions are not clear, things can go horribly wrong! If the instructions need to be translated into another language, make sure that the words used have comparable meaning and are culturally appropriate.

(6) *Pilot the diary.* Given the need for clarity, piloting with a handful of participants is ideal, as it allows you to iron out any issues, including clarity of instructions and viability of the method to collect the data you want. You may not need to pilot for the full planned data collection, but I highly recommend some form of piloting, if at all possible.

(7) *Decide how the diary writing task will commence.* A face-to-face meeting is ideal, in order to fully explain and discuss the method, and to cover ethical considerations and obtain consent. An online discussion may suffice, but the signed consent documents would need to be collected or returned separately. In my studies, diary writing was discussed with participants following their involvement in focus group discussions, and being physically present allowed diarists to ask us questions, to discuss the task with their peers, and to read through the instructions to check they understood what they had to do. This meeting also provided for a full and frank discussion of disclosure and ethics. However, unless part of an overall design (as ours was), this may not work – not least, group meetings are *hard* to set up! Ultimately, the key is finding a mode and way that suits participants, as well as you, and ensures any and all questions can be asked.

(8) *Agree on a time and date for collection, as well as when and how participants can contact the researcher during the diary writing phase.* Access to advice and support can prove invaluable for keeping participants on task and ensuring data are ultimately received (see Eidse and Turner, 2014). In my studies, some of the participants communicated by phone to discuss their diaries, and it was evident that some of them felt

---

Box 5.2 Example of diary instructions: 'Men's experience of violence in informal settlements in South Africa' study

Help on writing your diary

Dear diary-writer,

Thank you for agreeing to write this diary for my research. This is an unusual method of research but it is used because interviews only tell you about what a person is thinking on one day, not many days. Writing a diary allows you to tell your personal stories over a longer period of time. In the papers that are written at universities not much is known about what men think about violence and crime – and this is why I want to learn more about this.

You can write whatever you want in the diary, but what I am specifically interested in is to learn about your day-to-day feelings of fear, <u>and</u> experiences of, violence and crime. These fears and experiences could be ones that you suffered personally or that affected someone you know or heard of. These could be experiences that are happening now or even in the past. I am interested to know WHAT those experiences or fears were and HOW you managed or responded to them. This diary is a chance for you to write your personal stories about violence and crime – there is no right or wrong answer, anything you write will be useful and help us to understand your day-to-day experiences. I will keep your names secret, for example if your name is Mr Dlamini, I will call you Mr D when I am writing up my research reports.

Please can you try and fill in the following details about each description (if possible):

(1) WHEN was it? (date/time)
(2) WHO were you scared of? (other men/children/girlfriend)
(3) WHAT happened? (describe the event)
(4) HOW did you deal with it? (run away, fight back, call the police, hide, ignore it, pray, find your friends, avoid walking down a street, for example?)

Even though I want you to include something about the above four points, please write in full sentences if possible, and if there is anything else you want to say or elaborate on that is fine too.

Please keep a diary for six weeks and then return your diary as arranged. You will be paid for filling in the diary and returning it, as I do understand that writing a diary takes up time. I do not expect you to write in it every day. Some days you might write a lot and other days you might just write a few words or nothing at all, that is fine.

Thank you, Dr Meth.

Paula Meth's Diary (this is just an example for you):

On the 1 December 2002 I was driving in KwaMashu when a young man approached my car. He started to be friendly then he put his hand in the car and he pulled the keys out of the ignition. I jumped out of the car with my friend and left him to take the car. He couldn't start the car, so he jumped out and came towards me. I was very frightened. I gave him my bag so that he would not hurt me. He ran away, luckily he threw my keys back on the ground. My friend and I jumped back in the car and we drove away. We were both very upset and frightened. We were so happy that he did not hurt us.

anxious about what was expected of them. Talking this through with them helped to alleviate these concerns in advance, and meant that we got data that we may otherwise have lost.

(9) *Collect the diary data – this might be face-to-face or via post/email.* In my experience, the hand-over was a significant moment, as diarists were nervous but also proud of their 'work'. I'd thus encourage a face-to-face collection of diaries where possible; it also provides an additional ethical 'check in' moment for researchers, which may be valuable for highly sensitive topics.

(10) *Set up expectations around any on-going contact.* Researchers may want further access to participants after completion, in order to conduct follow-up interviews or informal discussions to check and clarify diary entries, something that usually occurs during translation and/or analysis. This ought to be explained in advance.

What Can Go Wrong with Solicited Qualitative Diaries?

Many of the challenges and issues with solicited diary research relate to the absence of the researcher during data production (i.e., diary-entry writing). One risk is that participants write unfocused and nonsensical entries, or write in an unexpected format that is not analytically useful. In my own work, all participants chose to write their entries in a way that wasn't chronologically organised. For example, the first page of Philani's diary featured the following subheadings: 'On 19th Sept 2003 . . .; In 1998 . . .; In June 2004 . . .; On Jan . . .; On Jan 2006 . . .' This temporally random sequence reflected his choice about what to focus on and when, as well as his understanding of what a diary was. If you require some specific format or focus in entries, this will need to be specified.

This relates to another risk: off-topic entries. Although I would argue that there is no such thing as a 'wrong' contribution – any contribution reveals *something* about the participant/issue – there may be cases where participants choose to write about something entirely different from the project's focus. As with all qualitative research, unexpected and off-topic entries can be seen as a potential challenge or an opportunity. Completed diaries may not contain the material that was hoped for in terms of the project's focus, but similarly, such unexpected entries can prove to be important opportunities for widening and rethinking original research questions, or the scope of relevance around the topic.

Participants' form of expression may also provide some challenges – for instance, they may use local jargon which you don't understand and which requires subsequent explanation. Contributions may be weakly linked, with gaps in stories or explanations, which may be confusing or even useless analytically. Relatedly, entries may provide very surface or glossed-over accounts, without depth and detail, and thus don't get to the heart of the experience or issue you're researching. All of these issues can, to some extent, be prevented by giving really clear instructions, but you don't want to provide so much that the participant feels straightjacketed in how they respond. Another way to address this might be build a follow-up interview or meeting into your research design, to deal with these issues.

Other risks relate to engagement and staying on task. Diary writing is time-consuming and potentially dull and repetitive for participants – it runs the risk of participants losing interest and failing to engage in the writing task, or even dropping out. Compensation of some sort (monetary or other) *may* prove effective in maximising diarists' willingness to complete the task, but raises ethical considerations, as discussed. It also carries cost implications for researchers, and is often difficult for student researchers.

A quite different risk is the potential for participants (or indeed the researcher) to lose the (hard copy) diaries – so the sooner safe copies are made, the better. This might sound overly cautious, but in my project with women, ten diaries were lost within thirty minutes of receiving them, through a car hijacking incident in South Africa. In the later project with men, I arranged for the collection of diaries to occur in a relatively safe place near to the residents' settlement, to reduce risk of theft in this way.

Finally, a somewhat different problem can arise from not budgeting time (or money) effectively. If diaries are handwritten, you'll almost certainly want to type up the content using a word processing programme – this is essential if you intend using computer-assisted qualitative data analysis software like NVivo during analysis. This takes time – but less time than audio data transcription, so take that into account if using audio or video diaries. If the diaries are written in another language, translation can prove very costly if you need to pay an interpreter to assist you. In my experience, this latter consumed a substantial portion of the project time and budget, as diaries were handwritten in Zulu, and were then translated and transcribed into English for analysis (see Figure 5.1). If such costs aren't effectively considered in the design phase, the analysis phase typically suffers – or the project drags out beyond your intended time-frame.

What Methods of Analysis Suit Solicited Qualitative Diary Data?

A variety of methods have been used by researchers to analyse their solicited diaries, including narrative analysis (Wiles et al., 2005), discourse analysis (Mason, 2002) and semiotic analysis, which explores absences, the study of signs and the constructions of meanings (Crang, 1997; Kellehear, 1993). In my research, I used thematic analysis, which involved reading and re-reading the texts searching for descriptive and subsequent analytic codes, and wider themes within the script (see Cope, 2003; Meth and McClymont, 2009). Qualitative analysis like this often takes place by hand, although computer software packages such as Nudist or NVivo can be used to facilitate the process. I found NVivo offered a useful mechanism to manage a substantial amount of data in the men's project.

During analysis, it is important that researchers ask questions regarding what types of participants – and hence what experiences, lives, situations, etc. – are *not* included in the data, and also what narratives are absent from individual diary accounts. These absences point to fascinating emphases in individuals' interpretations of events and can inform the nature of knowledge claims made. One example from my work is that in the participants' diaries, the role of the apartheid state was seldom ever mentioned, despite many diarists pursuing highly historical narrative strategies. This absence of discussion was intriguing, given the scale and dominance of the apartheid experience. It suggests that diarists focused on their immediate scale (their neighbourhood, their own lives) when seeking evidence or explanation of their experiences. As with all qualitative methods, it is critical to approach analysis with a very strong sense of the context of the research and the participants' accounts. My approach to diary interpretation and analysis required a constant appreciation of the subjective nature of diary entries, as well as the subjective role played by the researcher/s in shaping the material. This required me to actively acknowledge my own meanings and experiences, alongside those of my research assistant, and consider how these shaped my interpretations (Meth and McClymont, 2009).

Conclusion

This overview of solicited diaries as a method for qualitative researchers has outlined the benefits and challenges of this method, based on my actual use of this approach. The chapter has covered key practical as well as more methodological concerns, in order for researchers to make informed judgements

---

Box 5.3 Reflections on using solicited diaries

The qualitative diary method has been a significant journey for me personally, and it has inadvertently fuelled my interest in innovative qualitative methods and methodology. My decision to use the method was relatively arbitrary, in that I'd not come across it as a recommended method before my first project, and it wasn't at all clear to me that participants would embrace the method. The successful engagement with diaries by participants stands as evidence for me of the advantages of being creative, within a context of consideration of ethics, and also overall research purpose. Within the field of human geography, diary writing has become a more popular, albeit fringe, approach to researching complex issues. Within this field, my view is that diaries work best in combination with other methods, but that for my work, diaries 'trump' other methods in terms of data quality. As part of mixed method studies, I particularly value the added longitudinal insight that diaries provide, as well as the narrative depth available in diary contributions. I've recently (this month!) returned to using diaries in my work following my own critical evaluation of a few small-scale projects I've conducted over the past few years. These simply drew on focus groups and interviews, and in my view, yielded thinner and less insightful data. I hadn't turned my back on diaries for any reason other than cost, so driven by my motivations around data quality *and* practical limits (cost and time), I'm currently piloting diaries written over a two-week period; my early reflections are that these are very worthwhile, containing rich commentary which addresses my research questions. I'm relieved to be reacquainted with my favourite method, albeit, in a different form!

---

about the suitability of this method for their own work. In Box 5.3, I reflect on using this method, and just how beneficial I have found it.

Have a Go . . .

Read and reflect . . . Using a search engine (e.g., Google Scholar), search for journal articles that describe using and analysing, qualitative diaries as a primary technique. Search terms such as 'diaries research', 'solicited diaries', 'diaries qualitative methods' should work. Select an article each from three different disciplines (e.g., geography, psychology and sociology) and download them. Using these three articles, identify the following features of the diary method as described by the author/s:

(1) What was the overall *aim* of their research project? If available, what kinds of questions was the project seeking to answer?

(2) What were the diaries being used *for* within this project?
(3) What particular *insights* did the diaries offer the researchers?

Using this overview, reflect on your own particular research interests, aims and questions and consider the ways they are similar and different to the three projects you have looked at. Does this reflection suggest the diary method is a relevant data collection tool for you, and if so, why?

Turn yourself into a participant ... Testing out methods on *yourself* is useful for gaining insights into how the method works, and what participants might experience when engaging with a particular method. Aim to write a diary each day over a two-week period. Choose a topic that really interests you (e.g., participation in exercise, the joys and tribulations of friendship, experience of social media use, what and how you eat), and diarise this in different ways. For Week 1, try and record *the basic details* of your selected issue. For example, if you were recording your exercise over a week it might start like this:

Tuesday: Walked fast 45 minutes in am / nothing in pm / Pilates in evening.
Wednesday: No exercise am / walked 20 mins afternoon / 1 hour dance
               class pm

At the end of Week 1, assess the diary record, asking yourself how much you can learn from your entries and *what kinds of questions* they might help you answer. Consider what cannot be learned from them. Reflect on how you, as the participant, felt both writing the entries and while reviewing them at the end of the week.

For Week 2, record fuller narrative entries around the same topic – including not only what you did but your emotional and other relevant experiences or descriptions – write as much as you feel like, per day. These entries might look like:

Tuesday: Lovely walk this morning, icy wind but very bright, felt out of
               breath but invigorated. Sat down all day so I felt stiff and lazy,
               but Pilates class in evening really woke me up, back aches
               much better afterwards and great to chat to Claire.
Wednesday: Relied on car too much today, not good, but weather awful
               and am feeling tired again. Walked a little in the afternoon
               and then evening dance class good fun, although it was a bit
               technical so we didn't work up much of a sweat. The stretch
               at the end was great, reminded me that my hamstring was
               still sore. Even when I'm tired, I feel better after exercise.

At the end of Week 2, assess the second diary data, asking yourself again what can and cannot be learned from the entries. Reflect on the differences between the two diaries, in terms of content, depth, style and effort, seeing your diary entries as 'data'. Consider honestly how you felt writing these diaries – was the task onerous, engaging and/or something else? How might you alleviate any negatives around diary completion, if you were to use this method?

Further Resources: Online

For a range of videos, slides and documents relating to using diaries in research, visit the National Centre for Research Methods: www.ncrm.co.uk

Further Resources: Readings

For an extensive discussion of diaries as a research method, this book covers setting up diary research, collection of data and analysis. For advice on how to structure diaries to maximise participant engagement, see chapter 4: Alaszewski, A. M. (2006). *Using diaries for social research*. London: Sage Publications.

For an example of using solicited diaries in qualitative research with both male and female participants over relatively lengthy time periods (i.e., a median of 23 weeks), see Milligan, C., Bingley, A. and Gatrell, A. (2005). Digging deep: Using diary techniques to explore the place of health and well-being amongst older people. *Social Science & Medicine*, *61*(9), 1882–1892.

For an overview of various diary forms (video, audio, researcher diaries) and using diaries as part of a multi-method approach, see Meth, P. (2009). Methods: Diaries (video, audio or written). In R. Kitchin and N. Thrift, (eds.), *International encyclopedia of human geography* (Vol. 1, pp. 150–155). Oxford: Elsevier.

For an example of using solicited diaries in qualitative research, including accessing hard-to-reach spaces and situations, see Morrison, C.-A. (2012). Solicited diaries and the everyday geographies of heterosexual love and home: Reflections on methodological process and practice. *Area*, *44*(1), 68–75.

References

Alaszewski, A. M. (2006). *Using diaries for social research*. London: Sage Publications.

Bell, L. (1998). Public and private meanings in diaries: Researching family and childcare. In J. Ribbens and R. Edwards (eds.), *Feminist dilemmas in qualitative research: Public knowledge and private lives* (pp. 72–86). London: Sage Publications.

Braun, V. and Clarke, V. (2013). *Successful qualitative research: A practical guide for beginners*. London: Sage Publications.

Cope, M. (2003). Coding transcripts and diaries. In N. Clifford and G. Valentine (eds.), *Key methods in geography* (pp. 445–460). London: Sage Publications.

Crang, M. (1997). Analyzing qualitative materials. In R. Flowerdew and D. Martin (eds.), *Methods in human geography* (pp. 183–196). London: Longman.

Eidse, N. and Turner, S. (2014). Doing resistance their own way: Counter-narratives of street vending in Hanoi, Vietnam through solicited journaling. *Area, 46*(3), 242–248.

Elliott, H. (1997). The use of diaries in sociological research on health experience. *Sociological Research Online, 2*(2). Retrieved from: www.socresonline.org.uk /2/2/7.html

Gibson, B., Mistry, B., Smith, B., Yoshida, K., Abbott, D., Lindsay, S. and Hamdani, Y. (2013). The integrated use of audio diaries, photography, and interviews in research with disabled young men. *International Journal of Qualitative Methods, 12*(1), 382–402.

Hammett, D. and Sporton, D. (2012). Paying for interviews? Negotiating ethics, power and expectation. *Area, 44*(4), 496–502.

Harvey, L. (2011). Intimate reflections: Private diaries in qualitative research. *Qualitative Research, 11*(6), 664–682.

Kellehear, A. (1993). *The unobtrusive researcher*. Sydney: Allen and Unwin.

Kenyon, S. (2006). The 'accessibility diary': Discussing a new methodological approach to understand the impact of Internet use upon personal travel and activity participation. *Journal of Transport Geography, 14*(2), 123–134.

Mason, J. (2002). *Qualitative researching* (2nd edn). London: Sage Publications.

McDowell, L. (1999). *Gender, identity and place: Understanding feminist geographies*. Cambridge: Polity Press.

Meth, P. (2003). Entries and omissions: Using solicited diaries in geographical research. *Area, 35*(2), 195–205.

(2004). Using diaries to understand women's responses to crime and violence. *Environment and Urbanization, 16*(2), 153–164.

Meth, P. and McClymont, K. (2009). Researching men: The politics and possibilities of a mixed methods approach. *Social & Cultural Geography, 10*(8), 909–925.

Morrison, C.-A. (2012). Solicited diaries and the everyday geographies of heterosexual love and home: Reflections on methodological process and practice. *Area, 44*(1), 68–75.

Munyewende, P. and Rispel, L. (2014). Using diaries to explore the work experiences of primary health care nursing managers in two South African provinces. *Global Health Action, 7*, 1–10.

Odendaal, W., Hausler, H., Tomlinson, M., Lewin, S. and Mtshizana, Y. (2012). The use of audio and visual diaries to explore the adherence behaviours of HIV and TB patients: A South African study. *International Journal of Psychology, 47*(S1), 470.

O'Donnell, S.C., Marshman, Z. and Zaitoun, H. (2013). 'Surviving the sting': The use of solicited diaries in children and young people with oral mucosal disease. *International Journal of Paediatric Dentistry, 23*(5), 352–358.

Renzetti, C. (1997). Confessions of a reformed positivist: Feminist participatory research as good social science. In M. Schwartz (ed.), *Researching sexual violence against women: Methodological and personal perspectives* (pp. 131–143). Thousand Oaks, CA: Sage Publications.

Roth, A., Hensel, D., Fortenberry, J., Garfein, R., Gunn, J. and Wiehe, S. (2014). Feasibility and acceptability of cell phone diaries to measure HIV risk behavior among female sex workers. *AIDS and Behaviour*, *18*(12), 2314–2324.

Wiles, J. L., Rosenberg, M. W. and Kearns, R. A. (2005). Narrative analysis as a strategy for understanding interview talk in geographic research. *Area*, *37*(1), 89–99.

Worth, N. (2009). Making use of audio diaries in research with young people: Examining narrative, participation and audience. *Sociological Research Online*, *14*(4). Retrieved from: www.socresonline.org.uk/14/4/9.html

Part II

Media Data Collection

6 Making Media Data

An Introduction to Qualitative Media Research

Laura Favaro, Rosalind Gill and Laura Harvey

Overview

We live in a mediated world, and media offer an excellent source of data for qualitative researchers. This chapter introduces media research, focusing on the opportunities and challenges that it offers and capturing the experience of working critically with a form of data that we are all familiar with from everyday life, yet seldom pause to study. We illustrate our discussion of the broad field of qualitative media research in relation to three types of data – magazines (see Box 6.1), newspapers (see Box 6.2) and the increasingly pervasive *reader comments* sections of online news sites (see Box 6.3). Drawing on our own analyses and expertise in working with these kinds of data, we outline *what* they are, *why* they are *important, what* they can offer researchers and *how* to go about using them. As Boxes 6.1–6.3 show, our research is concerned with a nexus of questions about gender, sexuality and intimate relationships – but the potential of media data goes far beyond these domains. There are many advantages to media data – compared with interviews or focus groups, for instance: they are ubiquitous and often freely available; they are accessible and often time and 'resource-lite' – for example, not requiring lengthy transcription; and they have considerable value as data for the social and health sciences and beyond.

Introduction to Media Data

Media increasingly dominate our social world! Every day almost every person in the global North will have multiple interactions with media of various kinds: we may wake up to talk or music on a phone or radio alarm; we see newspapers and magazines all around us, and, even if we don't buy them ourselves, we may read them over the shoulder of the person next to us on the bus; we get news updates or check Facebook on our phones; we tweet, we blog, we snapchat and we upload pictures to Instagram and Pinterest; we watch TV and go to the

---

Box 6.1 The mediated intimacy and postfeminism study

This study was part of a wider project concerned with mediated intimacy – that is, the ways in which different kinds of intimate relations are constructed in and through different media and information and communication technologies. Here we explored sex and relationships advice in a popular women's magazine. *Glamour* is UK's best-selling women's monthly magazine, at the time of the analysis selling nearly 600,000 copies and gaining eight million 'hits' on its website each month. Articles about sex and relationships are a key part of its success, along with fashion, beauty and celebrity news. Each month sees this fare prominently displayed on the cover with headlines such as 'How good are you in bed? Men tell you what your partner won't' and 'We're coming to your sexual rescue: never be bored in bed again'. The analysis aimed to understand the kinds of messages about sex and relationships that were presented and to ask questions about the ideas and assumptions about sex, gender and sexuality that they relied on and imparted. Three broad interpretative repertoires (Potter and Wetherell, 1987; see 'analysis' section) were identified: the 'intimate entrepreneurship' repertoire, which was based on a language of goals, plans and strategies, and a 'professionalisation' of intimate life; 'menology' was organised around the idea that women need to study and learn about men's needs and desires; and 'transforming the self', which exhorted women to 'makeover' not simply their bodies and sexual practices, but their emotional lives too – in order to become confident and sexually adventurous. Our discussion focused in particular on the postfeminist nature of the advice, where pre-feminist, feminist and anti-feminist ideas are entangled and feminist politics are repudiated as currently unnecessary and obsolete. This makes gender ideologies – understood as 'the ways in which meaning is mobilized for the maintenance of relations of domination' (Thompson, 1984: 5) – pernicious and difficult to contest.

Source: Gill (2009).

---

cinema. In urban environments particularly, even the most reluctant media user cannot help glimpsing hundreds of commercial advertising messages every day on the billboards that dominate public space. Life for most of us is increasingly lived out in and through media – which makes media both a fascinating topic and an important source of data for social and health scientists.

Researchers use media as data to study all kinds of questions and issues, such as the political dimensions of computer war games (Machin and van Leeuwen, 2007), the 'sexualisation' of culture (Attwood, 2009), the representation of socially marginalised groups (Hall, 2000) and many more. Media analysis can be powerful and authoritative; significantly, it can be used to make a difference in the world, to highlight problems in society and to push for change. For instance, reports showing the underrepresentation of women in senior positions

---

Box 6.2 The everyday coupledom study[1]

As part of a broader project entitled 'Enduring Love? Couple Relationships in the 21st Century' (www.open.ac.uk/researchprojects/enduringlove), we systematically examined stories about couple relationships in top-circulating UK broadsheet and tabloid newspapers and magazines, which were aimed at a variety of audiences. The project aimed to find out how couple relationships were represented across a range of media during a specified time-frame. The data consisted of all stories and storylines about couple relationships in the selected publications and broadcasts from 10 November to 7 December 2012. From a total of 273 publications and episodes, 1,430 articles and storylines were sampled. Taking a social constructionist approach, the analysis is ongoing. Analysis we've conducted so far has examined how stories about celebrities' lives, problem pages, advice columns and comment pieces about the latest political scandal orient the reader towards the boundaries of normative coupledom – the social stories told about which kinds of couple relationships are 'normal'. This includes representing a world in which couples must be vigilant and unforgiving about infidelity, in which royal relationships are positioned as 'ordinary' at a time of increasing austerity and in which fertility and childcare remain central markers of contemporary coupledom.

---

within the news media – such as news anchor, producer or expert commentator – have been used to pressure broadcasters to hire or promote more women (Macharia, O'Connor and Ndanga, 2010). Media analysis can also be a key tool for activists, highlighting, for example, partiality in the coverage of climate change (McKewon, 2012), racism in news reporting of the killing of black people by white police officers (Noble, 2014), or the absence of media representations of lesbian, gay, bisexual, transgender, queer or questioning people (Fisher, Hill and Grube, 2007).

There is an enormous range of media, and their types are proliferating all the time. In the twentieth century, media research – or mass communication research as it was sometimes called – focused on television (and to a lesser extent radio), cinema, newspapers and magazines, along with public space (or 'outdoors') media, such as advertising billboards. Today our understanding of media is much broader and has extended to include YouTube, Facebook, Twitter, Instagram, computer games, the blogosphere (see also Chapter 8) and so forth. The digital revolution has not only generated entirely new kinds of

---

[1] The 'everyday coupledom' study (Box 6.2) was conducted as part of the *Enduring Love? Couple Relationships in the 21st Century* project, which was funded by the Economic and Social Research Council (ESRC RES-062-23-3056). We would like to express our gratitude to the MeCCSA (Media, Communication and Cultural Studies Association) mailing list contributors for a helpful discussion on copyright and comments section of news sites.

Box 6.3 The 'emasculation nation' study

This study examined constructions of men and masculinity in online discussions about the British feminist campaign *'Lose the Lads' Mags* (LTLM). LTLM aimed to get men's magazines, such as *Zoo, Nuts* and *Loaded*, removed from the shelves of major retailers, arguing that they are misogynistic and objectify women, fuelling sexist behaviours and attitudes. The campaign was widely debated across the British media, and online, becoming part of a national conversation related to the representation of women in public space, and ongoing concerns about 'sexualisation' and 'lad culture'. Our dataset comprised over 5,000 online reader comments to news reporting of the LTLM campaign and retailer responses to it. These comments were gathered from various national mainstream news websites, with those posted on the BBC and Yahoo UK accounting for more than half (56%). The analysis explored the repeated focus on men and masculinity as 'attacked', 'under threat', 'victimised' or 'demonised' in what was depicted as a sinister new gender order. Specifically, we identified four 'interpretative repertoires' (Potter and Wetherell, 1987; see analysis section) drawn upon by commentators in their posts: 'gendered double standards' in the campaign, media and public life; 'male sexuality under threat', pertaining particularly to heterosexual desire; 'the war on the normal bloke', which constructed white British straight men and their way of life as hated and under siege; and 'feminist tyranny', where feminism was presented as a looming menace for both men in particular and the UK more broadly. Throughout the analysis, we drew attention to the use of rhetorical strategies, key images and tropes that animated the sense of men under threat – for example, metaphors of war, or a conjuring of notions of extremism, fascism and totalitarianism. We suggested that the volume and nature of the commentary about 'men as new victims' or 'newly oppressed' does significant ideological work and may usefully be understood in relation to a rearticulated backlash against the current upsurge of feminist ideas and activism.

Source: García-Favaro and Gill (2016).

---

media; it has also transformed and multiplied existing and established media. In the past, an analysis of a television show – let's say *Doctor Who* – would have been a study of a broadcast programme or series of programmes. Today, the scope of that analysis might be expanded to include a huge variety of other material: the outtakes, 'bloopers', interviews and special features that come with the DVD; the TV programme's Facebook pages, its Twitter feeds; and the vast intertextual apparatus that surrounds its celebrity actors. It is likely that *Doctor Who* researchers could find hundreds of scripts online and access vast amounts of commentary, as well as a whole universe of homages, spoofs and fan fiction on sites like YouTube. To study *Doctor Who* would now not simply involve recording and analysing the programmes; it would involve engagement with a multiplicity of interrelated media productions, all of which shape how and what we understand *Doctor Who* to be. For you as a researcher, this represents a wealth of material, but also produces tough questions about how to draw the boundaries around what you're studying: the magazines, the children's toys, potato chips and cookies – or 'just' the broadcast programme? In other words, media researchers need to make choices about *what will count as data*. To illustrate this, we outline our choices around data for the example studies: magazines, newspapers and online reader comments.

Magazines today take many forms. The traditional glossy printed magazines we see on shop shelves and in doctor's waiting rooms still exist, but increasingly magazines are sold in digital forms for laptops or tablets and in online versions which feature not only the editorially controlled content but also a huge array of reader forums that are often lively and animated (Favaro, in press). Even in the printed versions, there are vastly varied types of content, offering rich pickings for researchers: the covers, articles of various kinds, advertisements, letters from readers and problem pages have all been topics of considerable interest in the past (e.g., McCracken, 1993). In our study of *Glamour* magazine's sex and relationship advice (see Box 6.1), we identified multiple kinds of texts – for example, 'how-to' advice pieces, quizzes, 'men's voice' pieces (which purport to explain to readers what men really want/feel), reports on surveys carried out by the magazine (e.g., *Glamour*'s sex survey or surveys on attitudes to pornography), as well as feature articles. This highlights the many different genres of writing found even in print magazines, and just looking at content focused around sex and relationships! Another point to bear in mind is the increasing resemblance between commercial messages and editorially authored content, which can make it difficult to draw distinctions. As with all data selection, you have to develop clear inclusion and exclusion criteria, but these are often best determined once you've identified the full spectrum of potential data.

Newspapers too have undergone a radical transformation in recent decades, and multiplied the range of data researchers can explore. While once *printed* newspapers were a primary source of mass-communicated information, developments in broadcast and digital technologies, and the globalisation of media, have provided more news platforms, many of which can be accessed for free. These new formats have transformed the nature of journalism, along with the content of newspapers themselves (Curran and Seaton, 2009). Some media scholars, for instance, have argued that a steady decline in newspaper sales has led to increasing competition and sensationalism (Rowe, 2011). Like magazines, newspapers offer a wide range of potential data, including the text in editorial stories and features, photographs and other visuals such as charts or diagrams, reader letters and a large variety of advertisements. Researchers might also want to consider the positioning and relationship *between* these elements, which can be of crucial significance. For example, in the reporting of the killing of black teenager Michael Brown by a white police officer in the US in August 2014, the use of different images had implications for the meaning of the story, including implicit criticism or justification of his death. Contrast the use of Michael Brown's graduation picture with CCTV footage reporting him stealing from a corner shop on the same day that he was shot. Like most print media, newspapers are now also readily available in *digital* downloadable forms and *online*, with interactive content such as journalists' social media feeds and reader-comment sections.

Online reader comments. Newspapers have long provided an outlet for public discourse, in the form of letters to the editor. With the advent of Web 2.0, online news media expanded this opportunity for public engagement with interactive features, notably the possibility to immediately comment on specific news stories, and on other people's comments (see also Chapter 9). Reader comment sections are now ubiquitous and highly valued by online news audiences, who are increasingly posting comments in response both to editorial articles and other readers' posts. These sections provide an unlimited number of users, often separated in time and place, a space to express their views and/or engage in debate on specific topics. Further, although only generated by a small number of people in comparison to the total site visitors, this commentary exerts an influential role in shaping public attitudes: it is widely read and, moreover, often seen by readers as illustrative of public opinion (Henrich and Holmes, 2013). In order to comment and rate other people's comments, users are typically required to register by providing a valid email address and self-selected username, which can present an anonymous 'face'. Indeed, when working with user-generated content such as this, it is important to keep in mind that the (relative) anonymity of the Internet induces a level of freedom of expression inhibited in other spaces, and that this can often mean that online discussion fora are highly affectively charged spaces (Jensen and Ringrose, 2014). Although comment-threads are often closed after a period of time, the archiving capacities of the Internet means they rarely disappear, remaining readily available for viewing – and analysing! Much like the editorial and reported content, reader posts become part of the discursive landscape of the site, and the web more broadly. Furthermore, they impact journalistic work, being used as triggers for the revision of content, such as fixing inaccuracies (Robinson, 2010) and sources of ideas for future stories. Overall, news sites' reader comment sections appear to be an increasingly important element of news journalism, as well as space for public deliberation – and thus a fascinating source of data.

There are notable distinctions in the production of different media, and thus the data they can generate. Magazine and newspaper content is usually (though not always) produced via multi-layered professional processes of journalism and editorial control. Television content is similarly the result of the work of a whole team involved in scripting, editing, performance and production; even 'reality' programming has a complex production process, despite its outwardly 'unscripted' performance. This contrasts with online discussions – and user-generated content more generally. With so-called new media, users enjoy increasing (but still limited and highly surveilled) control over content, and they interact, network, share information and co-create with other users.

Different media data also entail different text-audience relationships (see Box 6.4). This relationship has been long debated within cultural and media studies, with some scholars (e.g., Hall, 1997; Morley and Brunsdon, 2005) convincingly arguing that rather than passively consuming media, audiences actively negotiate their meaning. For example, there is a strong tradition of feminist research showing that girls and women not only critically read but often also actively transform meanings from commercial texts, such as magazines, in creative, transgressive and resistant ways (e.g., Durham, 2004; McRobbie, 1991). Digital and Internet communications and technologies further complicate this relationship, increasingly challenging the very idea of a clear distinction between consumption and production. This has given rise to a whole new vocabulary – for example, notions like *produser* (producer/consumer; Bruns, 2008) and *Pro-Am* (professional/amateur; Leadbeater and Miller, 2004) – to try to capture the idea of people simultaneously *consuming and producing* content (see Jenkins, 2006, on 'participatory culture' and 'media convergence'). The rapid changes we are seeing in the field of (digital and online) media make it a really exciting focus for qualitative researchers with many different research questions.

What Do Media Data Offer the Qualitative Researcher?

Media data offer an extraordinarily valuable source of information for social, health and many other researchers. More than at any other time in history, we live lives that are 'mediated' – that is, we increasingly create and communicate meaning in and through media sites and technologies. Most directly, social media such as Facebook, Snapchat or Twitter have become key to how many of

Box 6.4 What about media audiences?

Although this chapter focuses on media *content*, it's important for media researchers not to forget about audiences. The relationship between audiences and texts is an ongoing topic of debate. Nowhere is this more apparent than on the issue of 'media effects' – whether, and how, our media consumption affects our views, understandings, practices, etc. There are polarised positions between those who suggest that media are directly implicated in causing particular behaviours or transformations (e.g., Bandura, Ross and Ross, 1961; Dworkin, 1981) and those who point to the active agency of viewers/readers/consumers and their capacity to resist even dominant messages (e.g., Buckingham and Bragg, 2004).

It is now widely recognised that the 'effects' of a particular message or type of media content cannot be 'read off' from an analysis of that media and, furthermore, that there is no one fixed and unitary meaning to be discovered by the media analyst. Instead, there are multiple ways of reading or interpreting a media text. Most media scholars would say, however, that certain readings are 'dominant' or 'preferred' (Hall, 1980). For example, in their research on the reality TV programme *Wife Swap*, Wood and Skeggs' (2011) found that when showing particular episodes to different people, the same emotions would frequently be expressed at the same points – for example, one section would elicit anger, another would prompt tears from viewers and so on. The show did not *force* anyone to react in a particular way, but reactions could be said to be strongly 'preferred' by features of the programme, such as repetition, close-ups or musical score.

When working with media data, researchers may also usefully explore who the assumed, or ideal, reader, viewer or listener is (Litosseliti, 2006). One useful technique can be to ask 'Who does this text think I am?' in order to reveal the assumptions about (for example) race, class, age, gender or able-bodiedness that may be in the text. Another valuable strategy can be enacting 'reversals'. For example, look at an advert and, in your head, switch the gender of the people involved – see that scantily dressed woman, draped across that car or caressing that perfume bottle with one finger? Can you imagine a man posed like that? These kinds of critical questions can reveal some of the taken-for-granted ideas that might underpin a media text, along with the types of social identities, relations and ways of being/acting in the world they may (implicitly) promote. Scholars adopting a critical approach are likely to then interrogate how this relates to issues of power and inequality.

On the whole, textual and visual analysis of media data *can't* tell us about actual audience consumption and readings – or the intentions of producers: for that, one needs to do audience or reception research, or a production-based study. At the same time, we would argue, from a social constructionist perspective, that *representations matter* (Gill, 2007) and that the range of possible readings of a media text is constrained by the dominant norms and ideas within particular historical and socio-cultural contexts.

us relate to other human beings. More diffusely, media of all kinds – old and new – educate, inform, move and shape who we are and what we know (Gill, 2007). This media 'impact' involves our most intimate selves – shaping or mediating our understandings of love, sexuality, marriage, friendship and so forth. By analysing stories about couple relationships, the 'Everyday Coupledom' project (see Box 6.2) highlighted how only some specific forms of coupledom are represented in news media as 'normal' (e.g., monogamous, sexual, involving children). It also identified the key role of celebrity culture as a site for the expression of judgements about relationships, with, for example, many column inches devoted to morality tales of celebrity 'cheats'.

Studying media data can help us understand many social phenomena, practices and beliefs. Say we wanted to comprehend why there is such a low conviction rate for rape compared with other crimes. Exploring repeatedly circulated messages about sex crimes, their victims and perpetrators in the media would provide a valuable focus to further our insights of this problem. A broadly constructionist-orientated analysis might critically highlight pervasive victim blaming (e.g., positioning women as inviting or provoking rape for wearing 'sexy' clothing or walking somewhere alone), the 'women cry rape' myth, the tendency to trivialise or render invisible women's experience of the attack, and the construction of rapists as motivated by lust, or 'deranged strangers' or 'monsters' who are different from all other men (Gill, 2007).

Online media offer various additional possibilities. Online user comments, for instance, can provide insight into public views (perspectives or reactions) on specific topics, stories, public figures, etc. Our study of online comments posted in response to news articles dealing with the *'Lose the Lads' Mags* feminist campaign illustrates how exciting and illuminating such social inquiry can be. Beyond our direct aims (see Box 6.3), what emerged as most significant was a powerful and pervasive construction of *men as victims of a new gender order* – one where women rule, and men, masculinity and 'our whole way of life' are under threat. In other words, these data allowed us to investigate the expression of 'spontaneous' public opinion, untouched by the researcher's agenda. Indeed, all media usefully constitute 'naturalistic' or 'naturally occurring' data (see Given, 2008; and also Chapters 7–9).

A final advantage of media data is that they are relatively resource-lite. Large amounts of contemporary or historic (archived) materials can generally be accessed cheaply, easily, relatively quickly and without leaving the office or classroom! This becomes particularly important at a time of cuts to academic research funding – when we want to conduct high-quality research, but when time and money for research are increasingly scarce. In this sense, it can be valuable also for students. That said, although access can be fairly resource-lite, rigorous media data *analysis*, like all qualitative analysis, is time-consuming, laborious and needs to have proper time allocated to it.

What Research Questions Suit Media Data?

There are many different kinds of qualitative research questions that can be asked of media data; these intrinsically relate to the epistemological and ontological perspectives informing your research. Broadly speaking, it is useful to distinguish between realist and constructionist approaches in the use of media data. In the former, a notion of an independent, objectively discoverable 'reality' experienced by everyone is held up, which then serves as a point of comparison with media representations. A researcher adopting a realist position will be interested in: questions about the disjuncture between reality and representation, for instance of social groups (e.g., teenage mothers) and events (e.g., a national demonstration); questions about styles of portrayal and interaction; and questions about public opinion (e.g., as expressed online), among others. Studies that highlight the limited representation of people with disabilities on television, relative to their existence in the wider population (Cumberbatch, Maguire, Lyne and Gauntlett, 2014), are an example of such realist media research.

In contrast, media research adopting a constructionist perspective sets aside claims about a supposedly unmediated reality, and how media representations relate to it. Rather, it regards media as offering powerful constructions – rather than reflections – of the world. Researchers become interested in *media constructions in their own right*. In the three case-studies presented here (Boxes 6.1–6.3), our questions were informed by a feminist constructionist position and an interest in the increasingly mediated nature of social and psychological life. A concern with dynamics of power, inequality and oppression also runs throughout our examples. More specifically, our research questions were animated by the desire to understand how cultural constructions are connected to – and might help maintain – the operation of sexism, and how this intersects with other axes of oppression, such as racism, classism, ageism or heterosexism. In the 'mediated intimacy and postfeminism' study (Box 6.3), for example, this meant asking the following: How are sexual relationships constructed in this magazine? What assumptions are made about sexual orientation or about what is 'normal'? How – if at all – are women's and men's experiences represented differently? Might these representations work to sustain unequal gender relations and other social inequalities and injustices, and if so how?

Design, Sampling and Ethical Issues

Ethical Issues

Ethics are pivotal to research – broadly governed by the notion that one should 'do no harm' (Israel and Hay, 2006). Codes of ethical practice for qualitative researchers deal with questions such as anonymity and confidentiality, informed consent and the right of participants to withdraw, along with considering issues of power within the research process (Ramazanoglu with Holland, 2002). At first glance it would appear that media data pose fewer ethical challenges than other forms of data gathering, such as ethnography, interviewing or surveys. The fact that they are 'naturally occurring' data that can be gathered without impacting or disturbing participants in any way would seem to give them advantages over other data types. However, there are several key ethical issues to consider with media data, and particularly online material: challenges and controversies around defining 'public' and 'private', 'subject' and 'author'; safeguarding anonymity; and more (see also Chapters 8 and 9).

Using online user-generated content as data necessarily entails engaging with the unique challenges of Internet research ethics, which are constantly changing in light of rapid developments in Internet technologies, capacities, use and research activities; and are rendered increasingly complex by the blurring of conventional boundaries in digitally mediated environments. Indeed, the ethical considerations of using online discussions, such as from chat rooms, web forums, social networking sites, as well as news sites, as data for qualitative research are subject to ongoing lively debate, particularly when the selected analytic method requires direct quoting. A much-discussed (e.g., Snee, 2013; Sveningsson Elm, 2009) ethical complex arises when attempting to assess what constitutes online material as public or private, in light of changing cultural perceptions and the ever-developing and multifaceted character of online inter/actions. This task is notably complicated by Web 2.0 social media, along with divergences between site accessibility and user perception of 'public-ness'. To deal with such shifting terrains, authors have called for an understanding of the private/public as a *continuum* rather than two discrete points (Sveningsson Elm, 2009) and developed ethical principles such as that of 'perceived privacy' (Markham and Buchanan, 2012), which calls on researchers to consider users' privacy expectations regarding their communications/activities in the specific environment under study.

Another key debate concerns whether researchers are working with 'texts and authors' or 'human participants' (Snee, 2013). The former implicates dealing with issues of authorship and copyright, while the latter places the focus on privacy protection – and guaranteeing anonymity and gaining informed consent from participants emerge as important ethical measures to consider. However, obtaining consent is often not possible or warranted in 'e-research', and the distinct dynamics that emerge when dealing with online data – notably traceability, the possibility to locate inscriptions using search engines and other digital mechanisms – complicate anonymisation (Beaulieu and Estalella, 2012). Against this backdrop, the Association of Internet Researchers (AoIR) advocates a dialogic and adaptive, inductive, case-based approach to Internet research ethics, where ethical judgement is based on a detailed, situated assessment of the specific object, circumstances and context of a study (Markham and Buchanan, 2012). In addition to consulting guidelines for ethical practice in qualitative research generally (Israel and Hay, 2006), one's own discipline (e.g., British Psychological Society, 2014, for psychology in the UK), and in Internet-mediated environments (e.g., AoIR), critically examining existing scholarship on similar online spaces or data can be a useful resource for prompting reflection, and for developing responses to ethical conundrums (see Chapter 9 for other discussion of these issues).

How might this look in practice? In our study of reader comments posted in response to news articles about the *'Lose the Lads' Mags* campaign (Box 6.3), we approached online open-access mainstream news sites as *public* spaces. We considered it reasonable to assume that participants would likewise perceive this environment and their contributions as public, as well as locate the nature of the content/topic on the 'public' and 'not-sensitive' ends of the spectrum. Accordingly, we judged it ethically acceptable to collect and use the data without informed consent from those commenting. At the same time, grounded on the understanding that the content had been created for an audience and context different from the academic fora, we considered it more ethically sound to privilege adopting anonymising measures over attributing authorial credit. As such, in addition to the open accessibility criteria, we decided to only gather data from news sites that allowed anonymous commentary through pseudonymisation. Pseudonyms (and other names) were *not* included in the final report in order to further de-identify contributors, because they can be an important part of people's online persona and reputation. Furthermore, the comments were not, *at the time of writing*, traceable through search engines. However, digital data are increasingly archived, searchable and traceable. Researchers must keep this in mind.

Although emerging media technologies and uses pose new, unique challenges and tensions for ethical practice, media research shares fundamental tenets with other forms of scholarly inquiry. These include the understanding that different judgements can often be equally ethically legitimate and sound and that ethics should be approached as a *deliberative process*, involving assessment both of ongoing and emerging issues throughout each juncture of a research project (Markham and Buchanan, 2012). All researchers need to ensure that ethical decisions – along with methodological choices more broadly – are context-sensitive, well-informed, reflexively interrogated, rigorously expounded in reports and in close dialectical relation with the research questions.

Design and Sampling

In order to conduct good media research, you need to be meticulous and systematic concerning a number of areas and stages. Ultimately, this involves the following key steps in design and sampling: (1) formulating your research question(s); (2) designing your sample; and (3) gathering your data:

(1) *Formulating your research question(s)*. This first step, defines the scope of your project – and demarcates all following steps. Choosing your research question(s) is a matter of personal and intellectual interest. As already discussed, media data can be interrogated in a potentially infinite number of projects with very different questions. Take, for example, a newspaper or magazine problem page such as *Dear Deirdre* in *The Sun* – a UK tabloid newspaper. The problems in these pages focus almost exclusively on difficulties in intimate relationships. For some researchers, what will be interesting pertains to questions about sexuality: Why are same-sex relations so absent and silenced in these spaces? By what mechanisms is same-sex desire disparaged or invisibilised? These questions were central to the 'Everyday Coupledom' study (Box 6.2). Others will be interested in charting the *nature* of the problems presented in these pages and how they change over time. For still others, the content is less interesting than the *interactional style* between the 'agony aunt' and letter writers, and what it says about self-help or our changing relationship to 'experts' (Barker, Gill and Harvey, in press).

(2) *Designing your sample*. When you have identified the precise question(s) you want to answer, carefully consider what data you'll need to collect to answer it. Some questions specify the text(s) to be analysed (e.g., 'problem page constructions of sexuality'), while others leave this open (e.g., 'the representation of masculinity in the media'). Much media data can be relatively straightforward and quick to acquire – not needing

transcription, but merely needing to be located, selected and gathered, and then ordered into a usable dataset. However, for some (e.g., videos or radio broadcasts) data transcription is necessary and can be very time-consuming, particularly if one is trying to capture visual, musical *and* spoken aspects at the same time (QUIC, 2015a). Sometimes, programme transcripts are available online, and it is often possible to get hold of recordings programmes via online recording services such as the UK's Box of Broadcasts or even YouTube.

Although online content can offer an efficient and cost-effective way to collect data, researchers sometimes choose to collect hard copies of publications. This was the case in the 'Everyday Coupledom' project (Box 6.2), as the research aimed to examine the 'big' or leading stories and features in newspapers and magazines, which can often be identified by their inclusion in the print edition. We were interested in the language used to describe couple relationships and so collected news items, comment pieces, features, interviews, advice columns, obituaries and announcements in which couple relationships featured as the central focus. We did not include advertisements, since we were only interested in editorially authored texts. Whatever you are studying, it is crucial to be clear and consistent in your selection of media types and genres. Regardless of the nature of your data, sampling will *always* be a crucial issue – necessary both to ensure rigour and robustness, and to construct a manageable dataset.

There are different ways to sample qualitative media data (see Davies and Mosdell, 2006). One way is to select one particular media source and sample it across time. This is what we did in the *Glamour* magazine study (see Box 6.1). We initially collected three years of monthly editions, resulting in a total of thirty-six issues. This produced *more than 150,000 pages* – far too much for one researcher to handle in a short time. In order to cut into it, we selected only a few issues across the time period, but had to be careful to ensure they were spread over the year, as editions have distinct flavours and tone, and we wanted our final dataset to reflect this variety. Having selected the sample of magazines, a further matter was to select from *within* the magazines – to draw boundaries around the articles that could be considered to be 'about' sex and relationships. We wanted to avoid being bogged down with huge numbers of articles that were short film reviews or recipe suggestions, simply because they said 'your guy will love this feisty bolognese' or 'a great movie to see with HIM'. On the other hand we didn't want to exclude relevant and interesting data. It's good practice to keep notes about sampling criteria as they evolve, to develop a robust set of criteria for which data should count, and which should not, and to maintain a *consistent approach* to 'what counts' in your study – for instance, don't include some recipes or film reviews as data, but ignore others.

Another sampling approach is to select media at a particular moment in time, as in the 'Everyday Coupledom' study (Box 6.2), which included newspapers, magazines and soap operas. The newspaper sample, for instance, comprised the top four circulating broadsheet and tabloid daily newspapers (Monday–Saturday) and the top four Sunday newspapers. We decided to include all editions within a defined time-frame of one month, to provide a representative sample of the everyday, mainstream news coverage in the time period. The data included all stories and storylines about couple relationships in the selected publications from 10 November to 7 December 2012, generated by closely checking each edition and collecting those texts that matched the selection criteria. This produced a relatively large dataset for qualitative research: 1,161 stories from 208 newspaper issues. Newspapers can also often be sampled using *search* functions in the online versions, and via databases such as LexisNexis for print publications.

Sampling media covering a particular event is another possible approach. In our 'Emasculation Nation' study (Box 6.3), we narrowed our focus by concentrating on reporting of the decision by the Co-operative Group – one of Britain's largest magazine retailers – to only sell 'lads' mags' delivered to stores in individually sealed bags concealing the covers. Both this announcement (28 and 29 July, 2013) and its implementation (9 September, 2013) were widely covered by the media and stirred extensive public debate across online spaces – we decided therefore to look at public reactions and discussions around these. The dataset was generated through three queries on the *Google.co.uk* search engine – we used the search phrase 'Personal reflections on using Skype interviews mags Co-op' followed by each of the aforementioned key dates in the campaign's history. In light of the large amount of potential data these searches yielded, the search for relevant web pages was restricted to the first twenty obtained results or 'hits' for each search. Sixteen articles from thirteen different UK news sites, and all the accompanying reader comments, were collected: a total of 5,140 posts.

Note that the datasets discussed here are relatively large, particularly for student projects. Developing a feasible research project involves starting with a question that can be investigated using the time and resources available to you! The final size of your dataset will also depend on your method of analysis (discussed later) – a researcher looking at newspapers using a fine-grained linguistically oriented discourse analytic approach, for instance, might only explore a handful of articles.

(3) *Gathering your data.* As noted above, this may be a fairly straight-forward compilation task, or involve a bit more work. What you need for analysis are the data gathered together in such a way that you can work thoroughly with them, immerse yourself in them, take notes and easily find things. For example, in the 'Emasculation Nation' study, all the reader comments were copied and pasted onto a Word document. We then imported that document in *NVivo*, a computer-assisted qualitative data analysis software (CAQDAS) package that we used to facilitate the analysis. Other possible ways to collect online material include converting web pages to PDF files, taking screen shots or captures, and using other software tools such as *NVivo*'s web browser extension *NCapture*. To some extent how you compile the data depends on whether you'll analyse by hand or using CAQDAS. Data analysis methods and tools are discussed later.

What Can Go Wrong with Media Data?

Despite the exciting opportunities for qualitative media research, you may well encounter challenges, difficulties and problems when using media data – this section highlights these and ways to reduce their likelihood. A vital consideration for media research is understanding and avoiding *copyright* infringement. To avoid copyright infringement, researchers need to become acquainted with the national copyright legislation, the terms and conditions of the media or Internet companies under study, along with the guidelines and/or policy of the institutions where the research is being conducted. If the material is used for private study or non-commercial research, there may be statutory exceptions allowing the (limited) reproduction of copyright works without permission from the rights holder, for instance, under the terms of 'fair dealing' in many Commonwealth countries, or 'fair use' in the US (for the UK context, for instance, see GOV.UK, 2014).

Not designing and selecting an appropriate sample is a key thing researchers can get wrong. Selecting media texts without a clear rationale can make it difficult to answer your research questions – for example, if the data are not directly relevant to the questions, or if the dataset is too large or small, or too broad or narrow to enable rigorous analysis. Common to all types of media data analysis – and indeed research in general – is the need for *rigour*. This involves being transparent, disciplined and consistent in all aspects of the research process, from data selection to sampling to coding, analysis and writing up. In relation to sampling, rigour includes: identifying the broad relevant media landscape (e.g., media dealing with couple relationships), and the specific media types and genres within this (e.g., newspapers; then broadsheets and tabloids; then articles and advice columns; etc.); thinking about which of these will best provide the information you need to answer your question; and considering all available information to aid your decision-making. For example, if you're interested in mainstream news representation, looking at circulation or viewing figures can help you identify the most widely consumed sources.

Again, rigour is crucial in relation to the *analysis* of media data, as well as the writing up. In practice, for many qualitative researchers, 'writing up' is a central part of the shaping of the 'story' your research tells – part of, rather than subsequent to, the analytic process. Tempting as it might be to 'cherry-pick' the most intriguing bits of material or cite the 'juiciest' of quotes, it is absolutely essential to adhere to the practices described above for ensuring that the analytic 'story' is supported by the evidence – and, additionally, that it makes sense of *all* the data under consideration, not just the best or more quotable fragments. This is necessary for all researchers, but is perhaps even more salient for those using media as a form of data, since this is often disparaged (discussed further in Box 6.6). Relatedly, it's worth noting that the media analyst is *both researcher and audience*. Therefore, it could be said that their 'reading' (analysis) is one among other possible interpretations – and as such is open to debate. This means analyses must always be warranted by detailed attention to the material under study and developed from the application of particular analytic tools and associated theoretical frameworks, which should be clearly articulated in reports, alongside some reflexivity. The aim is to explicate and make clear one's assumptions, and the reasons for a particular interpretation.

Analysing Media Data

Finally, we briefly explore some issues to consider as you get ready to start analysing the data you've collected, and highlight some additional *things that can go wrong* at this stage. Following on from the design and sampling steps above, analysis will involve the following key processes: immersion in the data – intense reading; coding the data; developing the in-depth analysis; and writing up.

To begin with, it may seem like stating the obvious, but getting to know your media data is a *crucial* step in analysis: watching, reading, listening to them and making detailed notes about striking features. In interview research, the researcher has often conducted the interviews themselves, and possibly transcribed them, so frequently has a very good familiarity with the dataset at the outset of the analytic process. This may not be the case when working with media data, so the immersion stage is absolutely crucial to start forming ideas and making critical notes – even though it can feel like 'wasting time' (and many other people will helpfully point this out!). Trust us, it is not; it's vital!

Regardless of your analytic approach, working with media data will inevitably involve coding: a process of identifying (and marking) material or topics in the data that relate to your research question, as a step to organising your material. Some researchers do this 'by hand' and regard it as a craft skill that is part of immersing themselves in the material; increasingly, media researchers use CAQDAS software packages such as Atlas.ti or NVivo during coding (QUIC, 2015b). These originally enabled coding and note-taking on textual data; now they also work for video, image, sound and social networking data. Before deciding to use one, it is useful to consider the conceptual assumptions built into these packages, which are subject to debate (Soliman and Kan, 2004).

A common experience when starting out is to generate too many or too few codes. In our analysis of news site comments about the *Lose the Lads' Mags* campaign (Box 6.3), we initially coded the large volume of posts about 'men as victims' under a single heading. We subsequently refined our coding to reflect distinct nuances in the arguments being put forward – for example, some related specifically to sexuality, others to a perceived attack on 'our way of life' and others still were organised around the construction of feminism as a menace to society. We developed sub-codes to handle the extremely large number of posts on the topic, as well as to give a clearer and richer sense of the diversity and patterning in our data. However, while too few codes can be an issue, so can too many! We have all experienced the feeling that each individual item needs its own code to somehow capture its uniqueness: generally they don't! Sometimes it can feel hard to know 'when to stop' coding – it might seem possible to go on ad infinitum, digging deeper and deeper into the features of each category. To avoid this, keep in mind the idea of the *patterning* of data. Also, go back to your research question(s) and aims – is shedding light into such levels of intricacy necessary? Sometimes it helps to stop for a few days, and then return to our coding with 'fresh eyes'.

Coding is seen either as a precursor to, or the early stages of, analysis – depending on which analytic approach you take. Media data can be analysed in many different ways, and the approach you take will relate to your theoretical commitments and particular research question(s) – and the approach taken will necessarily and fundamentally shape the analysis produced. Suitable qualitative analytic methods may include semiology, developed from linguistics to analyse the meanings of both language and images (Penn, 2000), and multimodal social semiotics, which explores how particular aspects of communication, such as images and sound, work *socially* to produce shared understandings of reality (Kress and van Leeuwen, 2006). Media data can also be examined using thematic analysis (Braun and Clarke, 2006), which comprises a range of approaches that explore the patterning of meaning across texts. Some researchers who adopt a social constructionist perspective choose to conduct forms of discourse analysis (see Gill, 2017), such as critical discourse analysis (Machin and Mayr, 2012), connecting language use to broader patterns of power and inequality, rhetorical analysis (Billig, 1996), which explores how different ways of speaking are used to make claims, argue and persuade, or discourse analyses informed by poststructuralist frameworks – an example of which would be Nixon's (1996) Foucauldian-inspired study of representations of the male body. Media scholars also examine data using Marxist and psychoanalytic critique, among other things, respectively analysing the relationship between powerful social groups and media, and employing psychoanalytic concepts such as the unconscious (for introductions, see Berger, 2012).

The 'Mediated Intimacy and Postfeminism' (Box 6.1) and 'Emasculation Nation' (Box 6.3) studies used a discourse analytic approach which broadly drew upon the method and perspective elaborated by Wetherell and Potter (1992) in the social sciences, sometimes known as (critical) discursive psychology. A key unit of analysis is the 'interpretative repertoire' (Potter and Wetherell, 1987), which refers to 'a recognizable routine of arguments, descriptions and evaluations distinguished by familiar clichés, common places, tropes and characterizations of actors and situations' that become evident through repetition across a dataset (Edley and Wetherell, 2001: 443). Boxes 6.1 and 6.3 briefly discussed the interpretative repertoires we identified. Overall, each method of analysis has its own precepts and practical steps, levels and units of analysis, and hence also strategies and tools, which are beyond the scope of this chapter to elaborate – they are widely discussed elsewhere.

A final point to note: research does not always 'end' at writing up – as we explore in Box 6.5, those producing critical analyses can face a new set of challenges after publication.

Box 6.5 After publication . . .

Most books about research finish with 'writing up': publication of a book or article or submission of a dissertation is assumed to mark the end of engagement with the data. Good job – all finished! However, for many researchers, particularly those taking a critical perspective such as a feminist or queer approach, publication can mark the beginning of a different set of experiences – especially in an age of social media when universities are keen to see their research 'make an impact'. Sometimes this can be positive – when research seems to lift off the page and really make a difference in the world. But at other times, public 'engagement' and 'impact' can be difficult experiences (Phipps, 2014). Finding's experience exemplifies this. While a PhD student at LSE, she wrote a powerful critique of the British comedy series *Little Britain*, arguing that it was racist, class-shaming and homophobic. Her article was first published as part of a working paper series at LSE, and might have disappeared into relative oblivion had an eager press officer not seen its potential to generate publicity; soon *The Guardian* newspaper asked Deborah to write an article. Initially delighted, Deborah's feelings quickly turned to horror and anguish as her article attracted a barrage of hate speech, impugning her intellect, attractiveness and right to speak/write. Discussing the experience, she created a 'character' who talks in the first-person about all the things people said to her:

Hi I'm Deborah, and I'm a stupid humourless nitwit; an asinine political wonk who makes people want to vomit; a PC whinger with too much time on her hands; a worthless dickhead without even half a brain; a monotonous, bitter, narrow-minded academic who would do anything to become a celebrity . . . and a smug bitch with no life who doesn't know shit. (Finding, 2010: 273)

We reproduce this only partially, and edited, here, but it speaks powerfully of some of the challenges that may be faced when doing research that challenges the status quo. Equally, however, as we have shown in this chapter, research can be used to shed light on new questions, to challenge inequalities and, quite literally, to bring to attention new issues or patterns. The three studies reported on here are excellent examples of this.

Conclusion

Drawing on three case-studies that analysed magazines, newspapers and news websites' reader comments as qualitative data, we have offered an introduction to working with media data – highlighting the wide, and ever-expanding, range of material available under the term 'media data' in the contemporary net-worked, interactive, digital and online media environment, along with the potentials and challenges they offer. Media provide a rich, valuable and important source of data for qualitative research within and across multiple

---

Box 6.6 Personal reflections on using media data

Conducting media analysis can be fascinating work. Our research has enabled us to explore patterns in the media that confront us every day, and to make interventions in the production of meaning. However, media research can also often be positioned as 'non-work' ('you were just watching television!') or as trivial and ephemeral. Scholars can become identified with the supposed 'banality' of their object of study, as if it were inherently worth less intellectually than an analysis of, say, a historical text or a work of literary fiction. Even within cultural and media studies, there can be hierarchies of scholarly value, with particular forms or genres such as romance or reality television sometimes presented as less 'worthy' of research than, for example, news media. Feminist scholars have long challenged such distinctions – foregrounding how media associated with more socially marginalised groups tend to occupy a lower status in the academy (Wood and Skeggs, 2011).

Such evaluations about media studies can make it more difficult to talk about the emotional dimensions of research, for fear that analyses may be perceived as less 'serious' or 'scientific'. Feminist researchers have argued, however, that attending to emotions in the research process is crucial, and can provide rich, important insights; they are an integral part of feminist methodology (Ryan-Flood and Gill, 2010). For example, in our 'Emasculation Nation' study (Box 6.3), the data were steeped in anger. We were faced with an avalanche of misogynistic, sexist and xenophobic comments, along with fiercely hostile depictions of feminists and feminism. As feminist scholars and activists, working with these data was a sobering and challenging experience. We negotiated this through our conviction that academic work can have emancipatory social effects, and we hence focused on conducting high-quality analyses and advancing strong, well-grounded arguments. Our shared discussions and support were also fundamental. Indeed, this research experience is an example of the great value of collaborative work – intellectually, politically and affectively.

---

disciplines. This is perhaps more so than ever before, in light of the ever-growing ubiquity of media representations, technologies and use, as well as the increasingly mediated nature of social and psychological life.

From a constructionist perspective, researching media is additionally a worthwhile enterprise as the media are not seen as simply a neutral means of reflecting 'reality', but rather as a site for the construction – and contestation – of the social world. Media data can be utilised to explore manifold, innovative and exciting research questions, and critical media research has the potential to identify problems *and possible solutions* that may have a positive social impact. Against the backdrop of a continuously developing and unpredictable mediascape, working with media data is both a fascinating and an important activity for qualitative researchers!

Have a Go . . .

Identify the benefits and challenges of one of the types of media data outlined in the chapter. Next, write a feasible research question that could be answered by analysing that type of media data. Then:

(1) Devise a sample of the media data to answer this question. Think about *where, when and how* you could collect these data.
(2) Identify what would be the most appropriate *method of analysis* to use to answer your question. Why did you identify that approach? Write a short reflection exploring that question.
(3) *Collect a small sample* of the identified media data.
(4) Read and re-read to *immerse yourself* in the dataset; start to identify things that might be relevant to your research question.

Further Resources: Online

For more information about the 'Everyday Coupledom' project, see www.enduringlove .co.uk

The Association of Internet Researchers Ethical guidelines can be found here: http://aoir .org/reports/ethics2.pdf

The ReStore site offers material related to the assessment and development of new methods for the analysis of media content: http://www.restore.ac.uk/lboro/

Further Resources: Readings

To read more about the mediated intimacy case-study, see Gill, R. (2009). Mediated intimacy and postfeminism: A discourse analytic examination of sex and relationships advice in a women's magazine. *Discourse & Communication*, *3*(4), 1–25.

To read more about the *'Lose the Lads' Mags'* example study, see García-Favaro, L. and Gill, R. (2016). 'Emasculation nation has arrived': Sexism rearticulated in online responses to Lose the Lads' Mags campaign. *Feminist Media Studies*, *16*(3), 379–397.

For research methods for media analysis, see chapter 15 in this accessible introduction to media studies: Branston, G. and Stafford, R. (2010). *The media student's book* (5th edn). London: Routledge.

For a focus on media analysis from a gendered perspective, see Chapter 2, in particular, in: Gill, R. (2007). *Gender and the media*. Cambridge: Polity Press.

For a discussion of some theoretical perspectives around Internet and communications research, see: Rice, R. E. and Fuller, R. P. (2013). Theoretical perspectives in the study of communication and the Internet. In W. H. Dutton (ed.), *The Oxford handbook of Internet studies* (pp. 353–377). Oxford: Oxford University Press.

References

Attwood, F. (2009). *Mainstreaming sex: The sexualisation of Western culture*. London & New York: IB Tauris.

Bandura, A., Ross, D. and Ross, S. A. (1961). Transmission of aggression through the imitation of aggressive models. *Journal of Abnormal and Social Psychology*, *63*(3), 575–582.

Barker, M. J., Gill, R. and Harvey, L. (in press). *Mediated intimacy: Sex advice in media culture*. Cambridge: Polity Press.

Beaulieu, A. and Estalella, A. (2012). Rethinking research ethics for mediated settings. *Information, Communication & Society*, *15*(1), 23–42.

Berger, A. A. (2012). *Media analysis techniques* (4th edn). Thousand Oaks, CA: Sage Publications.

Billig, M. (1996). *Arguing and thinking: A rhetorical approach to social psychology* (2nd edn). Cambridge: Cambridge University Press.

British Psychological Society. (2014). *Code of human research ethics*. Leicester, UK: British Psychological Society.

Braun, V. and Clarke, V. (2006). Using thematic analysis in psychology. *Qualitative Research in Psychology*, *3*(2), 77–101.

Bruns, A. (2008). *Blogs, Wikipedia, second life, and beyond: From production to produsage*. New York: Peter Lang Publishing.

Buckingham, D. and Bragg, S. (2004). *Young people, sex, and the media: The facts of life?* Basingstoke, UK: Palgrave Macmillan.

Cumberbatch, G., Maguire, A., Lyne, V. and Gauntlett, S. (2014). *Diversity monitoring: The top TV programmes*. Birmingham: Creative Diversity Network. Retrieved from: http://creativediversitynetwork.com/wp-content/uploads/2014/08/CDN-diversity-portrayal-pilot-2014.pdf

Curran, J. and Seaton, J. (2009). *Power without responsibility*. London: Routledge.

Davies, M. M. and Mosdell, N. (2006). *Practical research methods for media and cultural studies: Making people count*. Edinburgh: Edinburgh University Press.

Durham, M. G. (2004). Constructing the 'new ethnicities': Media, sexuality, and diaspora identity in the lives of South Asian immigrant girls. *Critical Studies in Media Communication*, *21*(2), 140–161.

Dworkin, A. (1981). *Men possessing women*. London: The Women's Press.

Edley, N. and Wetherell, M. (2001). Jekyll and Hyde: Men's constructions of feminism and feminists. *Feminism & Psychology*, *11*(4), 439–457.

Favaro, L. (in press). Postfeminist sexpertise on the 'porn and men issue': A transnational perspective. In K. Harrison and C. Ogden (eds.), *Pornographies: Critical positions*. Chester, UK: University of Chester Press.

Favaro, L. and Gill, R. (2016). 'Emasculation nation has arrived': Sexism rearticulated in online responses to Lose the Lads' Mags campaign. *Feminist Media Studies*, *16*(3), 379–397.

Finding, D. (2010). 'Living in the real world?' What happens when the media covers feminist research. In R. Ryan-Flood and R. Gill (eds.), *Secrecy and silence in the research process: Feminist reflections* (pp. 273–290). London: Routledge.

Fisher, D. A., Hill, D. L. and Grube, J. W. (2007). Gay, lesbian and bisexual content on television: A quantitative analysis across two seasons. *Journal of Homosexuality*, *52*(3–4), 167–188.

Gill, R. (2007). *Gender and the media*. Cambridge: Polity Press.

    (2009). Mediated intimacy and postfeminism: A discourse analytic examination of sex and relationships advice in a women's magazine. *Discourse & Communication*, *3*(4), 1–25.

    (2017). Discourse analysis in media and communications research. In M.-C. Kearney and M. Kackman (eds.), *The craft of media criticism: Critical media studies in practice*. New York: Routledge.

Given, L. M. (ed.) (2008). *The SAGE encyclopedia of qualitative research methods*. Thousand Oaks, CA: Sage Publications.

GOV.UK. (2014, 18 November). *Exceptions to copyright*. Intellectual Property Office. Retrieved from: www.gov.uk/exceptions-to-copyright

Hall, S. (1980). Encoding/decoding. In S. Hall, D. Hobson, A. Lowe and P. Willis (eds.), *Culture, media language: Working papers in cultural studies* (pp. 128–138). London: Hutchinson.

    (ed.) (1997). *Representation: Cultural representations and signifying practices*. London: Sage Publications.

    (2000). Racist ideologies and the media. In P. Marris and S. Thornham (eds.), *Media studies* (pp. 271–282). New York: New York University Press.

Henrich, N. and Holmes, B. (2013). Web news readers' comments: Towards developing a methodology for using on-line comments in social inquiry. *Journal of Media and Communication Studies*, *5*(1), 1–4.

Israel, M. and Hay, I. (2006). *Research ethics for social scientists: Between ethical conduct and regulatory compliance*. London: Sage Publications.

Jenkins, H. (2006). *Convergence culture: Where old and new media collide*. New York: New York University Press.

Jensen, T. and Ringrose, J. (2014). Sluts that choose vs doormat gypsies: exploring affect the postfeminist, visual moral economy of My Big Fat Gypsy Wedding. *Feminist Media Studies*, *14*(3), 369–387.

Kress, G. and van Leeuwen, T. (2006). *Reading images: The grammar of visual design* (2nd edn). London: Routledge.

Leadbeater, J. and Miller, P. (2004). *The Pro-Am revolution*. London: Demos.

Litosseliti, L. (2006). *Gender and language: Theory and practice*. London: Hodder Arnold.

Macharia, S., O'Connor, D. and Ndangam, L. (2010). *Who makes the news? Global media monitoring project 2010*. London: World Association for Christian Communication.

Machin, D. and Mayr, A. (2012). *How to do critical discourse analysis: A multimodal introduction*. London: Sage Publications.

Machin, D. and van Leeuwen, T. (2007). *Global media discourse: A critical introduction*. London: Routledge.

McCracken, E. (1993). *Decoding women's magazines*. Basingstoke, UK: Macmillan.

McKewon, E. (2012). Talking points ammo: The use of neoliberal think tank fantasy themes to delitimise scientific knowledge of climate change in Australian newspapers. *Journalism Studies*, *13*(2), 277–297.

McRobbie, A. (1991). *Feminism and youth culture: From 'Jackie' to 'Just Seventeen'*. Basingstoke, UK: Macmillan.

Markham, A. N. and Buchanan, E. A. (2012). *Ethical decision-making and Internet research (version 2.0). Recommendations from the AoIR Ethics Working Committee.* Chicago: Association of Internet Researchers. Retrieved from: http://aoir.org/reports/ethics2.pdf

Morley, D. and Brunsdon, C. (2005). *The nationwide television studies.* London: Routledge.

Nixon, S. (1996). *Hard looks: Masculinities, spectatorship and contemporary consumption.* London: UCL Press.

Noble, S. N. (2014). Teaching Trayvon: Race, media and the politics of spectacle. *The Black Scholar, 44*(1), 12–29.

Penn, G. (2000). Semiotic analysis of still images. In M. W. Bauer and G. Gaskell (eds.), *Qualitative researching with text, image and sound* (pp. 227–245). Thousand Oaks, CA: Sage Publications.

Phipps, A. (2014, 4 December). The dark side of impact. *Times Higher Education.* Retrieved from: www.timeshighereducation.co.uk/comment/opinion/the-dark-side-of-the-impact-agenda/2017299.article

Potter, J. and Wetherell, M. (1987). *Discourse and social psychology: Beyond attitudes and behaviour.* London: Sage Publications.

QUIC (2015a). Qualitative innovations in CAQDAS – analysing audiovisual data using NVivo. Retrieved from: www.surrey.ac.uk/sociology/research/researchcentres/caqdas/support/analysingvisual/analysing_audiovisual_data_using_nvivo.htm

(2015b). Qualitative innovations in CAQDAS – support. Retrieved from: www.surrey.ac.uk/sociology/research/researchcentres/caqdas/support/index.htm

Ramazanoglu, C. with Holland, J. (2002). *Feminist methodology: Challenges and choices.* London: Sage Publications.

Robinson, S. (2010). Traditionalists vs. convergers: Textual privilege, boundary work, and the journalist–audience relationship in the commenting policies of online news sites. *Convergence: The International Journal of Research into New Media Technologies, 16*(1), 125–143.

Rowe, D. (2011). Obituary for the newspaper? Tracking the tabloid. *Journalism, 12*(4), 449–466.

Ryan-Flood, R. and Gill, R. (eds.,) (2010). *Secrecy and silence in the research process: Feminist reflections.* London: Routledge.

Snee, H. (2013). Making ethical decisions in an online context: Reflections on using blogs to explore narratives of experience. *Methodological Innovations Online, 8*(2), 52–67.

Soliman, J. and Kan, M. (2004). Grounded theory and NVivo: Wars and wins. *Proceedings of QualIT 2004: 24–26 November 2004.* Brisbane, Australia. Retrieved from: https://opus.lib.uts.edu.au/research/bitstream/handle/10453/7157/2004001837.pdf?sequence=1

Sveningsson Elm, M. (2009). How do various notions of privacy influence decisions in qualitative Internet research? In A. N. Markham and N. K. Baym (eds.), *Internet inquiry: Conversations about method* (pp. 69–88). Thousand Oaks, CA: Sage Publications.

Thompson, J. (1984). *Studies in the theory of ideology.* Cambridge: Polity.

Wetherell, M. and Potter, J. (1992). *Mapping the language of racism: Discourse and the legitimation of exploitation.* Hemel Hempstead, UK: Harvester-Wheatsheaf.

Wood, H. and Skeggs, B. (eds.) (2011). *Reality television and class.* London: Palgrave Macmillan.

7 'God's Great Leveller'

Talkback Radio as Qualitative Data

Scott Hanson-Easey and Martha Augoustinos

Overview

Talkback radio (TR), or 'talk radio' in the UK and in the US, offers qualitative researchers great potential for examining social life. It can be used to answer a range of research questions, using a number of different qualitative approaches. In our own discourse analytic research, we have found TR to afford rich insights into the features of lay and political talk, as it is used to complain about 'minority' groups and justify prejudicial and racist arguments (see Box 7.1). In this chapter, we provide a stepwise guide for qualitative researchers using TR as a data source in their research. We first provide a short, contextualising introduction to TR and then discuss some relevant theoretical approaches and research questions. Drawing on our own research (Hanson-Easey and Augoustinos, 2010, 2011, 2012), we then go on to clarify the distinct stages and processes involved in using TR as data.

Introduction to Talkback Radio

Talkback radio is an internationally popular radio format, which relies on 'call-ins' from the listening audience to discuss particular themes. TR covers a range of topics, including sport (e.g., talkSPORT), contemporary life (e.g., *Life Matters*, ABC Radio National – Australia), gardening (e.g., *Gardeners' Question Time*, BBC Radio 4), consumer affairs and health (e.g., *You&Yours*, BBC Radio 4). Many radio shows use the TR platform for politically-oriented talk, including sensitive and politicised issues such as social relations, immigration and 'race'. In the US, conservative talk radio (e.g., 'right talk') and liberal talk radio (e.g., Air America) are popular examples of this. Listener call-ins are combined with punditry, interviews and monologues by hosts (e.g., on *The Rush Limbaugh Show*).

Box 7.1 The discursive construction of Sudanese refugees in Australia on talkback radio

From a discursive perspective, we have used TR to explore how callers linguistically constructed 'narratives' about local events involving Sudanese refugees. We were interested in how callers developed these narratives in their talk and implicitly criticised this group on behavioural and moral dimensions. Through the vehicle of these narratives, we argued that such messages have the potential to bolster socio-political policies that have serious negative implications for Sudanese refugees. Talkback radio was a highly appropriate source of data to answer our research question, because the show invited people through call-ins to discuss anything on their mind, whether related to poor health, or a complaint they harboured about their neighbours' behaviours and cultural practices. We feel that qualitative research employing TR data is well-suited to a social constructionist approach, because it details the interactive and contingent nature of talk as it is deployed in constructing identities and phenomena.

Giving a voice to 'everyday' concerns, opinions and views, TR has been argued to play a democratising role in society (Turner, 2009). Dubbed by one of its earlier producers as 'God's great leveller' (Bodey, 2007: 15), radio's ubiquity has melded with talkback's perceived democratic, participatory footings, and has significantly popularised the format (Turner, 2009; Ward, 2002). Although TR does enable the general public to partially engage in its making, it also shares many of the 'elite' characteristics of other media formats: it is the host and producer who are empowered to select callers they wish to speak to, and leave on hold (sometimes indefinitely) those they do not. In the cruder, more populist version of TR, 'shock-jock' hosts make sport of denouncing callers they disagree with, provoking and ridiculing their views to entertain and rile their listeners. 'Shock-jock' talkback is not interested in being impartial; rather, it feeds on populist opinion, confrontation and the 'personality' of the host (Turner, 2009).

Talkback radio can have socio-political consequences beyond the immediate context, especially if the discussion resonates with pre-existing community anxiety. Political issues can often 'gain a new set of "legs" through being given a run on the radio: from time to time, this prolongs the life and extends the provenance of the story' (Turner, 2009: 421). Unsurprisingly, then, TR has had significant influence on government decision-making. For example, the longevity of the Howard conservative government in Australia (1996–2007) has often been attributed to Howard's close monitoring of public opinion as expressed on TR, and his routine early morning participation on programmes with a wide and popular reach (Lee, 2007).

What Does Talkback Radio Offer the Qualitative Researcher?

Talkback radio offers exciting opportunities for qualitative researchers who want to understand how people 'make sense of' their social worlds. It provides a forum for people to 'represent' their social worlds in various ways, by engaging in debates that (for example) describe social groups in particular ways, justify particular kinds of social actions and beliefs or enable people to manage or express particular aspects of their (and others') identities (e.g., see Hanson-Easey and Augoustinos, 2012). For this reason, TR is uniquely placed to provide qualitative researchers with important insights into the processes of representation; how people 'analyse, comment, and concoct spontaneous, unofficial philosophies' (Moscovici, 1984: 30) about their social worlds.

Talkback radio offers particular advantages for researchers who are interested in *language* – as is the case in our own research on constructions and representations of Sudanese refugees in Australia (see Box 7.1). TR is a unique and constantly fluid conversational context where social issues are introduced, opinions tabled and defended, and callers' subjective experiences described in interesting ways. Thus, it offers great potential for understanding the *discursive* – that is, how speakers use specific linguistic and cultural resources to construct *versions* of the world, and what actions these versions serve in local and global contexts (see Billig, 1987; Edwards and Potter, 1992; Wetherell and Potter, 1992). For example, our analyses of TR 'call-ins' afford important insights into how TR callers construct Sudanese refugees as 'problematic', and how such constructions justify support for various discriminatory practices against this group (Hanson-Easey and Augoustinos, 2010, 2012).

The inherently interactive nature of TR also offers great potential for (primarily discursive and conversational analytic) researchers interested in *talk-as-interaction* – that is, talk produced in social interaction. For example, researchers have looked at how interaction between hosts and callers on TR is organised in specific stages or sequences (Hutchby, 1991), how arguments and controversies on TR unfold and are managed (Hutchby, 1992, 1996) and how callers to TR shows use and display identity in strategic ways (Hanson-Easey and Augoustinos, 2012; Hutchby, 2001; Thornborrow, 2001). These analyses offer much insight into speakers' constructions of social realities and communicative activities, and their orientations to social contexts and identity relationships. As an example, consider the following extract that looks at how one TR caller manages the delicate issue of not sounding overtly 'racist', whilst concurrently complaining about a refugee group (see also Box 7.3 for an example of a TR caller failing miserably in this regard):

1. APRIL: ... so, look... we, they are very much in our area, and as much as
2. they keep to themselves. We see a lot – there are children just coming up left-
3. right and centre of Suda- Sudanese children are jus, ya-know, everywhere, and
4. they're beautiful children – but I think to a certain extent, they need to be more
5. educated.

Arguably, the caller in this extract is responding to the opportunity that TR provides to raise her concerns: consternation with her neighbour's children and, by association, their parents. What initially struck us when analysing this material was the way that the caller blends negative and positive evaluations of Sudanese children. The extract highlights one of the most interesting features of *modern-day racism*: the norm against sounding overtly racist (van Dijk, 1991). April's description of her problem, like many arguments in the social world, is attending to a number of potential issues and risks. For example, the evaluation of Sudanese children as both 'everywhere' and 'beautiful' is particularly telling. Why does she in one breath suggest there are too many Sudanese children in her ('our') area and then proclaim they are 'beautiful' in the next? We would argue that this talk works to soften her complaint, mitigating the risk of being heard as racist. In our research, speakers were rarely heard to overtly castigate Sudanese refugees without providing (sometimes elaborate) rationales for doing so. This highlights the complex and flexible nature of 'race-talk', as well as the ways in which people strategically organise their talk to avoid potential criticisms that may adversely impact on their identity (Billig, 1988). Talkback radio is saturated with this kind of *talk-in-interaction*, making it an attractive data source for researchers who want to try and understand the way in which talk is socially produced and organised.

Talkback radio can potentially provide easier access to controversial views and opinions than might be found in other contexts. This is because TR is a domain where the controversial can be more acceptable than it would be in other contexts (particularly for TR's 'shock-jock' versions). For example, through the course of our research, some callers on TR, we suspect, were relatively more willing to articulate their views on controversial topics when they affiliated with the host, assuming that he would be sympathetic to their views – even when this kind of talk is, in other contexts, such as the work-place, socially precarious. Some callers made this apparent when they initiated their call by praising the host, or announcing that they are 'big fans'. Others would 'pick up' a previously discussed topic, and the tone used, to base their call on – for example, 'you were speaking about the Sudanese before'. This pattern of talk led us to argue that callers may have spoken in such a way because they had some 'licence' to do so – felt like they were of 'like mind' – or that they were simply extending the theme initially broached by the host.

For researchers wanting to collect *naturalistic data*, TR offers a rich (and relatively accessible) data source. The TR data are *naturalistic* or *naturally occurring* because the researcher has not elicited them – they occurred for reasons separate to the researcher. This makes TR different from many other forms of qualitative data collection (e.g., focus groups or interviews), which rely on creating specific opportunities to generate data, guided by the researcher's interests. Such interests are often removed from participants' everyday lives and require them to do things (such as talk to a researcher) that they would not normally do in the course of their ordinary lives. Naturalistic data, on the other hand, are *socially contextualised data* – that is, people's talk and, thus, behaviour, can be observed in the context in which it occurs. Put simply, the benefit of observing talk in a naturalistic setting is that we can be confident that the researcher is not influencing the 'raw' data – the views, beliefs and version of the speakers on TR are of their own making. This is not to say that knowledge we gain from TR data remains 'objective' or untouched by the researcher's hands; the researcher's interests, culture and historical background inevitably bound naturalistic observation (Burr, 1999). In addition, it is important to note that while the researcher is not involved in censoring, eliciting, muting or selectively recruiting participants, such calls are still mediated by the station and the host. Indeed, it is a commonplace for TR programme producers and the host to actively select callers they believe may provide 'entertainment value', and leave on hold those who they view as not. Nonetheless, the naturalistic nature of TR does offer researchers insights that would be difficult to replicate using other methods of data collection (e.g., interview or focus groups).

Talkback radio provides a useful setting for the 'expression of everyday experiences' (Lunt and Stenner, 2005: 63). Indeed, it is argued that TR provides a context where people may feel more comfortable sharing their experiences – particularly for socially isolated or marginalised groups, for whom TR can provide a valued sense of connection to the community (Ewart, 2011). These settings, and especially topic-specific stations (e.g., Health Radio), or 'agony aunt' programmes (e.g., Anna Raeburn on the UK radio station Capital Radio), critically depend on creating a perception of an open and welcoming 'community' of listeners where callers are warmly invited to share their experiences. For qualitative researchers then, TR can be a fertile context in which to gain in-depth understanding of particular aspects of people's lived experiences and concerns across the many and varied topics that can be found in this domain (e.g., see Kang and Quine, 2007, for an analysis of young people's concerns about sex in TR).

Finally, TR can also provide a unique window into the media's role in affecting and reflecting public opinion (see also Chapter 6). One of the most striking examples of TR's potential for manipulating popular opinion and debate was its role in 'the Cronulla riots' in Australia. In December 2005, over 5,000 'Anglo-Australians' (Australians who identify as possessing British heritage) physically attacked anyone who they discerned as 'Middle Eastern' in the southern Sydney beachside suburb of Cronulla. The mob violence was predicated on a fight between a group of lifesavers and a group of Lebanese-Australian youths that happened on the beach a week earlier. Alan Jones, Sydney's most listened-to TR host, read aloud to his audience one of the many inflammatory text messages that were widely circulated after the fight, beseeching Anglo-Australians to 'come to Cronulla to take revenge' (Poynting, 2006: 87). There were numerous causal factors that led to the pogrom-like events at Cronulla, and TR can only be partially implicated. Yet, there is evidence that when news media and TR engage in what Perry (2001) has called 'permission to hate' talk, this sends a condoning message to those who wish to perpetrate racial vilification and violence (Poynting, Noble, Tabar and Collins, 2004). What the Cronulla riots highlighted was TR's power to magnify, crystallise and transform, (often nascent) social events into significant 'moral panics' (see Cohen, 2002). Talkback radio, particularly through a focus on events such as these, can therefore offer qualitative researchers much insight into the powerful role the media has in shaping our political values and social beliefs, our ideologies of self and other, and the constitution of everyday social life.

What Research Questions Suit Talkback Radio Data?

Talkback radio can be used to address a range of different kinds of empirical research questions. Indeed, a key strength of TR is the diversity of topics, views and rhetoric pervading this media. This in turn opens up interesting opportunities for researchers to ask research questions from across a wide variety of different research areas, disciplines and interests. Further, the qualitative researcher can select from a range of theoretical lenses – from essentialism to social constructionism – depending on the nature of the research and the research question.

As discussed, TR is particularly well-suited to questions about how language and conversational interaction is socially (and structurally) organised and managed (e.g., Fitzgerald and Housley, 2002; Hutchby, 1992, 1996; Liddicoat, Dopke and Brown, 1994; Thornborrow, 2001). Thus, it can be used to address a range of research questions about the communicative activities that happen between host and callers. This can include questions such as: How are callers are positioned and introduced by hosts? (e.g., Hutchby, 1991); how is control of the interaction between callers and hosts organised? (e.g., Fitzgerald and Housley, 2002; Hutchby, 1996); and How do callers present and position themselves as 'authentic' witnesses based on their knowledge and experiences? (Hutchby, 2001).

Talkback radio tends to be a hotbed for debate about (often controversial) socio-political issues, including discussions of current political issues and government policy, as well as broader debates about race, religion, gender, sexuality, terrorism etc. It is therefore particularly suited to research questions that focus on how socio-political issues are understood (or conveyed, debated, discussed etc.) by 'ordinary voters' (or indeed by politicians and other political elites). It is also well-suited to questions about how particular social groups are constructed and positioned through these debates, for example, 'refugees' (Hanson-Easey and Augoustinos, 2012), racial minorities (McMillan, 2005; Poynting, 2006; Trigger, 1995), 'women' (Weatherall, Stubbe, Sunderland and Baxter, 2010) or 'homosexuals' (Nylund, 2004). Further, it is a useful setting for research questions about identity. Such as, how people strategically use and manage their own and other's social identities, or how TR (e.g., sports TR) is involved in the production and maintenance of particular kinds of normative identities (e.g., traditional forms of masculinity, see Nylund, 2004).

For the critical qualitative researcher, the socio-political nature of talkback can lend itself to ideological inquiry and, in particular, to questions about power. For instance, we can ask question such as: How do individuals and the media interact to generate and reproduce representations of social groups in subordinate power relations to other groups to perpetuate the status quo? (e.g., Gill, 1993). Or, in terms of the Cronulla riots, we could potentially ask: How were Muslim Australians positioned as 'not belonging' in Australia? (see Due and Riggs, 2008); How were historically constituted 'discursive resources' invoked on TR to incite and legitimise racist hate and violence to reclaim control of Cronulla beach for 'white' Australians? (Poynting, 2006).

First and foremost, TR is intended as a forum for public participation, and therefore callers to TR are expected to express their *personal* opinions on a range of different topics such as health, finance, legal issues or issues of public concern (Thornborrow, 2001). Thus, TR can be used to address a range of research questions where the aim is to gauge personal perspectives or opinions on particular phenomenon (e.g., see Kang and Quine, 2007). In addition, some political opinions are more likely to be expressed on specific political talkback programmes, such as *The Rush Limbaugh Show* in the US, that are well known to support conservative political views (Barker and Knight, 2000). Such programmes effectively provide a concentrated sample of political opinion, enabling qualitative researches interested in such thinking a fertile source of data.

Design, Sampling and Ethical Issues

The most pressing research design consideration is determining whether TR is a suitable data reservoir to address your research question. Research questions can be broad and exploratory, or narrow and topic-specific – such as our research question: 'How are Sudanese Australians spoken about in essentialist terms on TR?' (Hanson-Easey, Augoustinos and Maloney, 2014). The kind of research question you ask will need to be conceived alongside sampling considerations, such as whether TR will provide the setting where this research issue or process is likely to occur. To determine this, a preliminary inquiry should be conducted into whether your topic of interest is represented in enough calls, and in adequate depth, to warrant further investigation – so listen to TR for a bit, casually, either 'live' (online or on traditional radio) or as a podcast, to get a general feel for what is available on TR. If the feature or issue you are interested in has been socially topical, receiving attention in the mainstream media, it is also likely that this issue has been discussed somewhere on TR.

Take again, for example, our research on how Sudanese refugees were being represented in the context of controversial and salient political and social events in Australia (Hanson-Easey and Augoustinos, 2011, 2012). Because this issue had received widespread media attention, which was confirmed by searching the print media database Factiva with key terms including 'Sudanese refugees', we were reasonably confident that the topic was being discussed on TR – our experience suggests that 'cross-fertilization' of discussion topics between news media and TR is common. Topics that had received less wide-spread media attention may have had only a limited number of mentions in a specific time period, and it may prove problematic to collect enough data to satisfy the methodological requirements of your research.

Unfortunately, there is no sure-fire way to determine what potential data exist in the domain unless you listen to the radio and garner an impression for what topics are prevalent. Searching for podcasts of TR shows on the respective station's website, or on an Internet radio website such as TuneIn, is another effective option. Our approach was to use a media monitoring database (iSentia) to search for topical calls on particular stations over a timescale that we knew the issue was receiving attention in newspapers and on the television. The downside of using a media monitoring service (as we discuss later in further detail) is that it often requires an account to access the media database, or payment on a call-by-call basis.

Decisions related to sampling will be dependent on your chosen methodology and its assumptions pertaining to appropriate sample size. In much qualitative research, quantitative concerns about the requirement for a large 'representative' sample take a back seat to the imperative to collect data that lend itself to detailed examination (Flyvbjerg, 2006). What is important, though, is that the sample – its size and features – is congruent with your research aims and methodological priorities (Seale, 2012; Silverman, 2005). For example, if your research uses a qualitative case-study methodology, it would be perfectly justifiable to select a small number of cases (calls, or parts of calls), so that a rich and detailed description of these data could be generated. In this instance, the selection of calls would be determined less by achieving a particular size of sample, than by whether the calls provide adequate insight into the relevant issue. For qualitative researchers at the undergraduate level, one reasonably lengthy call (five minutes or longer) may provide enough rich data for an in-depth analysis. In fact, a number of classic qualitative studies have wholly relied on a single case (e.g., Woolgar, 1981). For researchers at the postgraduate level, a larger call sample may need to be considered in order to explore more complex and extensive research questions.

In qualitative research, the question of when to stop looking for data – what is sometimes called 'data saturation' – is contested and controversial (Morse, 1995). There are no hard and fast guidelines for what constitutes an adequate sample size in qualitative research. However, what seems to be broadly agreed upon is that the *quantity* of cases is not nearly as important as the level of interest or novelty a particular case has. As we see it, sampling decisions should always be flexibly geared to how to best answer your research question or develop an argument or theory that is emerging from the research process.

One of the advantages of using TR data is that they exist in the *public domain*. As such, a human research ethics proposal is rarely necessary because the research does not involve human participation per se (but local requirements vary widely, so check yours before collecting data). Rather, the data have been generated in the course of public debate, in a forum that is accessible to the public and the researcher, and the subsequent analysis of these data is unlikely to present any serious risks to the speakers. Importantly, however, because TR research does not actively involve the recruitment of participants in the traditional sense, this does not mean that researchers can divest themselves of all ethical considerations (see also Chapter 6). Ethical principles, such as respect for participants, would be one benchmark of good scholarship; to achieve this principle in practice, it is critical to keep the object of analysis focused on the sense-making of speakers, rather than any speculative criticisms of the speaker's personality or moral orientation. For example, in our discursive research, we often found ourselves incensed by some of the views promulgated on TR. Some of the hosts' and callers' opinions of humanitarian refugee groups were truly noxious and unsettling. However, it was important not to let our emotional responses to the data undermine the focus of our analysis – it was imperative to analyse the *talk*, and not the speaker (see also Antaki, Billig, Edwards and Potter, 2002). This can be a tricky but important distinction to make. Analysis that appears to the reader as being motivated by personal criticism can be easily dismissed as pejorative or lacking academic rigor (British Psychological Society, 2014). Most university human research ethics committees provide guidance for researchers using data available in the public domain, and we strongly recommend consulting with them before you begin your research.

Steps to Using Talkback Radio

(1) *Decide what radio stations to target.* In the previous section, we touched on some general sampling considerations that need to be attended to before you contemplate the data collection phase. Hopefully, as part and parcel of listening to a number of TR programmes, it will become easier to identify the kinds of radio stations that would host shows that suit the needs of your research. If not, even a quick search of radio stations' websites can provide indications of what topics are typically broached, and what flavour of TR can be expected, such as argumentative, 'therapeutic' (e.g., agony aunt) or anecdotal.

For example, in our discursive research on lay representations of Sudanese refugees, we wanted a TR context where speakers might feel less conspicuous about advancing potentially prejudicial or pejorative claims about Sudanese refugees. At the same time, we wished to examine how local events in Adelaide were being made sense of by local people. This led us to the well-known (in Adelaide, anyway) *Bob Francis Show*, broadcast on FIVEaa. FIVEaa is a popular commercial radio station that services the Adelaide region and features a mix of 'interactive' talkback programmes, news and sports.

By selecting this particular show for sampling, we were fully aware that the dataset would only capture a particular range of views on the topic of Sudanese refugees in Adelaide. Charting a spectrum of opinions across the social milieu was not the objective of the research; instead, we were interested in how a recently arrived social group in Australian society was represented by participants in a forum that ostensibly gave them permission to 'speak their mind', against a prevailing norm of not sounding overtly prejudiced.

(2) *Decide where to retrieve TR data from, and how to construct a sample.* As we have discussed previously, TR recordings can be accessed quickly and inexpensively by simply listening to the programme directly, or through online radio services such as TuneIn. Data can then be recorded onto a digital recorder, or on a mobile device that has a similar function. Some radio stations now host *podcasts* of their shows on their websites, some of which include talkback sessions on a particular topic. These are typically free and can be downloaded and saved for analysis. Otherwise, if you are interested only in one well-publicised call, it is possible that it has been downloaded onto another social media platform, such as YouTube. If you are working within the university sector, some libraries or departments will have access to media tracking services such as iSentia. Media monitoring services are, as the name suggests, in the business of tracking and recording news media, television and radio programmes.

Gathering TR data requires thinking about potential repositories of calls that could be searched with specific terms or words (e.g., 'Sudanese refugees'). Our discursive approach required recordings that could be transcribed in great detail, enabling fine-grained analysis of speakers' talk. What the study also required, ideally, was a set of calls that featured a range of different ways of talking about an issue. With these criteria in mind, we identified a media monitoring service that could provide actual TR recordings – these recordings could be transformed into detailed transcriptions for analysis. In this research, the decision about what is an adequate sample was very much a pragmatic one, informed by our theoretical framework, resources to pay for calls and how well the calls elaborated some feature of the research question we were pursuing. Initially, our research focus was exploratory – our only guide was that we were interested in how politicians and lay people represented and accounted for Sudanese refugees, especially in terms of a well-publicised political controversy centred on a reduction of the Sudanese humanitarian refugee quota, and the murder of a young Sudanese-Australian. Both of these controversies raised 'concerns' about how well the Sudanese-Australians were fitting into Australian society. The parameters for the search made through the media monitoring company were closely tied to the actual dates of the political or social events our research programme was focusing on, ending on the date we requested the search. The media monitoring company held what are called 'call summaries' – short descriptions of the call and its contents. Our first search involved a search for key terms in these call summaries. We initially searched for all calls that included the phrase 'Sudanese refugee(s)'.

A second sampling phase assessed the relevance of the call summaries to our two research interests: (a) political interviews by the Minister for Immigration on the topic of the Sudanese refugee intake, and (b) calls about Sudanese refugees' behaviour in Adelaide on one TR programme. Calls were simply included or omitted on this basis, and at this point purchased from the media monitoring company for further analysis. Different media monitoring companies impose different rules on this process. Some companies demand full payment for calls matching search words or phrases even before they hand over the call summaries. This, obviously, has implications for the cost-effectiveness of using TR as a data source.

The aim of our sampling procedure was to build a TR dataset that provided an empirical basis from which we could explore any number of features of people's talk about Sudanese refugees. In this way, what was most important was not the size of the sample as such, but whether the corpus could provide enough data for discursive and rhetorical *patterns* to be observed: patterns either in terms of consistency or variation (Potter and Wetherell, 1987). The sample would need to have at least enough calls to allow for these essential analytic processes to proceed, enabling us to construct a theory about how these patterns functioned in the calls and what effects they produced.

(3) *Sorting 'call summaries' for core analysis.* In our research, twenty-three 'call summaries' (synopses) met our first sampling criteria ('Sudanese refugees'). As we were chiefly concerned with how Sudanese refugees are constructed in the Australian context, further reading of the calls was undertaken to omit calls that: (a) only made passing reference to Sudanese refugees, or discussed this group in countries other than Australia; or (b) were assessed not to provide adequate detail for analysis. Fifteen calls were eventually selected for full analysis. Again, this step was based on what could be identified from the call summaries. These summaries were of variable quality and depth, as they were written by 'monitors' employed by the media monitoring agency to listen to multiple calls and summarise them. So the detail of these call summaries was inevitably contingent on the methods adopted by the individual monitors, leading to some features of the

call being emphasised and others neglected. This is clearly not a precise exercise, and we suspect that some calls meeting our criteria could have been missed. For researchers using this data collection method, the nature of this process should be recognised, and the implications for data sampling acknowledged. However, as each full recording represented a significant cost of the project, a 'decision line' was set. Ultimately, our decision to stop data collection at fifteen calls was informed by a preliminary analysis of the data material, which indicated that adequate variation and complexity existed amongst the calls and allowed for a detailed, discursive examination of how speakers represented Sudanese refugees on TR. A second rationale for stopping data collection at fifteen calls was less theoretically informed: the cost of fifteen calls came close to exceeding the budget.

(4) *Preparing the data for analysis.* Audio files should be securely kept on a computer where they can be accessed and imported onto an audio player designed for transcription, such as the cross-platform software Audacity, which is free. It is always wise to make a number of duplicate files and store these in different locations; losing expensive and critical data because of a computer crash would be a mournful experience indeed.

From the call summaries, hopefully some features of the data might have already begun to stand out. One of the exciting aspects of analysing TR is the ability to hear data expressed in real-time, and the opportunity to re-listen to the original recording as many times as you want. Transcription and analysis go hand in hand at this stage, and this process can be a fundamental stage in your inquiry.

What Can Go Wrong with Talkback Radio?

There are a few potential pitfalls using TR data, but these can often be avoided with some considered research design. First, one potential sampling problem confronting researchers using TR is not finding enough data to satisfy your research question. This is especially problematic if your research specifically addresses a problem that may not have received much attention on TR. This can be avoided by starting you research from an 'exploratory' (inductive) position – that is, keeping your research focus or question *flexible* until you find enough data to sharpen your inquiry into a specific aspect of the phenomenon you are interested in.

Second, although data collection does not necessarily require the services of a media monitoring service, going down this track can prove to be an expensive undertaking. At the time we conducted our study, we were mindful that we could not spread the sample parameters too widely because of potential cost implications. Compared to other forms of media data (e.g., newspapers; see Chapter 6), the cost associated with accessing TR data in this way *can* constitute a serious limitation. A reasonable degree of risk is also associated with paying for calls before they can be fully vetted against a sampling criterion, and you can end up with calls that are not relevant to your research question. Data collection costs are not unique to methods using TR. Traditional social scientific research, employing questionnaires or focus groups, is inherently costly in terms of the research time spent recruiting participants, catering, paying honorariums and so forth. In our experience, the potential costs associated with TR are well worth it, especially when considering the contextual richness of the data.

What Methods of Analysis Suit Talkback Radio Data?

A wide range of qualitative methods are suitable for analysing TR data. Indeed, it lends itself equally well to approaches such as thematic analysis (Braun and Clarke, 2006) that focus on the identification of broad patterns and themes, and more fine-grained analytic approaches such as conversation analysis (CA) (Hutchby and Wooffitt, 2008) and various forms of discursive analysis (Wetherell, Taylor and Yates, 2001) and narrative analysis (Riessman, 1993). As we touched on earlier, TR is particularly well-suited to CA (Heritage, 2005). CA is a research approach that studies the organisation of conversation by analysing, in close detail, recordings and transcription of social interaction. For example, CA has fruitfully explored how people create 'identities' on TR (Atkinson and Kelly-Holmes, 2011; Fitzgerald and Housley, 2002), and how TR hosts routinely use their position – by virtue of being the first to ask a question in a call – to win arguments with callers (Hutchby, 1992).

Talkback radio as a *media genre* has received much academic attention, especially its role in determining social opinion (e.g., Barker and Knight, 2000); yet, beyond conversation and discourse analytic research, empirical examinations of actual call data are far less prevalent. In Box 7.2 we provide an illustrative example from our work, presenting insights into what one method – discursive analysis – can achieve with TR. As the analysis in Box 7.2 hopefully elucidates, TR can provide rather novel insights into the dynamics of argumentation as it is practised in situ. Normative values about what can be said, and not said, about social groups in the public sphere can be discerned and elaborated upon.

Box 7.2 An illustrative example of a discursive analysis of talkback radio

The following analysis illustrates how TR data can be usefully employed as a means for examining how particular views and attitudes are used in conversation. In particular, what is clearly on display here is how some attitudes are now considered out of step with what could be considered acceptable speech. The TR extract analysed in this Box is taken from *The Bob Francis Show* on FIVEaa. Dee is calling in to add her voice to the host's earlier editorial on a stabbing murder of a young Sudanese refugee by a peer in the Central Business District of Adelaide. The extract has been transcribed in accordance with simplified Jeffersonian transcription conventions (Jefferson, 2004). In short, the underlined words are emphasised by the speakers, and the CAPITALISED WORDS are nearly shouted.

DEE: ... There's not enough support workers to take me elsewhere
FRANCIS: Aaaw, that's a pity
DEE: Yeah, anyway, I didn't phone about me
FRANCIS: OK, what did you phone for?
DEE: Ah, well, when I came out in sixty-four
FRANCIS: Yeah
DEE: Um, I regarded Adelaide as a lovely country town
FRANCIS: Heh heh heh
DEE: I'm sorry, I can't regard it as a lovely country town anymore
FRANCIS: It's a bit like Chicago, isn't it
DEE: What on earth's happening Bob?
FRANCIS: It's a bit like bloody Chicago, isn't it?
DEE: Now, I did hear you say, before I phoned about the Sudanese
FRANCIS: Yeah ...
DEE: Now, I see, I'm not at all racist, but ...
FRANCIS: But ...
DEE: I think they all should be gathered up and sent back
FRANCIS: Aaw, you see that's jus, that is a total racist comment
DEE: I'm, I'm sorry
FRANCIS: ABSOLUTELY RACIST COMMENT
DEE: I'm sorry, but
FRANCIS: BLOODY STUPID AND RACIST
DEE: Bob, we don't need them here
FRANCIS: YOU ARE STUPID FOR SAYING THAT
DEE: Oh, don't call me stupid
FRANCIS: YOU'RE STUPID FOR SAYING THAT, GO BACK AND LEARN SOMETHING ABOUT HISTORY AND WHY PEOPLE LIKE THAT COME TO THIS COUNTRY, AND GIVE THEM A CHANCE TO GET GOING HERE
DEE: But they, don't ...

FRANCIS: ONE CHILD HAS DONE SOMETHING WRONG AND <u>YOU</u> HAVE
         SAID SOMETHING THAT IS <u>ABSOLUTELY RIDICULOUS</u>
DEE: Bob, the Italians and the Greeks came out and soon they did very well
FRANCIS: AH, I'LL BET YOU, YOU HAD PROBABLY THE SAME IDEA
         ABOUT THE ITALIANS AND GREEKS WHEN THEY FIRST
         COME OUT
DEE: No, I didn't
FRANCIS: NAH, NOT INTERESTED IN TALKING TO YOU. I THINK YOUR
         ATTITUDES, YOU'RE A DICKHEAD.

Analogous to many of the call beginnings in our TR corpus, this starts with an amiable conversation about personal matters; in this instance, about the host's recent leg injury and the caller's own health problems. The host demonstrates empathy for Dee's problems, uttering 'aaw, that's a pity' and Dee progresses the call to what is her primary topic: the stabbing and 'the Sudanese'. Dee begins her complaint by making a claim about the changing social nature of Adelaide, stating that when she 'came out in sixty-four' she saw 'Adelaide as a lovely country town'. But now, without explicitly uttering it, she implies that a stabbing was an exemplar of why things are now different, and thus why she 'can't regard it a lovely country town anymore'. Francis, deploying a jocular tone agrees, and retorts, it's 'just like bloody Chicago isn't it'.

Until this point, the call has progressed without trouble, in that both speakers are sharing and agreeing upon similar representations about Adelaide becoming a dangerous place, just like 'Chicago'. The caller's next turn relates to a previous segment of Francis' show that introduced the topic of the stabbing, and then progresses to deploy a disclaimer, 'I'm not at all racist, but'. This disclaimer has been widely noted in the race-talk literature (see Hewitt and Stokes, 1975; van Dijk, 1984, 1995; Wetherell and Potter, 1992) where it has been observed to function as a defence against inferences that the speaker is motivated by a deeply held prejudice. What is particularly noteworthy is how this rhetorical device *fails* so dramatically to mitigate as designed. Even before the caller has the opportunity to finish her turn of talk, Francis pre-empts what is to follow and both speakers utter 'but'. As Francis has correctly anticipated, Dee moves to deliver advice that indeed could be heard as racist: 'they should all be gathered up and sent back'.

From this point in the call, Francis is oppositional, deriding and accusing Dee of uttering a '<u>total racist comment</u>' and challenging the status of her intelligence, asserting that she is 'STUPID FOR SAYING THAT'. Moreover, Francis chides Dee for prejudicially generalising from one event (the stabbing) to recommend that 'all' the Sudanese should be removed from Australia. Francis is responding to Dee's lack of nuance when making causal sense of the stabbing, and her crudely formulated proposition that 'I think they should all be gathered up and sent back'. What usually functions at these moments to lubricate the interaction, such as a recognition that what is about to be said could be heard as 'racist', and a pre-emptive 'I'm not racist ... but ...', used to ward of potential criticism (see Hewitt and Stokes, 1975), is not present in this call.

It is this lack of delicacy that flags Dee as an individual who is displaying an antipathy for Sudanese refugees that Francis deems as so unacceptable – or at least, this is considered an opportunity to deploy his trademark 'shock-jock' rebuke. Unlike other calls in the TR corpus, there is no sketching of any personal encounters with 'the Sudanese', or any lay sociological theory explaining why this group is having trouble 'fitting into' Australian society, and thus, why they should be expelled. This call is unique in this TR corpus with regard to the caller's blunt opinion, and the complete rejection of it by Francis. What is more, Francis orientates to a notion of (in)tolerance in his attack on Dee, and in particular, her gross categorisation or stereotyping of all 'Sudanese' on the basis of one event (the stabbing). We suspect that without a softening formulation to manage the risk of this complaint being heard as motivated by Dee's own interests, or disposition (i.e., her irrational personality), Dee is left open to a range of accusations that are predicated on her views being heard as deeply intolerant.

Conclusion

Talkback radio is an underutilised reservoir of potential qualitative data that lends itself to being analysed by a broad range of methods. It is a media genre firmly planted in the public domain, providing individuals with opportunities to voice their opinions, tell their stories and join the 'public conversation'. It represents a forum for public, political and ideological debate and, in some instances, can play a part in agitating for social change. Talkback radio provides qualitative researchers relatively easy access to, often with minimal outlay of resources, a diverse array of data topics that are sometimes difficult to access using alternative methods. As we see it, TR is an exciting incarnation of social behaviour as it occurs 'in situ', and holds great promise for qualitative inquiry (see Box 7.3).

Have a Go ...

Some scholars have described TR as a public medium through which citizens can enhance their civic participation by having their voices heard (e.g., Turner, 2009). In Australia at least, talk radio has also become a preferred medium through which politicians can test and market their policies to a wide audience (Lee, 2007). Increasingly too, talk radio has become a communication platform for professionals to disseminate knowledge about health and well-being. This

---

Box 7.3 Personal reflections on using talkback radio

As we have written this chapter, it has been interesting to reflect on what drew us to TR in the first place, and what challenges were presented when working through what was, at the time, a very unfamiliar method of collecting and working with data. Re-reading the extracts from our journal articles using TR has reminded us of the relatively organic, naturalistic (i.e., not concocted for the specific needs of a research project, but occurring 'naturally' in the social world) nature of these data, and their usefulness for asking questions about how speakers mould language to meet situated (conversational) and global (ideological and social) ends. Put another way, TR data proved well-suited to a fine-grained analysis of conversation (Hutchby, 1996), and the construction of complaints and representations that we believed resonated with wider narratives running through the community.

What is more, as a function of reflecting on this past TR research, we are reminded of how interesting and, for want of a better word, *enjoyable* analysing this form of data can be for qualitative researchers. In part, this can be attributed to the nature of people's talk as it manifests in real-time communication and the endlessly fascinating ways speakers formulate and adapt their talk contingent on the interaction at hand. Moreover, and more generally, analysing and interpreting TR data can be a deeply engaging experience, in that it provides a unique window into the views, perceptions and beliefs of people as they wrestle with day-to-day issues affecting them in some form or another. For us, insights garnered from such analysis bring us closer to understanding the 'lived experience' of people and, thus, this is exciting and important research.

Lastly, one of the most compelling aspects of TR is that it reflects upon the broader social and political conditions currently being experienced by social groups. In our work, this provided the unique opportunity to observe 'the thinking society' (Moscovici, 1984), as its members argued about which social groups were deemed acceptable, which were not, and why their judgements were justifiable. Put another way, TR allowed us to closely examine the *logic* people used to build their arguments and advance their particular position on an issue. For the critical or politically minded qualitative researcher, TR is an intriguing analytic context for unpicking the logic of arguments that function to support the social and political order.

---

includes professionals working in the psy-disciplines who offer scientific knowledge and advice about mental health, personal and family relationships, parenting, etc.

Choose a talk radio programme that has a wide and popular reach, and download the programme's podcast for a one to two-week period. Save the podcast audio files onto your computer and spend some time reviewing the content, topics and concerns that are aired during that period. Use audio software such as Audacity to listen to, select and collate topics of interest (e.g., political participation and deliberation; the communication and dissemination of scientific knowledge). Build a data sample containing these selected segments for further analysis. These segments could include calls from listeners, interviews by the programme host with politicians or experts, or editorial comments by the host. Listen to the selected files repeatedly and start to ask some questions about the nature of the data you have collected. Questions such as:

- How are certain issues or social phenomena represented in people's talk? What descriptions, categories, metaphors and 'turns of phrase' are used?
- How do participants rationalise and justify their views?
- How and when are 'facts' mobilised in people's talk?
- Are there notable argumentative patterns that reoccur?
- How does the host orient to dissenting views, and are competing views offered the same air time?

Of course, in order to answer these questions in a scholarly fashion, you would need to transcribe your data. Depending on the kinds of questions you want to ask, and your epistemological preferences and analytic approach, this may require the use of a transcription system such as the 'Jeffersonian system' (Jefferson, 2004), which uses a range of symbols to represent not only what is said but also how things are said, and is widely used in CA and some forms of discourse analysis (e.g., discursive psychology).

Further Resources: Online

TuneIn is an Internet radio website that allows you to search for podcasts of particular TR shows. It provides a good way to find data or to get a feel for what TR feels and sounds like: http://tunein.com

Further Resources: Readings

To read more about the example study, see Hanson-Easey, S. and Augoustinos, M. (2010). Out of Africa: Accounting for refugee policy and the language of causal attribution. *Discourse & Society*, *21*(3), 295–323. See also: Hanson-Eusey, S. and Augoustinos, M. (2012). Narratives from the neighbourhood: The discursive construction of integration problems in talkback radio. *Journal of Sociolinguistics*, *16*(1), 28–55.

For a critical analysis of how men negotiate masculinity on TR, see Nylund, D. (2004). When in Rome: Heterosexism, homophobia, and sports talk radio. *Journal of Sport & Social Issues*, *28*(2), 136–168.

For a fascinating examination of the role of TR in the Cronulla riots, see Poynting, S. (2006). What caused the Cronulla riot. *Race & Class*, *48*(1), 85–92.
To read more about the influence of TR on politics in Australia, see Turner, G. (2009). Politics, radio and journalism in Australia: The influence of 'talkback'. *Journalism*, *10*(4), 411–430.

References

Antaki, C., Billig, M., Edwards, D. and Potter, J. (2002). Discourse analysis means doing analysis: A critique of six analytic shortcomings. *DAOL Discourse Analysis Online*, *1*(1). https://extra.shu.ac.uk/daol/articles/open/2002/002/antaki2002002-paper.html
Atkinson, D. and Kelly-Holmes, H. (2011). Codeswitching, identity and ownership in Irish radio comedy. *Journal of Pragmatics*, *43*(1), 251–260.
Barker, D. and Knight, K. (2000). Political talk radio and public opinion. *Public Opinion Quarterly*, *64*(2), 149–170.
Billig, M. (1987). *Arguing and thinking: A rhetorical approach to social psychology*. Cambridge: Cambridge University Press.
  (1988). The notion of 'prejudice': Some rhetorical and ideological aspects. *Text*, *8*(1–2), 91–110.
Bodey, M. (2007, 19 April). Four decades of 'God's Great Equaliser'. *The Australian*. Retrieved from: www.theaustralian.com.au%2Fbusiness%2Fmedia%2Ffour-decades-of-gods-great-eq&Horde=18db92b40dfb4eb796fca720e492bc17
Braun, V. and Clarke, V. (2006). Using thematic analysis in psychology. *Qualitative Research in Psychology*, *3*(2), 77–101.
British Psychological Society. (2014). *Code of human research ethics*. Leicester, UK: British Psychological Society.
Burr, V. (1999). The extra-discursive in social constructionism. In D. J. Nightingale and J. Cromby (eds.), *Social constructionist psychology: A critical analysis of theory and practice* (pp. 113–126). Buckingham, UK: Open University Press.
Cohen, S. (2002). *Folk devils and moral panics: The creation of the mods and rockers*. London: Psychology Press.
Due, C. and Riggs, D. W. (2008). 'We grew here you flew here': Claims to 'home' in the Cronulla riots. *Colloquy*, *16*, 210–228.
Edwards, D. and Potter, J. (1992). *Discursive psychology*. London: Sage Publications.
Ewart, J. (2011). Therapist, companion, & friend: The under-appreciated role of talk-back radio in Australia. *Journal of Radio & Audio Media*, *18*(2), 231–245.
Fitzgerald, R. and Housley, W. (2002). Identity, categorization and sequential organization: The sequential and categorial flow of identity in a radio phone-in. *Discourse & Society*, *13*(5), 579–602.
Flyvbjerg, B. (2006). Five misunderstandings about case-study research. *Qualitative Inquiry*, *12*(2), 219–245.
Gill, R. (1993). Justifying injustice: Broadcasters accounts of inequality in radio. In E. Burman and I. Parker (eds.), *Discourse analytic research* (pp. 75–93). London: Routledge.

Hanson-Easey, S. and Augoustinos, M. (2010). Out of Africa: Accounting for refugee policy and the language of causal attribution. *Discourse & Society*, *21*(3), 295–323.
   (2011). Complaining about humanitarian refugees: The role of sympathy talk in the design of complaints on talkback radio. *Discourse & Communication*, *5*(3), 247–271.
   (2012). Narratives from the neighbourhood: The discursive construction of integration problems in talkback radio. *Journal of Sociolinguistics*, *16*(1), 28–55.
Hanson-Easey, S., Augoustinos, M. and Moloney, G. (2014). 'They're all tribals': Essentialism, context and the discursive representation of Sudanese refugees. *Discourse & Society*, *25*(3), 362–382.
Heritage, J. (2005). Conversation analysis and institutional talk. In L. Fitch and E. Sanders (eds.), *Handbook of language and social interaction* (pp. 103–147). London: Psychology Press.
Hewit, J. P. and Stokes, R. (1975). Disclaimers. *American Sociological Review*, *40*(1), 1–11.
Hutchby, I. (1991). The organization of talk on talk radio. In P. Scannell (ed.), *Broadcast talk* (pp. 119–137). London: Sage Publications.
   (1992). The pursuit of controversy: Routine scepticism in talk on 'talk radio'. *Sociology*, *26*(4), 673–694.
   (1996). *Confrontation talk: Arguments, asymmetries and power on talk radio*. New Jersey: Lawrence Erlbaum Associates.
   (2001). 'Witnessing': The use of first-hand knowledge in legitimating lay opinions on talk radio. *Discourse Studies*, *3*(4), 481–497.
Hutchby, I. and Wooffitt, R. (2008). *Conversation analysis*. Cambridge: Polity Press.
Jefferson, G. (2004). Glossary of transcript symbols with an introduction. In G. H. Lerner (ed.), *Conversation analysis: Studies from the first generation* (pp. 13–31). Amsterdam: John Benjamins Publishing Company.
Kang, M. and Quine, S. (2007). Young people's concerns about sex: Unsolicited questions to a teenage radio talkback programme over three years. *Sex Education*, *7*(4), 407–420.
Lee, C. (2007). Mornings with radio 774: Can John Howard's medium of choice enhance public sphere activity? *Media International Australia*, *122*(1), 122–131.
Liddicoat, A., Dopke, S. and Brown, A. (1994). Presenting a point of view: Callers' contributions to talkback radio in Australia. *Journal of Pragmatics*, *22*(2), 139–156.
Lunt, P. and Stenner, P. (2005). The Jerry Springer Show as an emotional public sphere. *Media, Culture & Society*, *27*(1), 59–81.
McMillan, K. (2005). Racial discrimination and political bias on talkback radio in New Zealand: Assessing the evidence. *Political Science*, *57*(2), 75–91.
Morse, J. M. (1995). The significance of saturation. *Qualitative Health Research*, *5*(2), 147–149.
Moscovici, S. (1984). The phenomenon of social representations. In R. M. Farr and S. Moscovici (ed.), *Social representations* (pp. 3–69). Cambridge: Cambridge University Press.
Nylund, D. (2004). When in Rome: Heterosexism, homophobia, and sports talk radio. *Journal of Sport & Social Issues*, *28*(2), 136–168.
Perry, B. (2001). *In the name of hate: Understanding hate crimes*. New York: Routledge.
Potter, J. and Wetherell, M. (1987). *Discourse and social psychology: Beyond attitudes and behaviour*. London: Sage Publications.

Poynting, S. (2006). What caused the Cronulla riot. *Race & Class*, *48*(1), 85–92.

Poynting, S., Noble, G., Tabar, P. and Collins, J. (2004). *Bin Laden in the suburbs: Criminalising the Arab other*. Sydney: Sydney Institute of Criminology.

Riessman, C. K. (1993). *Narrative analysis*. Newbury Park, CA: Sage Publications.

Seale, C. (ed.) (2012). *Researching society and culture*. London: Sage Publications.

Silverman, D. (2005). *Doing qualitative research: A practical handbook*. London: Sage Publications.

Thornborrow, J. (2001). Questions and control: The organisation of talk in calls to a radio phone-in. *Discourse Studies 3*(1): 119–143.

Trigger, D. (1995). 'Everyone's agreed, the West is all you need': Ideology, media and Aboriginality in Western Australia. *Media Information Australia*, *75*, 102–122.

Turner, G. (2009). Politics, radio and journalism in Australia: The influence of 'talk-back'. *Journalism*, *10*(4), 411–430.

van Dijk, T. A. (1984). *Prejudice in discourse*. Amsterdam: John Benjamins.

(1991). *Racism and the press*. London: Routledge.

(1995). Elite discourse and the reproduction of racism. In R. K. Slayden and D. Slayden (eds.), *Hate speech* (pp. 1–27). Newbury Park, CA: Sage Publications.

Ward, I. (2002). Talkback radio, political communication, and Australian politics. *Australian Journal of Communication*, *29*, 21–38.

Wetherell, M. and Potter, J. (1992). *Mapping the language of racism: Discourse and the legitimation of exploitation*. New York: Harvester Wheatsheaf.

Weatherall, A., Stubbe, M., Sunderland, J. and Baxter, J. (2010). Conversation analysis and critical discourse analysis in language and gender research: Approaches in dialogue. In J. Holmes and M. Marra (eds.), *Femininity, feminism and gendered discourse: A selected and edited collection of papers from the Fifth International Language and Gender Association Conference (IGALA5)* (pp. 213–243). Cambridge, UK: Cambridge Scholars Publishing.

Weatherall, M., Taylor, S. and Yates, S. J. (eds.) (2001). *Discourse as data: A guide for analysis*. London: Sage Publications.

Woolgar, S. (1981). Discovery: Logic and sequence in a scientific text. In K. Knorr-Cetina and M. Mulkay (eds.), *Science observed: Perspectives on the social study of science* (pp. 239–269). London: Sage Publications.

8 Archives of Everyday Life

Using Blogs in Qualitative Research

Nicholas Hookway

Overview

This chapter focuses on blogs – now the 'elder statesman' of Web 2.0 – and the opportunities and challenges they offer the qualitative researcher. Drawing on a research project that used blogs to examine everyday understandings and experiences of morality (see Box 8.1), the chapter introduces blogs as contemporary multimedia 'documents of life'. I argue that blogs provide qualitative researchers with unique access to first-person textual accounts of everyday life. In addition, they provide large amounts of instantaneous data that are global, archived, searchable and relatively resource-lite. Suitable research questions and steps for conducting blog research are discussed, along with ethical issues involved with handling blog data. I then go on to consider problems and solutions involved with blog methodologies and suitable methods for analysis, before finishing with some personal reflections on my use of blog data in the everyday morality study (see Box 8.2).

Introduction to Blog Research

Over the last ten years, Web 2.0 has seen the development of a range of user-generated digital genres, where users can produce and consume content at the same time as communicating and interacting with one another (Beer and Burrows, 2007; see also Chapters 6 and 9). These new participatory forms of the Internet include social networking sites (e.g., Facebook and MySpace), social bookmarking services (e.g., Delicious and Bundlr), video and photo sharing sites (e.g., YouTube and Instagram) and blogging and microblogging services (e.g., Blogger and Twitter). These developments in Internet culture have not only dramatically reshaped social life but also fundamentally shifted and challenged how social and health scientists 'do' research (Fielding, Lee and Blank, 2008; Liamputtong and Ezzy, 2005). In this chapter, I report on the

---

Box 8.1 Exploring everyday morality

Blogs offered a specific set of advantages for my own qualitative research into everyday Australian moralities. The aim of this project was to 'thickly describe' (Geertz, 1973) how individuals 'write' and 'talk' their everyday moral worlds into existence from their own perspectives. The study was based on a qualitative analysis of forty-four Australian blogs combined with twenty-five online in-depth interviews (see Chapters 10-13 on virtual interviews). Blogs were sampled using a combination of searching, trawling and solicitation. The final age range for the forty-four sampled bloggers was nineteen to fifty-three, with a mean age of thirty-one. Twenty-five of the bloggers were female and nineteen were male. The key methodological issue for this research project was *how* to empirically capture the moral reality of everyday life. Blogs offered an original empirical lens through which to investigate the contemporary production of morality and selfhood in late-modernity. The blogs were selected as a form of personal life record (Thomas and Znaniecki, 1958 [1918]) that allowed access to spontaneous accounts of everyday life that reflected what was important to the blogger without the intervention of a researcher. The blogs were sampled from the blog hosting website LiveJournal due to the ability to perform searches by location and age, and a reputation for hosting personal and reflective style blogs. Blogs were selected that contained at least two incidents, moments, descriptions or experiences that shed light on the blogger's everyday moral constructions and practices (e.g., apologising to an ex-partner; helping a homeless person; reflecting on morality without a religious framework). Blog data collection comprised two main phases: a passive trawling phase and an active phase of blog solicitation, through advertisements placed in LiveJournal communities. The data generated from the blogs were complemented with twenty-five in-depth online interviews to further develop and explore important themes identified from the textual accounts. The central finding was that bloggers constructed morality as an actively created, non-conforming and autonomous *do-it-yourself* project that highlighted the ethical significance of self, body, emotions and ideals of authenticity (see Hookway, 2014, 2015).

---

use of one such Web 2.0 application, the 'weblog' or 'blog', in a study exploring everyday understandings and experiences of morality.

The year 1999 will be remembered as the year of the blog. In this year, blogs became a significant feature of online culture, driven by the twin motors of free, user-friendly blogging applications such as Blogger and LiveJournal, and the global media exposure of 'A-list' celebrity bloggers like Salam Pax (aka the 'Baghdad Blogger') and the actor Wil Wheaton (Blood, 2002a; Serfarty, 2004). The popularity of blogs can be connected to a wider cultural shift – think celebrity, reality TV, talk show and confessional cultures – in which private sentiment has come to colonise the public sphere (Bauman, 2000; Beer and

Burrows, 2007). The public telling of personal life has become so prominent that some theorists even suggest we now inhabit an 'auto/biographical' (Plummer, 2001) or 'interview' (Atkinson and Silverman, 1997) society. As the popular slogan goes, 'everyone has a story to tell'.

Evan Williams, co-creator of popular blogging programme Blogger, argues that the defining features of blogs are 'frequency, brevity and personality' (quoted in Turnbull, 2002: 82). More formally, a 'blog' refers to a website which contains a series of frequently updated, reverse chronologically ordered posts on a common webpage, usually written by a single author (Hookway, 2008). Somewhere between the individual-focused personal webpage and the interactivity of social networking sites, blogs are characterised by: instant text/ graphic publishing; a month-by-month archive; feedback through 'comments'; an expectation to link to other blogs and online sources; and a personal and candid writing style (Hookway, 2008).

Blogs are textual, but also interactive, and multimedia, forms of text (Scheidt and Wright, 2004). Blogs encourage not only personal written expression but also visual and other forms of expression via blog design and style customisation, embedding online content such as images, video and audio and linking to other blogs (see Figure 8.1). As Badger (2004: 1) claims, 'if we think of weblogs as being homepages that we wear then it is the visual elements that tailor the garment to fit the individual'. Figure 8.1 shows the basic visual template and features of a blog from Blogger.

While the format is relatively consistent, the content of blogs is wide-ranging and diverse. Rebecca Blood (2002b: xii), the author of pioneering weblog Rebecca's Pocket, captures this diversity:

Weblogs are the place for daily stories, impassioned reactions, mundane details, and miscellanea. They are as varied as their maintainers, and they are creating a generation of involved, impassioned citizens, and articulate, observant human beings.

The diversity in content means there are a variety of weblog genres from 'mommy' blogs, warblogs and celebrity blogs, through to food, travel, educational, professional, corporate and pornographic ones. However, typically blogs take the form of online diaries or life narratives, where private and intimate content is posted in daily, monthly or yearly snippets (Hookway, 2008). The online diary is a type of blog that is generally light on links with the focus being on the 'drama' (Goffman, 1959) of everyday interactions, selves and situations. While new social media like Facebook and Twitter are characterised by the brevity of the 'status update' or 'the tweet', the blog format encourages a deeper engagement with self, personal expression and community (Marwick, 2008).

Figure 8.1   Example blog post from Blogger

Blogs can be located as a contemporary 'document of life' (Plummer, 2001). Plummer defines documents of life as those personal artefacts of lived experiences that are produced as part of everyday life. For example, diaries, letters, biographies, self-observation, personal notes, photographs and films. For the qualitative researcher, documents of life offer insight into how people understand and experience the world, and the creative ways in which people express these understandings and experiences.

What Do Blogs Offer the Qualitative Researcher?

Blogs offer a range of practical and methodological benefits for the qualitative researcher. Blogs provide an unobtrusive method to capture unsolicited and naturalistic narratives unadulterated by the scrutiny of a researcher. Blogs provide access to spontaneously-generated narratives that provide insights and access to participants' own language, reflections and stories. Further, blogs capture situated understandings and experiences of everyday life, converging traditional self-reflective forms of data like diaries, letters, biography, self-observation, personal notes, images, photographs and video, into a multi-media and interactive archive of everyday life.

There is a paradox built into blogging: the majority of non-celebrity bloggers are anonymous, or relatively unidentifiable, but at the same time are typically writing for an audience and are therefore potentially engaged in a type of 'face-work' (Goffman, 1959). This tension between visibility and invisibility can give blogging a revelatory or confessional quality, where a less polished and even 'uglier' self can be verbalised. One can express one's faults, one's mishaps – whatever might be difficult to tell as we 'enter the presence of others' (Goffman, 1959: 1). As one blogger in my research reflected: 'the point of my blog is to have a space in my life where I can be anonymous and express the 'real' me, however confronting or ugly that might be' (twenty-eight-year-old male, LiveJournal, 2009).

In addition to providing access to spontaneous and candid accounts of everyday life, blogs can help avoid some problems associated with collecting sensitive information via interview or focus-group methods (Elliot, 1997). Like 'offline' diaries (see Chapter 5), blogs capture an 'ever-changing present' (Elliot, 1997: 3), where there is a tight union between everyday experience and the record of that experience (Toms and Duff, 2002). This proximity between event and record means that blogs are less susceptible to problems of retrospective recall and reconstruction than interviews and focus groups, which might be important if the goal of the research is to capture external 'truth' (Verbrugge, 1980).

One of the key strengths of using blogs is that they are an instantaneous, publicly available and low-cost technique for collecting documents of life. Blogs allow for the creation of immediate text without the resource intensiveness of tape recorders and transcription (Liamputtong and Ezzy, 2005). And, like other online research methods, blogs enable access to populations otherwise geographically or socially removed from the researcher (Hessler et al., 2003). The archived nature of blogs also makes them amenable to examining social processes over time, meaning they can be useful for conducting longitudinal forms of research.

For my own qualitative research on everyday Australian moralities, blogs offered a unique way to analyse the sources, strategies and experiences of modern moral decision-making. Blogs helped overcome methodological issues related to studying lay normativity using traditional qualitative methods like face-to-face interviews. As Phillips and Harding (1985: 93) pointed out, asking people directly about their moral beliefs and actions is difficult, and raises issues of validity and sensitivity. For example, people may be unwilling to share intimate moral details with a researcher in an interview, as they conform to 'the very obligation and profitability of appearing always in a steady moral light' (Goffman, 1959: 244). Instead, people may be inclined to frame themselves as having desired qualities, such as 'good', 'moral', 'kind', 'normal' and 'respectable'. There is also the difficulty of how to contextualise the topic in a meaningful way for informants in an interview setting. In relation to my research, I was struck with how challenging it would be for face-to-face interview participants to talk 'off-the-cuff' about their moral lives with a stranger, without some form of concrete prompting and situating.

Blogs can overcome some of the difficulties associated with finding or soliciting everyday biographical accounts (e.g., through diaries; see Chapter 5) because of their location in the public domain. As previously noted, they had for me the advantage of not being 'contaminated' by the interests of the researcher. In addition, they enabled easy access to informants from the major urban centres of Australia.

What Research Questions Suit Blog Data?

There are two broad types of research questions that blog data are appropriate for: (1) projects focused on analysing blogs and blogging as a phenomenon and how it is implicated in a range of practices and behaviours; and (2) projects focused on using blogs to examine an aspect or feature of 'offline' life. The first type of research question typically involves projects that investigate the qualities and characteristics of blogging and their uses and implications across broad areas of social life from identity and community building, education, health and travel, to commerce, business and marketing. For example, Hodkinson (2007) investigated the symbolic and practical significance of online journals for young people, Sanford (2010) explored weight-loss blogs as a support tool for people diagnosed as 'morbidly obese', and Sharman (2014) analysed blogs as a source of contestation to mainstream climate science.

The second type of research question is more focused on bloggers as both observers and informants of everyday life (Toms and Duff, 2002). The everyday morality project is an example of this type of blog analysis. Other examples are blogs being used to analyse health and illness (Clarke and van Amerom, 2008), weight loss (Leggatt-Cook and Chamberlain, 2012), global sporting events (Dart, 2009), cosmopolitanism, travel and tourism (Enoch and Grossman, 2010; Snee, 2013) and bereavement and religion (Bakker and Paris, 2013) (see Table 8.1).

Design and Sampling: Steps to Doing Blog Research

Table 8.2 outlines the key steps involved in conducting blog research. This is not a prescriptive model but an attempt to offer a set of guidelines for researchers who are new to blog research. I now discuss these steps in more detail.

Table 8.1 Blog research examples

Authors	Topic	Research question	Sample
Clarke and Van Amerom (2008)	Depression	Investigates and compares how men and women who self-identify as depressed describe their experiences in their blogs.	Fifty blogs (twenty-five women; twenty-five men) sampled using the search phrase 'depression blogs'.
Leggatt-Cook and Chamberlain (2012)	Women's weight loss	Explores how female weight-loss bloggers negotiate discourses around fatness and represent their bodies and identity online.	Ten women's weight-loss blogs sampled from a review of 180 weight-loss blogs. Blogs were sourced from blog lists (e.g., 'the top 100 weight-loss blogs'), relevant blog sites (e.g., BlogHer.com), blogrolls (links to similar blogs) and popular weight-loss blogs (e.g., watchmybuttshrinking.com).
Dart (2009)	2006 World Cup Finals	Examines the extent to which football fans embedded in Germany used the Internet to blog their World Cup experiences.	Used generic Internet search engines alongside specific blog search engines (e.g., Feedster; Blogdigger) to identify World Cup football blogs from independent, organisational and corporate blogs. Size of blog sample not given.
Enoch and Grossman (2010)	Backpacker tourism	Investigates cosmopolitan discourse among Israeli and Danish backpackers who have visited India.	Twenty-nine backpacker blogs (fifteen Israeli and fourteen Danish) written between 2003 and 2008. No information is given on how the blog sample was collected.
Snee (2013)	Gap year tourism	Explores debates about contemporary cosmopolitanism using gap year narratives from young Britons.	Thirty-nine travel blogs sampled using the search phrase 'gap year' on blog search engines and host platforms.
Bakker and Paris (2013)	Religiosity and parental loss	Examines the impact of stillbirth and neonatal death on parental religiosity.	A sample of 148 parent blogs (253 entries) was drawn from the website Glow in the Woods.

Table 8.2 Blog research steps in brief

Steps	Action
(1) Develop selection criteria	Use research question(s) to determine selection of blog type and content and intended blogger characteristics.
(2) Conduct blog data collection using 'searching', 'trawling' and/or 'solicitation'	Generate blog sample through blog platform or web-based searching, 'trawling' within defined parameters or 'active' solicitation via online and offline adverts.
(3) Establish an online presence	Set up research website to disseminate relevant project information (e.g., information sheet), provide a site to 'meet the researcher' and legitimate researcher's identity.
(4) Conduct blog analysis	Convert sampled blogs into text files for textual analysis within a word-processing program or for coding in qualitative data analysis software.

(1) *Develop selection criteria.* The first step for the blog researcher is to determine the selection criteria to guide sampling. It is important that researchers put in place careful search parameters and guidelines for data collection at the selection criteria stage. There can be a compulsive quality to blog searching; an irrational sense that the next post or the next blog will 'strike gold', which can prove time-consuming and ineffective. Developing clear selection criteria is important, not only in terms of meeting the goals of the research but also as means to save time and prevent frustration.

(2) *Conduct blog data collection using 'searching', 'trawling' or 'solicitation'.* There are three main ways to sample blogs and I used all of these in my research. I sampled blogs from LiveJournal. LiveJournal has a significant share of the global blog market, claiming to host over twenty-one million accounts, of which over two million are considered active (Livejournal.com, 2009). I made the decision not only to limit data collection to one blogging application, to simplify the process, but also because LiveJournal has a number of advantages. These include: (1) a user-friendly interface; (2) a systematic search engine that enabled identification of blogs by location (country, state, and city) and age; (3) a sizeable share of the blog market in Australia; and (4) a reputation as a site purely for online diaries. *Blog search-ing* involves using either a blog-specific, search engine (e.g., the now-discon-tinued Google Blog Search) and/or a blog host search engine (e.g., LiveJournal search) to identify relevant blog posts (e.g., doing a search for 'gap years'; 'volunteering'; 'dieting'; 'depression' etc.). I joined LiveJournal

as a paid account holder to allow the use of advanced search tools. LiveJournal did not allow searching by gender or ethnicity so I had to manually sample bloggers by gender and ethnicity to capture a diversity of experiences. This was difficult as Australian LiveJournal bloggers appear predominantly to be Anglo-Australian and often you only have visual cues to guide ethnic identification.

Platform search engines (e.g., LiveJournal search) and specific blog web-sites (e.g., weight-loss blog sites like 'The 100 most inspirational weight-loss blogs') are useful for projects focused on analysing a definite type of experi-ence or process such as those provided in travel, weight-loss or parenting blogs. However, blog researchers need to be cautioned that even when using search engines, a degree of blog 'weeding' is needed as these searches produce not only a range of irrelevant results, but also spam blogs, fake blogs, discarded blogs, access-restricted blogs and non-traditional blogs (e.g., blogs hosted on news websites or social networking sites) (Snee, 2012).

Blog trawling involves identifying a pool of bloggers by a set of particular characteristics (e.g., location and age), using a platform search engine, and then reading within that selected group for research-relevant posts (e.g., on everyday moral decision-making such as ending a romantic relationship or choosing not to eat meat). The trawling phase of my data collection involved examining Sydney and Melbourne LiveJournal blogs, within different age ranges, for concrete incidents of moral decision-making or more abstract discussions of moral thinking. I read the first two or three posts to determine background information. If this content contained material that indicated some reflexive moral content, then the latest year of posts was perused.

This 'trawling' approach proved time-inefficient and produced limited results, so I adopted blog solicitation as a more active form of recruitment. *Blog solicitation* involves inviting participants to identify their blogs to the researcher using online advertisements (e.g., advertising on LiveJournal for bloggers who write on everyday moral concerns). This strategy is particu-larly appropriate for projects like mine where the content is not linked to explicit blog types (e.g., weight-loss blogs or travel blogs) or easily retrieved via web-based blog search engines like Google Blog Search.

I posted a research invite (see Figure 8.2) to fifty-five Australian LiveJournal communities. Permission was sought from community mod-erators before posting the invite. If permission was given, I joined the community because posting access was restricted to community member-ship. Posting requires some basic skills in HTML coding, such as using an LJ cut (which conceals part or all of a post), creating a hyperlink,

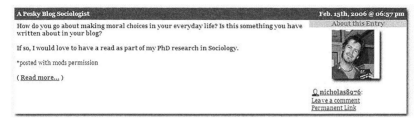

A Pesky Blog Sociologist   Feb. 15th, 2006 @ 06:57 pm

How do you go about making moral choices in your everyday life? Is this something you have   About this Entry
written about in your blog?

If so, I would love to have a read as part of my PhD research in Sociology.

*posted with mods permission

(Read more...)

Ω nicholas8976:
Leave a comment
Permanent Link

Figure 8.2   'Front' of blog invite

bolding text and uploading a user icon. Instructions for doing this were provided by the LJ help service, which made the process easy. Getting the 'blogger to come to the researcher', rather than the other way around, proved productive, generating forty-nine responses and a further eight recommendations for other possible blogs. While recommendations for sample size depend on the aims and analytical approach taken, ten blogs would be suitable for a small project (e.g., undergraduate/honours); twenty to twenty-five for a medium project (e.g., masters, professional doctorate); and forty to fifty for larger projects (e.g., PhD). For my PhD project I sampled forty-four blogs; this sample was combined with twenty-five online interviews.

(3) *Establish an online presence.* For my research, the creation of a basic research website and a LiveJournal blog was useful to establish an online presence, legitimate my identity, disseminate research materials and recruit participants. For researchers doing blog trawling or searching – where there is no interaction with bloggers – creating a website/blog may not be necessary. My weblog (http://nicholas8976.LiveJournal.com) included a brief biographical sketch of my research interests, a photo and a link to the research website. Creating a blog username was also necessary to access the premium search feature, which allowed searches by location and age. An information sheet and consent form (for bloggers being interviewed) could also be downloaded from the research website. One LiveJournaler commented in email communication with me: 'I googled you and found http://fcms.its.utas.edu.au/arts/sociol ogy/pagedetails.asp?lpersonId=3035 so you seem legit.'

(4) *Conduct blog analysis.* Blog data can be easily converted into text files for analysis or imported into computer-assisted qualitative analysis software (CAQDAS) tools like NVivo or ATLAS.ti. I gave consideration to using NVivo7 for the everyday morality study, but in the end adopted a 'manual' approach to analysis. My experience was that the fractured and unstructured nature of the blog data was unworkable with the linear and highly structured demands of the software. It seemed to do an injustice to the

contextual richness of the blog narratives, 'thinning' the data into fragmented codes (Ezzy, 2000: 118) and infringing the creative and playful dimensions of the research. However, other social researchers like Snee (2012) have successfully used CAQDAS to analyse blog narratives. Projects dealing with more sharply defined topics – for example, gap years, weight loss or depression – may be more amendable to CAQDAS due to their more focused and structured nature.

Ethical Issues in Blog Research

With the emergence of online tools like blogs come new and challenging ethical dilemmas (King, 1996; Walther, 2002; Waskul and Douglass, 1996), including questions about what conventional notions of private and public mean in online research venues (British Psychological Society, 2013; Markham and Buchanan, 2012; see also Chapter 6). For example, is authorial permission required from bloggers when using their posts as research data? Is blog material academic 'fair game' or is informed consent needed? Is a blog a public or private space? (Markham and Buchanan, 2012).

While there is no consensus among social scientists (see Chapters 6 and 9), responses to the broader question of what is private and what is public online tend to fall into one of three camps (Hutchinson, 2001). First, there are researchers who argue that archived material on the Internet is publicly available, and therefore participant consent is not necessary (Walther, 2002). This position often rests on an analogy between online forums and public space, where publicly accessible Internet content is treated like television content, a piece of art in a public gallery or letters to the editor. Second, some researchers claim that online postings, though publicly accessible, are written with an expectation of privacy and should be treated as such (Elgesem, 2002; King, 1996). Last, there are those who argue that online interaction defies clear-cut prescription as either public or private. Waskul and Douglass (1996: 131), for example, argued that cyberspace is simultaneously 'publicly-private and privately-public'. They warn online researchers of mistaking the public accessibility of online forums for the public nature of the interactions, instead emphasising the need to consider how actors themselves construe their participation in online environments.

Both the British Psychological Society ([BPS], 2013) and the Association for Internet Researchers (AoIR) (Markham and Buchanan, 2012) provide a useful set of guidelines for thinking about the significance of the private/public distinction for blog researchers. The BPS (2013: 7), one of the few professional bodies to currently provide a set of ethical guidelines for online research, suggests that where there is doubt about the public nature of online content, researchers should consider potential harm for participants caused by 'undisclosed observation', and whether informed consent is needed. But when 'there is likely no perception and/ or expectation of privacy, use of research data without gaining valid consent may be justifiable' (BPS, 2013: 7).

The AoIR ethical guidelines (Markham and Buchanan, 2012) are somewhat less prescriptive, instead advocating a case-based approach and highlighting a series of questions researchers should ask in regard to different online venues/ contexts. The AoIR guidelines provide a useful chart that addresses common questions about ethical practice for different types of data and online venues. In regards to 'personal space/blogs', the AoIR encourages researchers to consider: whether analysis, publication or availability of content beyond the confines of the venue could cause harm to participants; 'personal networks of connection sensitive'; content or the venue to be private or public; whether terms of service conflict with principles of ethical research; and whether the author is a child.

In my research, there was a strong case to adopt the 'fair game–public domain' position. The blogs I was sampling were located in the public domain, with little expectation of privacy, and with little potential for harm, so I considered that consent should be waived. Further, LiveJournal blogs are public not only in the sense of being publicly accessible, but also in how they are defined by users. LiveJournal blogs that are interpreted by bloggers as 'private' are made 'friends only'. Thus, accessible blogs may be personal, but they are not private. In saying that, I am ambivalent about this position; this is evident in my decision to protect the identity of participants by using pseudonyms.

Further, I made the decision to sample only adult bloggers (eighteen plus). Having a minimum age of eighteen for participation not only provided a convenient cut-off point for excluding a population group that might be expected to tap a different set of cultural and social dynamics related to moral construction, it was also an ethical decision. It was deemed potentially more harmful to sample blogs from minors, despite the content being public. This position is consistent with the BPS (2013) and AoIR (Markham and Buchanan, 2012) guidelines, which suggest that researchers must carefully consider potential harm caused to minors or children through Internet research.

The question of whether to preserve anonymity or credit bloggers for their work is another sticky ethical area that needs to be considered. In Australia, the Copyright Act (1968) stipulates that creators of 'works' have 'moral rights', which include right to attribution of authorship (Australian Copyright Council, 2005). There is an evident tension therefore between the research norms of protecting participants' identity (e.g., by using pseudonyms) and acknowledging blog authorship (e.g., by citing links). I adopted a position of 'moderate' disguise that privileged the protection of participants' identity over credit to the author (Bruckman, 2002). From the same position, Snee (2012: 190) suggested that citing blog links could potentially expose participants to 'the direct scrutiny of an unintended audience'. This meant that in my research, online pseudonyms (blog usernames) were changed and any potentially identifying information in blog quotations was disguised.

What Can Go Wrong with Blog Research?

There are four general areas that researchers need to be wary of when deciding to use blogs for their research. The first two areas relate to difficulties matching research aims to blog content and analysing large volumes of multimedia blog content. The second two relate to potential problems with the 'representativeness' of blog populations and how authentic or trustworthy blog accounts are, which is particularly of concern in research seeking some kind of external 'truth'. This section makes clear that these issues are not stable or unresolvable, but are rather shaped by the specific research design and aims of a particular piece of research.

Matching Blogs to Research Aims

One of the biggest challenges in conducting blog research is the sheer volume of blog data available, and the difficulties this presents for matching blog content to research aims. This posed a significant issue for the everyday morality project. During the trawling phase of data collection, I read approximately 200 blogs, which translated to an incalculable number of individual posts and comments. Of these, only eleven blogs were deemed relevant to the aims of the project. Part of the struggle to identify relevant blogs was due to my inexperience and cultural unfamiliarity with the world of blogs, but also because of the nature of the content sought. Finding blogs that reflected 'everyday moral concern' was like looking for a 'needle in a haystack'.

Identifying and Analysing Masses of Multimedia Text

Sampling blog data produces large volumes of multimedia text, which can pose challenges for researchers when it comes to data analysis. For the everyday morality project, I sampled a wide-ranging collection of moral encounters, moments, descriptions and reflections, which were collated into an electronic file. This produced a substantial amount of data – over 100,000 words and 200 pages. The blog data were combined with the text produced from twenty-five online interviews, making a total of 350,000 words. This is small compared to other blog research. For example, Snee (2012) reports a final blog word count of one million words! The mass of textual material, and in my case, the highly fragmented nature of the data, represented a challenging and daunting analytical task. I had hundreds of examples of moral decision-making and reflection – from people reflecting on the ethics of a relationship breaking up, choosing to be vegan, and being 'loyal' to friends at work, to the prospects of living a moral life as an atheist. How was I to make sense of this material and what was the story to be told? I decided to develop spheres of analysis (e.g., moral individualism; love and morality; morality and animals) and to conduct a thematic analysis within these discrete areas. These areas were developed as they were the dominant areas of moral decision-making reflected in the blogs that I sampled. This issue of data fragmentation is less of a concern when researching a more focused topic with dedicated blogs (e.g., weight-loss blogs; 'mummy' blogs; running blogs).

The multimedia and interactive nature of blog 'text' can also present challenges for data analysis. A typical blog post may comprise a text entry, images, video and audio clips, memes, hyperlinks, quiz results and advertisements. Each post also contains a comments section, where authors can comment and interact with readers. Further, blogs have a 'live' quality (Snee, 2012: 183), where content can change daily and between audiences, depending on what the blogger has decided to edit and make available to readers. The multimedia, interactive and live qualities of blogs represent analytic challenges for the blog researcher. In regards to the everyday morality project, a decision was made to focus only on written text captured on a specific date and time, and to only include interactive comments where they complemented or added to the moral position developed in the original post. There is certainly scope for researchers to take better advantage of the multimedia qualities of blogs, for example, through visual methods of analysis (Snee, 2012). However, researchers need to balance the appeal of these non-textual dimensions of blogs with pragmatic and methodological concerns about time, cost and how to best meet the aims of the project.

Homogeneity of the Blog Population

Another issue that blog researchers need to be wary of is the relatively homogenous nature of the blogging population. Research suggests that bloggers tend to be young (54% are under the age of thirty) and female (Henning, 2003; Lenhart and Fox, 2006). LiveJournal's (2009) own statistics confirm this picture, showing that more women (65%) than men (35%) blog and that most bloggers are under the age of thirty. These data are broadly consistent with my own experiences of sampling from LiveJournal, and with research by Lenhart and Fox (2006: 14), which shows that LiveJournal is the most popular blogging application among young women compared to other blogging platforms like Blogger or Xanga, which attract a slightly older population.

The concentration of young and female bloggers on LiveJournal posed a problem for the everyday morality project. The aims of the project were to capture a wider and more diverse range of moral experiences than those articulated by young women. A way around the issue of blogger homogeneity was to use LiveJournal's search engine to sample older bloggers and to manually select male bloggers (LiveJournal's advanced search engine does not allow searches by gender).

While the search engine enabled me to sample for a more diverse range of experiences, the bloggers included in the study do not in any way capture the range and diversity of the broader Australian population. The sample generated was highly homogenous and comprised predominantly white, urban, mainly tertiary educated, middle-class, and young service professionals. Non-bloggers, particularly those from less privileged social backgrounds, might articulate morality and selfhood in very different ways. Researchers thus need to consider the limitations of blogger populations when thinking about employing blog methodologies and what implications this has for achieving the aims and objectives of the research.

Online Authenticity and Verifying Background

The question of the trustworthiness of blog expression was a typical query from colleagues when presenting the everyday morality study. These concerns about the truthfulness of blog data need to be contextualised in terms of early Internet research, which emphasised online 'identity play' (Turkle, 1995) and recent 'moral panics' regarding the predatory potential of the Internet 'stranger'. Common to these accounts is the idea that the Internet gives rise to an experimental or playful online presentation of self with distinct implications for authenticity and credibility.

One response to this question of online authenticity is 'Does it really matter?' Even if bloggers do not tell the 'truth', these 'fabrications' still tell us something about the manner in which specific social and cultural ideas about morality are constructed. Here issues of 'truth' are not really at stake, as the emphasis is on how the constitutive elements of blogs work to produce 'particular effects' (Silverman, 2001: 122). The issue of deception might, however, be an important consideration for a researcher who wants to read external realities from the textual data – for example, the researcher seeking authentic accounts of weight loss or becoming a parent.

A further consideration in relation to online authenticity is issues related to verifying the identity of bloggers (Snee, 2013). Most blog authors explicitly state their age and gender. This information can usually be found on the profile homepage or can be found through reading the first couple of posts. However, there is no guarantee that this background information is truthful or accurate. This may pose problems for researchers who are looking to make conclusions, for example, about the social position of participants in relation to the chosen area of study. The validity of the 'Does it matter?' question depends then on whether a researcher is looking at how blogs work to produce particular effects, or whether they are looking at how blogs correspond with an 'offline' reality.

One strategy to alleviate concerns around authenticity is to supplement blog data with interviews. This approach was adopted in the everyday morality study. As the blogs were limited to whatever the author had chosen to record, interviews provided a means to seek clarification, to explore absences and implicit meanings, and to contextualise online representations in terms of articulations of offline experience. For these reasons, the interview material enabled a deeper and more nuanced account of how the bloggers understood and practised their everyday moral lives.

What Methods of Analysis Suit Blog Data?

While most blog analysis is focused on text, some researchers have investigated the visual aspects. For example, Scheidt and Wright (2004) explored visual trends in blogs, and Badger (2004) investigated how images and illustration shape the construction and reception of blogs. The visual aspects of blogs – photos, videos, images – provide researchers with a wider 'bandwidth' in which to capture identity and experience outside of text. In my experience, visual content also works to connect the researcher to the blogger. However, researchers need to consider whether non-textual elements such as image, video and music are integral to the goals of the project, and how these dimensions are to be best incorporated into the analysis. As Snee (2012: 183) writes, there is 'a need to balance the potential of blog data and what is methodologically interesting with pragmatic concerns'. It is easy to get excited about the visual elements of blogs but, in practice, analysing non-textual content can be difficult and time-consuming.

In terms of analysing text, conventional qualitative methods of text analysis like narrative analysis, discourse analysis, qualitative content analysis and thematic analysis are all suitable for analysing blog data. The focus of narrative inquiry, for example, is how participants use stories to interpret their biographical experience, create meaning and construct identity (Riessman, 1993). The chronological sequencing of biographical experience that defines blogging – each blog post adds to a sequential account of self and experience – makes blogging practices amenable to different modes of narrative inquiry. An example of the application of narrative analysis to blogs is Tussyadiah and Fesenmaier (2008: 303) who analysed blog travel stories according to story characterisation (e.g., hero or heroine), temporal dimension (morning, afternoon and evening), relational organisation (why and how of character action) and space categorisation (spatial plotting of attractions and places).

I contemplated using narrative analysis in my research, but the segmented nature of the blogs did not seem to lend itself to a form of analysis premised on analysing how the parts of a biographical past are 'storied' into a meaningful and coherent whole (Riessman, 1993). The blogs sampled exemplified narratives of self, but they tended to develop as a 'database narrative' (Lopez, 2009: 738), where posted fragments of self are disconnected from each other. Narrative analysis may prove more worthwhile for particular blog types organised around specific phenomenon or experience (e.g., travel blogs, weight-loss blogs etc.), where posts are less sequentially and thematically fractured.

Other blog researchers have employed pattern-based approaches such as qualitative content analysis and thematic analysis. Qualitative content analysis is popular in the qualitative analysis of travel blogs, used to decipher the subjective meanings bloggers attach to their travel experiences and how these might differ from official accounts (see Enoch and Grossman, 2010). Snee's (2013) blog research on gap years, and my own everyday morality project, are examples of using thematic analysis (which can be very similar to qualitative content analysis) to identify general themes and concepts in blog data. Largely inductive in nature, my use of thematic analysis provided room for theory to be built according to new patterns and themes that were developed from the data themselves (Liamputtong and Ezzy, 2005), and enabled me to draw a picture of the ways in which everyday morality is formulated and practised in the blogosphere.

Conclusion

Blogs are an exciting and innovative research method, offering practical and methodological benefits for developing qualitative insights into a range of experiences, processes and practices. With an awareness of the problems that blog research can present, and with a clear strategy to navigate them, blogs offer considerable potential for researchers interested in accessing unmediated first-person accounts of experience. At the same time, blog researchers can benefit from the general practical advantages of online research, including cost and time savings, and the existence of, and extended access to, instantaneous text. In sum, blogs provide a powerful way to do 'bottom-up' research, generating naturalistic data that is 'uncontaminated' or unprovoked by a researcher.

Have a Go ...

(1) Develop a research question suitable for blog research.
(2) Using the free basic search features of a blog platform, (e.g., LiveJournal) or a search engine which allows you to search by website type (i.e., blogs), perform a search on a relevant research topic.

Box 8.2 Personal reflections on blog research

As a sociologist, using blogs for the everyday morality study felt at times like a poisoned chalice. When I started my PhD, I was one of the first researchers in sociology to use blogs in social research. Blogs offered the promise of accessing unprompted moral narratives that are difficult to access through traditional methods, and the convenience of instantaneous text and access to bloggers geographically removed from me. However, blogs presented key challenges at both data collection and data analysis stages. Many of these problems were related to unfamiliarity with the research environment. Entering the blogosphere as a blog 'newbie' was like gazing into a dark and tangled labyrinth. The endless crisscrossing hyper tracks and trails of the blogosphere were overwhelming and disorientating. Blogs offered sociologically rich insights into the nature of contemporary self-identity and experience, but it was frustrating matching relevant blogs to the research aims. With little research precedent to steer research design, I often felt – and *was* – making it up as I was going along. A key breakthrough was when I switched to soliciting bloggers through advertisements in LiveJournal communities. This solved the 'digital needle in the haystack' issue, where I spent long periods of time trawling and searching in the vain hope of finding relevant posts.

> My sense is that many of the difficulties I encountered finding blogs were related to my research aims, rather than blog research per se. As discussed in this chapter, blog researchers focused on a specific type of blog/experience (e.g., travel blogs, weight-loss blogs, 'mummy' blogs etc.) should not have too many difficulties in finding relevant research content. However, researchers will still need to contend with issues related to the volume of blog data, as well as how to analyse multimedia/interactive blog text and negotiate ethical issues around consent, anonymity and authorship. The novelty of blog methods also means that the medium can take precedence when sharing research findings, and that researchers need to be prepared to justify their chosen method (perhaps more so than if an established method had been used!).
>
> Blog methodologies may play a modest role in responding to claims of a 'coming crisis of empirical sociology' (Savage and Burrows, 2007). This crisis refers to social scientists losing their monopoly on empirical research as new forms of data embedded in multiple information technologies, and the routine transactional data of organisations (e.g., Facebook, telecommunications data, credit cards, loyalty card data, online transactions etc.), surpass the empirical capacities and resources of researchers. Embracing new 'confessional' technologies like blogs is part of 'rethinking the repertoires of empirical sociology' (Savage and Burrows, 2007: 895) and enabling research into the 'liquid' (Bauman, 2000) and fluid nature of contemporary selves, identities and relationships.

(3) Sample 1–2 relevant blog posts, from two to three different bloggers.
(4) Identify three main analytic insights from the data in relation to your research question.

Further Resources: Online

The Association of Internet Researchers (AoIR) has a useful website where researchers can subscribe to a free, open-access mailing list, download papers from the association's annual conference, and access the AoIR Guide on Ethical Online Research: http://aoir.org

The Blog Analysis Toolkit is the University of Pittsburgh's Qualitative Data Analysis Program – a free online system for researchers to capture, archive and share blog posts: www.ibridgenetwork.org/university-of-pittsburgh/blog-analysis-toolkit

The web resource ReStore provides online training resources for researchers. The section 'resources for learners' (www.restore.ac.uk/orm/learnerresources/) is particularly valuable, providing overviews of key journals and texts in the field of online research, a glossary, links, FAQs and bibliographies on online research methods, including blogs (see Bibliography section 'online methodological futures': www.restore.ac.uk/orm/learnerresources/bibliography.htm): Madge, C., O'Connor, H. and Shaw, R. (2006). *Exploring online research methods in a virtual training environment*: www.restore.ac.uk/orm/

Further Resources: Readings

For an overview of the strengths and weaknesses of using blogs in social scientific research, particularly as a strategy to access accounts of everyday life, see Hookway, N. (2008). 'Entering the blogosphere': Some strategies for using blogs in social research. *Qualitative Research*, *8*(1), 91–103.

For an excellent overview of the opportunities and challenges blogs offer researchers in the context of a sociological study on young people's gap year narratives, see Snee, H. (2012). Youth research in Web 2.0: A case study in blog analysis. In S. Heath and C. Walker (eds.), *Innovations in youth research* (pp. 178–194). Basingstoke, UK: Palgrave.

The following two articles are from my everyday moralities project, and provide insight into how blog data can be used and presented within a qualitative research project: Hookway, N. (2014). Tasting the ethical: Vegetarianism as modern re-enchantment. *M/C: Journal of Media and Culture*, *17*(1). Retrieved from: http://journal.media-culture.org.au/index.php/mcjournal/article/view/759.

Hookway, N. (2015). Living authentic: 'Being true to yourself' as a contemporary moral ideal. *M/C: Journal of Media and Culture*, *18*(1). Retrieved from: http://journal.media-culture.org.au/index.php/mcjournal/article/viewArticle/759.

For an overview of how researchers might use blogs as a reflexive writing tool in the research process, see Wakeford, N. and Cohen, K. (2005). Fieldnotes in public: Using blogs for research. In N. Fielding, R. M. Lee and G. Blank (eds.), *The SAGE handbook of online research methods* (pp. 307–326). London: Sage Publications. (NB The chapter does not consider blogs as a source of data, but does offer an accessible introduction to blogs, relevant literatures and their social and cultural context.)

References

Atkinson, P. and Silverman, D. (1997). Kundera's immortality: The interview society and the invention of the self. *Qualitative Inquiry*, *3*(3), 304–325.

Australian Copyright Act (1968). SECT 195AR. Retrieved from: www.austlii.edu.au/au/legis/cth/consol_act/ca1968133/s195ar.html

Australian Copyright Council (2005). Information sheet: Moral rights. Retrieved from: www.copyright.org.au/pdf/acc/infosheets/G043.pdf

Badger, M. (2004). Visual blogs. In L. J. Gurak, S. Antonijevic, L. Johnson, C. Ratliff and J. Reyman (eds.), *Into the blogosphere: Rhetoric, community, and culture of weblogs*.

Bakker, J. K. and Paris, J. (2013). Bereavement and religion online: Stillbirth, neonatal loss and parental religiosity. *Journal for the Scientific Study of Religion, 52*(4), 657–674.

Bauman, Z. (2000). *Liquid modernity.* Cambridge: Polity Press.

Beer, D. and Burrows, R. (2007). Sociology and, of and in Web 2.0: Some initial considerations. *Sociological Research Online, 12*(5). Retrieved from: www.socresonline.org.uk/12/5/17.html

Blood, R. (2002a). Weblogs: A history and perspective. In J. Rodzvilla (ed.), *We've got blog: How weblogs are changing our culture* (pp. 7–16). Cambridge, MA: Perseus Publishing.

(2002b). Introduction. In J. Rodzvilla (ed.), *We've got blog: How weblogs are changing our culture* (pp. ix–xiii). Cambridge, MA: Perseus Publishing.

British Psychological Society (2013). *Ethics guidelines for internet-mediated research.* Leicester, UK: British Psychological Society.

Bruckman, A. (2002). Studying the amateur artist: A perspective on disguising data collected in human subjects research on the Internet. *Ethics and Information Technology, 4*(3), 217–231.

Clarke, J. and van Amerom, G. (2008). A comparison of blogs by depressed men and women. *Issues in Mental Health Nursing, 29*(3), 243–264.

Dart, J. J. (2009). Blogging the 2006 FIFA World Cup finals. *Sociology of Sport Journal, 26*(1), 107–126.

Elgesem, D. (2002). What is special about the ethical issues in online research? *Ethics and Information Technology, 4*(3), 95–203.

Elliot, H. (1997). The use of diaries in sociological research on health experience. *Sociological Research Online, 2*(2). Retrieved from: www.socresonline.org.yk/socresonline/2/2/7.html

Enoch, Y. and Grossman, R. (2010). Blogs of Israeli and Danish backpackers to India. *Annals of Tourism Research, 37*(2), 520–536.

Ezzy, D. (2000). *Qualitative research methods: A health focus.* Melbourne: Oxford University Press.

Fielding, N., Lee, R. M. and Blank, G. (2008). *The SAGE handbook of online research methods.* London: Sage Publications.

Geertz, C. (1973). *The interpretation of cultures.* New York: Basic Books.

Goffman, E. (1959). *The presentation of self in everyday life.* Harmondsworth: Penguin.

Henning, J. (2003). The blogging iceberg: Of 4.12 million hosted weblogs, most little seen, quickly abandoned. *Perseus Development Corp.*

Hessler, R. M., Downing, J., Beltz, C., Pelliccio, A., Powell, M. and Vale, W. (2003). Qualitative research on adolescent risk using e-mail: A methodological assessment. *Qualitative Sociology, 26*(1), 111–124.

Hodkinson, P. (2007). Interactive online journals and individualization. *New Media Society, 9*(4), 625–650.

Hookway, N. (2008). 'Entering the blogosphere': Some strategies for using blogs in social research, *Qualitative Research, 8*(1), 91–103.

(2014). Tasting the ethical: Vegetarianism as modern re-enchantment. *M/C: Journal of Media and Culture, 17*(1). Retrieved from: http://journal.media-culture.org.au/index.php/mcjournal/article/view/759

(2015). Living authentic: 'Being true to yourself' as a contemporary moral ideal. *M/C: Journal of Media and Culture*, *18*(1). Retrieved from: http://journal.media-culture.org.au/index.php/mcjournal/article/viewArticle/759

Hutchinson, R. (2001). Dangerous liaisons? Ethical considerations in conducting online sociological research. In C. Browne, K. Edwards, V. Watson and R. van Krieken (eds.), *TASA 2001 Conference Proceedings, The Australian Sociological Association*.

King, S. (1996). Researching Internet communities: Proposed ethical guidelines for the reporting of results. *The Information Society*, *12*(2), 119–127.

Leggatt-Cook, C. and Chamberlain, K. (2012). Blogging for weight loss: Personal accountability, writing selves and the weight-loss blogosphere. *Sociology of Health & Illness*, *34*(7), 963–977.

Lenhart, A. and Fox, S. (2006). Bloggers: A portrait of the Internet's new storytellers. *Pew Internet and American Life Project*.

Liamputtong, P. and Ezzy, D. (2005). *Qualitative research methods*. Melbourne: Oxford University Press.

Lopez, L. K. (2009). The radical act of 'mommy blogging': Redefining motherhood through the blogosphere. *New Media & Society*, *11*(5), 729–747.

Markham, A. and Buchanan, E. (2012). *Ethical decision-making and Internet research: Recommendations from the AoIR Ethical Working Committee (Version 2.0)*. Chicago: Association of Internet Researchers. Retrieved from: http://aoir.org/reports/ethics2.pdf

Marwick, A. (2008). LiveJournal users: Passionate, prolific, and private. *LiveJournal research report*.

Phillips, D. and Harding, S. (1985). The structure of moral values. In M. Abrams, D. Gerard and N. Timms (eds.), *Values and social change in Britain* (pp. 93–108). London: Macmillan.

Plummer, K. (2001). *Documents of life*. London: Allen and Unwin.

Riessman, C. K. (1993). *Narrative analysis*. Newbury Park, CA: Sage Publications.

Sanford, A. (2010). 'I can air my feelings instead of eating them': Blogging as social support for the morbidly obese. *Communication Studies*, *61*(5), 567–584.

Savage, M. and Burrows, R. (2007). The coming crisis of empirical sociology. *Sociology*, *41*(5), 885–900.

Scheidt, L. and Wright, E. (2004). Common visual design elements of weblogs. In L. J. Gurak, S. Antonijevic, L. Johnson, C. Ratliff and J. Reyman (eds.), *Into the blogosphere: Rhetoric, community, and culture of weblogs*.

Serfaty, V. (2004). Online diaries: Towards a structural approach. *Journal of American Studies*, *38*(3), 457–471.

Sharman, A. (2014). Mapping the climate sceptical blogosphere. *Global Environmental Change*, *26*, 159–170.

Silverman, D. (2001). *Interpreting qualitative data: Methods for analysing talk, text, and interaction*. London: Sage Publications.

Snee, H. (2012). Youth research in Web 2.0: A case study in blog analysis. In S. Heath and C. Walker (eds.), *Innovations in youth research* (pp. 178–194). Basingstoke, UK: Palgrave.

(2013). Doing something 'worthwhile': Intersubjectivity and morality in gap year narratives. *The Sociological Review*, *62*(4), 843–861.

Thomas, W. I. and Znaniecki, F. (1958[1918]). *The polish peasant in Europe and America*. New York: Dover Publications.

Toms, E. G. and Duff, W. (2002). 'I spent 1½ hours sifting through one large box . . .': Diaries as information behaviour of the archives user: Lessons learned. *Journal of the American Society for Information Science and Technology, 53*(4), 1232–1238.

Turkle, S. (1995). *Life on the screen: Identity in the age of the Internet.* New York: Simon and Schuster.

Turnbull, G. (2002). The state of the blog part two: Blogger present. In J. Rodzvilla (ed.), *We've got blog: How weblogs are changing our culture* (pp. 81–85). Cambridge, MA: Perseus Publishing.

Tussyadiah, I. P. and Fesenmaier, D. R. (2008). Marketing place through first-person stories – an analysis of Pennsylvania Roadtripper blog. *Journal of Travel & Tourism Marketing, 25*(3), 299–311.

Verbrugge, L. M. (1980). Health diaries. *Medical Care, 18*(1), 73–95.

Walther, J. B. (2002). Research ethics in Internet-enabled research: Human subjects issues and methodological myopia. *Ethics and Information Technology, 4*(3), 205–216.

Waskul, D. and Douglas, M. (1996). Considering the electronic participant: Some polemical observations on the ethics of on-line research. *The Information Society, 12*(2), 129–139.

9   Online Discussion Forums

A Rich and Vibrant Source of Data

David Giles

Overview

Wherever you look on the Internet, you find discussion! Vast regions of cyber-space are devoted to the exchange of comments on anything and everything: from extreme topics such as suicide and alien abduction, to more mundane hobbies and interests, responses to requests for information or shared experiences, or critical commentaries in response to blogs, videos or news stories. Most of these exchanges are tightly organised into networks of threads and topics, or themes, subthemes and overarching themes, grouped within a discrete section of a website typically referred to as a *discussion forum*. In this chapter, I discuss and outline the use of discussion forums as data in qualitative research – a very rich, but very specific, form of data – and reflect on my experience of using these data (see Box 9.4). Throughout, I draw on my own and others' research to illustrate the use and potential of forum data – including one study of an Asperger online community, which is introduced in Box 9.1.

Introduction to Discussion Forums

The modern-day discussion forum began life during the late 1970s on bulletin boards, which were interactive systems where users could post messages and develop online discussions on specific topics. Bulletin boards evolved into electronic mailing lists and newsgroups, where contributions to discussions were posted to all the members of the group, any of whom could respond, thus building up the now-familiar 'threads' of interaction that we see on more contemporary forums. While some of these groups are still in existence, they now constitute a minority in the online environment. What dominates instead are (large) discussion forums devoted to specific topics, which are hosted by relevant websites (the term 'message board' is also used on some sites, though with decreasing regularity).

Box 9.1 The online Asperger community reacts to being reclassified in the DSM5

Every decade or two, the American Psychiatric Association updates its *Diagnostic and Statistical Manual* (DSM) of psychiatric disorders. This is the 'bible' for many psychiatrists and other mental health professionals, in that it legitimates what can and cannot be diagnosed: what *counts* as a psychiatric disorder. In 2013, the 5th edition, the *DSM5*, sparked controversy in the very lively online community around Asperger's syndrome, when they reclassified Asperger's disorder as autism spectrum disorder. Given the very complex identity issues around being diagnosed with these different labels (can you still refer to yourself as an 'aspie', for example?), I was interested to understand what the online community had to say on the matter. I researched this by visiting a number of the most popular Asperger forums, and searching for discussion threads whose title referred to the DSM. This produced nineteen threads of conversation on the topic. By analysing the rhetorical positions each community member adopted in their contributions to the discussion, I drew up a list of six categories that represented the different arguments. Broadly, a third of the posts were in favour of the DSM5 reclassification, another third were strongly critical and a further third undecided. Much more interesting, however, were some of the heated exchanges that went on within the threads themselves (see Giles, 2014).

Discussion forums vary in terms of whether they are publicly visible, visible to members only or some combination, such as publicly visible, but with contributions only possible by members. This is important, since there are ethical implications for accessing and reproducing (particularly for research purposes) material on forums where access is restricted in some way (see 'ethics' section). Forums also vary in the extent to which they are moderated. Some are heavily policed by the owners of the parent website, even to the extent of censoring specific taboo words and terms (see Stommel and Koole, 2010, for an example in the online eating disorders community). Others are much more laissez-faire. For this reason, it helps to be informed about the broad culture of the community before conducting any research, and to remain sensitive to the context in which data are or were produced.

How are forums put together? There is no single model, so bear in mind that the following terms are rather loose. A *forum* refers to a website or section of a more general website, where people discuss things related to a particular topic. A forum can be broken down into any number of *subforums*, each of which deals with a specific topic. A *thread* refers to a delimited (i.e., with a clear beginning and end) discussion within a (sub)forum. And finally, a *post* refers to an individual comment within a thread.

What does this look like in practice? Let's take the 'Fan Forums' from official website of singer Taylor Swift (http://taylorswift.com) as an example of a discussion forum – I encourage you to have a look at the site (http://taylorswift .com/forum) as you're reading this chapter, if you can (NB: the live nature of the Internet means that there's a chance the site won't look identical to how it did at the time of writing). A typical discussion forum will be accessed by a menu link from the homepage of the website. Swift's forum is slightly unusual, in that it is not explicitly referenced on the homepage – you need to go via the menu item 'Taylor Connect' (this *was* the case at the time of writing; one slightly irritating, though obviously exciting, feature of researching online communication is that you can guarantee that some details accurate 'at the time of writing' will have changed before something appears in print!). The 'Fan Forums' page then provides links to twenty-one subforums, each dedicated to a specific topic – such as discussion about her latest album, tour, or just 'all things Taylor'. The total number of posts for each forum is recorded, along with the most recent post: most of the forums on the Taylor Swift site were posted to within hours of my visit to the page – a sign of vitality in any discussion forum.

The forum title suggests the – at least *intended* – focus of discussion. If you go deeper into the forum site, you start to see list of threads. Take, for instance, the forum '*1989 Discussions*': the title indicates the content is intended to relate to Taylor Swift's most recent album, although the threads make it clear that fans are using it to discuss tour details, and intriguingly, '*conversations with fake fans*'. Figure 9.1 reproduces the first three posts under '*conversations with fake fans*' (http://taylorswift.com/forum/1989_discussions/3130563) to illustrate some key aspects of forums. The first post, known as the opening post (OP), appears at the top of the page. Here, it relates a time-honoured complaint of fans everywhere: that other, less authentic, fans are muscling in on their territory. However, subsequent posts can engage in quite different ways. Here, the initial ones seem to be critical of the original author, alluding to her tone and likely age, but later ones develop the theme more in line with the OP. The thread eventually runs to twenty-seven posts ('replies'). There is much variation in the length of discussion threads: some have no replies to the OP; others have over 100 posts.

This variability in thread length is typical of discussion forums. Although most of the threads on taylorswift.com seem to have generated some replies, other forums may have hundreds of OPs that sit there, unresponded-to, until the moderator takes pity on them and terminates their brief existence. Others attract a few early responses and then die off, either because the OP asks a simple question, and an early response satisfies, or because the initial response(s) fails to stimulate sufficient interest for anyone to prolong the conversation. However, in other cases, threads are allowed to sit on a forum for months or

---

Opening Post (from fan xcswift)
CONVERSATIONS WITH FAKE FANS.
Mon, May 11, 2015 at 7:15 PM
I know more than 15 people who only like Taylor because of 1989.
I asked one girl if if I had no tickets to the tour and she did and had an extra, who would she give it to?
Her response? Probably skylar because she has a poster and the 1989 album and she's the biggest taylor swift fangirl I know. She knows more than you.
I asked, does she know where she lives?
her response: Yeah. New York.
Me: Anywhere else?
Her: No where else. Duh. You're not the biggest swiftie I know.

She should bring me. LUCKILY I HAVE LOWER LEVEL TICKETS. HAH TO HER.
~The ligh reflects the chain on your neck~

Reply 1 (from fan MiddleOfstartingOver)
RE: CONVERSATIONS WITH FAKE FANS.
Mon May 11, 2015 AT 8:19 PM
Well I wouldn't take someone who seemed to be insulting me
I hate Diney

Reply 2 (from fan nooneknows)
RE: CONVERSATIONS WITH FAKE FANS.
MON, MAY 11, 2015 AT 10:03 PM
How old are these people?
….[continues with graphics, quotes and links to fan's various social media]

Figure 9.1   Reproduction of text of first three posts in thread 'Conversations with Fake Fans' (from http://taylorswift.com/forum/1989_discussions/3130563)

even years, and generate hundreds of posts, sometimes drying up for months, and then being reactivated. How might this happen? The example of a different type of website, www.badmintoncentral.com, a community for badminton players worldwide to promote tournaments and discuss the finer points of the sport, offers some insight again, look at it as you read.

'Discussion Forums' show up on the homepage menu of badmintoncentral .com, as a set of drop-down topics ranging from 'tournaments' to 'rules and techniques' (or it can be accessed via www.badmintoncentral.com/forums/ index.php). The site organisation is broadly similar to the Taylor Swift forum, although there are considerably more subforums, and at first sight, it appears to be more active – with far more posts – than at taylorswift.com. If we select the option 'equipment' and then 'strings' from the drop-down menu, we find over *100 pages* of threads on the topic of badminton string. Clicking on the top thread (at the time of writing; '*Let's together answer: what is the*

ideal tension?'; see www.badmintoncentral.com/forums/index.php?threads/
lets-together-answer-what-is-the-ideal-tension.12569/) reveals this to be a
matter of deep history: the OP dates from 2003; the posts continue for
twenty-six pages, and the discussion is still topical with ongoing recent
posting. Clearly, there is still broad disagreement on the subject of badminton string tension! A final point to note about forum structure is that this is
a thread the site moderators have deemed a '*sticky*'. *Stickies* have priority on
a (sub)forum, and appear *at the top* of the list of threads. It is useful to be
aware of such practices, because they tell us about the values and priorities of
the community, which topics are deemed important, and why they are prized
over other topics.

What Do Discussion Forums Offer the Qualitative Researcher?

A fairly recent book on 'netnography' (Kozinets, 2010) is scathingly dismissive of discussion forums, referring to them as 'geeking communities', 'offering their member [*sic*] and readers deeply detailed information about a
particular set of activities, but not deeply engaging them most of them in
meaningful social relationships' (2010: 36). I disagree. Discussion forums
can, I believe, offer a lot to qualitative researchers, provided there is a good
fit with research question, sample selection and analytic approach, and depending on how you theorise them as data. They give access, in a fairly 'straightforward' way, to people's views and experiences around a topic of interest,
without a researcher asking about it. As a discursive psychologist, I find they
offer exciting examples of communities interacting, exhibiting all the complex
negotiations between individuals and groups that social psychologists have
been desperately trying to recreate in the laboratory for decades. They also
offer researchers a wonderful site for exploring the articulation of *identity* and
group membership. For instance, we can see how *identities* are 'worked up' in
posts: the author of the OP in Figure 9.1 refers to herself as a 'swiftie' –
presumably a recognisable label for Taylor Swift fans; age-based identity is
also made relevant in reply 2. This might seem rather arcane, but for some
communities, group membership is a very *important* matter – both for the
cohesion of the community and for the well-being of individual members.
Indeed, within the Aspergers communities I discussed in Box 9.1, there was
a lot of tension around the identity of 'aspie' (person with Asperger syndrome/
disorder). Some members felt that the term 'aspie' should include anyone on
the autism spectrum, even if self-identifying as 'low functioning': differentiat-
ing between labels was thought to be elitist. Others found such a broad identity

unhelpful and misrepresentative. Charting their debates and arguments gives the researcher access to a range of things: valuable insight into the function of online communities; the huge importance of group identity in mental health; as well as the range and variation in identities – or experiences or perspectives – expressed within the community.

What Research Questions Suit Discussion Forum Data?

Researchers using discussion forums for qualitative research can ask all sorts of questions, from trying to understand the views and perspectives of individuals, through to an interrogation of ways that language interaction is structured, or achieves certain functions! The latter is a more micro, discursive take on the data, and focuses on the nature of discussion forum data themselves, rather than treating the language data as evidence of something else. I offer four illustrations of questions we can answer with forum data. The first illustrates one way we can read forum data as evidence of the opinions of the users . . . I focus on what people think; it could similarly be used to understand what people *do*, or to access shared collective (or contested) understandings of a topic. The other three illustrate the sorts of questions we can ask if we treat forum data more discursively.

More 'Straightforward' Types of Research Questions: Focused on Content

If you are interested in the way a specific social group really *thinks about* a topic – their expressed views, experiences etc. – then a publicly accessible source of naturally existing dialogue, like a forum, seems to offer a good place to gain access to this. Indeed, it gives 'fly-on-the-wall' access to data not impacted on by the researcher – we haven't asked people their opinions in a focus group, for instance! Threads of discussion on the relevant topic can give you access to the diversity of views expressed by members of certain online communities, and the kinds of discussions that take place. Take care, though, not to over-interpret or over-estimate what discussion forum data represent: a *'pro-ana'* forum, for instance, is a community of 'like-minded' individuals who advocate an anti-recovery perspective on eating disorders. Therefore, the discussion forum will capture the views of this group, but cannot capture the views of 'people with anorexia' in any clear way. There are limits as to how far you can extend what you have sampled from a forum to the whole of that population, online and offline.

You can also explore the reported experiences of people around a particular topic, as discussed on a forum. For instance, a forum devoted to *'eating disorder' recovery* might contain discussion around the practices members report engaging in to develop better relationships with food and eating practices. But again, you need to take care around what you think data mean – any mapping of forum data to assumptions about real-life behaviour needs to done with caution, and with a sound theoretical framework.

More Discursive Questions: Interrogating the Workings of Forums Themselves

Researchers concerned with how much forum data can map onto real-life practices or meanings have often turned their focus to the nature of forums themselves, and a more discursive orientation in their research question(s). Through questions like 'How do forum discussions get going?', 'How do communities use forums to promote group norms and values?' and 'How do members manage conflict?' the research focus is firmly focused inward, on the nature of forums themselves – which is important as social life increasingly gets done online. I now provide illustrations of research addressing these questions.

How Do Discussions Get Going?

The OP in a discussion thread is of particular interest to researchers, because it does a substantial amount of work in shaping subsequent discussion (Horne and Wiggins, 2009), and hence the OP can potentially 'give life to' or 'kill off' a thread. Does it matter whether a thread is 'successful' or not? On a general interest forum, probably not! However, organisations like healthcare providers and local government increasingly use discussion forums as effective ways of communicating with users of their services, and it is important for them to be able to maximise their potential.

Researchers have identified certain *formats* to OPs. Horne and Wiggins' (2009) study of threads on a suicide forum classified the OPs according to their format: over half provided some kind of personal narrative; some contained an immediate threat of suicide, and a small number made an explicit request for shared experience. Vayreda and Antaki (2009), studying a bipolar disorder forum, identified a more common theme to OPs on that forum: members disclosed their diagnosis, described their situation and ended with a general request for help. They found also that most first responses provided the same information, along with some advice (which was not always welcomed by the

---

> **Box 9.2** Opening post-thread . . . and first reply
>
> 1 Hello . . . I just signed up to this site. I was wondering . . . is rage a normal effect of
> 2 depression? I've always had a quick temper, but it seems multiplied with
> 3 depression.
> 4 The tiniest little thing will suddenly set me off, like dropping something, or the
> 5 store being out of an item, or pushing the wrong button on the remote.
> 6 Plus, when one thing happens, I'll notice tons more throughout the day, and
> 7 they'll build up in my head until I could just cry with frustration, and end up
> 8 slamming doors & cursing a lot. Is this just me?
>
> 1 It's hard to say what's normal. I've always been pretty pissed off in general. I
> 2 think it just means you're paying attention in a f***ed up world.
>
> Source: Giles and Newbold (2013).

original poster). A different kind of pattern can be observed in Box 9.2, which contains the OP of a thread entitled '*Is rage normal?*' from one of my studies looking at a depression-related forum (Giles and Newbold, 2013). In that study, the first response consisted of a rather tangential, and not particularly welcoming, direct reply (see Box 9.2). It was not until after the third response, a more sympathetic message along with much self-disclosure, that the original poster returned to the thread in order to continue the discussion.

Although the *style* of the OP itself is important for shaping discussion, the difference between success and failure of a thread may (also) have something to do with the online community itself, and the appropriateness of the topic posted about. In the example in Box 9.2, it seems as though the original poster required just the right kind of response from someone to keep the thread going. In responses to OPs posted by 'newbies' to established communities, much of the work involves the community deciding what kind of person they are, and whether they are worth engaging in dialogue with, much like any social group introduced to a new individual. This highlights the social operation of 'the group'.

How Do Communities Use Forums to Promote Group Norms and Values?

One of the most fascinating features of forums is their use by communities as a way of establishing, and reinforcing, the normative values of the group. This is vitally important if the group is to be successful and supportive, especially where members perceive a threat to the group's cohesion or even its existence (Giles, 2006). As with the question of what makes a thread successful, understanding

---

Box 9.3 An example of identity contestation from the pro-ana site

1 there is deffy one person on this site, who you can just tell has NOT got an
2 ED (eating disorder). I know, you cant tell over the web, but you can by her
3 comments & herstupid posts on the subjects etc. A number of people on my
4 msn who visit
5 this site have also spoken about her on numours [*sic*] occasions, so I know
6 for a fact, I am not the only one who has noticed this . . .

Source: Giles (2006).

---

such concerns, and their resolution or prevention, may be crucial to the survival of a community initiative in, for example, healthcare or local government.

The 'pro-ana' community provides a nice example (see Giles, 2006) to explore how forum members maintain a degree of group cohesion through establishing clear norms and values. Because so many people were, and are, hostile to pro-ana as a concept, it is essential for this forum that community members are united in their beliefs and values. What we see on the site is pro-ana discussion forum members 'policing' their boundaries – identifying people who don't belong there, either because they are overly critical ('haters', 'trolls'), or because they fail to meet essential criteria for group membership (e.g., 'wannabes'). The fairly typical post in Box 9.3 highlights the way member identity is scrutinised and challenged.

Fan communities are another type of forum, particularly concerned with establishing group norms. In another study, I explored the dynamic tensions among the online fan community for the singer Morrissey (Giles, 2013). Hundreds of fans were 'jumping ship' from the long-established Morrissey-solo.com site, because of what was perceived as an over-critical tone towards Morrissey's most recent recordings and various controversial statements he had made in the press at the time, including a damning rejection of Morrissey-Solo itself. Supporters of the Morrissey-Solo site defended the owner and his policy of allowing unrestrained dialogue: some even claimed that a 'true' fan of Morrissey should be disappointed by the dip in quality of his recent work. Meanwhile, a new website had appeared, All You Need Is Morrissey, which imposed much tighter restrictions on the kinds of comments that were tolerated, in order to create a more genial atmosphere.

Norms are important to fan communities, because fans' identities are bound up with those of the fan object itself, and with what it means to be a fan of that object. In Bennett's (2011) study of the online community for US rock group REM, she cited the band members themselves describing their fans as 'intelligent' and sharing liberal and tolerant views. But when the online forum introduced explicit strategies for reinforcing these norms (e.g., a rating system for posts), they were strongly resisted by members. Explicit strategies for enforcing normative behaviour, it was argued, went against the liberal ethos of the community.

How Do Members Manage Conflict?

Online discussion is much more open and uninhibited than most of the discussions that take place offline, where people's fragile formal and informal relationships can only bear so much strain. Protected by physical distance and, in some cases, anonymity, online commenters seem unconcerned about hurting the feelings of other users and shoot straight from the hip (Kayany, 1998). Because they are, first and foremost, communities, forums do not suffer from quite the same level of outright abuse that is found on social networking sites, such as Twitter, or from open comment streams found on sites like YouTube and online newspapers. However, even in well-established and orderly communities, stinging arguments sometimes take place, which provide rich material for the analyst, particularly someone wishing to explore the strategies used to win an argument, or to defend an established position.

The business of online community conflict has been examined in some depth by Weber (2011), who described the '*insider's fight*' that can take place during a discussion thread. Weber identified three criteria for distinguishing an '*insider's fight*': (1) the two 'combatants' are clearly familiar with each other within the community (and may have clashed before); (2) they use emoticons to demonstrate playfulness; and (3) they are polite towards other members within the same thread. The most salient characteristic of such 'fights' is that they do not disrupt (too much) the interactional business of the thread – do not allow it to drift too far off topic – and are not regarded as disruptive to the purpose of the thread by other users.

Examining disputes in online communities can reveal much about the social organisation of the community. Even the most heated disputes can build cohesion, as they seemed to in Weber's (2011) study – although one of the things a researcher might want to explore here is the practice of *bullying*. In the Asperger community I researched (see Box 9.1), a tussle between two particularly opinionated and long-established community members descended into personal insults by one member, who was trying to steer forum opinion *against* his rival. Part of this process involved accusing the other of bullying – although that term could just as easily have been applied to his own behaviour! Indeed, the rival was effectively silenced, leaving the thread after the last attack and not returning. The study of conflict on forums show that ostracising critical or deviant members can, again, be another way of obtaining group cohesion and establishing reinforcing norms. Forum moderators have a role here, being able to step in and intervene if they think a member is being unfairly treated (this didn't happen in the Asperger case).

As I have illustrated here, the research questions that can be addressed using forum data range from the broad and/or topical, often focused conceptually on the people who are making the postings, or they can be more micro-focused, looking at the text in the very local context of the forum itself. Each question requires a different conceptual and theoretical rationale – a point I illustrate further later in the chapter.

Design, Sampling and Ethical Issues

What counts as good design when researching forum data? Much of the design consideration relates to sampling, and this also comes back to what your research question focuses on. If your interest in forums is to explore expressed opinions, your sampling frame needs to cover a broad enough timescale and you need to ensure that you have sampled as much of the selected forum, or forums, as relevant to the topic. If you are more interested in studying interaction at the 'micro-analytic' level (using something like conversation analysis [CA] or discourse analysis [DA]), I would advise working with a thread itself as your primary data (or maybe a selection of threads), taking more of a case-study approach.

How to Collect Forum Data: Five Sampling Steps

(1) *Select your forum.* This is not necessarily as straightforward a matter as it sounds. Do you want your forum to be typical of a particular *online* community (e.g., pro-ana) or do you want to take it as indicative of a much *broader* population (e.g., people with anorexia, people with eating disorders more generally)? If it's the former, you need to set out with a clear working definition of what a typical pro-ana site consists of, as you may find that, in practice, the websites are quite diverse. If it's the latter, a pro-ana website would not be the place to go, not least because pro-ana is a phenomenon pretty much peculiar to the Internet – even if some of the arguments have a longer history – and claims made by pro-ana community members are unlikely to be endorsed by individuals in 'recovery' or with very different types of eating disorder. If in any doubt as to the typicality of your forum for

the phenomenon of interest, it is always a good idea to sample from more than one forum to build up an indicative database.

(2) *Identify a time-frame*. Limit your dataset by specifying a time period within which you are going to select your data. The length of this period may be determined by your research question (e.g., you're examining responses to a specific event), but in most cases it will depend entirely on the activity level of the community and on the prevalence of the topic. A site like Mumsnet (www.mumsnet.co.uk), a hugely influential British parenting website, is so busy that, unless you're researching a relatively obscure topic, you may only need to sample across several days. Other sites are far less active and you might be looking at time periods closer to a year. A good idea of forum activity can be obtained by glancing at the number of posts associated with each thread. A low-activity site will have mostly single figure threads, while a high-activity site like Mumsnet will have several threads on each subforum stretching to over 1,000 posts.

(3) *Select your thread(s)*. How do you analyse a thread consisting of 1,000 posts? Or multiple threads with 100s of posts? That scenario could form an analyst's dream of a rich dataset … or a nightmare of being buried under too much data! How much material you *need* will depend largely on the scope of your project, your research question and your method of analysis. If you're doing a close analysis of interaction, perhaps drawing on techniques from CA or DA (see Giles, Stommel, Paulus, Lester and Reed, 2015) you might be able to base your study around a single, short, but very interesting, thread. If you're using an approach looking broadly at patterns across the dataset, for example, using a method like thematic analysis (TA) (Braun and Clarke, 2006), you will need to ensure that your selection of threads spans a suitably wide scope, taking into account time (depending on the activity level of the community) and subforum topic. Guidance as to sample sizes is not yet well established, but some suggestions in general can be found in Braun and Clarke (2013).

(4) *Download and format*. This is a pragmatic step, as forums exist only in an online environment, and you have to extract the data for the purpose of analysis. In most cases this is a simple, if laborious, task of cutting and pasting text from the browser into an offline document (e.g., a Microsoft Word file). However, decisions do need to be made about non-textual information, as, increasingly, forums allow users to include all kinds of links, emoticons and images in their posts. Indeed, an individual post may consist of nothing more than a link or an emoticon. Is such analysable material? Again, it depends on the level of analysis. For a micro-analytic study, it will be valuable, but for a broad-based TA, it can probably be safely discarded, unless you're coding pictures thematically as well as text.

(5) *Select relevant materials for deeper analysis.* If you're sampling widely from a busy forum, you will almost certainly end up with far more data than you require for your analysis. You need to consider what you want to do with that data, and what you need to answer your research question. If your analysis is broad-based/thematic, your coding process will exhaustively identify all relevant aspects of the dataset. A more micro or discursive orientation is quite different. As an example, in one study I explored the way online mental health forum users built up lists of 'characteristics' around different mental health 'conditions' – community members with 'emetophobia' (fear of vomiting), for instance, described how they carried round a set of props that worked as a coping strategy to reassure them, in case they were actually sick while out with friends. I chose to focus on *only two threads*, as despite a very broad research question, the analysis needed very close scrutiny of the OPs and responses to show just how *carefully* this discursive work was done by community members (see Giles and Newbold, 2013).

Ethical Issues

The ethics of research into forum data is a highly contested domain – one of the most contested in contemporary qualitative research! In the early days of my research on pro-ana communities, I often became irritated that other academics seemed more interested in the ethics of reporting data from the forums, than in the actual phenomenon itself. It was as if I were sneaking into teenagers' bedrooms with a tape recorder and divulging their personal conversations. However, there is increasing acceptance by Internet users that unprotected forum data is in the public domain and freely accessible by potential billions of web users (Jowett, 2015). Of course, what one *says* about that data is another matter entirely, and for that reason it is essential to consider what 'status' the data have, once they have been extracted from their online source and reproduced as part of an academic publication.

Many guidelines exist for researchers using online material. These take their cue from traditional ethical considerations in offline research, where surreptitious recording of conversation, 'covert' participation, and so on are regarded as breaches of etiquette and invasion of privacy. The British Psychological Society ([BPS] 2013) has published a set of guidelines, which I feel take a cautious approach considering the routine use of authentic web data in research articles. They advise researchers to consider the possibility that exposing a forum in a study might constitute 'harm' to the community:

'even the seemingly unproblematic highlighting of the mere existence of a discussion forum in a quiet corner of the web somewhere may be unwelcome to its users' (BPS, 2013: 16). Ultimately, however, both the BPS and the Association of Internet Researchers ([AoIR] 2012) agree that the one-size-fits-all approach in traditional (offline) ethical guidelines does not work well with online data, where context is all-important, and ethical judgements need to be made on a case-by-case basis. This, of course, doesn't make it any easier for researchers themselves!

The Status of Forum Data

The *status* of forum data – and by this, I mean exactly what we conceptualise them as being – is very important, from both an ethical standpoint, related to how we obtain and report these data, and an epistemological sense. It forces us to consider what we think the study of forum data can tell us about society, behaviour or about the nature of the specific topic under discussion. There are two divergent positions on this (of course, positions between these poles are also possible).

The first treats the data as essentially the private property of the *individuals* posting on the forum, and the researcher as effectively a 'fly on the wall', eavesdropping from a covert location on someone else's business. This is largely a traditional line taken by academics whose primary concern is the invasion of privacy and the anonymous status of the individuals implicated in research. Any form of dialogue online is treated much the same way as personal emails, or even handwritten letters. In terms of the status of the data, then, this position implies that they represent the authentic voice of the contributors on the site (and to some extent, the general public, the population that would typically be recruited for social scientific research via surveys, interviews, experiments etc.). In this sense, they are often taken to represent 'what people really think' about a topic.

The second position sees online discussion as public information available to be analysed like any other *media* content – the transcripts of TV or radio broadcasts, articles in newspapers and magazines, or indeed other publicly available online material such as blogs and articles on websites (see Chapters 6–8). Researchers' concern here is not the privacy of the individuals involved in the forum, who rarely contribute under their offline identities. Instead, they focus on exploring the rich cultural materials produced by Internet users on these sites, and theorise these materials as texts that contain, and convey, culturally located meaning, sidestepping the question of whether they are an expression of their authors' 'true beliefs'.

You could see these two positions as reflecting the interests of researchers from different disciplines, or differing intellectual traditions: the flies on the wall are behaving in much the same way as we would expect certain psychologists to do, objectifying individuals, studying behaviour, inferring motives and internal dispositions; the 'forums as media' researchers bypass the person, and focus on data as 'texts' to be analysed, focus on meaning, representation, culture and language practice, orientations more familiar to sociology, cultural/ media and communications studies. Psychologists Gavin, Rodham and Poyer (2008: 326), for instance, claim that the 'relative anonymity and the lack of social consequences can allow individuals to more ably express aspects of their "true self" while communicating online'. In contrast, White (2006), a communication scholar, compared the computer user to a spectator in front of a film or television screen, and argued that researchers need to consider whether they are actually studying texts ('representations') or 'people'. This distinction intersects with ethics: in the latter case, I would have no more ethical qualms about reproducing verbatim forum discussion than, for instance, quoting – and indeed naming – the participants in a reality TV show. However, as noted above, views on this are quite divergent, depending on the status given to data (see also Chapter 6, for discussion on this issue).

Dealing with Ethical Decision Makers

Notwithstanding your disciplinary or theoretical perspective on forum data, the issue may be taken out of your hands when presenting your research proposal to an ethics panel. When faced with a project outline that involves a researcher visiting a forum, reading discussions and then cutting and pasting them into a separate file, panels used to deliberating on the ethics of experiments, surveys and interviews may ask questions about 'the people' whose discussions are being scrutinised. Have they consented to having their contributions snipped out of their forum, taken to pieces by a researcher, and reproduced verbatim in research articles? Could they be 'harmed' in any way by having this information made public? Could a reader simply enter their words into a search engine in order to trace their origins? Might the contributors be identified even by their anonymised user names? Above all, might they *object* to the things you say about them?

By the time these sorts of (difficult) questions have been chewed over, it is not uncommon for ethics panels to insist on absolute protection of the identities, utterances and online sources of all 'the people' whose data are to be used in the research. Practice in line with these ethical concerns can be seen throughout the current literature on online communities. Researchers typically report that they contacted the 'gatekeepers' of the website involved for permission to 'lurk' on the forums, solely in order to cut and paste from the discussions (e.g., Mulveen and Hepworth, 2006). Some even say that they cannot provide direct quotation from the forum because of potential 'traceability' (Markham, 2012). Throughout the literature, source details, such as the title of the parent websites, their URL addresses and detailed description of the different sites (at least, enough detail to establish the kind of phenomenon under investigation) are withheld in the interests of ethical concerns about privacy violations. As a result, readers are given minimal detail about the nature of the forums or even of the websites hosting them, let alone any sense of the context in which the discussions take place (I will admit to having done this in my own research – see Giles, 2006). This means that readers often have to take it on trust that the forums involved are typical of a particular category of website. During the research on eating disorders, as an example, it is common for authors to refer to 'pro-ana websites', and refrain from providing details of these in order to protect both the vulnerable community, and readers who are theorised as vulnerable to the seductive allure of such sites. I believe this is problematic. The term 'pro-ana websites' covers an enormously diverse collection of online material, ranging from single homepages to large-scale stand-alone websites, and the domain itself is always in flux: even the term pro-ana was rejected by most sites by the late 2000s. Without details of the websites analysed, it can be very hard to judge quality of the claims made.

Despite the limited information often provided by studies of online discussion, some researchers argue for *further* limits on what is reported, and how. The highly experienced and established Internet researcher Markham (2012) recently recommended that researchers actually *fabricate* (i.e., invent fictitious) data, rather than quoting verbatim from websites, in order to provide 'illustrative colour' to analytic reports. This is a controversial position, and it has provoked lively debate within the communication discipline and elsewhere (e.g., Livingstone and Locatelli, 2014). It raises all kinds of questions about authenticity (of data; of analysis), and what is acceptable as a social science research document (Why not write novels?). Markham's objections rest largely on the need to protect vulnerable Internet users from, among other things, criminal investigation. She cites the example of a study of Swedish teenagers that fabricated their accounts of illegal activity (drug taking etc.) so that prying eyes would not use the quotes as ways of tracing the source, and thereby the individuals concerned. However, much of the research discussed by Markham and others involves situations where researchers intervene – that is, they *generate* data online, rather than analysing already-existing data, or data produced without researcher input, such as those on forums.

My position is that ethical restraints should be applied only when it comes to password-protected forums. In that case, we should contact site owners and members to get their permission to cite from their source (AoIR, 2012).

However, when forums offer unrestricted public access, it should be our duty as researchers to describe the data in as much detail as necessary for the reader to be able to make sense of the data, given their cultural context. It is not enough simply to state that the data come from, for example, 'a pro-ana website'. I advocate instead the kind of 'thick description' more commonly associated with ethnography (Geertz, 1973), that takes into account the mediated nature of the material we are dealing with. This might include information like user-names, which have been long problematic in online research due to concerns about 'traceability' (Markham, 2012). A good case for doing this comes from the opening chapter in Jenkins's (2006) *Convergence Culture*, where he describes in great detail the interaction on a particular forum dedicated to a particular reality TV series, in which a specific forum user had become notorious for sniffing out the filming locations of subsequent series. This user was so well known by forum members that it would seem churlish to anon-ymise him simply for the sake of 'protection' – and he was clearly revelling in his status as a bit of a local online celebrity.

Ultimately, the ethics of research on forum data is something that should be decided on a case-by-case basis, both by researchers and those responsible for ethical approval (AoIR, 2012; [BPS] 2013). Your decisions about how much detail to disclose about forum interaction will depend on a variety of factors: the nature and focus of the forum and its constituent community; the level of disclosure among posters, your research question; and, of course, the value added to the research by quoting real data. But whatever you decide, you will need to put a strong case to the ethical decision makers. The information I've provided should guide you to make a strong case to an ethics panel not only for conducting research using forum data, but also against the need for anonymity, if that's your position.

What Can Go Wrong with Discussion Forums?

Once immersed in the gloriously rich data-fest that is offered by Mumsnet or other highly active forums, it's tempting to feel that one has found the perfect data source for a lifetime of researching – and a glorious research career with few hiccups and glitches will follow . . . Ah, were it so! Forum data do not answer all research questions and problems, by any means. But they do offer a fairly easy-to-use data source. By and large, if you follow all the good guidance around design, base your research in sound theoretical and ethical considerations, and analyse the data in a rigorous and robust way, there's very little that can go *wrong* in using forum data. One key way it can is if there is a mismatch between research question (e.g., wanting to establish some cause-and-effect type theory) and what forum data can offer; another is between the aims or purpose of the research (e.g., wanting to generalise to a certain [sub]population) and what the data give you access to. A more pragmatic issue you may encounter is an inactive or low-level activity forum – if you want to collect data *prospectively* (rather than retrospectively), this may prove problematic. So make sure you research potential forum sites and choose one (or more) that has enough activity, *and* relevance to your research topic/question, that you can collect the data you need and justify well the sample selection. Finally, forum research can be problematic if it contravenes good ethical practice – as an example, if you occupy multiple roles in relation to a forum (e.g., moderator, contributor, researcher) you need to think very carefully through the ethical considerations – and make sure any undue influence from conflicting roles is avoided.

What Methods of Analysis Suit Discussion Forum Data?

Thematic analysis is the most useful approach if you have a very broad, or largely descriptive, research question, and are primarily focused on the *content* of what is expressed by posters. An approach like TA seeks to identify, and make sense of, patterns of meaning across the dataset. For example, Attard and Coulson (2012) were interested in the broad *content* of discussion forums used by people with Parkinson's disease (PD), as they wanted to know if this type of communication was positive or negative. They collected as much data as possible from the four forums they had identified: a total of 1,013 messages posted over a seven-year period, excluding only messages that were not clearly posted by those with PD (relatives, friends, health professional etc.). Using Braun and Clarke's (2006) thematic analytic procedure, they identified six themes: three positive (sharing experiences; sense of bonding/friendship; and optimism/hope) and three negative (absence of information; frustration that the interaction is only online; and lack of non-verbal feedback).

Discourse analysis suits questions where you are interested in language practices and the construction of reality, either locally or broadly. There are many different types of DA, ranging from the broadly oriented (Parker, 1992) to the micro (Potter and Wetherell, 1987), and any of these is suitable for analysing forum data (alone or in some combination). My analyses of forums are broadly discursive, but I also draw on other analytic methods, such as membership categorisation analysis (Stokoe, 2012) or rhetorical analysis (Billig, 1987). For instance, in the Asperger study described in Box 9.1, I was specifically interested in the way that community members organised their arguments for and against the proposed changes to the DSM. To answer this, I coded the messages in terms of their rhetorical function – how they *constructed a case* for or against the changes. This way I was able to organise their positions into 'for', 'against' or 'neutral' and to examine more closely the precise arguments they came up with.

For those interested in an even more micro-level, *conversation analysis* (CA) can provide a key tool. Stommel and Koole's (2010) analysis of an eating disorder website, for instance, outlines techniques for exploring things like who the intended recipients of each message are. Conversation analysis is, however, a somewhat controversial method for doing online analysis: some CA 'purists' have argued – off the record, largely – that their methodology is incompatible with anything that is not actual (and 'naturally produced') *talk*. To try and overcome some of these restrictions, and provide a way to use the elements of CA to offer key insight into the structure and organisation of *online* 'conversation', we have developed a version of CA specifically for use with such data (see Giles et al., 2015).

Conclusion

Discussion forums offer researchers a treasure trove of textual information and interaction (see Box 9.4). You may be interested in the *topics* discussed in them and/or you may be interested in *how* they work as communication. Either way, they provide insight into human activity in 'naturally occurring' groups – groups not put together by researchers! They enable us to identify and analyse the kind of discussions and arguments that go on about topics in contemporary society, from the seemingly arcane, to the socially important. If you decide to research using forums as data, try never to lose sight of their mediated, public context: you are not eavesdropping on private chat, and they are not conversations produced outside of their context.

Box 9.4 Personal reflections on discussion forums

I've discussed already the ethical issue of whether one is analysing *people* or *texts* when doing this kind of analysis. Although I adhere broadly to the 'texts' position myself, it is hard to avoid the obvious fact that there is a flesh-and-blood author behind every post, and when studying mental health forums, that author is often clearly in a state of considerable mental distress. Of course, there is nothing you can do but observe, even though it is very tempting at times to sign up to the community and deliver what you hope is useful advice! Anthropologists refer to this dilemma as 'going native' (Tresch, 2011) – where a researcher gets too immersed in the field and ends up joining the society they are studying. It hasn't happened to me yet . . .

Have a Go . . .

Follow the steps below to conduct a two-part study on a forum topic of your choice.

(1) Select a topic based on your own *interests*. This could be a cultural topic (e.g., musical; sporting) for which you can find one or two forums – preferably with slightly different angles on the topic. Select a subforum that appears on each site, and identify a research question based around the general content of the two subforums. Select a sample of 10–20 threads to each subforum (depending on length of each) that address the research question. Conduct a thematic analysis to identify the issues that are most important to the community as a whole.

(2) Take a more micro-approach. Select *one* thread from each of the subforums that illustrates one of the themes you identified in part one. What sort of structure does the thread have? Which members participate in the thread? How do they interact with one another? How are disagreements resolved (or not)? Compare the data selected from the two different subforums – do they share a broad consensus on the issues they are discussing, or can you identify distinctive sets of norms and values for each site? How might you characterise each site to someone thinking of joining an online forum devoted to your selected topic?

(3) Reflect on what you gain – and what you lose – taking these different analytic approaches to forum data.

Further Resources: Online

The website MOOD: The Microanalysis of Online Data is an international network of researchers from various disciplines who use methods such as conversation and discourse analysis to conduct 'microanalysis' of online data, including things like social media as well as discussion forums: (http://moodnetwork.ruhosting.nl/)
For another, more recent, scholarly network that offers a more linguistic orientation to discourse analysis, see http://adda.blogs.uv.es/

Further Resources: Readings

To read more about the study presented in Box 9.1, see Giles, D. C. (2014). 'DSM-V is taking away our identity': The reaction of the online community to the proposed changes in the diagnosis of Asperger's disorder. *Health*, *18*(2), 179–195.

For a study using thematic analysis to explore male accounts of infertility on a forum, see Malik, S. H. and Coulson, N. S. (2008). The male experience of infertility: A thematic analysis of an online infertility support group bulletin board. *Journal of Reproductive and Infant Psychology, 26*(1), 18–30.

For a study that exemplifies a discursive psychology perspective applied to forum data, see Horne, J. and Wiggins, S. (2009). Doing being 'on the edge': Managing the dilemma of being authentically suicidal in an online forum. *Sociology of Health & Illness, 31*(2), 170–184.

For a study combining elements of conversation analysis with 'membership categorisation analysis', see Giles, D. C. and Newbold, J. (2013). 'Is this normal?' The role of category predicates in constructing mental illness online. *Journal of Computer-Mediated Communication, 18*(4), 476–490.

References

Association of Internet Researchers (AoIR) (2012). *Ethical Decision-Making and Internet Research: Recommendations from the AoIR Ethics Working Committee (Version 2.0)*. Chicago: Association of Internet Researchers. Retrieved from: http://aoir.org/reports/ethics2.pdf

Attard, A. and Coulson, N. S. (2012). A thematic analysis of patient communication in Parkinson's disease online support group discussion forums. *Computers in Human Behavior, 28*(2), 500–506.

Bennett, L. (2011). Delegitimizing strategic power: Normative identity and governance in online R.E.M. fandom. *Transformative Works and Cultures, 7.* Retrieved from: http://journal.transformativeworks.org/index.php/twc/article/view/281/226

Billig, M. (1987). *Arguing and thinking: A rhetorical approach to social psychology.* Cambridge: Cambridge University Press.

Braun, V. and Clarke, V. (2006). Using thematic analysis in psychology. *Qualitative Research in Psychology, 3*(2), 77–101.

(2013). *Successful qualitative research: A practical guide for beginners.* London: Sage Publications.

British Psychological Society (2013). *Ethics guidelines for Internet-mediated research.* INF206/1.2013. Leicester UK: British Psychological Society.

Gavin, J., Rodham, K. and Poyer, H. (2008). The presentation of 'pro-anorexia' in online group interactions. *Qualitative Health Research, 18*(3), 325–333.

Geertz, C. (1973). *The interpretation of cultures: Selected essays.* New York: Basic.

Giles, D. C. (2006). Constructing identities in cyberspace: The case of eating disorders. *British Journal of Social Psychology, 45*(3), 463–477.

(2013). The extended self strikes back: Morrissey fans' reaction to public rejection by their idol. *Popular Communication, 11*(2), 116–129.

(2014). 'DSM-V is taking away our identity': The reaction of the online community to the proposed changes in the diagnosis of Asperger's disorder. *Health, 18*(2), 179–195.

Giles, D. C. and Newbold, J. (2011). Self- and other-diagnosis in user-led online mental health communities. *Qualitative Health Research, 21*(3), 419–428.

(2013). 'Is this normal?' The role of category predicates in constructing mental illness online. *Journal of Computer-Mediated Communication, 18*(4), 476–490.

Giles, D. C., Stommel, W., Paulus, T., Lester, J. and Reed, D. (2015). The microanalysis of online data: The methodological development of 'digital CA'. *Discourse, Context & Media, 7*, 45–51.

Horne, J., and Wiggins, S. (2009). Doing being 'on the edge': Managing the dilemma of being authentically suicidal in an online forum. *Sociology of Health & Illness, 31*(2), 170–184.

Jenkins, H. (2006). *Convergence culture: Where old and new media collide.* New York: New York University Press.

Jowett, A. (2015). A case for using online discussion forums in critical psychological research. *Qualitative Research in Psychology, 12*(3), 287–297.

Kayany, J. M. (1998). Contexts of uninhibited online behavior: Flaming in social newsgroups on Usenet. *Journal of the American Society for Information Science, 49*(12), 1135–1141.

Kozinets, R. V. (2010). *Netnography: Doing ethnographic research online.* London: Sage Publications.

Livingstone, S. and Locatelli, E. (2014). Ethical dilemmas in qualitative research with youth on/offline. *International Journal of Learning and Media, 4*(2), 67–75.

Markham, A. (2012). Fabrication as ethical practice. *Information, Communication & Society, 15*(3), 334–353.

Mulveen, R. and Hepworth, J. (2006). An interpretative phenomenological analysis of participation in a pro-anorexia internet site and its relationship with disordered eating. *Journal of Health Psychology, 11*(2), 283–296.

Parker, I. (1992). *Discourse dynamics: Critical analysis for social and individual psychology.* London: Routledge.

Potter, J. and Wetherell, M. (1987). *Discourse and social psychology: Beyond attitudes and behaviour.* London: Sage Publications.

Stokoe, E. (2012). Moving forward with membership categorisation analysis: Methods for systematic analysis. *Discourse Studies, 14*(3), 277–303.

Stommel, W. and Koole, T. (2010). The online support group as a community: A micro-analysis of the interaction with a new member. *Discourse Studies, 12*(3), 357–378.

Tresch, J. (2011). On going native: Thomas Kuhn and anthropological method. *Philosophy of the Social Sciences, 31*(3), 302–322.

Vayreda, A. and Antaki, C. (2009). Social support and unsolicited advice in a bipolar disorder online forum. *Qualitative Health Research, 19*(7), 931–942.

Weber, H. L. (2011). Missed cues: How disputes can socialize virtual newcomers. *Language@Internet, 8*, article 5. Retrieved from: www.languageatinternet.org /articles/2011/Weber

White, M. (2006). *The body and the screen: Theories of internet spectatorship.* Cambridge, MA: MIT Press.

Part III

Virtual Data Collection

10 'Type Me Your Answer'

Generating Interview Data via Email

Lucy Gibson

Overview

Email interviewing is an exciting development in qualitative data collection, offering researchers an inexpensive and convenient method of generating in-depth qualitative data. This chapter draws on my experiences of using email interviews in a qualitative, mixed-method study of older (thirty plus) music fans (described in Box 10.1). I found email interviewing was a great means of producing rich written accounts of participants' music experiences and memories. The chapter focuses on how this method works *in practice*, the type of data produced and issues relating to data collection and analysis. In addition, I reflect on the differences between written and oral data, the *practicalities* of conducting email interviews, and discuss the benefits and potential pitfalls of using email interviews to collect qualitative data.

Introduction to Email Interviewing

There has been a huge growth in information and communication technologies and, specifically, Internet technologies, in recent years, with a significant increase in the use of email in both personal and professional arenas (Bakardjieva, 2005). Such developments have led to new opportunities for researchers to examine how traditional research methods, like interviews, can be re-worked in online environments, in ways that allow researchers to obtain in-depth, descriptive data online, and gain new understandings of the human experience (Mann and Stewart, 2000). The Internet, and in particular the World Wide Web, has 'enabled social scientists to create a virtual laboratory, where data can be collected twenty-four hours a day across the globe . . . Just as the video revolutionised observation methods, so the Internet is fundamentally changing the ways in which we can observe, measure and report on the human condition and societal structures' (Hine, 2005: 21).

> **Box 10.1** Understanding popular music fandom and the life course
>
> This study explored the significance, meaning and long-term social uses of popular music for people aged over thirty (Gibson, 2010a). I used participant observation, and both face-to-face and email interviews, to explore fans' long-term involvement in three particular music 'scenes': northern and 'rare' soul, rock, and electronic dance music. The research used the Internet in two ways – to recruit participants and to collect data. Internet-generated data consisted of two types: (a) email interviews (which I focus on in this chapter) and (b) online discussion forums and message boards (not discussed, but see Chapter 9). Participants were given a choice of being interviewed face-to-face or via email. Email was favoured by the vast majority (fifty-five out of seventy), and it was suggested they preferred its unobtrusive nature and flexibility. In terms of the intersection of sampling, data collection and pragmatics, I decided to use *both* face-to-face and email interviews, to gain the opinions and experiences of a wide range of participants in a project where I was limited in time and financial resources. As I used email interviews alongside more traditional face-to-face interviewing, I was able to reflect on the differences in the kinds of data produced using each of these approaches to interviewing, and also helped to tease out the advantages and drawbacks of using email interviews.

Email interviewing is one such method that offers great potential to the qualitative researcher, although to date they have been used less frequently than other online variations of traditional qualitative data collection methods (see also Chapters 11–13).

Email interviewing goes by various aliases: online interviewing, e-interviewing, electronic interviewing and asynchronous computer-mediated communication. In simple terms, email interviewing refers to conducting interviews via email, and there are two main 'styles': asynchronous (the approach I used; other examples include James, 2007; Ratislavová and Ratislav, 2014) and synchronous (for instance, Bowker and Tuffin, 2004; Madge and O'Connor, 2002). Asynchronous email interviewing is *not* conducted in 'real-time': a researcher sends a series of questions, usually sequentially, but sometimes all at once, to a participant via email; the respondent is able to answer questions at their own pace and convenience, over a period of time. Synchronous email interviewing *is* conducted in real-time: both the researcher and participant log in to their email at a mutually convenient time; the researcher poses questions and the participant types responses. This chapter focuses primarily on asynchronous email interviewing, but I will note key comparisons between the two at certain points. Synchronous email interviews share many similarities with IM (instant messaging) interviews, so I recommend also consulting Chapter 11.

The time-frame of asynchronous email interviews is stretched out – the interview may take place over days, weeks or *possibly* even months, depending on how the project is set up (e.g., Olivero and Lunt 2004 reported that some of their interviews took place over more than six weeks and involved between seventeen and twenty-four exchanges). You will likely be running *multiple* interviews simultaneously. In addition, the total time directly 'collecting' data – which in email interviews means posing questions, reading responses, and posing further questions – *may* actually be more, in total, than the typical one-and-a-half-hour face-to-face interview, but there are factors that make up for this additional time – including not needing to transcribe audio data.

What Does Email Interviewing Offer the Qualitative Researcher?

Email interviewing offers qualitative researchers access to data that are both similar and different to those produced by face-to-face interviews, with a whole range of advantages attached. Advantages for the researcher include convenience, cost and time savings, access to more diverse samples, reduction in certain ethical concerns, reflective data gathering and the production of a written data record. Advantages from the participant's point of view include convenience, flexibility, and anonymity and control over the telling of their story, including the potential to edit, revise and reflect before sending a response.

Email interviews ultimately offer an efficient, cost-effective and convenient means of gathering rich and detailed data (Meho, 2006). They are unequivocally flexible, and a major advantage is that they are convenient and often more acceptable to people who are unable, or do not want, to attend a face-to-face interview – for both participants and researchers, there is reduced impact of time, travel and space (Bampton and Cowton, 2002). In my research, participants overwhelmingly favoured email interviews due to their expediency and ease. This hints at another key feature: email interviews offer the ability to reach a geographically dispersed group or population (Gibson, 2010b). My participants were recruited via online message boards and forums, and were based in various locations in the UK, as well as European countries and the US. Since the email interviews were carried out from my home or office, I didn't have to spend time or money travelling to interviews, and could interview people from a geographically wider area than if I were only collecting face-to-face interview data. This meant the interviews could capture a better variety of music fans' experiences and opinions, rather than being restricted to those who could be recruited in a specific local area (though it also raises some important considerations, see

---

> **Box 10.2** Where your email interview participants come from can matter
>
> Geographical variance does, raise questions around sampling, as you shouldn't just recruit random people from all over, without thinking about what this means and its implications – especially if your research explores local cultures and meaning, or aims to provide a deeply locally-contextualised analysis. In my research, the sample was based on self-identifying as a specific music fan; people were connected via their interest and age. However, I also used a quota sample that considered age, gender and occupation, in an attempt to obtain a diverse sample.

Box 10.2). The virtual location of email interviews means that they are convenient for both the researcher and participant in various ways. They are often completed in a familiar environment with technological access, and at a time that suits. There is also often less (physical) intrusion into participants' lives, as there is usually no need to meet face-to-face. Moreover, this aspect means they can also be considered less dangerous for the researcher, since the potential vulnerability of research sites (e.g., participant homes) and times (e.g., evening) is removed.

Another *practical* advantage for the researcher is that email interviews produce textual data (Bampton and Cowton, 2002) – you only need to print out emailed responses to produce a data record, though this may also involve some cutting and pasting into a more user-friendly format. Given that time is not spent on transcription of audio data, the ready-made 'transcripts' created by email interviews afford the researcher more time for both data collection and analysis (Hamilton and Bowers, 2006). The typical pitfalls of transcribing audio-recorded interview data, such as difficulties like ambiguity or audibility (see Poland, 2002), are likewise removed, meaning the data analysed are exactly the data produced by the interview process. Email 'transcripts' may thus be more 'accurate' than those generated via face-to-face means (see also Chapters 5 and 13).

Using email for interviewing offers advantages related both to your own research skill(s) and to the type of information you might obtain, which intersects – and things often messily do in qualitative research – with ethics. Face-to-face interviewing is a skill and can be demanding on qualitative researchers; it is potentially really challenging for *inexperienced* researchers, especially for sensitive topics. Nervous or anxious researchers don't necessarily make great interviewers, and can fail to put participants at ease, or establish rapport, which often reduces data depth and quality. Doing interviews via email can reduce the sense of pressure experienced by researchers, and possibly also by participants – though there are differing opinions in terms of what this latter point might mean for openness and anonymity when using email interviews (Bampton and Cowton, 2002), as well as the broader implications of it. On the one hand, an ethical case can be made that (particularly asynchronous) email interviews allow participants to protect themselves from over-disclosure, or making comments they later regret, because they write considered responses and are in control of what they send. Others suggest you are likely to get more disclosure from email versus face-to-face interviewing. Bampton and Cowton (2002: para 17) contended that as email interviews are less intrusive than face-to-face ones, 'the direct lack of contact means that Internet methodologies generally permit a degree of anonymity, which has been associated with respondents being more likely to admit to socially undesirable behaviour' (see also Hodgson's, 2004, email interview research on self-injury). In my research, for instance, a number of interviewees frankly discussed recreational drug consumption and other similar activities concerning intoxication, and this tended to happen in the email rather than the face-to-face interviews; although drug use was briefly alluded to during some face-to-face interviews, it typically occurred once the tape recorder had been switched off! The removal of face-to-face interaction during email interviews appeared to encourage participants to discuss a wide range of experiences in popular music scenes, including illicit ones. Ethically, if illegal activities are disclosed during the interview process (whether via email or face-to-face), researchers have the same legal obligations as any other research context: confidentiality for participants prevails, but if there is expressed intended harm to participants, specific third parties or the general public, there are obligations to report to authorities (see ethicsguide book.ac.uk for more details).

Participants in asynchronous email interviews can choose to devote specific periods of time to responses (Walther, 1996), or may choose to complete email interviews sporadically, fitting them in as and when time permits, and potentially writing responses over many days. This means the method allows participants a great degree of flexibility, and makes them particularly useful for people with busy lives, or people with complex schedules that don't easily accommodate a face-to-face interview in regular working hours (Madge and O'Connor, 2002). But don't assume a participant who is dedicatedly sitting at a computer or tablet, typing fully-fledged answers to every question. In my study, some participants would take up to a month to provide detailed responses, which appeared to be the result of contemplation, time, and effort spent in writing, reviewing and editing their response.

This ability to review and revise responses is a key feature of asynchronous email interview data, and makes the data – as well as the *process* – quite different to those produced in other ways. Overall, email interviews tend to be

---

Box 10.3 Written answers are carefully considered

I had time out of the scene from about 1970 to about 1995 – I know it sounds a long time but in 1970 I was getting worn out from the all-nighters and the pills – I happened to start playing rugby union and also got married and bought a house which meant I couldn't pursue the 'scene' . . . Music and events that I have been involved with in my youth have certainly stuck with me through the years, but interestingly most of us whether it be northern soul or Ibiza sound or punk or whatever, seem to take some sort of break from it at some point. Whether or not this is to recover as we have feasted on it and need a break or maybe other things appear like buying houses, getting married, having children getting more responsibility in the jobs I don't know. Although we go along the path of different relationships, different social scenes and different music I don't think anybody forgets their 'roots' and as I have found, once the children are grown up (and you have paid for the little sods to go through university – sorry Lucy) and the mortgage is small or paid for and you retire or control your job easily you find you have a little more time to do what you want . . . (male, 59, northern soul fan).

---

less 'spontaneous' than face-to-face interviews in terms of the data produced – they are typically more structured and considered, as the respondent is able to contemplate their response, and scroll through and edit their narrative, both immediately and over time. This can be a considerable advantage when researching people's past experiences and relying on memory, as my research did, as it affords the respondent time to reflect and consider before they compose a response (see also Wicksteed, 2000). Time for reflection and editing can allow participants to create *polished* accounts of their experiences, in their own words and direction (see example extract in Box 10.3). Despite the conversational tone and occasional slang words used in the extract in Box 10.3, the written account appears carefully structured and considered; the participant thoughtfully reflects on the part that music has played in his life over several decades.

This example, along with the example in Figure 10.1, demonstrates the *depth* and richness you can find in email responses. It also highlights, in comparison to typical face-to-face data, the 'articulate' nature of email data, which is also far more obviously driven by the participant's agenda, without interruptions or involvement from the researchers in the moment-by-moment interactional sense. Good face-to-face interviewing typically has minimal researcher *interruption*, but probes and prompting shape the flow of the discussion. The presence of the researcher is, arguably, always *directly* there, and potentially more directly and immediately impacts the ways

No probs Lucy.

It was cool to do and made me really think about the scene in a way that I suppose I always do, but not all at once.

Been around a long time and have seen a lot of things happen. But like I said it's the same as it ever was, just faces, tunes and venues come and go. The one thing I will say is that I possibly forgot to mention is that the best times for me were the acid house/rave years (88 - 89/90) because that's when it was a totally new concept for everybody from all races, social backgrounds coming together and partying as one. It didn't matter what music you liked, where you lived, what job you did, you just knew you were part of something special, a secret world that only a few knew about. That had never happened before........

In 1988, parties like Shoom, Sunrise and Energy catered for 700–1000 people and were considered massive. And we were the only people out dancing to the music that was being played. The drugs played a huge part, obviously but it was something never witnessed before. If I'm really honest, I and a lot of people my age who still go out are trying to find/recreate somewhere that's close in vibe to those early days but alas it's not going to happen because the main thing is was it was new.

Figure 10.1   Screen grab of participant's positive feedback and further reflection

participants discuss the topic at hand, when face-to-face. In my study, many participants wrote eloquent and luxuriant prose recording their opinions, beliefs and experiences, and the data did vary in this way from those generated in the face-to-face interviews. As the researcher, I *also* had the chance to reflect on participants' responses, read through our previous email conversations and then choose how to continue the interview. This is potentially quite demanding, but it likewise contributes to the shape of the data. It can also be used as an analytic tool, affording the researcher time to consider possible analytic directions in the research they wish to consider, and thus the questions they ask.

Synchronous email interviews generate somewhat different kinds of data, as although they allow a participant to consider their response and read through or edit before pressing send, they do not necessarily offer the same opportunity to spend time contemplating an answer, or to add points post-interview. However, despite being 'real-time', email interviews using synchronous methods can still be slow: 'The exchange of questions and responses was clearly influenced by the reading, reflection and typing skills of the respondents. In some exchanges, quite some time elapsed before a response appeared, sometimes as a result of computer crashes' (Davis, Bolding, Hart, Sherr and Elford, 2004: 947). Delayed responses could indicate time spent on reflection; likewise, it could indicate distraction and multi-tasking (see also Chapter 11).

Given that a 'line of communication' is established in email interviews, this approach also offers participants an established means of ongoing morning lucy!

just wanted to add a few things that i think i forgot last night!

   i would still go to concerts & buy cd's & collect- even if i was not employed on the distribution side. don't see the freebies anymore anyway LOL! so from that side- yes things have greatly changed. music biz is not that great anymore- all the downloading is hurting ALOT.

but on the other hand, internet can help promote more among the fans- egroups & fan sites, etc.

when i got out of high school, i did not have a clear idea of what i wanted to do.. needed a job & well- it all fell into place.lots of ups & downs.. not a lot of money., but i still enjoy my job. hope to be doing this for awhile yet.

remember, BUY – don't just download!!

back to work,
have a great one,

Figure 10.2   Screen grab of participant's additional reflection and comment

communication, should they wish to use it – which in my experience can happen in two ways. Some participants emailed additional information regarding their experiences, opinions and thoughts, following their first response – this seemed to happen when they remembered something additional, or thought of points they wished to share but hadn't raised (see an example in Figure 10.2). This is an advantage over traditional face-to-face interviewing, where both the researcher and participant can often think of issues they wished they had raised, but do not get the opportunity to do so. Even if a participant emails additional information following a face-to-face interview, the data form is out of context with the data production process, and any conclusion would need to be carefully considered. In *email* interviews, this sort of later reflection response fits with the process and logic of data collection; they can easily be incorporated into the dataset. This highlights the earlier point that we need to consider email interview data as effectively reflective, or 'multi-layered', rather than spontaneous, narratives.

Another way this communication occurs is through participants providing post-interview feedback – this final point relates also to the 'emotional' experience of the participants. In their analysis of virtual ethnography, Crichton and Kinash (2003) claimed that their participants enjoyed the process of being interviewed online and often found it hard to quit their interactions with the researcher. Similarly, in my study, a small number of participants maintained an active interest in the research process by occasionally emailing to enquire about the progress of the research and the study's findings. Overall, my sense is that participants had enjoyed the experience of writing their personal histories of music involvement, experiences and documenting their tastes, deriving a sense of plea-sure from 'authoring' their life experiences – some emailed me and directly told me, following the completion of the interviews. Some also expressed gratitude for providing the opportunity to document their opinions and experiences, and stated that they took pleasure in the process of answering questions via email (Figure 10.2 shows an example).

What Research Questions Suit Email Interviews?

As with most data collection methods, email interviews are more suited to certain research topics and questions than others. Email interviews are a great way of generating rich written accounts of participants' *experiences and memories*. They were particularly well-suited to my research, as fans could recollect their long-term involvement in music scenes, and would equally suit other research questions dealing with past experiences, memories and recollec-tions. Research questions focusing on *perceptions, experiences* or exploring *sensitive topics* lend themselves well to email interviews. They can also be used for those interested in how meaning or experience is constructed: they have been successfully used to explore topics such as experiences of the grieving process in Czech women following perinatal loss (Ratislavová and Ratislav, 2014), associations between seeking sex through the Internet and HIV trans-mission risk (Davis et al., 2004) and the construction of academic identities (James, 2007).

Alongside experience and memory, I was also interested in the *views* of various specialist interest groups who had a long-standing enthusiasm for specific music cultures; my research question explored how music tastes are formed and maintained through the life course. The topic of music could easily be swapped with other forms of cultural consumption: leisure activities or fandom cultures seem well-suited for email interviewing, where people are encouraged to engage and reflect on their participation, meaning around it and sense of identity associated with it. Email interviews are also highly suited to research questions that are tied in to understanding geographically dispersed groups, or other groups who may not wish to participate in traditional face-to-face research (e.g., shy participants; those whose activities are illegal or socially sanctioned). Such questions and topics could include a sample of people who have experienced particular circumstances or share similar inter-ests but do not live in the same location, such as the information-seeking process of social scientists (Meho and Tibbo, 2003), or the experiences of young people with cerebral palsy (Ison, 2009).

Design, Sampling and Ethical Issues

The online environment potentially requires new ways of thinking outside of the boundaries of traditional research (Gaiser and Schreiner, 2009) and email interviewing raises various design, sampling and ethical issues (James and Busher, 2007). Some of these are methodological – for instance, Will the method produce a kind of data appropriate for your research question? Some are practical – for instance, Have you got enough *time* to collect data this way? Research participants can take relatively long periods of time in replying to email questions, especially, and sometimes even, if clear response boundaries are not set. More specific design decisions related to the designing and doing of an email interview study are indicated in the 'Steps to Using Email Interviews' section that follows.

Participants, Sampling and Recruitment

Many of the issues associated with sampling and recruitment closely relate to concerns found in more traditional qualitative research approaches (Hooley, Marriott and Wellens, 2012), but for email interviews, there are key considerations related to *who* your participants are. Asking respondents to write lengthy accounts – which this method does – raises key questions: Who feels comfortable writing accounts? Who has time to devote to lengthy descriptions? And, who is able to do so? Hunt and McHale (2007: 1417), for instance, identified that 'for prison populations, groups with disability, or children, there are issues that the researcher must consider before deciding on whether to use the e-mail interview'. Email interviewing potentially favours the more articulate and those who are confident about writing, and it's commonly thought it is more suited to young participants. In my study, interviews were popular with participants across the full spectrum of ages, from thirty to sixty-two. The age of participants does, however, need to be considered – email interviews are not *necessarily* suited to very young children, or the elderly, but do consider this point carefully. In Great Britain, for instance, although the '65 and over' age group has the smallest proportion of daily Internet use overall, the number engaging in daily Internet use is growing, and sending/receiving emails is the most popular online activity for all age groups (Office for National Statistics, 2013). Whilst some populations of very young children and the elderly will feel comfortable using email, researchers need to consider carefully whether email interviews would be the most appropriate method, and not assume comfort of use, or, likewise, lack thereof. Email interviews also rely on participants having access to, and feeling confident using, computers, which likewise cannot be assumed. It's important to also consider whether participants will feel *at ease* and/or confident writing accounts of their experiences: respondents in my study enjoyed this process, but it will not suit all projects.

Researchers need to consider the most appropriate recruitment strategy for their topic; this links to the make-up and location of the sample too. It can be difficult to access a broad sample of the research population if they are geographically dispersed. It can also be difficult to recruit certain 'hard-to-reach' populations unless you are part of them (Braun and Clarke, 2013). In my study, where the sample was diverse but also connected to particular real-world and virtual sites, I created recruitment flyers to hand out to potential email interviewees at music events, and displayed posters in relevant venues. I decided flyers and posters offered a fairly quick and efficient means of being seen by a large number of potential participants, and were also minimally intrusive (unlike direct contact!). Researchers can also recruit using online methods such as message boards, Internet forums and groups related to the research topic. This can be less intrusive than other approaches: my face-to-face recruitment disrupted fans' leisure-time activities, which may have put them off participating. I set up accounts on relevant message boards and created usernames that differed from my real name – common practice when using message boards – and my real name was only revealed to those who contacted me to express interest. Using your real name *may* be more appropriate for a formal university study, so potential participants can look you up before getting in touch. The key point about recruitment is that any recruitment approach has pros and cons, and needs to be considered both in relation to the topic, and the potential participant population of interest.

With online research, where there is no face-to-face contact no visible indicators of identity or social characteristics, verification of identity has been raised as a concern – something that is shared with more traditional social and health research methods, such as postal questionnaires (Bampton and Cowton, 2002). If this is a vital consideration – and it isn't always – recruitment and sampling strategies can overcome this. One way could be to recruit face-to-face prior to commencing the interview – this offers some identity information. In my face-to-face recruitment, I assessed the age of attendees and approached people who appeared over thirty years old – a potentially problematic task and ethical concern, as people can be sensitive about their age – although, no one ever gave a negative reaction! I then used snowballing, asking people interested in the research to introduce friends and acquaintances from the scenes they were involved in. Identity would have been hard to fake in my research, and this is potentially true for any qualitative research asking participants' to relay in-depth memories and experiences. It would be difficult to fabricate convincing accounts of being a long-term and committed music fan, given the amount of detail about venues, events and musicians that were included.

Overall, sample sizes for email interview studies resemble those for face-to-face interview studies, intersecting with data analytic approach and overall research framework. So follow relevant guidance for selecting a sample that is appropriate (e.g., Braun and Clarke, 2013).

Ethical Issues

Researchers should always work within the ethical frameworks and guidelines of the institution and/or funding body under which the study is being carried out. Certain institutions will have policies regarding confidentiality and online research, which take into consideration the potential for hacking, protecting privacy and minimising harm to participants. The British Psychological Society (2013) ethical guidance document for 'Internet-mediated research', for instance, covers such issues in some detail. It distinguishes between online research carried out in the private and public domain; email interviews are considered to be relatively private, since data are not extracted from public forums (see also Chapters 6, 8 and 9). Due to the designated private nature of email data, confidentiality of replies for both the researcher and participants is of concern – notably due to anxiety about hackers, and the potential fraud that can occur with email accounts. That anonymity is often cited as a key advantage of email interviewing (Bampton and Cowton, 2002) highlights an ethical complexity: the relationship between research and participant can be 'anonymous' but the risk of hacking, as well as potential identification through IP address, means they cannot be considered truly anonymous. Another key ethical consideration is protecting participants' privacy during interactions (James and Busher, 2007). The ethics of online research is a live, evolving area. I'd advise consulting resources such as the Association of Internet Researchers wiki – where you can debate issues relating to the use of online methods in research (Hooley et al., 2012) – and ensuring your process is in line with current ethical thought.

Finally, related to data security, it's crucial to ensure you have *as secure* an email account as possible, and to consider password protecting or encrypting any files saved onto computers – some ethics bodies *may* even require this as a minimum. You may also consider encrypting emails themselves. General software for email encryption is available (e.g., produced by McAfee), or researchers can use software specifically designed to cooperate with their email programme. A Google search of 'email encryption software for Outlook', for instance, leads to various software programs that can be used for email encryption. An abundance of online review articles evaluates such software and explains how it can be used effectively to protect email data. Finally, passwords should be changed regularly to avoid hacking: strong ones use a combination of upper and lower case letters, and numbers/symbols.

Steps to Using Email Interviews

You need to make various decisions before and during a study using email interviews – I now outline ten key steps/decisions:

(1) *Choose a format for the email exchange.* Questions and responses can be delivered either *in* the email (as the text itself) attached to email as a separate word-processed document, or sometimes a combination of both. Each has pros and cons. Attached Word documents make emailed interview data easier to manage, analyse and reproduce. But it's important to consider the different devices people now use for email – such as tablets or smartphones – which can make an attachment-based format difficult or impossible for some participants. The format of sending questions/responses directly in emails is easier to manage if using a tablet or phone – or indeed for responding across different devices over the course of the interview – but they make your task of managing and preparing data for analysis potentially harder. I used a combination of attached documents and embedded text in emails. A set of initial questions were sent via an attachment; follow-up questions were sent embedded within the email. Whatever approach you take, participants need clear guidance about how to respond – whether to embed their answers into emails, or write in an attached document and send it back. This helps to avoid any confusion for the participant and to increase the chances of a consistent style of data across the dataset.

(2) *Choose an email account.* It may be worth setting up a dedicated project email account, whose email address reflects the research topic. A dedicated account means the research and data are contained in one space, which is uncontaminated by any other email traffic. This makes management of both data collection and the data themselves far easier – particularly if your inbox is anything like most academics'. I used a Gmail account and found this useful as it groups all back-and-forth email sequences together in chronological order, creating a conversation thread. The *label* function allowed easy grouping of emails into particular clusters, and identification of relevant emails. Overall, I found it easy to use and navigate. Note though: sometimes ethical bodies prefer or require the use of an *institutional* account, so check that out!

(3) *Decide how to recruit.* From the range of options available (discussed already), select the most appropriate ones for your sample and topic.

(4) *Design an interview guide.* Follow standard guidance for designing interview questions (e.g., Braun and Clarke, 2013), with some tweaks. Questions need to be geared towards providing data that will answer the *overarching* research question and provide rich information on the topic. Questions work best when they are open and exploratory (e.g., tell me about ..., can you describe how ...) and specify that you want the participant to answer in as much detail as possible. It's also vital they are worded in a clear and accessible format, because there's less chance of clarifying any misunderstanding than in face-to -face interviews. A useful way to check the viability of your interview questions for generating the sort of data you want, and their clarity, is to conduct a small pilot study – this may need to happen *following* ethical approval. A pilot can also help inform on practical design issues, such as how many questions to send at once, and whether to send as attachment or in the email itself.

(5) *Seek ethical approval.* Once the study is conceptualised and designed, seek ethical approval from the relevant local body. Note that this can take some time, so build this into the timescale for time-limited projects.

(6) *Start recruiting participants.* This step can be a mix of active and passive, depending on your recruitment strategy – many of the ways we recruit involve some kind of advertising and distribution of information, then it's a 'wait and see' game to see if anyone gets in touch. However, it's good to regularly assess the viability of our recruitment strategies, and keep them active – for instance, reposting on forums, putting up new flyers – if recruitment is slow. If recruitment doesn't work, reassess your strategies (which may require seeking additional ethical approval). For those who express interest, provide all relevant information about the study and parti-cipation (e.g., timescale of the study; time allocated for starting the inter-views) – usually in the form of a participant information sheet – and give them the opportunity to ask any questions.

(7) *Gain consent.* As standard ethical practice, gain informed consent from participants prior to starting the email interviews. Depending on local ethics, the participant information sheet and consent form can often be attached to an email during initial interaction (if you do not meet parti-cipants face-to-face) and then signed and returned before participation. Participants do, however, need to have the opportunity to ask questions at this point. Consent forms generally need to clearly specify the parameters of participation and withdrawal, as well as agreed use of data – but local

requirements can vary, so consult specifically (e.g., www.ethicsguidebook .ac.uk/Consent-72). Once consent has been given, you're free to begin.

(8) *Start the interview and collect your data.* In comparison to face-to-face interviews, email interviews allow you to provide a fairly detailed and structured introduction to the topic, if you wish. This gets sent to all participants in the same way, orienting them to the research and task at hand. Then it's onto the distribution of questions! It's important not to overwhelm participants – so you need to decide how many questions to initially send – while one-at-a-time might seem logical, sending three or four simultaneously can encourage broader and detailed answers (Hunt and McHale, 2007). I initially sent all participants, no matter what their musical affiliation, a list of *fifteen* open-ended questions in a document attached to the email. Participants were asked to answer them at their own pace and convenience. I also tried sending one or two questions at a time, and this allowed for a more conversational style and produced richer, more detailed data. Each time I got a response from a participant, I replied with further questions: clarifying their responses; asking for more information on something they had mentioned and/or asking new questions from my interview guide, or entirely new ones, to gauge more detail and about their experiences. This general process continues until you feel you have covered all the topics on your interview guide, and any (new) follow-up points that participants' responses have generated.

In general, I'd recommend specifying a time-frame for response, and doing a follow-up if you have not heard back from participants – either by the 'due' time, or by sending a reminder a day or so earlier. Some of my interviewees sent their answers back on the same day, while others took days or weeks to email their response. Those that took longer to respond tended to let me know their intentions to write detailed responses slowly, so follow-up emails were unnecessary.

(9) *Finish data collection.* In face-to-face interviews, researchers are able to close the interview and part company with participants, once they feel conversations have come to a natural end and sufficient data have been gathered. With email interviews, online conversations could, theoretically, continue for a far longer time, as both participant and researcher are able to continue sending more thoughts, reflections or questions, for an indefinite period of time. This makes clarifying the point of closure important. Determining – and sticking to – a strict timescale for data collection from each individual can be useful here; participants should be made fully aware of this time-frame, and any deadlines. That said, the flexibility of the email interview format does allow lenience for messy

real-life things that get in the way of completing the interview. What you don't want, however, is still to have not finished any interview months after you started!

(10) *Compile data for analysis.* The final step before 'jumping in' to analysis is to prepare and compile your data. In general, compilation will involve the production of a chronological 'transcript' for each participant, clearly labelled and possibly anonymised. If you have a sense of the particular focus of the analysis – or part of it – you might also want to compile all relevant data for each topic/issue across all your participants, or group participants into certain types. In my study, Gmail was used to label interviews, and group them according to participants' musical taste and gender. I could then easily select data related to, for instance, male northern soul fans, without having to look through all my 'transcripts'. Whether or not you pre-cluster a selection of data depends on your analytical approach. Once your data are compiled, you're set to go for analysis!

What Can Go Wrong with Email Interviews?

Although email interviewing has certain distinct advantages over face-to-face interviews, and offers a range of cost and time benefits, there are also practical and methodological challenges in using email interviews. Successful email interviewing is dependent on available and reliable technology, and competence on the part of both researcher and participant (Bampton and Cowton, 2002), not to mention willingness and commitment to participate over time. Technology can fail or crash; data can get lost. Not planning across the multiple devices that people now access email on (smartphones, tablets, computers) risks frustrating and therefore alienating participants. This may also risk the quality of data – you need to be clear if you expect more in terms of responses than might be likely to be 'typed' on a smartphone. Participants need to be technologically proficient and have regular access to the Internet to participate in email interviews. And your time-frames do need to be flexible, to allow for possible technological failure. Data need to be backed up regularly.

Participants losing interest and engagement is a real risk of asynchronous email interviews (Hunt and McHale, 2007) – but less so in synchronous. There are two potential risks: a decrease in the quality of the data, or the participant completely dropping out, either deliberately and letting you know, or simply by stopping making contact with the researcher. To combat potential fatigue, boredom and waning commitment on behalf of participants, you can set expectations of time taken over replies. This expectation can be set during the setting up of participation, prior to commencing the interview. You can also reduce this risk by building rapport with participants. Rapport can be established in various ways in email interviews, including synchronous contact and chats, as the email interview gets set up, starts and even progresses, or by asynchronously emailing respondents with research updates and gentle reminders to encourage them to maintain interest with the study. Regular online contact can help participants to actively engage with questions.

The loss of voice inflections and other non-linguistic features is seen by some as a further limitation of both synchronous and asynchronous email interviewing – with some suggesting a decline in the quality of data (Bampton and Cowton, 2002; Crichton and Kinash, 2003). Others, however, suggest email interviewing produces rich and high-quality data that are in no way lesser than other interview forms (Madge and O'Connor, 2002; McCoyd and Kerson, 2006). With email interviews, there is a risk of poor-quality data due to lack of engagement, and misinterpretation during analysis due to textual, as opposed to spoken, data. But this disadvantage can be – and often is –counteracted, since 'emoticons created from normal keyboard characters are commonly used to inject a degree of personality into email (e.g., ☺' or 'smiley' to indicate humour) or to clarify the way in which a given phrase should be interpreted' (Bampton and Cowton, 2002: para 16). Numerous participants in my research used 'smileys' and other typographical symbols to convey meaning, tone and humour in their answers (e.g., Fig 10.2). Colloquialisms and relatively non-standard language such as 'textspeak' are often used in mobile technology and online communication. Such vernacular may be commonly used by respondents, reflecting the social world they participate in, as well as slang or jargon particular to the topic. Participants should be told that such e-communication norms are acceptable, or they may treat the email interview in a more 'formal' way, and such locally relevant and nuanced responses may be excluded. You can clarify intended meaning if unsure. In my research, as an example, past and present experiences of drug use were described by some using 'street' names and textual abbreviations – something a researcher could misunderstand, if not familiar with an area. Moreover, the 'street' names for drugs varied among the different music scenes! Online forums and urban dictionaries can be useful to 'bring you up to speed' on something that may not be that familiar; you can also ask participants to clarify/confirm, if necessary.

Finally, the disembodied nature of email interviewing can raise problems. The dislocation of the interviewer and interviewee opens up an increased possibility of misunderstanding when compared with the face-to-face interview (Bampton and Cowton, 2002), or at least misunderstanding that isn't relatively quickly identified and resolved. As the researcher and participant are not together during the email interview process, participants could make assumptions about, or misread, questions – which then impact on their responses; the researcher could do the same! To counteract this limitation in asynchronous email interviews, researchers can encourage participants to check whether anything's unclear – this creates a thread of emails back and forth that can help to overcome any ambiguity, and be useful for analysis. The same goes for researchers clarifying ambiguity or uncertainty in participant responses. In my study, I set the project up so participants knew I might email them to clarify, and that they could likewise email to ask for clarification or further information to aid accurate interpretation of questions and responses. As synchronous email interviews happen in 'real-time', they are more like traditional face-to-face interviewing, and such clarification can occur as the interview and conversation progresses.

What Methods of Analysis Suit Email Interview Data?

Methods of analysis suitable for use with data generated by email interviews are similar to those for analysing many other forms of qualitative data, and especially other forms of interview data. In my own research, interview data from both face-to-face and email interviews were analysed using thematic analysis (Braun and Clarke, 2006), using categories from the interview topic guide, including 'descriptions of changing music taste', 'involvement in youth', 'gendered experiences' and 'changes in drug/alcohol use', to identify patterned meanings. Qualitative analysis methods such as narrative analysis (Chase, 2005) and certain versions of discourse analysis (Silverman, 2005) would also be appropriate to analyse email interview accounts. Each offers something different. Narrative analysis, for instance, might highlight participants' complex stories; discourse analysis could show how people construct their experiences and everyday lives in the context of the language used to discuss the research topic; thematic analysis might provide a means to explore more obvious patterns across participants' experiences, or critically interrogate these. If appropriate, computer-assisted qualitative data analysis software, such as NVivo, Atlas/ti or HyperResearch, can be used to facilitate the coding of data; this process is otherwise done by hand. Consider the compatibility between your skills, your research question, your data and analytic approach, and research such technology before jumping in and using it.

Conclusion

Email interviewing is a highly convenient and inexpensive mode of generating rich and valuable data (see Box 10.4). A key advantage is that it allows access to a geographically dispersed group, or people who might otherwise be unwilling to participate in face-to-face interviews – and it still generates rich and in-depth personal narratives. If you consider using email interviews, you need to be aware of the limitations of email interviews, how they might be overcome, and the ethical issues that this method can raise. Researchers can also consider *combining* email interviews with more traditional research methods, such as face-to-face interviewing methods, rather than replacing them – but there should be a good rationale for that, such as a means of obtaining a diverse sample of research participants.

Have a Go . . .

Using one of the following research questions (or your own), consider whether email interviewing might be an appropriate research method, and identify the practical implications of using this method to address the research question, with that population group:

Research Question 1: What impact do breastfeeding support initiatives have for first-time mothers?

Research Question 2: Why do students use social media?

Research Question 3: How is cannabis use perceived by adolescents living with a mental health issue?

Consider the following specific issues, alongside any others that might occur to you:

- Is email interviewing a suitable research method for this question? If so, which *mode* of email interviewing would you choose? Why would email interviews potentially work or not work?
- Who would your participants be?
- Might there be any technological issues specific to the participants that you'd need to consider?
- What particular ethical issues might arise if you were to use email interviewing?
- How would you recruit participants for the project? Are there any existing online forums/groups that you could use to recruit?

- What retention issues might you face?
- How might email interviewing compare to other methods of collecting qualitative data on the topic? Do you think email interviews should be used in collaboration with another research method, or alone? Why?

Box 10.4 Personal reflections on using email interviews

Email interviews are a great way to collect data, but I would always consider combining them with face-to-face methods and offering participants a choice of interview method. Managing data via an email account is relatively easy and the lack of transcription is definitely a key advantage. Whilst extant literature tends to compare email interview data to face-to-face interview data, it would be better, in my view, to compare email interview data to diary accounts or mass observation directives, as they both comprise written rather than spoken data.

Further Resources: Online

The Research Ethics Guidebook is a resource for social science researchers; for students, it provides help with writing a research proposal or ethics application and dealing with ethical dilemmas: www.ethicsguidebook.ac.uk

The British Psychological Society provides ethical guidance for Internet-mediated research: www.bps.org.uk/&/inf206-guidelines-for-Internet-mediated-research.pdf

Further Resources: Readings

For a comparison of face-to-face, telephone and email interviews, see McCoyd, J. L. M. and Kerson, T. S. (2006). Conducting intensive interviews using email: A serendipitous comparative opportunity. *Qualitative Social Work*, 5(3), 389–406.

For a useful comparison of face-to-face and email interviews by focusing on issues relating to time, space and technology, see Bampton, R. and Cowton, C. J. (2002). The e-interview. *Forum Qualitative Sozialforschung/Forum: Qualitative Social Research*, 3(2), article 9. Retrieved from: http://nbn-resolving.de/urn:nbn:de:0114-fqs020295

For a useful discussion of various practical benefits and ethical issues around email interviews for researchers, as well as participants – especially those with disabilities – see Bowker, N. and Tuffin, K. (2004). Using the online medium for discursive research about people with disabilities. *Social Science Computer Review*, 22(2), 228–241.

For a paper that explores email interviews amongst other online research methods, and draws on three research projects over ten years to suggest online, textual interactive interviews are worthy of research consideration, see Crichton, S. and Kinash, S. (2003). Virtual ethnography: Interactive interviewing online as method. *Canadian*

Journal of Learning and Technology, 29(2), Spring/Printemps, www.cjlt.ca/index
.php/cjlt/article/view/40/37
For a discussion of inclusivity in email interviews, showing how email interviews can be
used to facilitate research participation by people with impaired verbal communication, see Ison, N. (2009). Having their say: Email interviews for research data
collection with people who have verbal communication impairment. *International
Journal of Social Research Methodology, 12*(2), 161–172.
For a discussion of some challenges of email interviewing, see James, N. (2007).
The use of email interviewing as a qualitative method of inquiry in educational
research. *British Educational Research Journal, 33*(6), 963–97.

References

Bakardjieva, M. (2005). *Internet society: The internet in everyday life.* London: Sage
Publications.
Bampton, R. and Cowton, C. J. (2002). The e-interview. *Forum Qualitative
Sozialforschung/Forum: Qualitative Social Research, 3*(2), article 9. Retrieved
from: http://nbn-resolving.de/urn:nbn:de:0114-fqs020295
Bowker, N. and Tuffin, K. (2004). Using the online medium for discursive research
about people with disabilities. *Social Science Computer Review, 22*(2), 228–241.
Braun, V. and Clarke, V. (2006). Using thematic analysis in psychology. *Qualitative
Research in Psychology, 3*(2), 77–101.
   (2013). *Successful qualitative research: A practical guide for beginners.* London:
Sage Publications.
British Psychological Society (2013). *Ethics guidelines for Internet-mediated research.*
Leicester, UK: British Psychological Society.
Chase, S. E. (2005). Narrative inquiry: Multiple lenses, approaches and voices.
In N. K. Denzin and Y. S. Lincoln (eds.), *The SAGE handbook of qualitative
research* (3rd edn, pp. 651–679). Thousand Oaks, CA: Sage Publications.
Crichton, S. and Kinash, S. (2003). Virtual ethnography: Interactive interviewing online
as method. *Canadian Journal of Learning and Technology, 29*(2). Retrieved from:
www.cjlt.ca/index.php/cjlt/article/view/40/37
Davis, M., Bolding, G., Hart, G., Sherr, L. and Elford, J. (2004). Reflecting on the
experience of interviewing online: Perspectives from the Internet and HIV study in
London. *Aids Care, 16*(8), 944–952.
Gaiser, T. J. and Schreiner, A. E. (2009). *A guide to conducting online research.* London:
Sage Publications.
Gibson, L. (2010a). *Popular music and the life course: Cultural commitment, lifestyles and
identities* (Unpublished PhD thesis). Manchester, UK: University of Manchester.
   (2010b). *Using email interviews to research popular music and the life course.*
'Realties' toolkit, ESRC National Centre for Research Methods (NCRM).
Hamilton, R. J. and Bowers, B. J. (2006). Internet recruitment and e-mail interviews in
qualitative studies. *Qualitative Health Research, 16*(6), 821–835.
Hine, C. (ed.) (2005). *Virtual methods issues in social research on the Internet.* Oxford:
Berg Publishers.

Hodgson, S. (2004). Cutting through the silence: A sociological construction of self-injury. *Sociological Inquiry, 74*(2), 162–179.

Hooley, T., Marriott, J. and Wellens, J. (2012). *What is online research? Using the Internet for social science research.* London: Bloomsbury.

Hunt, N. and McHale, H. (2007). A practical guide to the email interview. *Qualitative Health Research, 17*(10), 1415–1421.

Ison, N. (2009). Having their say: Email interviews for research data collection with people who have verbal communication impairment. *International Journal of Social Research Methodology, 12*(2), 161–172.

James, N. (2007). The use of email interviewing as a qualitative method of inquiry in educational research. *British Educational Research Journal, 33*(6), 963–976.

James, N. and Busher, H. (2007). Ethical Issues in online educational research: Protecting privacy, establishing authenticity in email interviewing. *International Journal of Research & Method in Education, 30*(1), 101–113.

Madge, C. and O'Connor, H. (2002). On-line with e-mums: Exploring the Internet as a medium for research. *Area, 34*(1), 92–102.

Mann, C. and Stewart, F. (2000). *Internet communication and qualitative research: A handbook for researching online.* London: Sage Publications.

McCoyd, J. L. M. and Kerson, T. S. (2006). Conducting intensive interviews using email: A serendipitous comparative opportunity. *Qualitative Social Work, 5*(3), 389–406.

Meho, L. I. (2006). E-mail interviewing in qualitative research: A methodological discussion. *Journal of the American Society for Information Science and Technology, 57*(10), 1284–1295.

Meho, L. I. and Tibbo, H. R. (2003). Modelling the information-seeking behaviour of social scientists: Ellis's study revisited. *Journal of the American Society for Information Science and Technology, 54*(6), 570–587.

Office for National Statistics (2013). Internet access – Households and individuals, 2013.

Olivero, N. and Lunt, P. (2004). Privacy versus willingness to disclose in e-commerce exchanges: The effect of risk awareness on the relative role of trust and control. *Journal of Economic Psychology, 25*(2), 243–262.

Poland, B. D. (2002). Transcription quality. In J. F. Gubrium and J. A. Holstein (eds.), *Handbook of interview research: Context and method* (pp. 629–649). Thousand Oaks, CA: Sage Publications.

Ratislavová, K. and Ratislav, J. (2014). Asynchronous email interview as a qualitative research method in the humanities. *Human Affairs, 24*(14), 452–460.

Silverman, D. (2005). *Doing qualitative research* (2nd edn). London: Sage Publications.

Walther, J. B. (1996). Computer-mediated communication, impersonal, interpersonal and hyperpersonal interaction. *Communication Research, 23*(1), 3–43.

Wicksteed, A. (2000). Manifestations of chaos and control in the life experiences of individuals with eating disorders: Explorations through qualitative email discourse. *Feminism & Psychology, 10*(4), 475–480.

11   A Productive Chat

Instant Messenger Interviewing

Pamela J. Lannutti

Overview

Instant messenger (IM) programs are Internet-based applications that allow people to conduct text-based interactions in real-time. An IM interaction may be limited to two individuals or, depending on the specific IM program, may allow for groups of people to interact simultaneously. Instant messenger offers researchers a convenient and inexpensive tool for conducting interviews with one or more participants; yet, there are also some important issues to consider. Throughout this chapter, I draw on my own experience with conducting IM interviews on same-sex marriage in the US (see Box 11.1) to discuss the uses of IM in interviewing, as well as the positives and negatives of IM as an interviewing tool .

Introduction to Instant Messenger Interviews

Qualitative interviewing as a research method depends on an interviewer building rapport with a participant and asking questions that encourage them to share their experiences in their own words. Kvale (1996) described this type of qualitative interviewing as 'travelling', with a participant who can be understood as a local inhabitant of the 'territory' being explored, and the interviewer as the traveller who asks questions of the local guide to better understand the 'territory'. As use of the Internet and its applications has become part of daily interactions for many people, researchers have been using online tools in innovative new ways to conduct their research (Jankowski and van Selm, 2005; see also Chapters 10, 12 and 13). Interviews using IM programs have been increasing in usage across the social sciences (James and Busher, 2009).

Instant messenger programs allow people to use a text-based chat to have an exclusive and simultaneous conversation online. Interviewing via IM is attractive to researchers for many reasons, including the ability to conduct

---

Box 11.1 Legal recognition of same-sex marriage in the US

I have spent much of the last decade researching how the legal recognition of same-sex marriage and the debates surrounding legally recognised same-sex marriage have impacted US gay, lesbian, bisexual and transgender (GLBT) people, same-sex couples and their social networks (see Lannutti, 2008, 2001, 2013, 2014). In this chapter, I use two of my studies on same-sex marriage as examples. The first study examined interactions between same-sex couples and members of their extended social networks (acquaintances, neighbours, co-workers etc.) regarding a ban against legal recognition of same-sex marriage in their US states (Lannutti, 2011). I conducted IM interviews with fifty-seven couples living in various US states that had passed bans on same-sex marriage. The second study examined privacy management in interactions among same-sex couples and their family members when discussing the couples' same-sex marriage and/or marriage plans (Lannutti, 2013). For this study, I conducted IM interviews with forty-eight married or engaged same-sex couples.

---

synchronous (real-time) interactions with participants. However, given some characteristics of IM interactions, there is debate about the usefulness of IM as an interviewing tool (Mann and Stewart, 2000). For example, interacting via IM removes many of the nonverbal signals that help us to understand another person's self-presentation in face-to-face interactions, as well as things like age and ethnicity-related cues (Hinchcliffe and Gavin, 2009; James and Busher, 2009). Some researchers argue that, as a result, the degree to which an interviewer and participant can build rapport via IM is limited (see James and Busher, 2009). Further, IM interview detractors point out that IM interviews do not take place with the interviewer and participant sharing the same physical space, so the degree to which an IM interviewer can experience the same 'territory' as the participant is also limited (see Salmons, 2010).

Based on my own experiences with IM interviewing, and my review of the IM interviewing literature, I agree with James and Busher (2009: 19) who argue that 'the development of research relationships and interactions online are still embedded in everyday lives'. Thus, like face-to-face interviews, online interviews allow researchers to learn details about participants' experiences through a conversation that may feel similar to other daily conversations in many ways. Further, research comparing face-to-face and online data collection methods consistently shows that these methods share more similarities than differences (Hinchcliffe and Gavin, 2009; see Chapters 10, 12 and 13). Instant messenger interviews can be used to address similar research topics and questions, can use similar structure and types of interview question and the IM interviewer can make similar choices about methods of participant recruitment, sampling, data analysis and reporting.

Given the similarities between IM interviewing and face-to-face interviewing, an understanding of general interviewing research designs, techniques and issues is an important foundation for successful IM interviewing (e.g., Gubrium and Holstein, 2001; Seidman, 2012). Some IM platforms also provide the ability to run IM *focus groups*, in which many participants interact with the researchers and each other simultaneously (see Mann and Stewart, 2000). However, many of the uses, pros and cons of IM focus groups differ from those of IM interviews with one participant, or even a small group of participants. Thus, this chapter will focus on IM interviews with one participant or a small group of no more than three participants, not IM focus groups (see Chapter 13 for a discussion of online focus groups).

What Do Instant Messenger Interviews Offer the Qualitative Researcher?

The majority of qualitative interviews use open-ended questions and allow for at least some adjustment in either the questions themselves, or the order of questions, depending on information shared during the interview interaction (Baxter and Babbie, 2004). Moreover, IM offers several advantages to researchers wishing to conduct this type of open-ended semi-structured, or even unstructured, interview. The main advantages that IM interviewing offers are: the ability to more easily overcome distance; convenience for the researcher(s), and participants; increased possibility for data confidentiality and anonymity; suitability for hard-to-find and/or -reach populations of participants; integration of Internet-based recruitment and data collection; and ease of data capture.

(1) *Ability to more easily overcome distance.* Perhaps the most obvious, and the most important, advantage that IM interviews offer is that they do not require the interviewer and participant to be in the same physical location. While it is possible for one interviewer to travel in order to conduct face-to-face interviews in a variety of different locations, or for multiple interviewers to conduct face-to-face interviews in different locations, it is seldom possible to do these types of studies without spending considerable financial and time resources. Further, the use of multiple interviewers for the same study can increase the time needed for interviewer training and lead to inconsistencies in the data generated across the interviews. Instant messenger interviews allow a researcher to considerably widen the scope

of possible locations from which participants may be recruited, with little to no financial resources and with little additional time required. Plus, the ability for one interviewer to conduct all of the interviews helps to better maintain consistency and control of the interview experience, if that is important for the research.

The ease with which IM interviewing allows a researcher to overcome the challenge of physical distance may make some studies possible that would not otherwise be within their grasp. For example, I wished to conduct interviews with same-sex couples who lived in a US state that had recently passed a state constitutional amendment banning the legal recognition of same-sex marriage (Lannutti, 2011), but I was not living in or near one of these states. I had no source of funding for the study, so it was not possible for me to travel to, or hire an interviewer, in these locations. Using IM allowed me to complete interviews with fifty-seven couples, who lived in one of seven states, within three months.

(2) *Convenience for researcher(s) and participants.* Another advantage of IM is the convenience that IM interviewing offers to both participants and researchers. Although an interviewer and participant may live in the same area, it does not necessarily mean it is easy for them to meet in the same physical location. The researcher's university campus may not be conveniently accessible to all participants and it may not be affordable for the researcher to rent a space that is accessible to the participants. Public meeting places, such as coffee shops or parks, potentially create concerns about data confidentiality, sensitivity of the topic or the presence of interruptions and distractions. It may be uncomfortable and/or inappropriate to conduct a face-to-face interview in either the interviewer's or participant's home. In contrast, IM interviewing offers a way for an interviewer and participant to interact while each is in a location that is safe, convenient and comfortable (and quiet!).

Also, IM interviewing may be more convenient than other types of interviews due to an increasing use and preference for computer-mediated text-based communication among some groups (Hinchcliffe and Gavin, 2009). Schwarz (2011) argues that interpersonal communication is increasing shifting from face-to-face and phone conversations to IM, especially for younger people, and that this shift is associated with changes in ways people express intimacy, organise conversations and present examples in interpersonal interactions. Kelly, Keaten, Hazel and Williams (2010) offer further support for the importance and integration of IM into our daily interpersonal interactions by showing that IM is used not only for mundane interactions but also for interactions related to difficult personal situations, such as conflict and grief expression, as well. Thus, IM interviewing may be increasingly perceived as a 'natural' and convenient way to interact with a researcher about a range of topics that vary in intimacy. This may be especially true among certain segments of the population, such as teenagers, who have been shown not only to increasingly use IM but also to rely on IM for building and maintaining personal relationships (Schwarz, 2011; Valkenburg and Peter, 2009).

(3) *Increased possibility for data confidentiality and anonymity.* The protection of privacy is a concern for all researchers who work with human participants. In face-to-face interviews, the level of privacy protection that interviewers can offer is (at best) limited to maintaining data confidentiality, so that only the researcher can link a participant's identity to the information they shared. Factors such as participant recruitment procedures and interview location can limit confidentiality in face-to-face interviews. For example, an interviewer and participant who meet in a coffee shop, or even a university office, may be observed and overheard by others in the area. In contrast, IM programs create an exclusive 'space' in which the interviewer and participant may interact, therefore providing easier data confidentiality protection than many face-to-face interviews.

Instant messenger interviewing also offers the possibility of maintaining participant anonymity, something not possible with face-to-face interviewing. *Completely* anonymous IM interviewing is not possible because IP addresses *can* be traced, but in terms of the relationship between the interviewer and the participant, an anonymous interview may be achieved if the research team consists of more than one person, and if steps are taken to protect the participant's identity from the interviewer. One research team member should schedule the interviews, and be the only member of the team to have access to the participant's usual email address; another should conduct the interviews. The participant should create and use an IM username for the interview that is not linked to their identity in any way, and be instructed to avoid sharing identifying information, such as their full name. Interview questions should not require disclosure of such information about the participant.

A common limitation of interview research is that participants may be reluctant to discuss *sensitive* topics via interviews because their identity would be linked to the information that they shared (Kvale, 1996). This limitation may be partially or completely overcome by IM interviews (Hinchcliffe and Gavin, 2009). Not all researchers, however, see IM interviewing as appropriate for discussing sensitive information. Wilson (1997) argued that being physically separate from the other person you are conversing with online creates a disconnection that might make discussion of sensitive topics online difficult. Further, Davis, Bolding, Hart, Sherr and Elford (2004) argued that text-based online interviews may not be the best platform for the discussion of sensitive information, where clarity is important, because text is potentially more ambiguous than spoken words. However, face-to-face interviews are also influenced by social and cultural norms that may affect the discussion of sensitive information (Denzin, 2003). Thus, if the researcher decides that interviews are the best method for their research, IM interviews offer anonymous, and therefore more private and protected, data collection, making them an attractive option for research on sensitive issues.

(4) *Suitability for hard-to-find/hard-to-reach participants.* Researchers often wish to conduct interviews with participants who are relatively difficult to identify and contact compared to others. This difficulty in finding and reaching participants may be because the participants are part of a socially marginalised group, such as members of the GLBT community, or because the participants are part of a very specific and/or relatively small group, such as female chef/owners of Asian fusion restaurants. Because IM interviewing is not limited by physical con-straints of time and space, it facilitates drawing a sample from this kind of hard-to-find and/or hard-to-reach group of participants, who can be dispersed over a wide geographic area (Hinchcliffe and Gavin, 2009; Riggle, Rostosky and Reedy, 2005). Furthermore, the convenience (and greater anonymity) offered by IM interviewing may encourage more of these people to participate in the study, particularly if social stigma is a concern.

(5) *Integration of Internet-based recruitment and data collection.* Additionally, IM interviewing allows for integration of Internet-based participant recruit-ment and data collection (Hinchcliffe and Gavin, 2009). Using IM to inter-view participants recruited online allows researchers to have all interactions with participants using the same platform. Researchers do not need to risk losing the advantages gained in reaching hard-to-find and/or hard-to-reach participants through Internet-based recruiting, by switching to non-Internet-based data collection. For example, if you were to try to recruit GLBT people for a study using non-Internet-based recruiting, you might recruit through community centres, support groups and bars. However, Internet-based recruiting methods offer expanded opportunities, because they go beyond limited geographic locations such as community centres and bars, and enable the recruitment of GLBT people who do not frequent support groups, bars or other GLBT community organisations (Riggle, Rostosky and

Reedy, 2005). Further, Internet-based recruitment procedures may help researchers gather a sample of GLBT participants that captures more of the diversity (including age, socioeconomic class, level of 'outness') of the community than 'offline' recruiting methods, such as placing signs in community centres, because of the wide reach of Internet-based recruitment (van Eeden-Moorefield, Proulx and Pasley, 2008).

(6) *Ease of data capture.* Another advantage that IM interviewing offers researchers is ease of data capture. Researchers traditionally use audio recording, and occasionally video recording, of (face-to-face, or telephone) interviews in order to capture the information shared by participants. Although technological advances have provided inexpensive, small, and easy to use high-quality audio and video recorders, there are still possible difficulties presented by these recording devices. The sight of these devices may make some participants nervous or distracted. Depending on the setting of the face-to-face interview, recording devices may pick up background or environmental noise that may make later playback unclear. And, of course, there is always the possibility that a recording device may malfunction, or that user error may occur such that the recording does not take place or only partially takes place.

Instant messenger interviewing eliminates the possibility of all of these recording difficulties: the text-based nature of the IM interview means that the interview unfolds and is simultaneously captured within the IM tool. In addition to the ease of data capture, IM interviewing eliminates the need for data transcription. For some qualitative researchers, the data transcription process is a useful part of becoming familiar with the data at the beginning of data analysis (Kvale, 1996). Yet, the transcription process is usually time-consuming, may be expensive, and even small errors in transcription can radically alter the meaning of the data (Poland, 2002). For researchers who do not wish to transcribe their interview data, IM interview data are ready for analysis much more quickly, inexpensively and more accurately.

What Research Questions Suit Instant Messenger Interviews?

Research questions that are appropriate for IM interviews are those that are appropriate for any qualitative interview study, such as those focused on participants' thoughts, feelings and behaviours. Although IM interviewing techniques are still relatively new in the social scientific research world, IM interviews have already been used to address a wide range of research questions, including self-reported Internet use and addiction (Chou, 2001), reactions to deception in online dating ads (Stieger, Eichinger and Honeder, 2009) and the communication of persons with disabilities (Bowker and Tuffin, 2007). In my own research, I have used IM interviewing to investigate research questions that vary from the broad, such as 'How have older same-sex couples reacted to legally recognized same-sex marriage and the debates surrounding legally recognized same-sex marriage?' (Lannutti, 2011: 67), to the narrower, such as 'During interactions with family members about same-sex marriage, how do married and engaged couples manage their regulation of their private information?' (Lannutti, 2013: 62).

Design, Sampling and Ethical Issues

After you have formed research questions that are appropriate for interviewing, the next consideration should be whether or not the target participants are an appropriate group for IM interviewing. As discussed further below, using IM for interviews may mean that the sample will be more likely to include those who are financially comfortable, technologically savvy, well-educated and physically able. This possible limitation may be a more important for some studies than others. For example, a researcher studying the effects of standardised testing in education may find IM interviewing more problematic in terms of generating a diverse sample than might a researcher studying the communication styles of large corporation CEOs. You need to carefully consider the possible impact of these potential sample limitations on your study *before* choosing to interview via IM. Ethical issues are discussed later.

Steps to Using Instant Messenger Interviews

If you decide that IM interviews are appropriate for your research question and potential participants, then there are a series of steps you should follow to conduct the IM interview (see also James and Busher, 2009; Salmons, 2010). I now outline the four steps that I followed in my own research, as an example of the process:

(1) *Design an appropriate interview protocol.* Most of the IM interviews I conduct are semi-structured, meaning that an interview protocol, (or 'guide'), with some predetermined questions and question order, is used for all interviews, but each interview ultimately develops in reaction to participants' responses (see Box 11.2 for a sample interview protocol). Researchers using IM could also use an unstructured interview protocol in which they at

---

Box 11.2 Example Internet Messenger interview protocol

(1) How old are you?
(2) How would you describe your racial/ethnic background?
(3) How long have you been together?
(4) How long have you been in a committed relationship with each other?
(5) Have you ever had a commitment ceremony or wedding?
  • Please describe the ceremony.
  • How did you decide to have this type of ceremony?
(6) Why did you decide to get married (or not get married)?
  • Tell me more about your decision process.
  • Who did you communicate with about your decision? What happened in those interactions?
(7) How has the legal recognition of relationships in your State impacted your relationship?
  • your sense of self?
  • the GLBT community?
  • the larger community?
  • your friends?
  • your family?
(8) How have you been affected by same-sex marriage bans?

Standard probes: Can you tell me more about that? Can you give me an example of that? I'd like to hear more about that. Why? Do you agree? Is that how you would also describe what happened?

Source: Lannutti (2011).

---

most have a list of topics to cover and specific questions are spontaneously created *during* each individual interview, dependent on the flow of the conversation. Semi-structured interviews are very common and have the advantage of keeping the core of the interviews similar from participant to participant, while still allowing some flexibility (Baxter and Babbie, 2004). Unstructured interviews allow researchers and participants more flexibility than do semi-structured interviews, but unstructured interviews may lack consistency from interview to interview, which may complicate data analysis.

(2) *Interact with potential participants: recruit and gain consent.* First, when recruiting participants through various methods, I ask that people interested in participating in the study to send me an email. I respond by sending a consent form (see Box 11.3 for an example) with details about the study and ask them to complete and return it. Procedures for informed consent vary widely – for instance, some ethics bodies will expect a *separate*

Box 11.3 Example informed consent document

Informed Consent for Participation in Same-Sex Marriage, Couples, Families
Investigator: Pamela J. Lannutti, Ph.D.

Introduction: You are being asked to be in a research study of the impact of relationship recognition on same-sex relationships and the families of same-sex couples. You were selected as a possible participant because you are over eighteen and have been in a same-sex romantic relationship for over one year or because you are a family member of a person in a same-sex couple. We ask that you read this form and ask any questions that you may have before agreeing to be in the study.

Purpose of Study: The purpose of this study is better understand the impact of relationship recognition on same-sex couples and their families.

Description of the Study Procedures: If you agree to be in this study, we would ask you and your partner to participate in a forty-five to sixty minute interview with the researcher via an IM program.

Risks/Discomforts of Being in the Study: There are no reasonable foreseeable (or expected) risks. There may be unknown risks.

Benefits of Being in the Study: You should expect no direct benefits for participating in this study.

Payments: You will receive no payment/reimbursement for participation.

Costs: There is no cost to you to participate in this research study.

Confidentiality: The records of this study will be kept private. In any sort of report we may publish, we will not include any information that will make it possible to identify a participant. Hard copies of research records will be kept in a locked file. All electronic information will be coded and secured using a password protected file. Access to the records will be limited to the researchers; however, please note that regulatory agencies, and the Institutional Review Board and internal College auditors may review the research records.

Voluntary Participation/Withdrawal: Your participation is voluntary. If you choose not to participate, it will not affect your current or future relations with the University. You are free to withdraw at any time, for whatever reason. There is no penalty or loss of benefits for not taking part or for stopping your participation. You will be provided with any significant new findings that develop during the course of the research that may make you decide that you want to stop participating.

*Dismissal From the Study: If you do not follow the instructions you are given you will be dismissed from the study.

Contacts and Questions: The researcher conducting this study is Pamela J. Lannutti, Ph.D. For questions or more information concerning this research you may contact her. If you have any questions about your rights as a research subject, you may contact: Director, Office for Research Protections.

Copy of Consent Form: You should save a copy of this form to keep for your records and future reference.

Statement of Consent: I have read the contents of this consent form and have been encouraged to ask questions. I have received answers to my questions. I give my consent to participate in this study. I will receive a copy of this form.

Consent agreement

By typing your IM name and date here, you give your consent to participate in the study:

IM name:_____

    Date:_____

Source: Lannutti (2013).

information sheet and consent form, so check your location requirements. After informed consent is received from the participant, I ensure that they have access to the IM program. If they don't, I sent them a link to download a free IM program, such as Yahoo! Messenger. Then, I schedule an interview time and share the ground rules for the interview (see Box 11.4). To help protect the participants' confidentiality, I ask them to create a new IM username to be used exclusively for the purposes of the interview.

(3) *Conduct the interview.* Most IM interviews that I have conducted lasted between forty-five and ninety minutes. Just as with face-to-face interviews, interview length should be determined by the content and goals of the individual research project. I usually begin IM interviews with questions about participants' demographic information, such as age and biological sex, and other background information, such as a brief employment history, to build rapport; I then spend the majority of the interview time discussing the key questions for my study. If you are short on time, or think asking the demographic questions at the start might be too threatening for your participant group, then keep the interview focused on key questions for the study and collect demographic information outside of the interview via an emailed demographic information form. An important skill for an interviewer, whether using an IM or face-to-face format, to learn is to be able to judge when to ask more follow-up probes for a topic, and when to move on to a new topic in the interview. This skill is best learnt through practice. One technique that I sometimes use is to directly ask a participant if she or he has anything more to say on a topic before I move on to the next.

(4) *Prepare the data for analysis and presentation.* After the IM interview is complete, it is easy to save the conversation for data analysis either by cutting and pasting to a word processing document, or saving within the

---

Box 11.4 Example ground rules for an Internet Messenger interview

During the interview, I ask that you please adhere to the following ground rules:

(1) Do not share any identifying information about yourself, such as your full name, address, etc.
(2) The IM program will let you see when another person is typing. Please do not type while another person is typing. Instead, wait to see what that person has written before you respond.
(3) If you need to take a break, please type that. Do not just walk away from your computer. Please don't use other programs on your computer while we are having the interview.
(4) Please refrain from using emoticons or other pictorial symbols. It's okay to say how you feel, but please type it out.
(5) It is okay to use common abbreviations and shorthand on IM, such as typing 'u' instead of 'you'. If someone types something that is unclear to you, please ask for clarification.
(6) The more information you can give, the more you will help the research project. I know that typing can get tedious, but it is really important to learn as much detail about your experiences as possible. So, please write at length in response to questions.
(7) If you do not wish to answer a question, please type 'no comment' in response rather than just ignoring the question.
(8) It is okay to disagree with another person, but please do so respectfully.
(9) Please do not share the information from the interview with anyone else.

Source: Lannutti (2013).

IM program itself. Following analysis, I usually edit quotations from the IM interviews to replace any IM language conventions, such as 'u' for 'you', with standard English. For example, a participant wrote: 'idk. she talked abt us differently. things just werent the same w my sister after we told her abt getting married'. I would present this quotation as, 'I don't know. She talked about us differently. Things just weren't the same with my sister after we told her about getting married'. I choose to edit the IM quotations to standard English spelling and grammar to make them more understandable to a wider audience of readers. I am, however, always careful to note that these editorial changes have been made to IM language conventions in my reports, to ensure that the reader understands the data representation fully. You should decide whether or not making such edits is appropriate for your study. A goal of many interviews is to capture the exact language that participants use to describe their experiences, within the medium they are using to construct their narratives. In these cases, editing exactly what the participant writes in the IM interview would not be appropriate. Like most researchers, I also use pseudonyms to replace participants' names in reports, to protect participant identities.

What Can Go Wrong with Instant Messenger Interviews?

Many of the things that can 'go wrong' in IM interviewing are things that could be problematic in any interview format. All researchers may be faced with difficulties such as problems in recruiting participants, participants failing to meet at the scheduled interview time, participants who are reluctant to answer questions or those who keep on sharing various and unrelated thoughts regardless of the questions actually being asked, and struggles to identify and explain the best themes and categories to describe and report the data. There are, however, some potential difficulties that are *specific* to IM interviewing, including: managing the flow of the interview; distractions and interruptions to the interview; concerns with data security; and possible sampling limitations. I consider each of these in turn:

(1) *Flow of the IM interview.* One challenge of IM interviewing is that the flow of an IM conversation is different from that of a face-to-face conversation because of the text-based nature of IM interactions. During a face-to-face conversation, people rely on a host of nonverbal cues, such as eye contact and gestures, to regulate turn taking, which are not available in an IM interaction. Thus, it can be difficult to have what feels like a natural and relaxed flow of conversation using IM, especially if the users are not accustomed to communicating via IM or communicating with each other. What may result instead is a type of stuttered interaction in which one person is typing and posting their thoughts on a topic before the other person has finished typing and posting their full thoughts on that topic or another topic. Here is an (edited to standard English) example from an interview I collected as part of a study examining familial conversations about same-sex marriage (Lannutti, 2013):

ELIZABETH: The first conversation with my parents was really awkward.
INTERVIEWER: Did you tell them by yourself?

ELIZABETH: I started by asking them to come over for dinner. Be better
                to have a nice evening as part of it.
ELIZABETH: Yes. Just me and my parents.
INTERVIEWER: Sorry. You were talking about the dinner.
ELIZABETH: So, right, I asked them to dinner but couldn't figure out
                how to bring it up.

This type of stuttered interaction can not only be annoying to the people having the conversation but it can also be problematic to a research interview, because the interruptions in participants' thoughts may lead them to leave out important insights, lose track of their thought process or decide to respond using shorter and less descriptive statements. These things can be detrimental to a goal of most qualitative interviews: to gain an in-depth understanding of participants' experiences.

In my research, I have worked to reduce the possibility of stuttered conversational flow by including specific instructions about how to handle turn taking in the IM interview at the onset (see Box 11.4). An interview, after all, is not a casual conversation between friends. Although it may seem unusual to set ground rules for an IM interaction, I have found that doing so helps the interview go much more smoothly. These ground rules include asking participants to wait to start typing any comments until their IM program stops indicating that another person in the interaction is typing. I ask participants to avoid using emoticons or pictorial representations of their thoughts and feelings so that ambiguity from pictures might be avoided. I also ask participants to type 'no comment' if they do not wish to answer a question or have no further responses to a question rather than just ignoring the most recent post. Although following this rule may add more time to the interview, this cost is outweighed by the benefit of smoother IM interactions.

In interactions with more than one participant – such as interviews with couples in my study of same-sex couples interactions with others about same-sex marriage bans (Lannutti, 2011) – I find that another way to help the IM interaction flow more smoothly is to direct a question to one specific participant at a time by using the participant's username before asking a question, rather than just typing the question. Here is an (edited to Standard English) example from the data collected for Lannutti (2011):

INTERVIEWER: Can you tell me more about the conversation you had with
                your neighbour?
LINDA: I kind of came in on the end of that conversation.

SUE:	Yeah, it was mostly me that started having the conversation, but I think that Linda was there for most of it. I don't remember it that well, but I remember being upset.
LINDA:	You were. We both were. Our neighbour didn't say anything rude, but he made it clear that he supported the ban.
INTERVIEWER:	Sue, do you remember what kinds of things he said?
SUE:	He said that he was going to vote. That people of faith needed to be heard on the issue. That's all I remember.
INTERVIEWER:	Linda, do you remember more of what he said?
LINDA:	Not really.

Even when the flow of an IM interview is a bit stuttered at the beginning, I also find that the flow tends to smooth out after participants adjust to the ground rules and the pace of the interaction itself after a few exchanges. It is helpful to practice interviewing a volunteer via IM before beginning actual data collection.

(2) *Distractions and interruptions to the IM interview.* Some of the distractions and interruptions that may impact face-to-face interviews may also, depending on the setting, affect IM interviews. Face-to-face interviews that take place in public places or even in private homes are vulnerable to interruptions and distractions caused by other people, noise or other events in the setting. People engaging in an IM interview may also be interrupted or distracted by these hazards because simply being part of an online conversation does not mean that you are completely removed from the environment around you. Your dog barking at you for attention is just as distracting if you are talking face-to-face or trying to participate in an IM conversation.

There are, however, some types of interruptions and distractions that *are* associated with the technology involved in IM interviewing, that are not likely to affect face-to-face interviewing. As with other Internet-based technology, IM programs are sometimes plagued with delays, freezes and other breakdowns that will interrupt an interview. Because people are using the IM program on their computers or other devices, there are also possible distractions caused by alerts and popups from other programs, and participants may be tempted to quickly check email or open a favourite game during the interview (James and Busher, 2009; Salmons, 2010). Although it is not always possible to fully avoid these distractions and interruptions, I suggest asking IM interview participants to refrain from engaging in other programs, or asking for a pause in the interview if they must engage another program, as part of the ground rules for the interview (see Box 11.4).

(3) *Concerns about data security.* Inherent in the promise of greater opportunities for data confidentiality and/or anonymity in IM interviewing is the ability to provide protection and security for the data collected during the research process. While almost all IM programs provide an exclusive 'space' for an interaction, information shared via IM is easily saved and copied by anyone involved in the interaction. So, if more than one participant is included in the interview, there is the risk of a participant breaching confidentiality and sharing others' responses outside of the interview. As part of the ground rules for the interview, you should ask those who participate in group IM interviews to refrain from unauthorised sharing of information from the interview, and warn all participants of the limits of data security in these interviews. In addition, you should be careful to protect your own copies of the interactions. It is important to review the privacy and data security information of the IM program you wish to use for the interviews. You should make sure that you are using a password-protected private device to conduct, save and store the IM interviews. All saved and stored IM interviews should be kept in a password-protected file and should be accessible only to those who are part of the research team. While no one person can guarantee total data security, taking these simple steps helps to ensure that you do your best to live up to the ethical obligations of data protection.

What Methods of Analysis Suit Instant Messenger Interview Data?

In my experience, data analysis methods do not vary for IM interviews and face-to-face interviews. There are a wide range of data analysis techniques that can be used for interview data, collected via IM and other methods, including thematic analysis (e.g., see Hussain and Griffiths, 2009) and interpretative phenomenological analysis (e.g., see Whitty, Young, and Goodings, 2011). Although it may not be appropriate for all interviewing studies, most of the studies that I have conducted using IM interviewing use grounded theory inductive method, where sampling is influenced by the data analysis process. In this process, the data from an initial set of interviews are analysed using a data-driven approach, where themes develop from the participants' responses rather than a priori conceptual categories or themes (Boyatzis, 1998; Charmaz, 2000). Using procedures recommended by Strauss and Corbin (2008), my first step in analysis for the initial interviews is open coding. Open coding is performed for each of the participants' responses to questions or each other's statements during the interview, to identify key concepts in the data. Consistent with Strauss and Corbin (2008), the relationships among concepts in the data are then analysed to form themes.

Once I have a set of themes based on data from the initial sample, I conduct interviews with more participants to ensure that the emerging data analysis categories are fully explored or 'saturated'. Saturation occurs when new data do not lead to new theoretical insights about categories or the relationship between categories (Charmaz, 2006; Strauss and Corbin, 2008). Participants' responses in the second set of interviews are analysed using comparative analysis (Strauss and Corbin, 2008). In this process, concepts that are similar to those already part of identified themes from the initial sample are included within those existing themes; and concepts that are not consistent with those or part of existing themes are used to form *new* themes. After all concepts from the second set of interviews are coded into themes, concepts from the initial sample are comparatively analysed to see if they fit better with those first generated from the *second* set of interviews. Thus, all of the concepts from the entire dataset are compared to all themes, and placed into themes representative of the entire dataset. Once all of the themes derived from the inductive comparative analysis process are established, theoretical linkages among themes are identified. Throughout the entire coding process, notes are made to identify exemplar quotations from the interviews, that will to be used to describe the themes.

As part of the final steps of IM interviewing, I also usually take steps to check the trustworthiness of the data analysis (Lincoln and Guba, 1985; Miles and Huberman, 1994). In most cases, I conduct 'member checks' of my data analysis. To do so, I ask a small section of participants to review the themes and exemplars that emerged from data analysis and confirm that the descriptions fit with their lived experiences.

Conclusion

Collecting data using instant messaging programs provides researchers with an opportunity to overcome distance and other obstacles to reach participants. While IM interviewing does present some unique challenges, I have found that the advantages of the method outweigh concerns introduced by the computer-mediated chat (see Box 11.5). For those already familiar with interviewing, or those just *beginning* to use interview methods, IM interviewing expands the toolbox available to qualitative researchers.

Box 11.5 Personal reflections on using Internet Messenger interviews

When I began my career as a communication researcher, online data collection methods were not available. Thus, I learnt how to conduct interviews either face-to-face or via telephone. When IM and other online tools became widely available, I wasn't sure that these would provide a viable means of interviewing participants. When I first considered using IM for research interviews, I was worried that the participants would be uninterested in IM interactions and that the interviews themselves would be flat and lack the rich detail I had previously only associated with face-to-face interviews. Quickly after starting to use IM for interviews, I realised that the participants were not only willing to interact with me via IM but also that many of the potential participants for my studies were *more* willing to be interviewed via IM than through another interview format. Further, I was impressed by the quality of interview that was possible via IM. Because of IM interviewing, I have been able to interview people from all over the US about their experiences with same-sex marriage without spending large amounts of time and money on travel. Like any research method, IM interviewing has pros and cons. There are times when the IM conversation seems to move more slowly than a face-to-face conversation might. Occasionally, I wish I could see my participants' face or hear their tone of voice to better understand a comment they are making without having to explicitly ask for clarification as I do when using IM. However, I have found IM interviewing to be an extremely productive and useful research tool.

Have a Go ...

The best way to become skilled at conducting IM interviews is through practice. To practice a semi-structured IM interview, complete the following steps:

(1) *Preparation.* Identify a topic you wish to learn more about. Use this topic for your interview. Create one or two research questions related to the topic you wish to answer. Create a set of five to eight key interview questions, with possible probing questions to use as follow-ups to your questions. You may also want to create three to five demographic questions to include in the interview, or in a separate demographic information sheet. Create an informed consent document (and participant information sheet, if necessary) that provides the participant with information about the interview purpose, procedure, estimated length and data protection. Create a set of ground rules for the interview.

(2) *Recruitment and informed consent.* Recruit a volunteer to act as the participant in your IM interview. Provide the potential participant with the informed consent document (and information sheet), and get their consent to be

interviewed. Share your ground rules and information about the IM program with the participant. Set up an interview time.

(3) *IM interview interaction*. Begin with reminding the participant about the ground rules for the interview. Conduct the interview as you planned in step 1. Be sure to save the interview interaction once it is complete.

(4) *Analysis*. Look for themes among the interview answers that relate to your research questions. Identify quotations from the interview that exemplify each theme. Do you want to translate the IM language to standard English? If so, do so in this step.

(5) *Reflect upon the interview*. What challenges did you face as you completed the steps above? How did you handle them? What did you enjoy about conducting an interview via IM?

Further Resources: Online

For an introduction to what IM is, see https://en.wikipedia.org/wiki/Instant_messaging

Further Resources: Readings

For further guidance on preparing for synchronous online interviews, see Chapter 6: Preparing for a live online interview, in: Salmons, J. (2010). *Online interviews in real time*. Thousand Oaks, CA: Sage Publications.

For useful guidance on creating and sustaining meaningful relationships with participants in online interviews, see Chapter 2: Engaging with research participants online in James, N. and Busher, H. (2009). *Online interviewing*. Thousand Oaks, CA: Sage Publications.

To read more about the example studies involving couple interviews, see

Lannutti, P. J. (2008). 'This is not a lesbian wedding': Examining same-sex marriage and bisexual-lesbian couples. *Journal of Bisexuality*, *7*(3/4), 237–260.

(2011). Examining communication about marriage amendments: Same-sex couples and their extended social networks. *Journal of Social Issues*, *67*(2), 264–281.

(2013). Same-sex marriage and privacy management: Examining couples' communication with family members. *Journal of Family Communication*, *13*(1), 60–75.

References

Baxter, L. A. and Babbie, E. (2004). *The basics of communication research*. Belmont, CA: Wadsworth.

Bowker, N. I. and Tuffin, K. (2007). Understanding positive subjectivities made possible online for disabled people. *New Zealand Journal of Psychology*, *36*(2), 63–71.

Boyatzis, R. E. (1998). *Transforming qualitative information: Thematic analysis and code development*. Thousand Oaks, CA: Sage Publications.

Charmaz, K. (2000). Grounded theory: Objectivist and constructivist methods. In N. K. Denzin and Y. S. Lincoln (eds.), *Handbook of qualitative research* (pp. 509–535). Thousand Oaks, CA: Sage Publications.

(2006). *Constructing grounded theory: A practical guide through qualitative analysis*. Thousand Oaks, CA: Sage Publications.

Chou, C. (2001). Internet heavy use and addiction among Taiwanese college students: An online interview study. *CyberPsychology & Behavior, 4*(5), 573–585.

Davis, M., Bolding, G., Hart, G., Sherr, L. and Elford, J. (2004). Reflecting on the experience of interviewing online: Perspectives from the Internet and HIV study in London. *AIDS Care, 16*(8), 944–952.

Denzin, N. (2003). The cinematic society and the reflective interview. In J. F. Gubrium and J. A. Holstein (eds.), *Postmodern interviewing* (pp. 141–155). Thousand Oaks, CA: Sage Publications.

van Eeden-Moorefield, B. V., Proulx, C. M. and Pasley, K. (2008). A comparison of Internet and face-to-face (FTF) qualitative methods in studying the relationships of gay men. *Journal of GLBT Family Studies, 4*(2), 181–204.

Gubrium, J. F. and Holstein, J. A. (eds.) (2001). *Handbook of interview research: Context and method*. Thousand Oaks, CA: Sage Publications.

Hinchcliffe, V. and Gavin, H. (2009). Social and virtual networks: Evaluating synchronous online interviewing using instant messenger. *The Qualitative Report, 14*(2), 318–340.

Hussain, Z. and Griffiths, M. D. (2009). The attitudes, feelings, and experiences of online gamers: A qualitative analysis. *CyberPsychology & Behavior, 12*(6), 747–753.

James, N. and Busher, H. (2009). *Online interviewing*. Thousand Oaks, CA: Sage Publications.

Jankowski, N. W. and van Selm, M. (2005). Epilogue: Methodological concerns and innovations in internet research. In C. Hine (ed.), *Virtual methods: Issues in social research on the Internet*. Oxford: Peter Lang Publishing.

Kelly, L., Keaten, J. A., Hazel, M. and Williams, J. A. (2010). Effects of reticence, affect for communication channels, self-perceived competence on usage of instant messaging. *Communication Research Reports, 27*(2), 131–142.

Kvale, S. (1996). *Interviews: An introduction to qualitative research interviewing*. Thousand Oaks, CA: Sage Publications.

Lannutti, P. J. (2008). 'This is not a lesbian wedding': Examining same-sex marriage and bisexual-lesbian couples. *Journal of Bisexuality, 7*(3/4), 237–260.

(2011). Examining communication about marriage amendments: Same-sex couples and their extended social networks. *Journal of Social Issues, 67*(2), 264–281.

(2013). Same-sex marriage and privacy management: Examining couples' communication with family members. *Journal of Family Communication, 13*(1), 60–75.

(2014). *Experiencing same-sex marriage: Individuals, couples, and social networks*. New York: Peter Lang Publishing.

Lincoln, Y. S. and Guba, E. G. (1985). *Naturalistic inquiry*. Newbury Park, CA: Sage Publications.

Mann, C. and Stewart, F. (2000). *Internet communication and qualitative research: A handbook for researching online*. Thousand Oaks, CA: Sage Publications.

Miles, M. B. and Huberman, A. M. (1994). *Qualitative data analysis: An expanded sourcebook.* Thousand Oaks, CA: Sage Publications.

Poland, B. D. (2002). Transcription quality. In J. F. Gubrium and J. A. Holstein (eds.), *Handbook of interview research: Context and method* (pp. 629–649). Thousand Oaks, CA: Sage Publications.

Riggle, E. D. B., Rostosky, S. S. and Reedy, C. S. (2005). Online surveys for BGLT research. *Journal of Homosexuality, 49*(2), 1–21.

Salmons, J. (2010). *Online interviews in real time.* Thousand Oaks, CA: Sage Publications.

Schwarz, O. (2011). Who moved my conversation? Instant messaging, intertextuality and new regimes of intimacy and truth. *Media, Culture & Society, 33*(1), 71–87.

Seidman, I. (2012). *Interviewing as qualitative research: A guide for researchers in education and the social sciences* (4th edn). New York: Teachers College Press.

Stieger, S., Eichinger, T. and Honeder, B. (2009). Can mate choice strategies explain sex differences?: The deceived persons' feelings in reaction to revealed online deception of sex, age, and appearance. *Social Psychology, 40*(1), 16–25.

Strauss, A. and Corbin, J. (2008). *Basics of qualitative research: Techniques and procedures for developing grounded theory* (3rd edn). Thousand Oaks, CA: Sage Publications.

Valkenberg, P. M. and Peter, J. (2009). The effects of instant messaging on the quality of adolescents' existing friendships: A longitudinal study. *Journal of Communication, 59*(1), 79–97.

Whitty, M. T., Young, G. and Goodings, L. (2011). What I won't do in pixels: Examining the limits of taboo violation in MMORPGs. *Computers in Human Behaviors, 27*(1), 268–275.

Wilson, M. (1997). Community in the abstract: A political and ethical dilemma. In D. Holmes (ed.), *Virtual politics: Identity & community in cyberspace* (pp. 23–57). London: Sage Publications.

12 'I'm Not *with* You, Yet I Am …'

Virtual Face-to-Face Interviews

Paul Hanna and Shadreck Mwale

Overview

This chapter is concerned with the use of Internet-based video-calling technologies, specifically Skype, in interview research. The chapter is based on our experiences of using Skype to conduct interviews in two research projects – one on sustainable tourism and another on volunteer involvement in Phase I clinical trials (see Boxes 12.1 and 12.2). In this chapter, we draw on theoretical and reflexive insights regarding our experiences of conducting Skype interviews, in order to show that video-calling technologies allow qualitative researchers to harness the potential of the Internet. We also use extracts from interviews with research participants conducted via Skype to explore their perceptions of the advantages and limitations of this method – these are all from Mwale's study (see Box 12.2). We outline steps in using Skype, and the practical challenges it presents. Finally, we conclude with our personal reflections on how we came to use Skype and what opportunities it opened up for us.

Introduction to Skype Interviews

It is often argued that the Internet is changing the nature of social and health research due to a range of characteristics, such as the ability to communicate with people across the world at the touch of a button (e.g., Evans, Elford and Wiggins, 2008). In this chapter we draw on two very different research projects in which using Skype to conduct interviews had the potential to be of specific benefit to our research and to the research participants. There is now a range of alternatives to Skype offering similar technologies, such as Apple's FaceTime. However, given our experience, we concentrate here on Skype as an example of video-calling technologies.

Box 12.1 Sustainable tourism

Paul Hanna's (2013a) research explores how people experience and understand sustainable and pro-environmental behaviour such as sustainable tourism. Sustainable tourism is explicitly labelled 'sustainable' and 'ethical', but at the same time, 'the holiday' is generally understood as a time and place to 'escape' from everyday struggles and relax, and often involves high-polluting air transportation. Hanna initially conducted sixteen interviews with self-defined 'sustainable tourists', but on reflection, decided it was extremely problematic to travel vast distances solely to collect data. Therefore, he decided to offer his future participants the choice of either a face-to-face, telephone or Skype interview. In the end, no participant located outside a five mile radius of the local area opted for a face-to-face interview, which suggests the importance of offering participants the choice between different interview mediums, particularly when environmental sustainability is a concern.

Box 12.2 Volunteer involvement in Phase 1 clinical trials

Shadreck Mwale's (2015) project investigated human involvement, particularly the experiences of healthy volunteers, in clinical trials – a testing regime which involves a set of practices required before new drug molecules can be declared safe and effective for marketing (Pocock, 2000). There were a number of challenges involved in conducting this research. For healthy volunteers, taking part in clinical trials is often socially perceived as reckless and irresponsible behaviour (Abadie, 2010), and thus participants were very conscious about sharing their experiences face-to-face with a researcher who is a stranger. In addition, the pharmaceutical companies involved were concerned that their volunteers may be lured by their competitors away from their units or that information about their clinical trial units given to the media, which may portray them negatively. Conducting interviews via Skype enabled Mwale to manage these concerns about confidentiality and access.

Skype was founded in 2003 and is free software that offers both audio and visual communication via an Internet connection. The software is available on computers (both Windows and Apple Mac), through Smart TVs, via video game consoles (such as PlayStation 3) and as an app on smartphones and tablets. We suggest that researchers use the software through a PC to utilise the recording software available. The participant, however, can use it through any form of technology that supports it. The basic download of Skype is free and simple to use, requiring only that a user account is set up. To use Skype you have to open an account and create a profile; this involves choosing a Skype username, selecting an image for your profile (if desired) and creating a secure password. After this, your profile is publicly available for people to use. Communication is then possible from individual to individual via their username contact details. It also has a platform for sending messages, which users can access at any time they log in.

As the software runs through the Internet, and does not 'make calls' over a standard phone-line, the locality of those wishing to communicate by calling or sending instant messages from Skype to Skype is irrelevant in terms of the potential costs of calls. However, the technology does include services for calling mobile phones and landlines, both local and international, at a fee (though generally greatly reduced compared to standard call charges). To make a Skype-to-Skype call, you need to be *connected* with the other user. After sending 'contact' requests to other Skype users, a connection is created when they accept your request – or you accept theirs.

To the best of our knowledge, the technology had not been used for research purposes until Hanna's 2008–2011 project and subsequent 2012 publication (Hanna, 2012). The technology appears now to be readily used in a vast range of research areas, with a number of papers reporting the findings of Skype interview research published in the last few years. For example, British geographers Deakin and Wakefield (2014) used Skype in their PhD research projects exploring 'academic networking for learning and teaching' and 'student work placement mobility in Europe', both of which had a focus on UK- and non-UK-based participants. Gkartzios (2013), a researcher in planning and development, used Skype to conduct in-depth interviews with participants in Greece to explore the ways in which the recent economic crisis has impacted the lives of individuals, and resulted in people moving from urban lifestyles to rural lifestyles, and returning to a greater reliance on the extended family unit. In his research on childcare and emotions, Australian educational researcher Yarrow (2013) used 'web-based video-calling services' to conduct semi-structured interviews with childcare staff (other examples include: Green and Young, 2015; Hill and Hemmings, 2015; van Riemsdijk, 2014).

What Do Skype Interviews Offer the Qualitative Researcher?

As a tool, Skype does not offer a radical alternative to conventional means for collecting interview data. Rather, what it offers is an *alternative* means for collecting data that uses the Internet to overcome many of the inherent limitations and challenges of face-to-face data collection, such as: difficulties of arranging a time and place to meet; participants not feeling comfortable sharing their experiences in person; and the challenges of noise and disruptions if interviewing in public spaces (Bryman, 2004). Therefore software such as Skype further advances the Internet as the medium that provides the most feasible alternative to face-to-face interviews, if issues such as distance, sensitivity/anonymity, time and funding resources are of concern.

We see five key benefits of using Skype in qualitative interview research:

(1) *Ease and flexibility of scheduling.* Skype interviews are much easier to arrange than face-to-face interviews, as the researcher and the participant do not have to travel to meet for the interview. Rather, the interview is conducted at the participant's convenience and in some cases the participant can be at home. Skype offers practical benefits in relation to scheduling interviews, and flexibility to shift times at the last minute with minimal disruption. This is important when people live increasingly busy lives and may not have time to meet face-to-face (Holt, 2010). In addition, Skype overcomes time zone differences. For instance, four interviews for the volunteer involvement in clinical trials study were with participants in Brazil, Sweden, India and the US. The participants considered the benefits of Skype in relation to time and space:

> 'I think I prefer Skype to face-to-face meetings, although I would probably choose a face-to-face meeting with an interlocutor if it was easy to arrange . . .' (Participant 2).

Whilst Participant 2 expressed some ambivalence over a preference for face-to-face or Skype, other participants noted the added value of Skype, even if they *could* physically meet the researcher, as it helped to overcome the inconvenience of travel, especially in big cities:

> '[I]t is a quick way to talk to people who may be in a distant location. In London it seems to take so long to get anywhere for meetings; thus saving time and money involved in travel to a meeting spot is a significant plus side' (Participant 4).
> 'I also like . . . the fact that I did not travel or spend any more than I usually do for using the Internet you know but still did the interview' (Participant 9).

In using Skype, the participants and researchers not only saved money, but also the time spent travelling to meet each other, enabling the participants to contribute to research with minimal costs on their part.

(2) *Virtual and visual interaction.* Software such as Skype provides not only synchronous (real-time) interaction between the researcher and participants, but also visual interaction. In their account of using online instant messaging to conduct interviews, Evans et al. (2008) noted that there are often problems

building rapport and trust (typically deemed crucial for good interviewing) between interviewee and interviewer, due to the lack of personal contact and/ or visual cues (but see Chapter 11). However, with a live video and audio feed, Skype largely overcomes this concern. Video calling gives access to cues (such as body language) that are deemed important in face-to-face interviews and thought to help facilitate and communicate feelings that would otherwise not be articulated (Knapp, Hall and Horgan, 2013).

(3) *Ease of data capture.* Researchers can easily record the audio and (if desired) video stream of the interview, through easy-to-use software down-loaded onto their workstation (e.g., Audacity). Whilst this may appear a relatively minor benefit, it does ease the apprehension we have felt in previous research when using an audio-recording device to record face-to-face interviews and the potential for 'disaster' resulting from flat batteries or corrupted files.

(4) *'Public' places and 'private' spaces.* Some participants may find the idea of inviting a researcher into their house intimidating or uncomfortable. They may also not wish to have a researcher interview them at their place of work, and may not have the time to travel to the researcher's office. Skype offers participants a space that is both (more or less) private and familiar *and* accessible to the researcher, who nonetheless remains removed from that space. Thus Skype provides a space for interviews that in some sense is both 'public' and 'private' and can potentially lessen feelings of intimidation for participants. Qualitative interviews – even those that aim to 'give voice' to participants and focus on how they make sense of their experiences – can be understood as retaining some degree of the hierarchies and unequal power relations associated with quantitative research, in which research is done *on* people, rather than *with*, or *for*, them. For example, even in qualitative interviews, the researcher determines the focus of the research and the questions that guide the interview. Having an 'expert' researcher enter your home, or being required to attend the possibly unfamiliar and intimidating environment of a university campus for the purposes of an interview, can serve to maintain such unequal power relationships, or at the very least leave the participant on the back foot (Elwood and Martin, 2000). Skype has the potential to sidestep such concerns and offer a more empowered experience for the interview participant, something argued to be a central goal of qualitative research (Rappaport and Stewart, 1997).

(5) *Greater control for participants.* In Hanna's sustainable tourism study, participants were given the choice of a face-to-face, telephone or Skype interview. This choice was deemed important because of the research topic – sustainable tourism. Conflict could have arisen between the

participants' ecological principles and Hanna travelling vast distances to conduct the interview. Offering the participant more say in the medium through which the interview was conducted may well have resulted in participants feeling more comfortable to respond to questions, creating a more open interview, and potentially the generation of more nuanced and detailed data.

In the volunteer involvement in clinical trials study, Mwale found that the use of Skype gave the participants liberty to choose the interview medium (video or just voice call; the latter enhanced the anonymity of the interview). They also had the option to end the interview at any time simply by clicking a mouse and, presumably, without feeling the same level of pressure and obligation that result from sitting opposite the researcher. As one participant commented:

'I like the fact that you . . . keep a certain level of privacy, both in terms of profile information and of the contents of a conversation, as far as I know, and whether to use the video or not, and you can end a conservation if you want anytime by clicking a button . . .' (Participant 1).

It is important to note, however, that Skype is not without its limitations. Relying (solely) on Skype to conduct your interviews means that only participants who can afford or access the necessary equipment will be included in the research – a concern that is raised around Internet research more generally (Evans et al., 2008; see Chapters 10, 11 and 13). Other potential problems with Skype interviews are discussed later.

What Research Questions Suit Skype Interviews?

As interviewing via Skype predominately draws on the approach and principles of qualitative interviewing more generally, the research questions appropriate for Skype interviews are largely similar to those guiding face-to-face interview research; there are no limitations inherent in the technology. The two example studies discussed in this chapter (see Boxes 12.1 and 12.2) use Skype as a method of data collection to address questions that focus on individuals' understandings, negotiations, experiences and constructions of social phenomena (related to sustainable behaviours and clinical trials). Hanna has continued to use Skype as a method of data collection on two additional projects, the first addressing the question 'How does the social economy function throughout the European Union?' and the second exploring 'In what ways are community organisations providing alternatives to statutory mental health services?'

As the software offers an interactive mode for data collection that is situated both in a 'public place' and 'private space', it is particularly suited for addressing sensitive research questions, which may be difficult or awkward to discuss in person. For example, Schuetz's (2013) doctoral research exploring the representations and experiences of HIV-positive women's journey into motherhood, or Wagemakers, Van Zoonen and Turner's (2014) study exploring the controversy surrounding two types of hearing implants, both allowed participants a degree of distance from the researcher and the intimacy of a face-to-face interview.

Design, Sampling and Ethical Issues

Sampling and ethics are little different in face-to-face and Skype interview research, and you will need to address all of the relevant ethical issues and design decisions associated with face-to-face interviews. For example, in terms of sample size in interview research, there is always the pragmatic question of the size and scope of your project (for students, this is usually tagged to level at which you are working – such as undergraduate, MSc, professional doctorate or PhD), as well as the need to consider the method of analysis you will be using. If you wanted to use thematic analysis (e.g., Braun and Clarke, 2006), or a similar approach that focuses on broad patterns in the data, we would typically recommend a sample of between five and ten interviews for undergraduate research. However, if you were interested in using a more ideographically-oriented approach like interpretative phenomenological analysis (e.g., Smith and Osborn, 2008), you may wish to interview just a few individuals in order to fully engage with their 'life world' (e.g., Eatough and Smith, 2006).

Recruitment

Possibly the biggest benefit to using Skype to conduct interviews is that the researcher is no longer geographically restricted, and thus the sampling frame can be very broad (see Deakin and Wakefield, 2014). Furthermore, if the researcher is using Skype to collect data, then using the Internet to recruit participants – advertising the research via discussion forums, social media and Internet pages – is entirely appropriate. For Hanna's research on ecological tourism, such a strategy proved fruitful in providing a range of diverse and willing participants from across the UK and even further afield. Hanna contacted a number of Internet-based companies, forums, social media

---

Box 12.3 Summary of guidelines on how to formulate interview questions

(1) Have a clear research question you wish to explore in your research project – this is important for directing the focus of the study and the questions to be asked in the interview.
(2) Have a set of clear aims or objectives that help you to focus the study further and will be the basis for formulating interview questions.
(3) Start by looking at your first aim and then make a list of two or three issues that pertain to the aim.
(4) Draft one or more questions that would seek to explore (directly or indirectly) each of the issues.
(5) Repeat the procedure for your other aims, until you have a list of questions that will allow you to address all of your aims.
(6) Arrange these in the order that you want to ask them, keeping in mind the importance of building up to more sensitive and/or threatening questions (Leech, 2002; Charmaz, 2014).
(7) Think of how these questions could be interlinked, and consider possible follow-up (probe) questions you may need to explore or clarify some issues further.
(8) Add one or two opening and closing questions.
(9) Finally, pilot your questions to test their suitability; you can also ask your pilot participants what they thought about the questions. Afterwards adjust your interview questions, and the schedule order, accordingly.

---

groups and email lists to seek help in advertising the research project. Not only did these methods of recruitment yield ample participants, but they were also free (a very important consideration for student researchers with little or no research budget) and did not use paper (which also means zero costs, and keeps your eco conscience clear!).

Design

As with any interview research, having well thought-out research questions and a well-designed interview schedule is vital. In Box 12.3, we outline a series of steps for designing good interview schedules.

Boxes 12.4 and 12.5 provide examples of interview schedules from our research. As you can see, each is structured very differently: Mwale (2015) opted for a list of questions that flowed in a logical order (Box 12.4); Hanna (2013) adopted a more 'narrative' approach to interviewing (Hollway and Jefferson, 2000), with questions organised around a beginning, middle and end Box 12.5. There are many ways to design an interview schedule (e.g., see the approaches discussed in Charmaz, 2014; Willig, 2013); the approach

---

Box 12.4 Example interview schedule from the 'volunteer involvement in Phase 1 clinical trials' study

(1) Will you tell me a bit about yourself?
(2) How did you hear about the clinical trials?
(3) How did you get involved?
(4) What do you think about the recruitment process?
(5) At what stage did you decide to take part in the trial?
(6) Is this your first time as a volunteer or have you taken part in other trials before?
   • If so, how long have you been doing this?
(7) What motivated you to take part in this/these trial/s?
(8) How important is the monetary reward on offer to you?
(9) Do you think you have all the information necessary to help you make a decision?
(10) What is your view about the risks involved in trials?
(11) Have you ever experienced any adverse effects from trial drugs in your time as a volunteer?
   • If so, how did you deal with that?
(12) Do you think you have adequate information about possible effects and what support you would have in case of severe effects?
(13) Do you know of any channels of communication/support available for you if you may have an issue with during or after the clinical trial?
(14) How do you ensure your voice is heard on issues of clinical trials if you have any concerns?
(15) What is your occupation? Current or previous.
(16) What would you describe your ethnicity as?
(17) What would you describe your social class to be?
(18) Is there something I have not asked that you think I should know to better understand your experience as a healthy volunteer?
(19) Do you have any questions for me?

---

you use should fit well with your style as an interviewer *and* your research question and aims.

You might be thinking that these examples seem extremely long for '*semi-structured*' interviews, but this is not the case. It is a good practice to have all potential questions mapped out, so that you can explore the issues you want to cover to the desired depth. An interview schedule is not rigidly followed; rather, it is more of a *guide* to the key elements that you want or need to cover. A participant may answer 'question 3', for instance, while responding to 'question 1', and you need to judge if you should still directly ask 'question 3' – perhaps in

Box 12.5 Example interview schedule from the 'sustainable tourism' study

Section 1 – The Holiday

(1) Can you describe how you booked your holiday – were there any difficulties?

(2) What made you book this holiday over a high street or package holiday?

(3) Did you see any conflicts with flying to the destination/what made you decide not to fly?

(4) Can you describe what you expected your holiday to be like?

- What did you expect to be doing day to day?
- Did you expect it to be different from holidays in the past?
- What was appealing about this specific holiday over others?
- What did you find appealing about the tour operator?

(5) What were the highlights of your holiday?

- Were there any experiences you didn't like?
- Shall we look at some of the photographs?
- Did you do any excursions or day trips?

(6) Overall do you feel that the holiday lived up to your expectations?

(7) Was this holiday different from holidays you have been on in the past?

(8) Do you feel this holiday has provided you with an insight and understanding of the local culture and environment?

(9) Do you feel that this holiday was different from a mainstream/high-street holiday?

(10) Do you think more people should be encouraged to go on this type of holiday?

- Should there be more of these holidays available?

Section 2 – Tourism and Ethics (explain that there are a range of labels)

(1) How would you define your particular holiday?

(2) How do you feel that differs from –

- Sustainable tourism
- Ethical tourism
- Eco tourism
- Green Tourism
- Responsible Tourism

(3) Are there any other labels which you feel are significant in this area?

(4) Do you have any preference over the labels used?

(5) What made you interested in this type of tourism?

Section 3 – Everyday Ethics

(1) In your general day-to-day life, do you feel you are conscious about:

- Environmental issues?
- Cultural issues?
- Issues around sustainability?

(2) Are:
  - Environmental issues
  - Cultural issues
  - Issues around sustainability

  important to you in your general life?
(3) Would you consider yourself as a responsible or ethical consumer in general?
(4) Do you feel your holiday has changed the way you view the environment or culture?
  - Do you feel it has changed any day-to-day practices? For example, made you recycle more?

Concluding Remarks
(1) Is there anything you would like to add that hasn't been discussed?
(2) Would you go on this type of holiday again?

a different way – or simply move on. The skills for making such judgements develop with practice.

Steps to Using Skype for Interviews

(1) *Develop a research question and aims.* Think of something that really interests you that is not already well addressed in existing research, and note what this is. From this area of interest, try to formulate a question that you are specifically interested in and write this down. Think about how you might break this question up into a set of three to four aims, and make a note of these.

(2) *Identify your participant group.* With your research question and aims in mind, decide which people you would select to interview in order to address your question and aims.

(3) *Design an interview schedule.* Reflecting on your research question, aims, and sample, write roughly ten questions, the responses to which would generate appropriate data to address your research question and aims (see Boxes 12.3, 12.4 and 12.5 for further guidance).

(4a) *Create a Skype account.* If you don't already have a Skype account, log on to your computer and create one. To do this you will need to visit www.skype.com and download Skype onto your computer. Create a new Skype account or login via your email or even your Facebook account.

(4b) *Familiarise yourself with Skype.* If you aren't familiar with Skype, take the Skype tour to explore its functions and get yourself familiar with

the software. Trust us, there is nothing worse that arranging to interview someone using a particular form of technology and then disco-
vering that you don't actually know how to make a call and thus have to
postpone the interview whilst you figure it out (not that this has
happened to either of us, of course . . .).

(5) *Prepare for data capture.* Now it is time to download recording software.
We have both used Audacity, but there is a range of similar software (such
as TotalRecorder or CamStudio) to enable you to record the audio and/or
video input to your computer – have a look and download whichever
seems the most user-friendly to use, and/or is widely used in your
institution. Be sure to also familiarise yourself with this software, as
you do not want to do the interview and find out you have not recorded it!

(6) *Practice makes perfect.* You should now be ready to go with your research
question, aims, interview schedule and knowledge of the software. Time
to try out your interview skills! Recruit a friend you can 'interview' via
Skype, and then reflect on your use, and the functionality, of the software
you have used, and make any necessary tweaks (e.g., to your interview
schedule, Skype setup etc.) before conducting a proper interview.

What Can Go Wrong with Skype Interviews?

Skype can only be an effective research tool if there is good Internet connection.
Poor connections can be frustrating for researchers and participants alike; sudden
interruptions to conversation can impact on rapport and ultimately on the quality
of data collected. The quality of Internet connections is fundamental, particularly
when conducting interviews with difficult-to-reach groups, such as in the volunteer involvement in clinical trials study – each opportunity to speak needs to be
taken full advantage of, with minimal disruptions. In one interview for the
sustainable tourism project, a faulty webcam created a situation in which
Hanna could be seen by the participant, but the participant could not be seen
by him. The quality of the connection determines not only the quality of the
picture but of the voice as well, thus potentially resulting in a missed opportunity
if the quality of the interview experience and subsequent data are hindered.
Furthermore, when there are poor-quality connections, interviews may take
longer than planned. For instance, in one interview for the volunteer involvement
in clinical trials study, the connection was so poor that an interview that could
have taken forty-five minutes took almost an hour and half. Consequently, when
organising Skype interviews, it is important to leave plenty of time for each

interview, and instruct the participant to do the same, in anticipation of such disruptions.

In another interview in that study, the conversation could not flow due to the 'glitchy' nature of the Internet connection and both the participant and researcher felt uneasy with the disjointed flow of conversation throughout – not to mention the extra time the participant needed to give to the research process. This meant that in some cases the quality of the data was compromised, as the exchange between the participant and the research was not of the desired depth and rapport was often hard to establish and/or maintain. Such potential issues should be discussed with the participant prior to the interview, to make the participant aware that should such a situation arise, a further interview may be needed.

In another of Hanna's interviews for the sustainable tourism study, the connection was so poor that it was difficult to observe basic telephone etiquette, such as waiting for the other person to speak or respond before asking another question. Furthermore, Hanna could not hear or see the participant clearly and often the connection would cut-out on the participant's side. This resulted in Paul not only missing out on vital data, but also having to *imagine* what the participant had said in order to try and maintain some flow to the conversation (an essential element to a good interview, see Flick, 2009), rather than continually asking the participant to repeat what they had just said. In addition, there were occasions where Hanna thought the participant had finished talking and would start asking a follow-up question, when in fact the participant was still answering the preceding question. Such exchanges not only felt unprofessional, they also resulted in the researcher appearing rushed and impatient to the participant. Mwale's experience was that on occasions when connection was disrupted, he felt anxious, as he did not want to lose the participants from the study. It was also awkward to restart conversations after such breaks, as sometimes both he and the participant would have lost their train of thought. Given such circumstances, discussing the issue of connection and potential for disruption before the interview begins can be useful in managing this problem. This can also be a good way to begin the interaction and establish rapport with the participant. Issues around connection quality were also of concern to the participants for instance:

'I think the only things that might have been improved by a face-to-face meeting would have been the clarity of sound and the fact that I was perhaps a little conscious of my housemates overhearing the discussion over Skype' (Participant 5).

This quotation also highlights that the researcher may not always be aware of the environment in which the participant is located and how this might affect the responses they are able and willing to make. Having other people in the vicinity could result in constrained responses, and/or distractions to the participant that may not be easily discernible to the interviewer. Thus setting the ground rules to the interview in advance, and being aware of the potential issues of having people in the vicinity of the interview, are key strategies for the researcher to manage such issues (Chapter 11 offers an example of ground rules for online interviewing).

What Methods of Analysis Suit Skype Interview Data?

Skype and other VoIP (voice-over-Internet protocol) software (such as FaceTime) generate data that can be audio and visual and invite a range of analytic methods and approaches. In the project on sustainable tourism, Hanna transcribed the interview data and 'tried out' a range of different theoretical and analytical methods, including thematic analysis (Braun and Clarke, 2006), interpretative phenomenological analysis (Smith and Osborn, 2008) and discursive psychology (Edwards and Potter, 1992). Whilst all of these approaches provided some interesting findings on the research area, he felt that there was still something missing in terms of really getting to the bottom of the specific issues he was interested in. In the end, he drew on a nuanced method of Foucauldian discourse analysis (see Hanna, 2013b) to reflect the primary focus on 'ethics' in the project. Whilst this is not the 'textbook' way of analysing data for a research project (and certainly is not something we would recommend for undergraduate or Master's dissertations), it does demonstrate that data obtained via Skype does not raise any specific issues with regard to the type of analysis one can conduct on the data. In his project exploring volunteer involvement in clinical trials study, Mwale adopted a thematic analysis, approach. This method was useful because unlike other forms of analysis, such as discourse analysis, it is not inherently attached to any theoretical framework (Braun and Clarke, 2006).

Whilst neither of us have encountered any specific issues in adopting a method of analysis suitable for Skype interview data, we suggest that for some of the more fine-grained methods of analysis, that rely on the nuances of interaction (e.g., some forms of discourse analysis), a more cautious approach may be needed. For example, within discursive psychology, the emphasis on a 'Jefferson' style method of transcription (Potter and Hepburn, 2005) to capture subtleties in how participants' say things (such as emphasis, rising and falling intonations, and laughter interpolated into words), as well as what they say, may prove difficult if the Internet connection is problematic and the recording is not of a high-quality. Moreover, with discursive psychologists increasingly turning to 'naturally occurring' talk and conversation analysis (e.g., Friesen, 2009; Wiggins and Potter, 2008), questions have been raised about the validity of all forms of researcher-generated interview data (see Chapter 8 for a discussion of the merits of 'naturalistic' data).

Conclusion

Throughout this chapter, we have highlighted what Internet-based video-calling technologies, and specifically Skype, can offer the budding social or health researcher as a medium through which to collect qualitative interview data. Following the initial description of Skype, we have presented a reflective account of the key benefits of conducting Skype interviews in social and health research. In addition, we have highlighted some of the practicalities of using Skype for interviews, and some of the design decisions you will need to make (e.g., what research questions suit Skype interviews; what methods of analysis are suitable for analysing Skype interview data). Drawing on our own experiences of using this technology, we have also highlighted some of the limitations of Skype as a research resource (e.g., poor Internet connections), and how best to manage these. Overall though, we hope that, on balance, we have demonstrated that Skype interviews offer a range of very exciting research possibilities, of which we have only just scratched the surface (see Box 12.6).

Have a Go . . .

(1) If you don't have one already, set up a Skype account, and invite a friend willing to participate in a practice interview to do the same.
(2) Develop a research question on a topic appropriate to a Skype interview, and design a brief interview schedule.
(3) Call your friend-participant, and conduct your interview with them (remembering to start up your recording software).
(4) Listen back over the interview; reflect on the process of conducting a Skype interview in terms of how you felt and how the participant might have felt. Were there any uncomfortable silences? Did you experience any technological glitches?
(5) Ask your friend-participant to give you feedback about their experience.
(6) Reflect on whether you would change the schedule, and how might you conduct a Skype interview differently in the future.

Box 12.6 Personal reflections on using Skype interviews

Paul: I originally came to use Skype for non-academic purposes due to the emigration of family members to Australia. During my PhD (Hanna, 2011), however, the usefulness of having something similar to a face-to-face encounter via the Internet seemed to me like a logical use of technology to overcome some of the recruitment and spatial issues I was encountering at the time. Since first using the technology in my PhD, I have used it on a range of additional projects and do genuinely feel that it offers something to researchers that cannot be understated. It has offered me the chance to interview people from all over the world without having to excessively increase my carbon footprint. It has also enabled me to take a flexible approach to scheduling interviews, whereby last-minute changes by participants no longer create undue stress, either to the participants or to me. I have also found the ability to record the audio and visual elements of the interviews as a real blessing and no longer have to hold my breath as I plug the dictaphone into the computer, praying that the file: (a) is actually on the device; (b) transfers to my computer without corrupting; and (c) is in fact audible and not clouded out by fuzz or the romantic conversation of the couple sitting next to me in the café. That said, I would be lying if I said the technology is an exact replacement for face-to-face encounters. The interactions can lack that intersubjective 'feel' you get when you are actually in the same room as someone else. However, there are also times when in fact it is precisely that 'feel' that both the participant and, at times, the researcher would like to avoid, due to the sensitive nature of the research project. In sum then, the technology has been of great benefit to me, and I can see a very exciting future for Skype and the ever-increasing array of possibilities the Internet opens up.

Shadreck: I started using Skype to keep in touch with my family and friends living in Zambia. When designing my research for my PhD (Mwale, 2015), I initially did not consider using Skype until I was presented with a situation where my participants were not within easy reach. In fact, *they* suggested using Skype when I contacted them to arrange an interview. Because of the sensitive nature of the study and the dispersed geographical locations of potential participants, using Skype meant that I was able to give these participants the opportunity to share their experiences, and I gathered valuable data that I would have otherwise missed if I had insisted on using face-to-face interview. In addition, Skype bridged the time factor that could have limited some participants' involvement in the research, and I was able to conduct the interviews at a time that was convenient for them. The ability to enhance further the anonymity of participants, by allowing them to choose to either use the audio and video stream or just the audio stream, was also a significant benefit to interviewing via Skype. However, using Skype has not been without its frustrations – sometimes a poor network connection meant that I was constantly having disrupted conversations that made it hard to retain the thread of both my thoughts and the participants' account. Sometimes it was frustrating to find myself talking over my participant, being unable to read their facial expressions or knowing when to interject without coming across as unprofessional. Furthermore, the information conveyed through body language is not always easily visible via Skype. Despite these limitations, it was a very useful tool that I would use again if I needed to interview participants at a distance.

Further Resources: Online

Skype: www.skype.com/en/

Further Resources: Readings

For a useful reflection from two PhD researchers on the strengths and weaknesses of using Skype in their research, see Deakin, H. and Wakefield, K. (2014). Skype interviewing: Reflections of two PhD researchers. *Qualitative Research*, *14*(5), 603–616.

For a short article that outlines the benefits of Skype for qualitative interviews in relation to face-to-face and telephone interviews, see Hanna, P. (2012). Using Internet technologies (such as Skype) as a research medium: A research note. *Qualitative Research*, *12*(2), 239–242.

To read about the results of the sustainable tourism study, see chapter 5: Identifying what and why: Reasons for engaging with sustainable tourism, in: Hanna, P. (2013a). *Being sustainable in unsustainable environments*. Charleston, NC: Amazon.

For more general advice on qualitative interviewing, see chapter 2: Crafting and conducting intensive interviews, in: Charmaz, K. (2014) *Constructing grounded theory: A practical guide through qualitative analysis* (2nd edn). London: Sage Publications.

References

Abadie, R. (2010). *The professional guinea pig: Big pharma and the risky world of human subjects*. Durham, NC: Duke University Press.

Braun, V. and Clarke, V. (2006). Using thematic analysis in psychology. *Qualitative Research in Psychology*, *3*(2), 77–101.

Bryman, A. (2004). *Social research methods* (2nd edn). Oxford: Oxford University Press.

Deakin, H. and Wakefield, K. (2014). Skype interviewing: Reflections of two PhD researchers. *Qualitative Research*, *14*(5), 603–616.

Eatough, V. and Smith, J. (2006). 'I was like a wild wild person': Understanding feelings of anger using interpretative phenomenological analysis. *British Journal of Psychology*, *97*(4), 483–498.

Edwards, D. and Potter, J. (1992). *Discursive psychology*. London: Sage Publications.

Elwood, S. and Martin, D. (2000). 'Placing' interviews: Location and scales of power in qualitative research. *The Professional Geographer*, *52*(4), 649–657.

Evans, A., Elford, J. and Wiggins, D. (2008). Using the Internet for qualitative research. In C. Willig and W. Stainton Rogers (eds.), *The SAGE handbook of qualitative research in psychology*. London: Sage Publications.

Flick, U. (2009). *An introduction to qualitative research*. London: Sage Publications.

Friesen, N. (2009). Discursive psychology and educational technology: Beyond the cognitive revolution. *Mind, Culture, and Activity, 16*(2), 130–144.

Gkartzios, M. (2013). 'Leaving Athens': Narratives of counterurbanisation in times of crisis. *Journal of Rural Studies, 32*, 158–167.

Green, A. R. and Young, R. A. (2015). The lived experience of visual creative expression for young adult cancer survivors. *European Journal of Cancer Care, 24*(5), 695–706.

Hanna, P. (2011). *Consuming sustainable tourism: Ethics, identity, practice* (Unpublished PhD thesis). Brighton, UK: University of Brighton.

   (2012). Using Internet technologies (such as Skype) as a research medium: A research note. *Qualitative Research, 12*(2), 239–242.

   (2013a). *Being sustainable in unsustainable environments.* Charleston, NC: Amazon.

   (2013b). Foucauldian discourse analysis in psychology: Reflecting on a hybrid reading of Foucault when researching 'ethical subjects'. *Qualitative Research in Psychology, 11*(2), 142–159.

Hill, D. M. and Hemmings, B. (2015). A phenomenological exploration of coping responses associated with choking in sport. *Qualitative Research in Sport, Exercise and Health, 7*(4), 521–538.

Hollway, W. and Jefferson, T. (2000). *Doing qualitative research differently: Free association, narrative and the interview method.* London: Sage Publications.

Holt, A. (2010). Using telephones for narrative interviewing: A research note. *Qualitative Research, 10*(1), 113–121.

Knapp, M., Hall, J. and Horgan, T. (2013). *Nonverbal communication in human interaction* (8th edn). Boston, MA: Cengage Learning.

Leech, B. (2002). Asking questions: Techniques for semistructured interviews. *Political Science & Politics, 35*(4), 665–668.

Mwale, S. (2015). *Risk, rewards and regulation: Exploring regulatory and ethical dimensions of human research participation in phase I (first-in-human) clinical trials in the United Kingdom* (Unpublished PhD thesis). Brighton, UK: University of Sussex. Retrieved from: http://sro.sussex.ac.uk/55221/

Pocock, J. (2000). *Clinical trials: A practical approach.* Chichester, UK: Wiley and Sons.

Potter, J. and Hepburn, A. (2005). Qualitative interviews in psychology: Problems and possibilities. *Qualitative Research in Psychology, 2*(4), 281–307.

Rappaport, J. and Stewart, E. (1997). A critical look at critical psychology: Elaborating the questions. In D. Fox and I. Prilleltensky (eds.), *Critical psychology: An introduction* (pp. 301–317). London: Sage Publications.

van Riemsdijk, M. (2014). International migration and local emplacement: Everyday place-making practices of skilled migrants in Oslo, Norway. *Environment and Planning A, 46*(4), 963–979.

Schuetz, S. (2013). *Representations and experiences of HIV-positive women on the journey to motherhood in Canada* (Unpublished PhD thesis). Alberta, Canada: University of Calgary.

Smith, J. and Osborn, M. (2008). Interpretative phenomenological analysis. In J. Smith (ed.), *Qualitative psychology: A practical guide to research methods* (2nd edn). London: Sage Publications.

Wagemakers, S., Van Zoonen, L. and Turner, G. (2014). Giving meaning to RFID and cochlear implants. *IEEE, Technology and Society Magazine, 33*(2), 73–80.

Wiggins, S. and Potter, J. (2008). Discursive psychology. In C. Willig and W. Stainton Rogers (eds.), *The SAGE handbook of qualitative research in psychology* (pp. 73–90). London: Sage Publications.

Willig, C. (2013). *Introducing qualitative research in psychology* (3rd edn). Berkshire, UK: Open University Press.

Yarrow, A. (2013). 'I'm strong within myself': Gender, class and emotional capital in childcare. *British Journal of Sociology of Education*, *36*(5), 651–668.

13 Meeting in Virtual Spaces

Conducting Online Focus Groups

Fiona Fox

Overview

In this chapter, I document the emergence of online focus groups (OFGs) as a qualitative method, drawing on my own experiences of running both real-time (or synchronous) and non-real-time (or asynchronous) OFGs with young people with chronic skin conditions (see Box 13.1). Face-to-face focus groups are a popular method for qualitative researchers, offering a way to capture a range of perspectives and to generate interactive data that provide insight into the process of collective sense-making (Wilkinson, 1998). Focus groups conducted in the online environment offer a more convenient mode of participation for some groups of people, such as young people with appearance concerns. In addition, the online environment offers an alternate way of engaging with populations reluctant or unable to participate in face-to-face data collection. Online focus groups can enhance participants' sense of confidence in, and control over, the participation experience, which is particularly important when researching vulnerable populations or sensitive issues. In this chapter, I consider differences between running OFGs as real-time and non-real-time discussions, and reflect on the practicalities of designing, recruiting, moderating and analysing both of these types of OFGs. Whilst advocating the potential of OFGs for qualitative research, I also suggest strategies to address the potential pitfalls of this method.

Introduction to Online Focus Groups

I use the term 'online focus group' (OFG) to describe a group discussion that is planned, hosted and moderated online by a researcher, with the aim of collecting qualitative data to answer a specific research question. Other terms used to describe OFGs include: 'computer-mediated' (Franklin and Lowry, 2001) or 'virtual' (Moloney, Dietrich, Strickland and Myerburg, 2003; Murray, 1997;

Box 13.1 Experiences of young people with chronic skin conditions

My PhD investigated the support needs of young people with chronic skin conditions. I found that this population was reluctant to participate in face-to-face focus groups. Therefore, through a process of trial and error, and with some technical support, I hosted seven real-time OFGs, with three to five participants in each, lasting an average of one hour. The participants were aged between eleven and nineteen years and had a diagnosis of either psoriasis or vitiligo. These real-time OFGs enabled me to explore the experience of living and coping with a chronic skin condition during adolescence. The ways in which the young people exchanged peer support in these OFGs captured my interest, and in subsequent data collection I explored how young people sought and provided emotional and informational support in online chat groups. To do so, I hosted, analysed and compared a non-real-time chat group (with nineteen young people with vitiligo) with a series of weekly real-time online chat groups (with four young people with psoriasis). These chat groups were not guided by a focus group schedule; instead, the participants were asked to discuss any aspect of their skin condition that they wished. Comparing real-time and non-real-time chat groups allowed me to reflect on aspects of the online environment that affect the sharing of peer support, with practical implications for organisations that support young people with chronic health conditions.

Turney and Pocknee, 2005) focus groups and 'electronic discussions' (Rezabek, 2000). Online focus groups differ from other kinds of online qualitative data sources such as blogs (Chapter 8) or online forums (Chapter 9), as these sources draw on data that occur regardless of the interests of a researcher and thus can be regarded as 'naturally occurring'. Instead, OFGs are more in keeping with the aims of traditional focus groups, where discussions are 'focused' on a collective activity for the purposes of data gathering (Adams, Rodham and Gavin, 2005; Adler and Zachrin, 2002; Fox, Morris and Rumsey, 2007a). The OFGs that I discuss in this chapter are text-based and do not include a visual element, and so are distinct from those conducted via web conferencing technology – the emerging use of which has recently been described by Tuttas (2014).

   I discuss two forms of OFG in this chapter: real-time (or synchronous) and non-real-time (asynchronous). In a real-time OFG, participants join the online discussion at the same time, for a defined period (typically around 45–90 minutes) (Fox et al., 2007a). These OFGs usually take place in a virtual 'space' using chat room technology, or are mediated via messenger systems (early examples include O'Connor and Madge, 2003; Stewart, Eckerman and Zhou, 1998; Williams, 2003). In contrast, non-real-time OFGs operate via online discussion boards or forums, which may run for a longer period of

Table 13.1 Data extract from a real-time OFG with young people with psoriasis

Moderator:	Is there anything that you don't do because of your psoriasis?
Emma:	u also learn wot not to do/use/eat and wot cream work and what to wear to cover it up
Ellie:	at least i dodnt think they wud not as much as teens and kids
Mark:	i try not to swim much, tho is sad as i do enjoy it
Emma:	yep!!! wear skimpy summer clothes (not sure i would anyway! lol!)
Mark:	:)
Emma:	be in a swimming team (started out but quit)
Moderator:	does swimming irritate it, or is the worry about how it looks?
Emma:	yeh – ilove swimming but in the summer as a fam we go to a vill aso i can sunbarthe without anyone seeing! sun cures it!
Mark:	the stares mostly
Ellie:	not reli i just live with it its a part of me i cud neva stop swimmin n i've just started scuba divin
Emma:	i dont like being in a cossie were skin and evrything is exposed!
Ellie:	the sun makes mine worse!!!!!!!!!!!
Mark:	oo wow sounds fun
Emma:	yeh! definately the stares
Mark:	really yeah i read that only happens in a small amount of cases

time than real-time chats – as long as several weeks or even months (Im, 2006). In non-real-time OFGs, participants and researchers contribute and respond at their convenience (early examples include Gaiser, 1997; Robson, 1999; Ward, 1999).

There are some notable differences in the characteristics of real-time and non-real-time OFGs (compare data the examples in Tables 13.1 and 13.2). Real-time group interactions (see Table 13.1) are frequently characterised by dynamism and immediacy (O'Connor and Madge, 2003; Stewart et al., 1998; Williams, 2003), contributing to a form of communication that has been described as 'more oral than literate' (Stewart and Williams, 2005), more like talk than traditional written communication. Real-time data are often full of 'text-speak', or 'informal representations of written language' (Williams, Clausen, Robertson, Peacock and McPherson, 2012: 371). This can include abbreviations, emoticons, popular acronyms, capital letters and punctuation marks, all of which communicate the emotional tone of a contribution. In contrast, messages posted to non-real-time OFGs are typically longer and more reflective (see Table 13.2), as participants can edit their messages before posting (Williams et al., 2012). Researchers therefore have the opportunity to clarify meaning and probe for additional responses. The degree of *interactivity* between participants may be lower in non-real-time OFGs (Fox, Morris and

Table 13.2 Data extract from a non-real-time online chat group with young people with vitiligo

Floyd:	Hey everyone, Katie just wondering how long have u been on the Protopic cream? cause i`ve been offered to use it but im a bit apprehensive . . . are the results worth the cost of the product? I would love to be able to comfortably and confidently be able to wear short clothes . . .
Chelsea:	Hi everyone . . . My doctor just told me that I had vitiligo. My Aunt has it real bad so I guess I am not suprised that I had it. I just don`t kno a lot about it. The doctor explained but it was all in medical jargon . . . can you guys explain it to me a little better??? Thanks
Chelsea:	'I myself find vitiligo uncomfortable and very isolating at times. Its very hard to be a teenage girl and have to wear long clothes and hats in the summer time . . . when my friends get to wear short skirts and bikinis'. This was a past post written and I have to comment on it . . .I agree with this 100%. My friends don`t get that I hhave to be careful and when I try to kinda explain to them that act like I am contagious. It`s no like I choose to wear jeans in the summer or a t shirt when I go into the water. But it something I have to do for my health!!!
Floyd:	Hey Chelsea, dont worry your not alone. I made that comment and it is a very isolating at times, and can also get extremely hot at times especially in the heat of summer. I wear long clothes for most of all of the day and it sucks . . . and even more so when my friends get to wear short clothes and I dont:-{ If there is any questions about vitiligo, anything you`d like to know just ask??? I`ve had it since I was little so I know a bit about it . . .
Chelsea:	Thanks Floyd!!! It is so nice to kno that I have people here to talk to!!
Katie:	Floyd, so sorry I haven`t gotten back to you quicker, oops! Any way, to answer your question, yes, the Protopic really does help and it is worth the money! You`ll know it`s working when you see little 'Islands' of brown spots inside the spots! But you also have to combine it with a little bit of sun-light.
Hayley:	Hey, everyone! My name`s Haley and I just turned sixteen a few days ago, and I`ve had vitiligo since I was four or five. At first, my mom tried to cover it up with make-up everyday, and I hated it so much that I still refuse to wear make-up to this day. First, it was only a few spots here and there on my arms, but by the time I was in second grade, it was around my eyes, lips, all over my hands and legs, my stomach . . . . . . As far as negative emotional events go, there was one a few years back, when a girl in my year was furious with me and commented, 'At least I`m only one color of skin' to which I only rolled my eyes in response. There are jerks in the world, and I`m very much used to it by now . . . . . . The positive experiences, however, you can`t exactly call positive, but they`ve helped me in a variety of different ways. By people being skiddish around me and not really knowing how to react, it`s helped me just walk up to people, hold out my hand, grin, and say, 'Hi! My name`s Hayley and

Table 13.2 (cont.)

I promise that I'm not contagious'. Once you do it once or twice, the entire thing just seems like this practical joke that the universe tried to pull on you, and you develop a sense of humor to get over it, as if laughing at the world that it didn't work because you're stronger that that. Without my vitiligo, I probably wouldn't know half of the people I do, and most likely wouldn't be as outgoing as I am . . .

. . . Honestly, I never want it to go away. Apart from sunburn being possibly the worst thing in the world anymore, vitiligo has become part of me and my life, and I really don't know how I'd live without it. It'd be like asking me to cut off my arm or my leg; I just couldn't do it.

Rumsey, 2010), and the resulting data may appear more 'formal' and less 'chat-like' than real-time OFGs. Researchers should consider whether participant spontaneity or reflection is more important for their research before choosing between real-time and non-real-time OFGs (Williams et al., 2012; see also Chapters 10 & 11, related to email and IM interviews).

What Do Online Focus Groups Offer the Qualitative Researcher?

Focus groups offer qualitative researchers the opportunity to study collective meaning-making, and allow participants to generate their own questions, challenge ideas and respond to each other's experiences (Kitzinger, 1995). Online focus groups share many of the characteristics of face-to-face focus groups but do have some additional unique qualities:

(1) *OFGs facilitate greater control and equality for participants.* Online discussions have the potential to produce a greater equality of participation, and more outspoken advocacy, than face-to-face group exchanges (Bordia, 1997; Keisler and Sproull, 1992). The lack of visual presence online can affect interactions as participants may experience less social pressures than they do in face-to-face social encounters (Reips, 2000). The Internet has been described as 'a level playing field with respect to physical attributes' (Wallace 1999: 138) and so status-based prejudices, social desirability bias and social discomfort may be reduced online (Mann and Stewart, 2000; Stewart and Williams, 2005; Tidwell and Walther, 2002). Researchers should be mindful that reduced social pressure also means that participants might feel able to terminate their participation before completion (Reips, 2000), and that the researcher may not know the reasons for withdrawal. Respondents in non-real-time OFGs might also value the flexibility and

convenience of logging in at their own pace, allowing time for reflection, to respond at length, and the opportunity to change or nuance their opinion (Tates et al., 2009).

(2) *OFGs facilitate participant disclosure.* The 'invisibility' of the online environment can enhance self-disclosure (Joinson, 2001; Tates et al., 2009), as participants may feel less inhibited (Williams et al., 2012) and may believe that their responses are more anonymous and secure (Davis, 1999). The sharing of more sensitive information online has been noted in research with adults (Fawcett and Buhle, 1995; Joinson, 2001). Similarly, research suggests that young people discuss sensitive topics online, which they might not feel comfortable talking about with friends or family face-to-face (Suzuki and Calzo, 2004) without fear of judgment or because of shyness (Sweet, 2001). In my research boys and girls of different ages interacted freely and discussed their appearance concerns without seeing one another; they were therefore unable to form judgements about, or compare the severity of, each other's condition (Fox, Rumsey and Morris, 2007b).

(3) *OFGs facilitate access to hard-to-reach and -engage groups.* OFGs can help researchers to access groups which might otherwise be difficult to engage in research due to health, mobility or time constraints (Gibson, 2007; Horrell, Stephens and Breheny, 2015; Kennedy, Kools and Krueger, 2001; Morgan, Gibbs, Maxwell and Britten, 2002). Some may be more unable than unwilling to take part in face-to-face groups, for example, pregnant women on bed rest whose physical functioning is compromised (Adler and Zarchin, 2002). Similarly, as I discovered, young people who are reliant on an adult to transport them to a focus group may find it easier to participate online (Nicholas et al., 2010). Online focus groups can reach people that other methods cannot, as they may be less intimidating or more acceptable for groups that feel marginalised, such as men who are gay or bisexual (Ybarra, DuBois, Parsons, Prescott and Mustanski, 2014), or those who lack the social confidence to participate in face-to-face groups, such as individuals with appearance concerns (Fox et al., 2007b; Montoya-Weiss, Massey and Clapper, 1999). Furthermore, the text-based communication offered by OFGs may be preferred by people who find it difficult to express themselves verbally, such as people with cognitive disabilities, or speech or hearing difficulties (Tanis, 2007).

(4) *OFGs are resource-lite.* The pragmatic advantages of using OFGs include reduced costs associated with venue hire and participant travel, and increased speed of data collection (Gaiser, 2008). The time and costs of transcription are eliminated due to the automatic and accurate capture of the discussion data (Tates et al., 2009).

What Research Questions Suit Online Focus Groups?

Many research questions that are suitable for face-to-face focus groups can also be addressed in OFGs. I provide some examples here from my own research area, that of qualitative health research. The heightened disclosure that is characteristic of online talk allows access to individuals' life-worlds (Adams et al., 2005) and enables researchers to explore aspects of illness and coping, especially where participants are too unwell to travel. For example, Tates et al. (2009) noted that their sample of paediatric cancer patients welcomed the opportunity to participate in non-real-time OFGs, and emphasised that the anonymity they experienced made them feel comfortable to express their views in detail (Tates et al., 2009). As noted, the sense of anonymity described by many researchers (Mann and Stewart, 2000; Stewart and Williams, 2005; Tidwell and Walther, 2002) means that OFGs are well-suited to the discussion of sensitive, or taboo topics (Nicholas, 2003) that participants may be reticent to discuss face-to-face. Therefore, OFGs have been used effectively to facilitate discussions about: smoking (Stewart et al., 1998); alcohol use and sex (Mann and Stewart, 2000); HIV/AIDS (Bosio, Graffigna and Lozza, 2008); sexual health (Thomas, Wootten and Robinson, 2013; Ybarra et al., 2014); and deliberate self-harm (Adams et al., 2005). The 'invisibility' experienced online can facilitate research exploring appearance concerns or body image (de Jong et al., 2012; Williams et al., 2012). In my research I observed the ease with which participants discussed the stigma that they experienced relating to their chronic skin conditions (Fox et al., 2007b, 2010). The perceived sense of anonymity afforded by OFGs has also been useful when investigating aspects of health service intervention and delivery (Boshoff, Alant and May, 2005) and participants' perceptions of participation in their treatment (Tates et al., 2009). Finally, in public health, OFGs have been used effectively to gauge the effectiveness of health information-seeking behaviour (Williams et al., 2012).

Design, Sampling and Ethical Issues

Recruiting Online

A range of online recruitment methods are appropriate for OFGs. In my own research, I wanted to recruit young people with psoriasis or vitiligo but found that they were geographically dispersed. Therefore, I set up a basic website, hosted by my university, which included information about the research and my contact details. I then requested permission from gatekeepers of relevant organisations (such as the Vitiligo Society and Psoriasis Association) to adver-tise a link to my website on their online pages, and waited for volunteers to respond. If researchers wish to recruit people who engage with a particular service, such as a dermatology clinic, they can ask the gatekeeper to circulate a direct email with information about the study. Additionally, snowballing may be appropriate, if participants are willing to use their online social networks to refer others to the researcher. However, in order to protect the anonymity of those referred, the researcher should wait for these individuals to demonstrate their interest by contacting the researcher, rather than the other way around.

In my own research, I was mindful that advertising and recruiting online would only attract participants with access to the Internet (Adler and Zarchin, 2002; Tates et al., 2009). Furthermore, only those with broadband and a reasonable degree of technical competence would be able to *participate* in my real-time OFGs. The issue of the digital divide reflects concerns that participation in online research is linked to socioeconomic status. However, Internet access is growing (Internet World Stats, 2014), with greater access in schools and libraries (Kenny, 2005) and increased ownership of smartphones and tablets. Thus, these inequalities in access to online research may be decreasing (see also discussions in Chapters 10–12).

Group Size

In real-time OFGs, a smaller number of participants is recommended, as size is crucial to the moderator's sense of control. Too many participants may result in such a high speed of dialogue that important issues are skimmed over (Horn, 1998). Based on my pilot group, I decided that five young people in each discussion would both be manageable and facilitate dynamic interaction. I over-recruited for each group, assuming that not everyone would 'turn up' on the day. The average size of my real-time OFGs was three young people, and this proved to be suitable for moderation, provided enough input for lively exchanges, and confirmed that smaller group sizes can facilitate a comfortable environment that encourages self-disclosure (Mann and Stewart, 2000). Had my real-time OFGs been larger (e.g., more than five participants), I would certainly have needed a second moderator to type questions, while I concen-trated on the content and flow of the discussion. This is consistent with recommendations for the moderation of face-to-face focus groups (Krueger and Casey, 2000). The young people in my OFGs ranged in age from eleven to nineteen years, which did not seem to impede the discussion, although other researchers advocate splitting young people into focus groups according to their age and developmental stage (de Jong et al., 2012).

Non-real-time OFGs can accommodate a much larger number of participants – I had nineteen young people in my discussion group. Williams (2009) identified an average of twelve participants per group across the literature, although as many as fifty-seven participants have taken part in a single non-real-time OFG (Robson, 1999). Whatever the number of participants, the level of interaction in non-real-time OFGs varies according to the number of times that each participant contributes to the discussion.

Ethical Issues

Online focus groups involve many of the same ethical considerations as face-to-face focus groups (Ess, 2002; Pittenger, 2003; Williams et al., 2012), although a number of concerns specific to OFGs have been identified:

(1) *Obtaining consent*. It can be difficult to secure signed informed consent for online studies (Williams et al., 2012). Finding the optimum way of consenting participants for my OFGs was a process of trial and error, and required several amendments to ethical approval. Young people who read information about my study on the research website could indicate their interest in participating by filling out an online registration form. I then requested that they print, sign and return a consent form by post, complete with their parent's signatures. This approach proved largely unsuccessful, which may have reflected a lack of access to a printer, or a lack of organisational skills we might take for granted in adults. I therefore began sending consent forms embedded in an email to those who registered. Although this achieved a better response, it greatly slowed the process of organising the OFGs. Subsequently, I linked an online consent form to the registration page on the research website, where an extra tick box required participants to confirm that they had read and understood the information about the study.

(2) *Participant identity*. Unfortunately, there is no fool-proof method for the verification of identity, age or gender in the online environment, but in my research I found that during the process of setting up the OFGs I was re-assured about my participants' identities through email contact with them and their parents. When young people registered and consented to take part in my OFGs, I sent them a link to the online forum and, in a separate email, a unique login and password. This ensured that only the people that I had recruited to the study were able to take part in the OFGs.

(3) *Potential conflict*. Disagreement and criticism are more common in OFGs than in face-to-face focus groups, and although conflict can spark idea

generation (Reid and Reid, 2005), there is greater potential for participants to use inappropriate language or to express offensive views. This results from the previously-noted perceived sense of anonymity afforded by the online environment (Bosio et al., 2008), and the moderator must have clear strategies to address this. Prior to the start of my OFGs, I clearly stated that any inappropriate or confrontational language would result in a 'warning' from me. Anyone receiving more than two warnings would be asked to leave the OFG. I was able to terminate their participation via a function on my moderator's screen, although I did not have to use this during any of my OFGs.

(4) *Participant distress.* Given the absence of visual cues, researchers using OFGs should take a vigilant approach to detecting distress in their participants (Fox et al., 2007a). Distress may be indicated if a participant starts to post fewer comments, or posts comments with a strongly emotional tone. Moderators need to be mindful of the range of non-verbal techniques that participants use to express their emotional state online, such as capital letters or emoticons. The moderator can respond by providing encouraging feedback and re-assuring participants of the value of their contributions. In addition, they should offer opportunities to discuss any concerns by email or phone after the OFG, and provide contact details of relevant support organisations. I gained encouraging feedback from participants in my study, and from their parents, that the potential risk of distress caused by participation was offset by the positive experience of interacting with others in a similar situation to themselves.

(5) *Online safety.* For young people and other vulnerable groups, it may be good practice to provide information about staying safe online, such as not disclosing any identifying information (see 'Further Resources' sections). Participants were advised not to share their contact details with one another. The forum that I used for my real-time and non-real-time OFGs did *not* have the facility for separate or side chats. I was therefore able to monitor all interactions between participants. However, researchers should make it clear to potential participants that it is impossible to guarantee complete confidentiality online (Mann and Stewart, 2000).

(6) *Distractions.* Finally, researchers should be aware that when conducting OFGs they may not know the conditions under which participants are responding (Fox et al., 2007a). It is possible that participants will login to an OFG from a shared computer, or will participate from a public space, where there is potential for distraction or influence from friends or family members. Researchers can remind participants at the start of OFGs that they should ideally take part in a private space that is free from distraction.

Steps to Using Online Focus Groups

I now outline the key steps for using OFGs, focusing on the unique features of real-time and non-real-time discussions, including: (1) choosing a venue and piloting; (2) moderating the discussion; and (3) ending the discussion. The steps are broken down further by time, and summarised in Table 13.3.

(1) *Choosing a venue and piloting*. Hosting an OFG requires an online venue and researchers therefore need to hire a virtual facility (Mann and Stewart, 2000) or design their own (Fox et al., 2007a). Options will depend upon the research budget, resources and the availability of IT support. Online venues offered by external providers vary in terms of costs and flexibility. For example, renting a virtual space to hold one real-time OFG costs around £350 (at the time of writing); to hire a non-real-time forum for three weeks for up to fifty participants costs around £1,000. Hiring software to independently design, moderate and analyse multiple real-time and non-real-time OFGs costs around £4,000. Clearly these figures contradict claims of reduced costs associated with OFGs (Gaiser, 2008; Tuttas, 2014), and therefore researchers may wish to consider alternatives. Existing virtual learning environments, such as Moodle or Blackboard, that are designed for educational purposes, can offer both real-time and non-real-time facilities for data collection (Williams et al., 2012), as well as a secure, confidential and safe environment for participants (Peacock, Robertson, Williams and Clausen, 2009). Other researchers have reported that their online forums and message boards were hosted by charities (Thomas et al., 2013) or by organisations supporting their research (Tates et al., 2009).

I was fortunate to have the technical support of a university IT technician, who created both the real-time forum and the non-real-time message board for my OFGs. When designing my forums I followed Krueger's (1988) principle for face-to-face focus groups that the venue should be free of distraction, easy to find and relaxed. I attempted to make the environment 'distraction-free' through a simple, functional design. Displaying university logos showed that the university was hosting my research, a strategy that is advisable to re-assure participants that the research is linked to a reputable institution. I ensured that the OFG was easy to find by sending a link to the online forum to all participants.

By piloting, or running practice OFGs, researchers can become familiar with the unique features of synchronous online chat and hone their moderating skills. I tested my real-time online forum with a group of students, which allowed me to check technical issues and get feedback on the forum.

Table 13.3 Steps for running real-time and non-real-time OFGs

Steps for running real-time OFGs	Steps for running non-real-time OFGs
Planning: • Find suitable online venue OR design online forum • Develop FG guide • Run pilot OFG and make any necessary changes to the forum and FG guide	**Planning:** • Find suitable online venue OR design online message board • Develop FG guide • Run pilot OFG and make any necessary changes to the message board and FG guide
One month to go: • Advertise for participants with participant information sheets • Consent participants • Agree time for real-time OFG to take place	**One month to go:** • Advertise for participants with participant information sheets • Consent participants
One week to go: • Email participants link to join OFG, username and password • Email reminders to join OFG at agreed time	**One week to go:** • Email participants username and password for non-real-time forum • Email reminders
One day to go: • Email reminders to join OFG at agreed time	**On the day:** • Open forum • Post welcome message • Email link to participants
On the day: • Get online before agreed time • Check participants' usernames and passwords as they login • Direct participants to the welcome page with reminders/codes of conduct etc. • Open the real-time forum at agreed time and begin OFG by asking participants to introduce themselves • Post questions and allow time for response but keep discussion focused • Summarise the discussion and agree when it will end • Thank participants • Close the real-time forum • Direct them to the final page with post-participation material • Email thanks and post-participation material to participants • Download and save the data ready for analysis	**Over the next week(s):** • Check incoming message before posting to message board • Send participation reminders • Post new questions daily/weekly • Prompt if necessary to stimulate discussion **A few days before the end:** • Email reminders that OFG will be ending soon **Final day:** • Post a message of thanks • Close the forum • Set up a re-direct message including post-participation material • Email thanks and post-participation material to participants • Download and save the data ready for analysis

On the basis of this, I refined some functionality on the moderator screen (see Figure 13.1). Most importantly, it gave me insight into the pace and flow of real-time online chat, prior to data collection.

(2) *Moderating the discussion.* As moderators are unable to create a comfortable *physical* environment, it is necessary to establish a welcoming and friendly atmosphere online (Mann and Stewart, 2000). For real-time OFGs, a welcome page, where participants wait between logging in and starting the discussion, offers researchers a space to identify the purposes and expected conduct of the group, and to encourage active participation. The moderator screen for my real-time OFG displayed the participants' names as they logged in (see Figure 13.1). After I checked their unique password and accepted them, participants saw the welcome page, which reminded them about the aims of the OFG and stated that all contributions were welcome, but that offensive or abusive language would not be tolerated. Once all (or most) participants had arrived, I opened the real-time forum and the participants could then access the main chat screen.

As previously noted, the dynamics of real-time online chat can be fast, furious and chaotic and 'the distinction between replying and sending becomes blurred as the interactivity defies conversational turn-taking' (Mann and Stewart, 2000: 102). To ensure that I could keep pace with the conversation, my moderator's screen allowed me to select questions and prompts from a drop-down list based on my focus group topic guide (see Box 13.2). It is common for participants to post their responses simultaneously, and to become distracted from the moderator's question in favour of responding to another thread of conversation. While interactivity is the key to a successful focus group, the moderator may need to re-focus the participants, by repeating or re-phrasing the question. Poor spelling and abbreviations can lead to misunderstandings during the discussion, and if contributions are incomprehensible it is important to seek clarification.

There can be periods in real-time OFGs where no one contributes, and the moderator may not know whether the silence is a result of participants thinking, typing or declining to answer (O'Connor and Madge, 2003). With experience I came to realise that extended silences meant that someone was usually typing a response, and so I learnt to wait a few seconds longer before posting another question or prompt. Additional functionality (that I did not have) indicating when a respondent is typing can help to inform the moderator's decision about when to post a question, probe for further information or wait for responses.

Although the opportunity to respond and contribute is potentially the same for all participants, in real-time OFGs the participant who is most

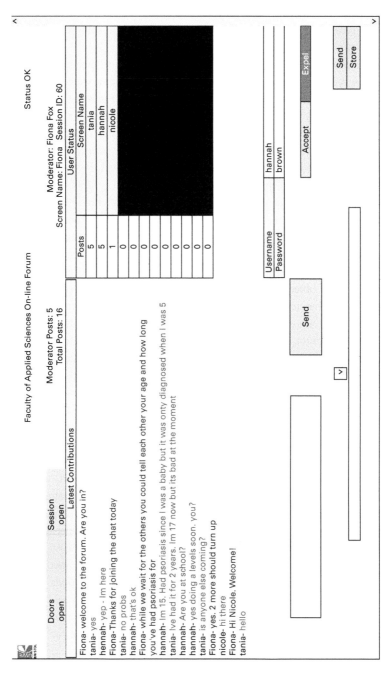

Figure 13.1 Moderator's screen for my real-time OFGs

proficient at typing has the ability to contribute the most. My moderator's screen displayed the number of contributions made by each participant (see Figure 13.1), allowing me to see who required additional encouragement. Depending upon the approach of the study, the moderator might encourage contributions from the quieter members of the group by asking them directly for their views, or instead may observe the group dynamics without prompting individual participants.

My non-real-time OFG remained open for three months, but studies report extended periods of data collection of up to six months (Im, 2006). This means that rapport between participants may be slower to develop than in real-time groups. It is the moderator's responsibility to help this process along, with questions and prompts to the group. Some researchers adopt a non-directed moderating style, in order to encourage participants to express themselves freely (Bosio et al., 2008). I adopted this approach and posted only a welcome message at the start and a brief message at the end of my discussion group, which thanked participants, notified them that the focus group had finished, and gave my contact details if they had any further comments or questions. Where online message boards are open for shorter periods of time, researchers typically report a more structured approach, posting a new question every few days, along with probing, asking additional questions and clarifying views. This encourages both sustained engagement with the discussion and interactivity between participants (de Jong et al., 2012).

In order to report accurately the numbers of participants in non-real-time OFGs, it is helpful for researchers to define what qualifies as participation – for example posting at least one message. My analysis of online peer support identified different types of participation in the non-real-time discussion group, from highly interactive to 'lurkers', or people who read other member's posts but did not actively contribute (Fox et al., 2010). To help define participation, it is useful if the moderator can view which participants are posting and which are reading the messages but not contributing to the discussion.

(3) *Ending the discussion.* The principles that are typically used when ending face-to-face focus groups (Kreuger and Casey, 2000) can be applied to OFGs. The moderator should attempt to summarise the discussion in order to elicit any additional experiences or views that participants wish to share, and should also remind participants that all their views will be useful for the analysis. Before ending the real-time discussion, the moderator should thank participants and let them know that the forum will be closing in the following minutes. When the forum closes, they can be

---

Box 13.2 Focus group guide for real-time OFGs

Introductions:
(1) Can you start by telling each other about when you first noticed your psoriasis/ vitiligo?

Opening:
(1) How does having a skin condition affect your day-to-day life?
(2) Is there anything that you do or don't do because of your skin condition?

Age and Development – Past/Future:
(1) How did you feel about your skin condition when you were younger?
(2) Can you imagine having different problems or concerns as you get older?

Appearance-Related Concerns:
(1) How important is your skin in terms of your overall appearance?
(2) Is there anything that you don't do because of your skin?
(3) How do other people react?
(4) What have they said/not said or done/not done that has been helpful?
(5) How does this affect the way you feel about yourself?
(6) What makes your life easier or harder?

Coping and Support:
(1) What has helped you to cope with your worries?
(2) Who helps you and how/what do they do?
(3) What kind of advice or support do you get from your GP/Consultant?
(4) What other advice or support would you find helpful?

Ending:
(1) Of all the problems we have talked about – which is the most important for you?
(2) Do you have any advice for other teenagers with skin conditions?
(3) Is there anything else that you would like to talk about?

Source: Fox et al. (2007b).

---

directed to a final screen that can include post-participation material, such as a reminder of the purposes of research, contact details for the researcher and information about appropriate support services. A few days before the end of a non-real-time OFG, the moderator can email all participants to remind them that they have limited amount of time left to make a contribution. Once the message board closes, a re-direct message should indicate that the discussion has ended. The researcher can then send a final email to participants, thanking them for taking part in the OFG and providing details of relevant organisations in case they require further information or support.

What Can Go Wrong with Online Focus Groups?

Researchers should be aware of the following potential problems associated with the use of OFGs:

(1) *Technical problems.* OFGs can be subject to a variety of technical problems both before and during the discussion. For example, participants may experience difficulties logging into the online discussion, reflecting computer literacy issues (Nicholas et al., 2010) or technical problems, such as computer viruses. In real-time OFGs, the Internet connection can fail, from either the participant's or researcher's end. I found it particularly useful that, if they lost their connection, participant names changed colour on my moderator's screen, alerting me that their status was offline. I found that in most cases, participants who lost connection to the forum were able to log back in and continue participating. However, during one of the OFGs, the entire forum shut down, and the OFG had to be rescheduled by email. Of course, it can be difficult to distinguish between participants who have lost connection, or those who have chosen to leave the discussion, although this can sometimes be clarified through follow-up emails.

(2) *Recruitment problems.* Ensuring that participants attend OFGs can be problematic, and researchers may be left guessing a participant's reasons for non-attendance, including: forgetting; changing their mind; having competing commitments and difficulty getting online or connecting to the online forum. I found that sending reminder emails to participants a few days before the real-time OFG, and then again an hour before it started, helped to minimise this. With non-real-time OFGs, researchers can encourage participation through regular reminder emails. For both forms of OFG, it is advisable to over-recruit, although the moderator must be prepared to cope with a situation where all those recruited do actually turn up, such as having a second moderator available to assist.

Organising real-time OFGs can be more challenging when participants are in different time zones, and it is crucial to use clear communication and reminder emails to ensure that all participants agree to join at the same time. Researchers should carefully consider cultural differences in online communication and engagement with technology, as well as language proficiency. In my research, participants from outside the UK were less interactive than their UK counterparts, and tended to direct their comments to me, rather than to each other. As a result, my moderating style became more directive and active.

(3) *Problems with participant behaviour.* As early as 1986, Sproull and Kiesler warned about episodes of 'flaming' in online discussions. More recently, Bosio et al. (2008: 200) reported exchanges in their real-time OFGs that were 'frenzied and characterized by provocations or insults'. As noted earlier, expected codes of conduct should be clearly stated in the information provided for participants before the OFG, and again on the welcome page, prior to entering the online forum or message board. Researchers should explain in the participant information that all messages posted to non-real-time OFGs will be checked by the moderator before they appear online. Although this process requires the moderator to regularly monitor incoming messages, it does negate the possibility of offensive or inappropriate comments affecting the other participants.

(4) *Unexpected problems.* In my real-time OFGs I noted two occurrences, which are unique to online communication. During one OFG a participant wrote '*brb*' – an abbreviation for 'be right back'. This left me wondering whether they had left the computer to answer the phone or the door, or for a bathroom or refreshment break. I was unprepared for this incident, but chose not to question the participant about their reasons for leaving. On another occasion a participant in a real-time OFG commented '*It's difficult to write when some annoying person is reading over my shoulder'*. This raises an important point about the privacy and confidentiality of online discussions, when participants may be taking part from a computer that is in a public or shared space.

What Methods of Analysis Suit Online Focus Group Data?

Data analysis for OFGs begins with the downloading of transcripts, saving on the time and cost associated with the transcription of audio files. In real-time discussions, the complexity of participant interactions may result in a chaotic transcript, characterised by overlapping conversations (see Table 13.1), which can be frustrating for the novice researcher to manage and interpret. Non-real-time discussions are likely to generate transcripts where individual contributions vary greatly in terms of length and depth of reflection (see Table 13.2). Both kinds of data are amenable to a range of analytic techniques, or indeed to a multiple analytic approach (Bosio et al., 2008), including those that are typically used for analysing face-to-face focus group data.

Analytic approaches, both deductive and inductive, which are oriented to describing, interpreting and finding patterns provide a good fit for OFG data (Tesch, 1991). Deductive analytic approaches typically involve the use of a preconceived coding frame to guide a content or thematic analysis of the data (Boyatzis, 1998; Hsieh and Shannon, 2005). In one study, I used content analysis to identify the frequency, patterns and sequence of support exchanged within the non-real-time group (Fox et al., 2010). This involved using relevant research findings to guide the development of my initial codes. In addition to coding using predefined categories of support, I also made detailed observations about the tone, content and development of the groups, which added contextual richness to the analysis. More inductive approaches are also possible (e.g., Braun and Clarke, 2006), where codes are generated from the data, rather than determined in advance of analysis.

The communication generated in OFGs also lends itself to more technical processes of conversational analysis (Collins and Britten, 2006). Linguistic features of online discourse, such as lexical choices, grammatical structure and conversational style can be analysed, as well as the dynamic features of conversation that are unique to OFGs, such as turn-taking, organisation and silence management (Bosio et al., 2008).

Finally, OFG data can also be analysed using theory-building approaches such as grounded theory (Glaser and Strauss, 1967); my work aligned with Charmaz's emphasis on 'constructing' grounded theory (Charmaz, 2006; see Fox et al., 2007b). As with face-to-face focus groups, there is no 'best' way to analyse data from OFGs, but choosing to focus on the content or the interaction process can help to guide analytic decisions (Wilkinson, 1998).

Conclusion

I have demonstrated that many of the research questions and analytic processes used for face-to-face focus groups can be applied to OFGs. I have highlighted some of the unique features of both real-time and non-real-time discussions, and have outlined key steps and considerations for the researcher when planning and hosting OFGs. Through examples from my own research, I have indicated that OFGs can offer a feasible alternative to face-to-face focus groups and may even be more inclusive for, and attractive to, some participant groups (see Box 13.3). I encourage researchers to continue to develop the OFG method.

Box 13.3 Personal reflections on using OFGs

The idea of running OFGs was a response to the challenges of engaging young people in face-to-face focus groups. My participants were young people with chronic skin conditions that potentially affected not only their appearance but also their confidence. Online discussions therefore seemed like a good option to offer to them. My own experience of real-time online chat was limited, so this was an 'experiment' that appealed to me, and with the support of a university technician and my supervision team I was encouraged to 'give it a go'. Waiting for participants to log in and join my initial OFG was a nerve-wracking experience, as I worried about how responsive they would be to me, and to each other. However, just minutes after opening the real-time OFG, responses and contributions started to fill my screen. Immediately I was struck by the speed with which this small group of strangers established rapport and how easily they began to disclose their experiences to each other. I recall thinking that I could probably just sit back and let them run the discussion without my intervention. Then came the first heart-stopping lengthy silence ... followed by several posts all hitting my screen at once! At points I felt that I was being left behind by the speed of their conversation, their shared understanding of abbre-viations and use of emoticons that were unfamiliar to me. What exactly did LOL mean (lots of love?) and why did they keep saying it? A quick Google search set me straight – these kids were Laughing Out Loud! I felt a mixture of being privileged to gain insight into their social world and mild panic that I needed to keep up with the kids!

I had anticipated that my research would start by exploring the experiences of young people with chronic skin conditions and would proceed with a neat series of studies that would ultimately define their support needs. However, it emerged that within the OFGs, participants were exchanging peer support and thus spontaneously meeting their own support needs. Therefore, my conceptual thinking and my research plans took a giant leap forward (and slightly to the left) as I planned subsequent studies to compare specific aspects of peer support and how they are negotiated in different online environments.

Throughout my subsequent research career, I have retained the sense that the Internet provides an important vehicle for reaching groups of young people. As a powerful communication and information-sharing tool, the Internet is also a social domain within which many young people exist (Pastore, 2002), and doing qualitative research online can enable young people to feel relaxed and in control of their own participation experience. On this basis, I am convinced that it should be considered as an appropriate space in which qualitative research can flourish.

Have a Go ...

Compare the data extracts from two separate OFGs (in Table 13.1 and 13.2):

(1) Note down your initial observations about the differences between the data from the real-time and non-real-time OFGs.
(2) What are the characteristics of the communication styles in each?
(3) How might you start to analyse these data?

Further Resources: Online

The following websites provide information for young people about online safety:
Stay Safe Online.org: www.staysafeonline.org/stop-think-connect/tips-and-advice
Safety Net Kids – staying safe online: www.safetynetkids.org.uk/personal-safety/st aying-safe-online/

Further Resources: Readings

For a further discussion of real-time OFGs, see Fox, F., Morris, M. and Rumsey, N. (2007a). Doing synchronous online focus groups with young people: Methodological reflections. *Qualitative Health Research*, *17*(4), 539–547.

To read more about the example study using real-time OFGs, see Fox, F., Rumsey, N. and Morris, M. (2007b). 'Ur skin is the thing that everyone sees and you can't change it!': Exploring the appearance-related concerns of young people with psoriasis. *Developmental Neurorehabilitation*, *10*(3), 133–141.

For an exploration and comparison of the different ways young people share support via real-time and non-real-time online groups, see Fox, F., Morris, M. and Rumsey, N. (2010). How do young people use disclosure in real-time and non-real-time online groups? *Internet Journal of Web-Based Communities*, *6*(4), 337–348.

For a discussion of the strengths and limitations of OFGs, see Gaiser, T. (2008). Online focus groups. In N. G. Fielding, R. M. Lee and G. Blank (eds.), *The SAGE handbook of online research methods* (pp. 290–306). London: Sage Publications.

For a comparison of face-to-face and non-real-time OFGs and an exploration of differences in participants' preferences, experiences and engagement with either approach, see Nicholas, D. B., Lach, L., King, G., Scott, M., Boydell, K., Sawatzky, B. J., Reisman, J., Schippel, E. and Young, N. L. (2010). Contrasting Internet and face-to-face focus groups for children with chronic health conditions: Outcomes and participant experiences. *International Journal of Qualitative Methods*, *9*(1), 105–121.

References

Adams, J., Rodham, K. and Gavin, J. (2005). Investigating the 'self' in deliberate self-harm. *Qualitative Health Research*, *15*(10), 1293–1309.

Adler, C. L. and Zarchin, Y. R. (2002). The 'virtual focus group': Using the Internet to reach pregnant women on home bed rest. *Journal of Obstetric, Gynaecologic, and Neonatal Nursing*, *31*(4), 418–427.

Bordia, P. (1997). Face-to-face versus computer-mediated communication: A synthesis of the experimental literature. *Journal of Business Communication*, *34*(10), 99–120.

Boshoff, K., Alant, E. and May, E. (2005). Occupational therapy managers' perceptions of challenges faced in early intervention service delivery in South Australia. *Australian Occupational Therapy Journal*, *52*(3), 232–242.

Bosio, A. C., Graffigna, G. and Lozza, E. (2008). Toward theory and technique for online focus groups. In T. Hasson (ed.), *Handbook of research on digital information technologies: Innovations, methods and ethical issues* (pp. 193–213). Denmark: Emerald Group.

Boyatzis, R. E. (1998). *Transforming qualitative information: Thematic analysis and code development*. Thousand Oaks, CA: Sage Publications.

Braun, V. and Clarke, V. (2006). Using thematic analysis in psychology. *Qualitative Research in Psychology*, *3*(2), 77–101.

Charmaz, K. (2006). *Constructing grounded theory: A practical guide through qualitative analysis*. Thousand Oaks, CA: Sage Publications.

Collins, S. and Britten, N. (2006). Conversation analysis. In C. Pope and N. Mays (eds.), *Qualitative research in health care* (3rd edn, pp. 43–52). Oxford: Blackwell.

Davis, R. N. (1999). Web-based administration of a personality based questionnaire: Comparison with traditional methods. *Behavioural Research Methods, Instruments and Computers*, *31*, 572–577.

Ess, C. and the AoIR ethics working committee (2002). *Ethical decision-making and Internet research: Recommendations from the AoIR ethics working committee*. Retrieved from: www.aoir.org/reports/ethics.pdf.

Fawcett, J. and Buhle, E. L. (1995). Using the Internet for data collection: An innovative electronic strategy. *Computers in Nursing*, *13*(6), 273–279.

Fox, F., Morris, M. and Rumsey, N. (2007a). Doing synchronous online focus groups with young people: Methodological reflections. *Qualitative Health Research*, *17*(4), 539–547.

 (2007b). 'Ur skin is the thing that everyone sees and you can't change it!': Exploring the appearance-related concerns of young people with psoriasis. *Developmental Neurorehabilitation*, *10*(3), 133–141.

Fox, F., Morris, M. and Rumsey, N. (2010). How do young people use disclosure in real-time and non-real-time online groups? *International Journal of Web Based Communities*, *6*(4), 337–348.

Franklin, K. K. and Lowry, C. (2001). Computer-mediated focus group sessions: Naturalistic inquiry in a networked environment. *Qualitative Research*, *1*(2), 169–184.

Gaiser, T. (1997). Conducting online focus groups: A methodological discussion. *Social Science Computer Review*, *15*(2), 135–144.

(2008). Online focus groups. In N. G. Fielding, R. M. Lee and G. Blank (eds.), *The SAGE handbook of online research methods* (pp. 290–306). London: Sage Publications.

Gibson, F. (2007). Conducting focus groups with children and young people: Strategies for success. *Journal of Research in Nursing, 12*(5), 473–483.

Glaser, B. and Strauss, A. (1967). *The discovery of grounded theory.* Hawthorne, NY: Aldine Publishing Company.

Horn, S. (1998). *Cyberville: Clicks, culture and the creation of an online town.* New York: Warner Books.

Horrell, B., Stephens, C. and Breheny, M. (2015). Online research with informal caregivers: Opportunities and challenges. *Qualitative Research in Psychology, 12*(3), 258–271.

Hsieh, H. F. and Shannon, S. E. (2005). Three approaches to qualitative content analysis. *Qualitative Health Research, 15*(9), 1277–1288.

Im, E. (2006). White cancer patients' perception of gender and ethnic differences in pain experience. *Cancer Nursing, 29*(6), 441–452.

Internet World Stats (2014). Internet growth statistics. Retrieved from: www .Internetworldstats.com/emarketing.htm.

de Jong, I., Reinders-Messelink, H. A., Janssen, W. G. M., Poelma, M. J., van Wijk, I. and van der Sluis, C. K. (2012). Activity and participation of children and adolescents with unilateral congenital below elbow deficiency: An online focus group study. *Journal of Rehabilitation Medicine, 44*(10), 885–892.

Joinson, A. N. (2001). Self-disclosure in computer-mediated communication: The role of self-awareness and visual anonymity. *European Journal of Social Psychology, 31*(2), 177–192.

Keisler, S. and Sproull, L. (1992). Group decision making and communication technology. *Organizational Behavior and Human Decision Processes, 52*(1), 96–123.

Kennedy, C., Kools, S. and Krueger, R. (2001). Methodological considerations in children's focus groups. *Nursing Research, 50*(3), 184–187.

Kenny, A. J. (2005). Interaction in cyberspace: An online focus group. *Journal of Advanced Nursing, 49*(4), 414–422.

Kitzinger, J. (1995). Qualitative research: Introducing focus groups. *British Medical Journal, 311*(7000), 299–302.

Krueger, R. A. (1988). *Focus groups: A practical guide for applied research.* Newbury Park, CA: Sage Publications.

Krueger, R. A. and Casey, M. A. (2000). *Focus groups. A practical guide for applied research* (3rd edn). Thousand Oaks, CA: Sage Publications.

Mann, C. and Stewart, F. (2000). *Internet communication and qualitative research: A handbook for researching online.* London: Sage Publications.

Moloney, M. F., Dietrich, A. S., Strickland, O. and Myerburg, S. (2003). Using Internet discussion boards as virtual focus groups. *Advances in Nursing Science, 26*(4), 274–286.

Montoya-Weiss, M. M., Massey, A. P. and Clapper, D. L. (1999). On-line focus groups: Conceptual issues and a research tool. *European Journal of Marketing, 32*(7/8), 713–723.

Morgan, M., Gibbs, S., Maxwell, K. and Britten, N. (2002). Hearing children's voices: Methodological issues in conducting focus groups with children. *Qualitative Research, 2*(1), 5–20.

Murray, P. J. (1997). Using virtual focus groups in qualitative research. *Qualitative Health Research*, *7*(4), 542–545.

Nicholas, D. B. (2003). Participant perceptions of online groupwork with fathers of children with spina bifida. In N. Sullivan, N. C. Lang, D. Goodman and L. Mitchell (eds.), *Social work with groups: Social justice through personal, community and societal change* (pp. 227–240). Binghamton, NY: Haworth.

Nicholas, D. B., Lach, L., King, G., Scott, M., Boydell, K., Sawatzky, B. J., Reisman, J., Schippel, E. and Young, N. L. (2010). Contrasting Internet and face-to-face focus groups for children with chronic health conditions: Outcomes and participant experiences. *International Journal of Qualitative Methods*, *9*(1), 105–121.

O'Connor, H. and Madge, C. (2003). Focus groups in cyberspace: Using the Internet for qualitative research. *Qualitative Market Research: An International Journal*, *6*(2), 133–143.

Pastore, M. (2002). Internet key to communication among youth. Clickz network: Solutions for marketers.

Peacock, S., Robertson, A., Williams, S. and Clausen, M. (2009). The role of learning technologists in supporting e-research. *ALT-J*, *17*(2), 115–129.

Pittenger, D. J. (2003). Internet research: An opportunity to revisit classical ethical problems in behavioural research. *Ethics & Behaviour*, *13*(1), 45–60.

Reid, D. J. and Reid, F. J. M. (2005). Online focus groups: An in-depth comparison of computer mediated and conventional focus group discussions. *International Journal of Market Research*, *47*(2), 131–162.

Reips, U. D. (2000). The web experiment method: Advantages, disadvantages and solutions. In M. H. Birmbaun (ed.), *Psychological experiments on the Internet* (pp. 89–117). San Diego, CA: Academic Press.

Rezabek, R. (2000). Online focus groups: Electronic discussions for research. *Forum Qualitative Sozialforschung. Forum: Qualitative Social Research*, *1*(1). Retrieved from: www.qualitative-research.net/fqs-texte/1-00/1-00rezabek-e.htm

Robson, K. (1999). *Employment experiences of ulcerative colitis and Crohn's disease sufferers* (Unpublished PhD thesis). Cardiff, UK: University of Wales.

Sproull, L. and Kiesler, S. (1986). Reducing social context cues: Electronic mail in organizational communication. *Management Science*, *32*(11), 1492–1512.

Stewart, F., Eckerman, E. and Zhou, K. (1998). Using the Internet in qualitative public health research: A comparison of Chinese and Australian young women's percep-tions of tobacco use. *Internet Journal of Health Promotion*, *12* [Online]. Retrieved from: www.rhpeo.org/ijhp-articles/1998/12/

Stewart, K. and Williams, M. (2005). Researching online populations: The use of online focus groups for social research. *Qualitative Research*, *5*, 395–416.

Suzuki, L. K. and Calzo, J. P. (2004). The search for peer advice in cyberspace: An examination of online teen bulletin boards about health and sexuality. *Journal of Applied Developmental Psychology*, *25*(6), 685–698.

Sweet, C. (2001). Designing and conducting virtual focus group. *Qualitative Market Research: An International Journal*, *4*(3), 130–135.

Tanis, M. (2007). Online social support groups. In A. Joinson, K. McKenna, T. Postmes and U. Reips (eds.), *The Oxford handbook of Internet psychology* (pp. 139–153). Oxford: Oxford University Press.

Tates, K., Zwaanswijk, M., Otten, R., van Dulmen, S., Hoogerbrugge, P. M., Kamps, W. A. and Bensing, J. M. (2009). Online focus groups as a tool to collect data in hard-to-include populations: Examples from paediatric oncology. *BMC Medical Research Methodology, 9*(15), 9–15.

Thomas, C., Wootten, A. and Robinson, P. (2013). The experiences of gay and bisexual men diagnosed with prostate cancer: Results from an online focus group. *European Journal of Cancer Care, 22*(4), 522–529.

Tesch, R. (1991). Software for qualitative researchers: Analysis needs and programme capabilities. In N. G. Fielding and R. M. Lee (eds.), *Using computers in qualitative research* (pp. 15–22). London: Sage Publications.

Tidwell, L. C. and Walther, J. B. (2002). Computer-mediated communication effects on disclosure, impressions, and interpersonal evaluations: Getting to know one another a bit a time. *Human Communication Research, 28*(3), 317–348.

Turney, L. and Pocknee, C. (2005). Virtual focus groups: New frontiers in research. *International Journal of Qualitative Methods, 4*(2), 32–43.

Tuttas, C. A. (2014). Lessons learned using web conference technology for online focus group interviews. *Qualitative Health Research, 25*(1), 122–133.

Ward, K. J. (1999). The cyber-ethnographic (re)construction of two feminist online communities. *Sociological Research Online, 4*(1). Retrieved from: www .socresonline.org.uk/4/1/contents.html

Wilkinson, S. (1998). Focus group methodology: A review. *International Journal of Social Research Methodology, 1*(3), 181–203.

Williams, M. (2003). *Virtually criminal: Deviance and harm within online environments* (Unpublished PhD thesis). Cardiff, UK: University of Wales.

Williams, S. (2009). *Understanding anorexia nervosa: An online phenomenological approach* (Unpublished PhD thesis). Edinburgh, UK: Queen Margaret University.

Williams, S., Clausen, M. G., Robertson, A., Peacock, S. and McPherson, K. (2012). Methodological reflections on the use of asynchronous online focus groups in health research. *International Journal of Qualitative Methods, 11*(4), 368–383.

Ybarra, M. L., DuBois, L. Z., Parsons, J. T., Prescott, T. L. and Mustanski, B. (2014). Online focus groups as an HIV prevention programme for gay, bisexual and queer adolescent males. *AIDS Education and Prevention, 26*(6), 554–564.

Afterword

Ruthellen Josselson

Qualitative researchers have vastly expanded their notions of *what* constitute data in the social and health sciences. Much can be learned about people in ways other than having a researcher sit down with them, either individually or in focus groups, and interview them. Why not look at diaries or ask people to respond in open-ended ways to surveys? Or to complete stories or respond to vignettes framed by the researcher? Why not tap the vast resources of interactive media such as blogs, discussion forums, talkback radio and other forms of media data – as well as all the talk that occurs online? In a thorough and thoughtful way, this book takes researchers through the steps of accessing widely varied manifestations of human life. That the 'how to' of these approaches – textual, media and virtual – are all gathered in this one volume is an enormous contribution to qualitative research.

The data of human experience and social practice are everywhere and, with the Internet, more accessible to researchers than ever before. Qualitative researchers in the social and health sciences have newly available to them recorded phenomena of social and personal life that open new vistas for exploring new questions. Those of us who immigrated, sometimes reluctantly, into the Internet (and media) age, are mindful that a generation of Internet natives are now coming of age in the academic world. These people, who grew up on the Internet as an integral part of their social world, are expanding our conceptions of how knowledge can be constructed – and from what sources. There are now new possibilities of making contact with previously difficult-to-reach populations and learning about them. There are new opportunities to witness how people are behaving and talking in natural settings.

The texts we analyse to gain understanding can be obtained in many ways, as this book details. How data are gathered (and what they are assumed to represent) is a crucial decision that anchors whatever interpretation we make of the observed phenomena. This book both expands the available databases and looks closely at the *actual processes* of collecting qualitative data in these

300

forms, thereby offering a crucial beginning for thinking about what we as scholars can understand from such research designs.

An emerging philosophical perspective in contemporary qualitative research can be viewed as what Ken Gergen (2014) calls *reflective pragmatism*: forgoing what has been called 'methodolatry', we evaluate research in relation to whether a given research practice fulfils its envisioned goals and whether it does so in a sufficiently rigorous way. Creativity in research practice becomes unlimited. The authors of the chapters in this book are engaged in reflecting (pragmatically) on various sources of data, considering what these data may represent and how they can be obtained most usefully to address meaningful research questions.

Most of the forms of data collection discussed in this book rely on language – and language embodies the assumptions of a society. Approaches like qualitative surveys, story completion, vignettes and diaries all sample natural use of written language, and thereby offer a window into foundational, socially constructed realities that reveal how people conceive of their social worlds. While asking for written samples of experience are already-established forms of data collection, particularly among quantitative researchers, the authors of these chapters (Chapters 2–5) bring them *newly* to the attention of qualitative researchers, and meticulously detail the mechanics of using them as a means for exploring participants' meanings around, and interpretations of, a particular phenomenon.

Tapping media and virtual data are more recent forms of data collection, particularly in psychology. These data can illustrate how people use language in natural settings, capturing the social construction of their realities with little or no impact of the researcher. One of the most intriguing aspects of many of these forms of data collection is that the researcher becomes a fly on the wall, a fully unobtrusive observer. These approaches to amassing data subtract from the research equation the research relationship, and its many influences on the data produced. Although we still need to be aware of to whom blogs or talk radio offerings or social media posts are addressed, our presence as researchers, because it occurs after the fact, is removed from the *production* of the data. We thereby gain access to something different from researcher-solicited data.

The Internet and related media provide documents that reflect how people make meaning of the world, and qualitative researchers, such as those who have contributed to this book, are creatively and avidly trying to harvest the riches that are strewn in the virtual world. These researchers remind me of the fifteenth-century explorers who knew there was a 'new world' out there, and built the ships and devised the maps to reach and document it (and yes, often claim/colonise it). In our contemporary world, an explorer's ship sits on everyone's desk. The challenge remains in the maps – where to explore, how to explore, and how to make sense of it all. Accessing this interactive archive of everyday life *responsibly* is the first step. It is to their credit that the authors are so mindful of the ethics involved – the ethics of virtual research can raise complex questions, particularly in relation to (social) media. Where are the boundaries between public and private in the virtual world? How do we maintain the anonymity of those we study when this virtual world is so searchable? These sorts of questions have evolving answers, and each scholar here has offered a thoughtful way of approaching them (despite not always agreeing!).

That many of these forms of data collection are so accessible – clicks can produce massive datasets in seconds – offers both opportunities and challenges. As the editors point out, these forms of data collection are particularly appealing in these days of limited time and money for research. Why travel to talk to someone, or do a face-to-face focus group, when we have Skype? Why spend a lot of money to ask people questions when people are posting what they think voluntarily in real-time? There may still be good reasons to collect qualitative data in more 'traditional' ways, but they may not be necessary in all cases; may not even be ideal. But important questions do need to be addressed if we go virtual – especially without researcher involvement in data production: how do we limit the amount of data we seek? How can we verify the authenticity of what we find – if that is important to our research question? How do we interpret what we obtain? These kinds of questions can only be answered with experience, and one particular value of this book is that the authors all share the perils of their investigations – the difficulties and problems – as well as the successes. The researchers whose voices we hear here all testify to the messiness of the research process, which, while true of all research, no matter its form, is often cloaked.

Qualitative researchers learn about people and social life by analysing the ways in which they construct their experience and the social world. This book is a compendium of new and evolving ways to access meaning-making and, with its carefully wrought detail, opens new vistas for qualitative researchers.

Reference

Gergen, K. J. (2014). Pursuing excellence in qualitative inquiry. *Qualitative Psychology*, *1*(1), 49–61.

Glossary

Account: participants' attempts to explain, justify or legitimate some action, experience or situation. (see also *Accountability*)

Accountability: in some qualitative analytic approaches (see *Conversation analysis, Discourse analysis, Rhetorical analysis*) this refers to the idea that the actions, words and experiences of individuals are always (in some way) accountable to others.

Analysis: the detailed examination of data. Can be quantitative, where the data analysed are numeric, or qualitative, where the data analysed are audio, textual or visual. (see *Conversation analysis, Discourse analysis, Grounded theory, Thematic analysis, Interpretative phenomenological analysis, Rhetorical analysis*)

Anonymity: protecting the identity of participants. There can be varying degrees of anonymity, ranging from designs where only the participants know that they have participated in the research, to designs where the researcher knows but takes active steps to ensure that only they know the identity of participants. Typically, a requirement of *ethics*.

Asynchronous: where interaction between the research participant and the researcher happens in different time periods – for example, where a researcher poses a question to a participant, but the participant provides their answer at a later point. An element of *email interviews* or *online focus groups*.

Audience effects: a social psychological term referring to the impact of an audience on the performance of a task.

Bias: associated with positivist research, bias refers to the idea that our research or data might be contaminated by our lack of objectivity. Bias as a concept does not apply as a valid critique of (*Big Q*) qualitative research. (see *Subjective; Subjectivity*)

Big Q qualitative research: the application of qualitative methods of data collection and analysis within a qualitative paradigm, rather than a *positivist* one.

Blog: a regularly updated website or webpage written in an informal or conversational style.

Blogosphere: a set of *blogs* considered to be a distinct online network or community.

Bottom-up: an approach to analysis that starts with, or is grounded in, the meanings and ideas conveyed within the dataset – and sometimes involves then developing theory (as in *Grounded theory*). Also called *inductive*, the opposite of a *deductive* or *top-down* approach.

Broadsheet: a newspaper in the UK with a large format, regarded as more serious and less sensationalist than *tabloids*.

CAQDAS: computer-assisted qualitative data analysis software.

Case-study: an in-depth study of a case or cases (a 'case' can be a programme, an event, an activity, an individual), studied over time using multiple sources of information (e.g., observations, documents, archival data, *interviews*).

Cherry-picking: to selectively choose from available evidence.

Code: the process of identifying and describing meaningful concepts in a dataset. Labels are given to 'data chunks' (e.g., lines, sentences or paragraphs) in order to capture and convey the meaning of that data chunk. Usually, one of the first steps in data *analysis*, after *familiarisation*.

Coding: the process of examining data, and identifying and noting aspects that relate to your research question. Coding can be *complete*, where the whole dataset is coded, or *selective*, where only material of interested is selected and coded.

Collective meaning making: refers to the social process whereby the meaning of an event, experience or situation is collectively negotiated and understood. Typically, a concern of those working from a *social constructionist* perspective, or where data are collected from groups. (see *Focus groups*)

Comments: the comments that are invited from readers after publication of story or opinion piece online.

Comparative design: a research design that involves comparing data from two or more groups of people (e.g., men and women), or two or more data sources.

Confidentiality: a promise, and set of processes, to limit access to participant data and information. Typically, a requirement of *ethics*.

Consent form: a form that participants are asked to complete and sign in order to indicate that they understand the purposes of the research and agree to take part. Typically, a requirement of *ethics*. (see *Informed consent*)

Construct: refers to a particular social artefact or object, which is the focus of analysis or interest. Fitting with a *social constructionist* position, meaning is seen not as inherent in the object, but as socially produced. For example, consider the construct 'the child': what westerners now understand as the essence and meaning of childhood is very different from the meanings ascribed 200 years ago; policies and practices around children similarly differ. (see *Construction, Constructionism, Social constructionism*)

Construction: can be used both to refer to a process and a product. As a process, it is about the production of meaning and reality through language, representation and other social processes, such as the production of meaning around 'obesity'. As a product, it refers to a particular or specific object or meaning that has been produced through this process – 'obesity' is a good example of a construction (or *Construct*). (see *Social constructionism*)

Constructionism: a socially-oriented theoretical approach, concerned with the production of meaning; understands truth as non-fixed, and meaning as interpersonally and socially produced (constructed) through language, representation and other processes. Sometimes used interchangeably with *constructivism*, although the approaches are different, and used differently across different disciplines. (see *Social constructionism*)

Constructivism: Often confused with *constructionism*, although the approaches are different (and used differently across different disciplines). Constructivism sees personal meanings and truths as produced through individuals' engagement with their worlds. It is often applied more individualistically and in psychologically-oriented ways than constructionism. (see *Social constructionism*)

Contextualism: a theoretical approach informing some qualitative research, which assumes that meaning is related to the context in which it is produced.

Convenience sampling: a very common way of sampling, where participants or data are selected based on *accessibility* rather than some other criterion. (see *Purposive sampling; Snowball sampling*)

Conversation analysis (CA): a form of qualitative analysis that attempts to describe the orderliness, structure and sequential patterns of interaction in everyday conversation or institutional (formal) talk.

Critical psychology: an umbrella term for a range of different approaches that challenge core assumptions of mainstream psychology. The key components of critical research are the questioning of taken-for-granted truths about subjectivity, experience and the way the world is, combined with recognition of the cultural, political and historical factors that shape experience.

Critical qualitative research: does not take data at face value. It takes an interrogative stance to the meanings expressed in data unpacking the ideas and concepts associated with them, and often relates them to broader social meanings.

Critical realism/Critical realist: a theoretical approach that assumes an ultimate reality, but claims that the way reality is experienced and interpreted is shaped by culture, language and political interests.

Cultural resources: the collective knowledge, experience, accomplishments and artefacts belonging to a specific group of people.

Data: materials collected, or generated, that are analysed.

Data breadth: data that provide a broad and general understanding of some phenomenon. Usually, the opposite of *data depth.*

Data depth: data that provide a thorough (in-depth) understanding of some phenomenon. Usually, the opposite of *data breadth.*

Data extract: short extracts from a dataset that provide evidence for particular analytic claims, or are the focus of detailed, specific analysis.

Data item: an individual unit of *data* (e.g., an interview; a newspaper story).

Dataset: all the *data items* collected for a particular study or analysis.

Deductive: generally, an approach that moves from the general to the specific. For example, testing a theory by generating specific hypotheses that are explored or tested in data. Theory-driven. Sometimes described as *top-down*; the opposite of *inductive.*

Demographics: the characteristics of a population or sample, including age, ethnicity, gender, economic status, level of education, income level and employment, among others.

Diary (solicited): a form of data collection where participants are asked to complete a diary over a given time period, for the purposes of addressing a specific research question.

Digital media: any media (e.g., text, audio, graphics and video) that is created, viewed or transmitted via computers or the Internet.

Discourse analysis (DA): a cluster of forms of qualitative analysis that centre on the detailed examination of patterns of meaning within texts, and the effects and implications of particular patterns of meaning. Theoretically underpinned by the idea that language creates meaning and reality, rather than reflecting it.

Discourse: a word with various meanings. Most broadly, it refers to patterned meaning within spoken or written language; to systems of meaning and talk which form readily identifiable ways of interpreting or understanding a particular object, or set of objects, in the world, which are theorised to create reality.

Discursive psychology (DP): the application of discourse analysis to psychological phenomena, associated with a 'fine-grained' approach to *discourse analysis* and detailed analyses of *textual data.*

Discursive resources: verbal, non-verbal and interactional resources that people use to construct particular *accounts* or particular versions of the world (and reality). (see *Discourse*)

Discussion forum (aka Internet forum or Forum): a type of online space where people with common interests can exchange open messages, by posting messages and receiving responses to them. Usually hierarchical in nature, a discussion forum will contain several *subforums*, each of which may have several topics. Within each topic, each new discussion started is called a *thread*.

Email interview: an interactive data collection method, with a researcher and a participant, that takes place over email. (see *Interview; Telephone interview*)

Emoticon: a typographic display of a facial representation, used to convey emotion in a text-only medium (e.g., ☺). (see *Emoji*)

Emoji: a standardised set of symbols or pictographs (a facial expression, a common object, places, types of weather, animals etc.) used to convey specific meaning in a text-only medium. (see *Emoticon*)

Empiricism: theoretical position that sees truth as revealed through observation and experimentation or empirical research.

Epistemology: a theory of knowledge, which determines what counts as valid or accepted knowledge, and also therefore how we go about obtaining or producing that knowledge.

Essentialism/essentialist: the idea that events result from fixed qualities 'inside' people (essences) that are impervious to the social context. Not the same as biology, but frequently closely linked to biology in explanations of human behaviour.

Ethics: theory, codes and practices concerned with ensuring we do research in a moral and non-harmful manner.

Experiential qualitative research: seeks to understand people's own perspectives, meanings and experiences.

Face-to-face: where the participants and the researcher meet up (face-to-face) for the purposes of interactive data collection.

Familiarisation: the process of getting to know (familiarising yourself with) your data. Also called *immersion*.

Feminism: broad range of theoretical and political approaches which at their core assume the equal rights of women and men.

Fine-grained analysis: see *Micro-analysis*.

Flaming: a hostile and insulting conversation between Internet users. Can be the result of an emotional conversation, or can be deliberate where individuals (known as flamers) specifically seek to incite controversy around specific topics.

Focus group: a method of collecting data, where a group of participants discuss a topic of interest, guided by a moderator, either face-to-face or virtually. A key and unique aspect of this method is the interaction and conversation between members of the group.

Focus group moderator: the person who guides the discussion in a *focus group* and moderates the group dynamics. Sometimes a member of a pre-existing group, rather than the researcher, can take on this role.

Focus group schedule (aka **focus group guide**): the topics, questions and prompts that the *focus group moderator* may want to ask during a *focus group*. There are three types: structured (a fixed list of questions that must be asked in the same order in every focus group), *semi-structured* (a list of topics that may be asked depending on the flow and content of the discussion) or *unstructured* (where questions are spontaneously created during each individual interview, dependent on the flow of the conversation). (see also *Interview schedule*)

Foucauldian discourse analysis (aka **Poststructuralist discourse analysis**): a form of discourse analysis based on the theories of Michel Foucault, focused on analysing power relations in society.

Generalisability: the ability to apply the results of a study to the wider population; most strongly associated with quantitative research. (see *Transferability*)

Grounded theory: a qualitative methodology that offers a way of developing theory grounded in data. As the theory evolves throughout the process of the research, data analysis and collection are linked. Often used in a 'lite' manner, without full theory development.

Hard-to-engage populations: groups who might not feel a strong connection to, investment in, or understanding of research, or might have had very negative experiences of research in the past, or for whom participation might be risky. (see *Hidden populations; Marginalised populations; Vulnerable groups*)

Hermeneutics: the theory and practice of interpretation.

Heteronormativity: a concept developed in queer theory that describes the social privileging of heterosexuality and the assumption that heterosexuality is the (only) natural and normal sexuality.

Hidden populations: those whose group memberships are not necessarily very visible, or may be stigmatised in some way, so people are not likely to be easy to identify as a member of that group. (see *Hard-to-engage populations; Marginalised populations; Vulnerable groups*)

Honorarium payment: payments to participants for volunteering to take part in the research. Typically, a small amount as compensation for their time, travel expenses etc. Also called a participant payment or incentive.

Ideology: an organised collection of ideas; a way of looking at things.

Instant messaging (IM): a form of private communication on the Internet where individuals can chat with one another in real-time using text-based communication.

Internet forum: see *Discussion forum*.

Immersion: a process where researchers *familiarise* themselves with their data by reading or examining (often repeatedly) some portion of the data in detail.

Inductive: a general orientation that moves from the particular or specific, to the general – often refers to the generation of new theory grounded in data (e.g., as in *Grounded theory*); in relation to qualitative analysis, refers to a *bottom-up* approach, where analytic meanings and concepts are derived primarily from the content of the dataset, rather than existing theory. Not a theory-testing/*deductive* approach.

Informed consent: consent given by research participants for their participation in research, and for their data to be used for research purposes; granted with full knowledge of all research procedures, and all risks and benefits of the research. An ethical requirement of research. (see *Anonymity, Confidentiality, Participant information sheet*)

Interpretation: a process of making sense of, and theorising the meanings in, data; goes beyond summarising the obvious semantic content of data and puts an interpretative framework around them.

Interpretative phenomenological analysis (IPA): an approach to qualitative research concerned with understanding experiences of the 'person in context'; prioritises participants' experiences and their interpretations of them. Theoretically developed from *phenomenology* and *hermeneutics*.

Intersubjective: the shared meanings constructed by people in their interactions with each other, used as an everyday resource to interpret the meaning of social and cultural life.

Interview schedule (aka **interview guide**): the topics, questions and prompts that an interviewer may want to address during an interview. There are three types: structured (a list of fixed questions that must be asked using the same wording and in the same order in every interview); *semi-structured* (a list of questions/topics that guide the discussion, but where the order is not fixed, and spontaneous questions may be asked in response to the participant's developing account); or *unstructured* (where some topics are determined in advance, but the precise questions are spontaneously created during each individual interview, dependent on the flow of the conversation). (see also *Semi-structured interview, Unstructured interview*)

Interview: a one-on-one method of collecting qualitative data, where a participant responds to a researcher's questions. Traditionally conducted in person, but can also be conducted virtually. (see *Email Interview; Telephone interview*)

IP address: a unique set of numbers that identifies each computer connected to the Internet.

Lads' mags: magazines aimed at or appealing to men, often featuring scantily dressed women.

LexisNexis: a digital database of legal and journalistic documents, including newspapers, magazines etc.

Linguistic resources: resources used when talking about, describing or accounting for various phenomena in the social world, in order to construct particular versions of phenomena – for example, the use of imagery or metaphor. Particularly of interest in *discourse analysis* and *rhetorical analysis*.

Lived experience: used to describe participants' first-hand accounts and experiences of phenomena.

Marginalised population: populations that are often not seen as part of the mainstream, or seen as unimportant, and so are often neglected in research. (see *Hard-to-engage populations; Vulnerable groups*)

Member check: where participants in a research project are asked to provide feedback on the findings of a study, in order to help improve the quality of a study. More commonly associated with *experiential qualitative research* and often more *realist* or *essentialist* approaches.

Message board: an Internet site where users can post comments about a particular issue or topic and reply to other users' postings.

Method: a technique or tool for data collection or analysis; often confused with *methodology*.

Methodology: theory of how research proceeds, including consideration of such things as *methods, participants*, the role of the researcher, *ethics* and so forth.

Micro-analysis: the very detailed, fine-grained, analysis of small amounts of data found in some versions of *conversation analysis, discourse analysis* and *rhetorical analysis*.

Mixed-method research: the combination of different methods of data collection and/or data analysis within a single study, frequently combining qualitative and quantitative approaches.

Multi-modal social semiotics: seeks to understand the different modes by which people communicate in particular social settings. An essential element of the theory is that modes of communication offer historically specific and socially and culturally shared options (or 'semiotic resources') for communicating.

Multi-textuality: qualitative data collection methods that offer the possibility of collecting data in more than one form (e.g., audio, visual, digital etc.). The aim being to examine the complexity of a phenomenon from more than one angle, or across more than one level of data.

Narrative analysis: uses the person as the unit of analysis, and looks within the person's account to find meanings; the analysis may draw together elements from multiple stories to construct an overarching narrative.

Narrative: an account of events or more than one event, characterised by having some sort of structure, often temporal in western cultures, and other story elements.

Naturalistic data: data that exist in the world (such as newspaper reports or doctor-patient interactions) rather than being collected specifically for the purposes of research. Also called naturally occurring data.

New media: media content available through the Internet, accessible on any digital device, usually containing interactive user feedback and creative participation.

Normative: what is widely considered and constructed to be 'normal' in society.

Non-normative: outside of what is considered and constructed as *normative*.

Online focus group: a *focus group* conducted using the Internet, rather than face-to-face.

Online interview: an *interview* conducted using the Internet or email, rather than face-to-face.

Ontology: refers to the study of being, and is concerned with the state/ nature of the world, with questions of what exists, and what relationship exists between the world and our human understandings and interpretations of it.

Open coding: one of the initial phases of a *grounded theory* analysis. The process involves the collection of raw data (e.g., interviews, field notes etc.) that are then systematically coded, labelled and defined on a line-by-line basis, in order to break the data down into segments that can then be interpreted for their meaning.

Opening post (OP): the first post in a *discussion forum, Internet forum* or *message board*.

Orthographic transcript: a written 'translation' of audio (or audiovisual) data that principally captures what was said, rather than how things were said. (see *Transcript*)

Paradigm: a conceptual framework within which scientific (and other) theories are constructed, and within which scientific practices take place. Major changes in thought and practice have been referred to as paradigm shifts.

Participant information sheet (PIS): Written information given to potential *participants* that specifies the parameters of a study and the scope of any involvement they might have, including the potential risks and benefits.

Participant: a person who takes part in research.

Participatory methods: involve the participants and/or the community the research is about as active members of the research, even as co-researchers.

Pattern-based discourse analysis: versions of *discourse analysis* primarily focused on identification of patterned features of language; often retain some interest in the content of language, not just its function.

Phenomenology: an influential philosophy in qualitative research. There are many varieties of phenomenology, but broadly speaking it is concerned with understanding people's subjective experiences.

Pilot: part of the research design stage that involves testing your data collection tool (e.g., survey, vignette, story completion task etc.) on a small sample of your *population* of interest, to ensure that it is meaningful to *participants* and that it is completed in the way that you expect.

Population: the collection of individuals or objects that you are interested in. Typically, determined by the focus of the research.

Positivism: a theoretical framework for making sense of the world which assumes a world that exists independent of our ways of getting to know it, and that if we observe it properly, we can discover its real and true nature.

Postmodernism: notoriously resistant to definition (and anti-definition in itself), postmodernism is a worldview that challenges the linear and 'progressive' model of the world promoted by modernism. Instead, it offers an approach to society and/or knowledge that stresses the uncertainty of knowledge and the existence of multiple truths. It theorises individual experiences as fragmented and multiple rather than coherent and linear. It is often seen as ironic and self-aware.

Postpositivism: beyond *positivism*, a theoretical position that acknowledges that researchers are influenced by their contexts, but still seeks (uncontaminated) knowledge about the true nature of the world.

Poststructuralism: refers to a loose collection of theoretical positions (and analytical approaches), developed in France in the 1960s from structuralist theories of language. The different approaches labelled poststructuralist share assumptions about language, meaning and subjectivity. Language (*Discourse*) is seen as constitutive of the world, the organisation of society and individual subjectivity. Meaning is thus produced and created within language and discourse.

Practice(s): a term that captures the very diverse 'things people do'; often used in place of the term 'behaviour' within critical psychology research, but is conceptually much broader than a traditional understanding of behaviour, because it includes things like language use.

Pro-Am: a contraction of professional and amateur, this term refers to the blurring of the boundaries between professional and amateur journalism and reporting in online environments.

Produsage: a contraction of producer and usage, this term refers to the creation of user-led content in online environments, where the boundaries between passive consumption and active production are blurred (e.g., in *blogs*).

Produsers: individuals engaged in the activity of *produsage*.

Projective test: a psychological test where words, images or situations are presented to a person in order to uncover some hidden or unconscious elements of their personality.

Pseudonym: a fake name used in place of a real name, to protect a participant's anonymity.

Pseudonymisation: A partial anonymisation of data source (e.g., anonymising participants' characteristics such as their age, their current and former occupations and the city where they live) that removes or alters key identifying features, but retains some features that are analytically important.

Purposive sampling: a mode of *sampling* typical of qualitative research; involves selecting participants or data on the basis that they will have certain characteristics or experiences. (see *Convenience sampling; Snowball sampling*)

Qualitative content analysis: qualitative data analysis method that typically involves classifying large amounts of text into categories that represent similar meanings. A qualitative form of *quantitative content analysis*.

Qualitative survey: a method of qualitative data collection consisting of a fixed series of open-ended questions that participants write responses to.

Quantitative content analysis: a form of analysis that usually counts and reports the frequency of concepts/words/behaviours within the data. (see *Qualitative content analysis*)

Rapport: the sense of positive emotional connection between people; often relates to interactive data collection and putting participants at ease and creating an environment where they feel relaxed, open and willing to answer questions.

Raw data: data in their original form, such as audio data before transcription.

Realism/realist: an *ontological* and *epistemological* position which assumes that the world has a true nature which is knowable and real, discovered through experience and research, that we 'know' an object because there are inherent facts about it that we can perceive and understand. (see *Relativism*)

Reflexivity: reflexivity has many meanings, but here it is concerned with a critical reflection on the research, both as process and as practice, and on one's own role as researcher, and on one's relation to knowledge. Reflexive research is that which acknowledges the role of the researcher in the production of knowledge, and in which the researcher reflects on their various positionings and the ways these might have shaped the collection and analysis of their data.

Relativism: a theoretical position that holds that there are multiple, constructed realities, rather than a single, knowable reality (see *Realism*) and that all we have is representations or accounts of what reality is, and that, at least *epistemologically*, all accounts are of equal theoretical value (even if they might not be based on other criteria); there is no foundation on which to claim some version of reality as more true and right than another version. (see *Ontology*)

Reliability: the extent to which the results generated could be generated again (e.g., by another researcher, in another context, at another time . . .); a key component of *positivist* research.

Representation: in writing up research, refers to the process of saying something about what participants think, feel, say, believe etc.; representation is what we do with research. As a form of qualitative research practice, refers to an interest in factors that shape or create meaning and the effects and implications of particular patterns of meaning in particular contexts.

Research design: effectively the plan for what a study will involve, and how it will be conducted. Ideally design should incorporate the goals of the study, the theoretical framework(s), the research questions, ethics and methods of generating and analysing data.

Research object: the thing that we are studying; the thing we want to understand more about. Can be theoretical or conceptual (e.g., love, creativity) or more concrete (e.g., cancer, eating).

Resource-lite: qualitative data collection methods that are not as onerous in terms of resources, like time or cost, particularly when compared to a *face-to-face interview* or *focus group*. These methods can be easier and faster to use, particularly when collecting data from a wide range of geographically dispersed participants.

Rhetorical analysis: a type of qualitative analysis that falls under the broad umbrella of *discursive psychology*. The focus of a rhetorical analysis is on the argumentative and persuasive nature of language, and the ways in which social interaction is located within a context of controversy containing discourses and counter-discourses.

Rhetorical device: a *linguistic resource* that is used to construct a particular kind of argument, or deflect a counter-argument. For example, the use of humour to deflect accusations of racism. Particularly of interest in *discourse analysis* and *rhetorical analysis*.

Rich data: data that provide detailed, complex and contradictory accounts about the *research object*. (see *Data depth*, *Thick description*)

Roll-off: a survey term that refers to participants who begin a survey but do not complete it.

Sample: the *participants* that are selected to take part in the research. A subset of a *population*.

Sample size: the total number of *participants* that are selected to take part in the research.

Sampling: the process of selecting *participants* to take part in the research, on the basis that they can provide detailed information that is relevant to the enquiry.

Saturation: commonly used criterion for size of qualitative sample. Generally used to refer to the point at which additional data items no longer generate any substantially new ideas. 'Saturation' developed out of *grounded theory*, with specific meanings, but has become used far more widely, and often without due theoretical consideration (e.g., that it relies on a *realist* position).

Secondary sources (of data): information that has been generated for purposes other than research, but that can be used as data in empirical research, such as parliamentary debates or *blogs*.

Semi-structured interview: A type of interview where some predetermined questions and question order is used for all interviews, but each interview ultimately develops in reaction to participants' responses. (see *Interview schedule*, unstructured interview)

Small q: the application of the qualitative methods of data collection and analysis within a *positivist-empiricist* orientation.

Snowball sampling: an approach to sampling where new participants are invited from the networks of people who have already taken part. (see *Convenience sampling; Purposive sampling*)

Social constructionism: a broad theoretical framework, popular in qualitative research, which rejects a single ultimate truth. Instead, it sees the world, and what we know of it, as produced (constructed) through language, *representation* and other social processes, rather than discovered. The terms in which the world is understood are related to specific socio-political, cultural, historical contexts, and meanings are seen as social artefacts, resulting from social interaction, rather than some inherent truth about the nature of reality.

Social desirability: the tendency for participants to respond to questions in a way that puts them in a favourable light, usually by over-reporting 'good' behaviour' or under-reporting 'bad' behaviour. This '*bias*' is usually seen as very problematic in quantitative or *realist/positivist* research, as it means that people are not giving 'truthful' responses, thereby limiting the *validity* of the research.

Social representation: a social representation is a theoretical concept in social psychology that refers to a set of values, ideas, beliefs, and practices that are shared among members of groups and communities. Based on the work of Serge Moscovici.

Sticky: a message on an Internet *message board* that contains important information about a particular *thread* (e.g., moderator rules). This message will remain (i.e., 'stick') at the top of all other threads, regardless of when it was last updated.

Story completion task: a method of data collection, where *participants* are given the start of a story and asked to complete (or continue) it.

Story mapping: a method of analysing *story completion* data that involves identifying patterns in the way in which stories unfold and progress.

Story stem (aka **story cue**)**:** the start of a story, involving a hypothetical scenario and characters, as part of the *story completion task* method.

Subforum: a subsection of an *Internet forum Discussion forum* that usually contains one or more topics.

Subject positions: effectively a 'way of being' or identity created by *discourse*, which individuals can take up; subject positions offer ways of thinking about oneself in relation to the world, and delimit the options available for action. (see *Subjectivity*)

Subjective: the idea that the researcher brings their personal and cultural history, values, assumptions, perspectives and mannerisms into their research, and these inevitably influence research, making it subjective, rather than objective; seen as a strength by most qualitative researchers. (see *Bias; Subjectivity*)

Subjectivity: people's sense of themselves; their ways of being in, and relating to, the world. Within *poststructuralist* (and *postmodern*) thought, the individual is a contradictory, fragmented subject, whose identity is constituted in and through *discourse*.

Survey: a (quantitative) data collection tool used to gather information about a population by collecting standardised data from a sample of that population. Commonly used to collect self-report data from participants, for example, about attitudes, opinions, beliefs, knowledge or practices. (see *Qualitative survey*)

Synchronous: where interaction between research participants and researchers happens in real-time. An element of *email interviews* or *online focus groups*.

Tabloid: a newspaper that is typically popular in style and dominated by sensational stories. (see *Broadsheet*)

Talk-in-interaction: a term in *conversation analysis* and some forms of *discourse analysis*, used to describe the interactive elements of communication between people.

Talkback (or talk) radio: radio shows that invite listeners to call in and make comment or provide opinion on some issue.

Telephone interview: an interactive data collection method between a researcher and a participant that takes place over the telephone. (see *Email interview; Interview*)

Temporal: relating to time.

Textual data: data collected in written (as opposed to audio) form. (see *Email interviews, Qualitative surveys, Vignettes, Media data*)

The 'usual suspects': the people who most regularly feature as the sample for western psychology: white, middle-class, heterosexual, able-bodied (and in the past, male) individuals; often psychology students.

Thematic analysis: a form of analysis which has the *theme* as its unit of analysis, and which looks across the dataset to identify themes.

Thick description: originally referred to data in which the contexts of behaviour were described; now often used to refer to detailed, complex, contradictory data. (see *Rich data*)

Thread: a new discussion started on a *subforum* on an *Internet forum Discussion forum*.

Top-down: a *deductive* orientation in qualitative analysis, whereby existing knowledge and theory guides what is looked for, or seen, and reported on, in the data. Sometimes associated with theory-testing. The opposite of an *inductive* or *bottom-up* orientation.

Transcript: a textual version of audio or audiovisual data, produced through the process of *transcription*. (see *Orthographic transcript*)

Transcription: the process of turning audio or audiovisual data into written text (a *transcript*) by writing down what was said (and if audiovisual material, what was done), and in some instances how it was said, so that data can be systematically coded and analysed.

Transferability: the extent to which qualitative research results can be 'transferred' to other groups of people or contexts. (see *Generalisability*)

Transphobia: prejudice against trans people.

Triangulation: using two or more data sources, methods or researchers to try to gain a fuller or multifaceted understanding of a topic.

Trolling: refers to comments 'designed' to provoke a negative reaction through 'objectionable' responses marked by misogyny, racism and heterosexism, prevalent in social media.

Unstructured interview: a type of interview where researchers may have, at most, a list of topics to cover, and questions are spontaneously created during each individual interview, dependent on the flow of the conversation. (see *Interview schedule, Semi-structured interview*)

Validity: refers most basically to whether research actually shows what it claims to show. There are different forms of validity, with ecological validity the most commonly used in qualitative research. Ecological validity is about whether or not research captures meaning in a way closely related to real-life situations.

Vignette: a short hypothetical scenario; as a method for qualitative *data* collection, a vignette is presented to *participants*, often in a series of 'stages', after which they answer a series of open-ended questions relating to it.

Visual methods: methods that try to incorporate some element of the visual – for example, drawings, maps, images or other types of graphic presentation – into the *data* collection process. This can either be a task for *participants* to complete (e.g., doing a drawing) or a task for participants to respond to (e.g., presenting an image and asking for responses to it).

Vulnerable groups: groups marginalised within society, or potentially at risk of harm. (see *Hard-to-engage populations, Marginalised groups* and *Hidden populations*)

Web 2.0: describes Internet sites that emphasise user-generated content.

Withdrawal: refers to a participant's right to withdraw their participation and their data from a research study. An ethical requirement of research with human participants.

Zinger: refers to short, bite-sized comments that are 'designed' to get a response on social media in the form of 'favouriting' or 'likes', and tend towards the superficial rather than the personal.

Index